Robert Walser

Robert Walser

A Companion

Edited by Samuel Frederick
and Valerie Heffernan

NORTHWESTERN UNIVERSITY PRESS
EVANSTON, ILLINOIS

Northwestern University Press
www.nupress.northwestern.edu

Printed in the United States of America

10 9 8 7 6 5 4 3 2 1

Library of Congress Cataloging-in-Publication Data

Names: Frederick, Samuel, editor. | Heffernan, Valerie, editor.
Title: Robert Walser : a companion / edited by Samuel Frederick and Valerie Heffernan.
Description: Evanston, Illinois : Northwestern University Press, 2018. | "This book was inspired by a number of panels titled "Reading Robert Walser" that took place at the conference of the German Studies Association in October 2010 and some subsequent conversations on both sides of the Atlantic about the growing recognition of Walser's work in the English-speaking world." | Includes bibliographical references and index.
Identifiers: LCCN 2017049797 | ISBN 9780810137127 (pbk. : alk. paper) | ISBN 9780810137134 (cloth : alk. paper) | ISBN 9780810137141 (ebook)
Subjects: LCSH: Walser, Robert, 1878–1956—Criticism and interpretation. | Modernism (Literature)—Germany.
Classification: LCC PT2647.A64 Z7865 2018 | DDC 838.91209—dc23
LC record available at https://lccn.loc.gov/2017049797

CONTENTS

Acknowledgments *vii*

A Note on Sources and Abbreviations *ix*

Introduction. Robert Walser: Modernist at the Margins *3*
Samuel Frederick and Valerie Heffernan

The Young Poet (1896–1899) *21*
Susan Bernofsky

To Pieces: Robert Walser's Correspondence with Frieda Mermet *47*
Elke Siegel

Robert Walser as Lyric Poet *65*
Samuel Frederick

Antechambers of Life: School and Living-On in *Fritz Kocher's Essays* *87*
Anette Schwarz

Robert Walser's Jewish Berlin *105*
Daniel Medin

Out of a Job: Giving Notice in *The Tanners* and *The Assistant* *125*
Paul Buchholz

Robert Walser's *Jakob von Gunten*: A "Zero" Point of German Literature *143*
Peter Utz

Robert Walser's Sceneries: "Kleist in Thun" and "The Walk" *171*
Bernhard F. Malkmus

Immersion, Interpolation, Philology: Losing Oneself in Robert Walser *191*
Jörg Kreienbrock

Parodies of Power: Robert Walser's Dramatic Scenes 211
Valerie Heffernan

Robert Walser and Violence: Strange Excursions into the Microscripts 229
Kai Evers

Robert Walser's *The Robber*: An Exercise in Camp 251
Anne Fuchs

Works Cited 269

Contributors 285

Index 289

ACKNOWLEDGMENTS

This book was inspired by a number of panels titled "Reading Robert Walser" that took place at the conference of the German Studies Association in October 2010 and some subsequent conversations on both sides of the Atlantic about the growing recognition of Walser's work in the English-speaking world. Our thanks are due first and foremost to Henry Carrigan Jr., then acquiring editor of Northwestern University Press, for encouraging Sam and Rebecca Schuman to pursue this project. Rebecca also deserves recognition for the pivotal role she played in getting the project off the ground and in persuading an impressive lineup of Walser researchers to contribute their expertise and their enthusiasm for Walser's work to the volume.

This work could not have been completed without the financial support of several associations. Publication grants from Penn State's Max-Kade Institute for German-American Studies, Penn State's Department of Germanic and Slavic Languages and Literatures, the National University of Ireland Publications Scheme, and the Maynooth University Publication Fund allowed us the additional scope to publish the volume in its most suitable form. Research funds provided by Penn State's Center for the Humanities and Information and by Maynooth University German Studies were used to pay for the translation of Utz's essay. We are very grateful to each of these associations for trusting in the academic merit of this project.

Two of the contributions to this volume are excerpted from publications that are under copyright with other presses. Susan Bernofsky's essay, "The Young Poet (1896–1899)," is taken from her forthcoming biography, *Robert Walser: Clairvoyant of the Small*. It is included here with the kind permission of Yale University Press. Peter Utz's contribution, "Robert Walser's *Jakob von Gunten*: A 'Zero' Point of German Literature," is a translation of the following article: Peter Utz, "Robert Walsers *Jakob von Gunten*: Eine 'Null'-Stelle der deutsche Literatur," in *Deutsche Vierteljahrsschrift für Literaturwissenschaft und Geistesgeschichte* 24, no. 3, ed. C. Kiening and A. Koschorke (2000): 488–512. Its translation is included here with the kind permission of J. B. Metzler Verlag, Stuttgart/Springer-Verlag GmbH Germany.

The Suhrkamp/Insel Verlag (Berlin) has also given their permission for the reprinting of the following texts by Robert Walser in this volume:

"Zukunft!," from Robert Walser, *Sämtliche Werke in Einzelausgaben*, edited by Jochen Greven, vol. 13, p. 48. © Suhrkamp Verlag, Frankfurt am Main.

"Ein Landschäftchen," from Robert Walser, *Sämtliche Werke in Einzelausgaben*, edited by Jochen Greven, vol. 13, p. 20. © Suhrkamp Verlag, Frankfurt am Main.

"Immer am Fenster," published as "Am Fenster (I)," from Robert Walser, *Sämtliche Werke in Einzelausgaben*, edited by Jochen Greven, vol. 13, p. 22. © Suhrkamp Verlag, Frankfurt am Main.

"Wie immer," from Robert Walser, *Sämtliche Werke in Einzelausgaben*, edited by Jochen Greven, vol. 13, p. 14. © Suhrkamp Verlag, Frankfurt am Main.

"Zeit," from Robert Walser, *Sämtliche Werke in Einzelausgaben*, edited by Jochen Greven, vol. 13, pp. 31–32. © Suhrkamp Verlag, Frankfurt am Main.

"Schildkrötelein," from Robert Walser, *Aus dem Bleistiftgebiet: Mikrogramme aus den Jahren 1924–1932*, transcribed and edited by Bernhard Echte and Werner Morlang, vol. 4, p. 277. © Suhrkamp Verlag, Frankfurt am Main.

Letter to Robert Seidel, from Elio Fröhlich, and Robert Mächler, eds., *Robert Walser zum Gedenken*, p. 14 © Suhrkamp Verlag, Frankfurt am Main.

We would like to thank the committed staff at Northwestern University Press, particularly Maggie Grossman, Trevor Perri, Nathan MacBrien, and Liz Hamilton, for the practical, legal, and moral support they offered us as we prepared the manuscript for submission. We would also like to acknowledge the two anonymous readers who kindly read the initial manuscript; their very insightful comments and useful suggestions added greatly to the quality of the volume. Special thanks go to James Kopf and Chrisann Zuerner for last-minute help with the index. We are also extremely grateful to Tilo Steireif for permission to use his marvelous Walser-inspired artwork for the cover.

Finally, we would like to thanks our families and our colleagues for their steadfast support, their encouragement, and above all, their patience.

A NOTE ON SOURCES AND ABBREVIATIONS

The titles of frequently cited works by Robert Walser are given throughout the text and notes using abbreviations. A list of these abbreviations and the editions used can be found on p. 269. Unless a published translation is cited, all English translations are by the authors.

Robert Walser

Introduction

Robert Walser: Modernist at the Margins

Samuel Frederick and Valerie Heffernan

Much has been made of the Swiss writer Robert Walser's (1878–1956) relatively recent arrival on the English-speaking literary scene and his recognition in the Anglo-American world as one of the great German-language writers of the modernist period. Although there can be no doubt that the wider popularity of Walser's writing is a recent phenomenon, aided in no small way by the publication of a number of high-quality English translations in the last couple of decades, Walser has been an open secret among writers in England and the United States for quite some time now. It is well known that Walser counted among his devotees some of the most prominent writers of the twentieth century, including Franz Kafka, Walter Benjamin, Hermann Hesse, and Robert Musil, and that contemporary German-language writers such as Elfriede Jelinek, Martin Walser, Elias Canetti, and W. G. Sebald have professed their admiration for Walser's writing and in some cases even its influence on their own work.[1] What is perhaps less well known is that in the Anglo-American world too, several important authors have been singing Walser's praises and calling attention to his work for more than twenty years now. To writers such as Harry Mathews, John Ashbery, William H. Gass, and J. M. Coetzee, the recent discovery of Robert Walser in the Anglo-American work cannot have come as a surprise; the only surprising thing is that it has taken so long.

As early as 1990, William H. Gass described his fascination for Walser's peculiar prose; the renowned American novelist and short-story writer penned the introduction to Susan Bernofsky's translation of some of Walser's prose pieces, *Masquerade and Other Stories*.[2] Like many other critics before him, Gass likens the Walser narrator's gaze to that of a stroller observing the world around him, and he marvels at the collage of apparently haphazard observations that make up each text. His praise for Walser's penetrating portrayal of the social order is unambiguous: "No writer I know employs the adjectives and adverbs of value so repeatedly, with such real appreciation and conviction, with such relentless resentment."[3] At the same time, Gass seems aware that the aspects of Walser's writing that attract him most may confound other readers. In particular, he remarks on the absence of a narrative thread in Walser's prose perambulations and the apparent lack of connection between the writer's sentences: "His transitions are abrupt as table edges;

non sequiturs flock his pages like starlings to their evening trees; the pieces turn, almost savagely, against themselves, or they dwindle away in apparent weariness."[4] Gass's sensitivity to the self-reflexive quality of Walser's prose and his unmistakable admiration for its idiosyncrasies make his introduction a resounding endorsement of one writer by another.

Though W. G. Sebald wrote primarily in the German language, his name is well established in the English-speaking world, since he spent most of his life living in England. In 1998, Sebald published *Logis in einem Landhaus* (*A Place in the Country*), which includes a chapter on Robert Walser.[5] After Jo Catling's translation of Sebald's volume appeared in 2014, the *New Yorker* published an adapted version of the Walser chapter.[6] Like Gass, Sebald also professes his profound admiration for Walser's prose, which, in words that echo Walter Benjamin's appraisal, "has the tendency to dissolve upon reading."[7] He writes in particularly glowing terms about the playful language of Walser's *The Robber* and highlights his creative exaggerations, skilled neologisms, and "almost manic loquaciousness."[8] Sebald also draws attention to the distinctive figures of Walser's texts who—and here his words again evoke Benjamin's—"flit through Walser's fragmentary stories and embryonic novels as people in dreams flit through our heads at night, never stopping to register, departing the moment they have arrived, never to be seen again."[9] Although Sebald writes about Walser's writing with evident appreciation, it is obvious that it is primarily the *writer* Walser to whom Sebald is drawn. He empathizes and even identifies with Walser; he describes him as his "constant companion" and claims, "I only need to look up for a moment in my daily work to see him standing somewhere a little apart, the unmistakable figure of the solitary walker just pausing to take in the surroundings."[10] That a distinguished writer such as Sebald looks to Walser for literary "companionship" bears witness to the quality and distinctiveness of Walser's literary ruminations.

In 2000, the celebrated South African writer and Nobel laureate J. M. Coetzee published an essay in the *New York Review of Books* that sought to introduce Walser the writer to an English-speaking readership through a review of two translations of his novels, Christopher Middleton's *Jakob von Gunten* and Bernofsky's *The Robber*.[11] Coetzee offers an overview of Walser's life story and focuses on the particularities of his method of producing the first drafts of his texts in pencil and in tiny script. He writes enthusiastically about *Jakob von Gunten*, which he proclaims to be "the best known of [Walser's] early novels, and deservedly so."[12] He compares Walser's Jakob to characters by Dostoevsky or Rousseau and, similar to Gass, he draws attention to the nonlinearity of the prose: "Walser's texts are driven neither by logic nor narrative but by moods, fancies, and associations."[13] Elucidating the delicate irony and narrative innovation of *The Robber*, Coetzee declares that if the novel had been published when it was completed in 1926, it might have influenced the course of modern German literature. Though he acknowledges that Walser is best known for his novels, Coetzee argues that it is in his short prose that Walser's true genius is most discernible.

Gass, Sebald, and Coetzee are three of a number of important writers—which now also includes those of a younger generation, such as Ben Lerner—who have sought to draw the reading public's attention to a truly original Swiss writer, Robert Walser—to his extravagant prose, his eccentric poetry, and his extraordinary little dramas. The admiration these three acclaimed authors express for Walser is by no means exceptional among the literati; indeed, the attention given to Walser by other writers has prompted critics to refer to him first and foremost as a "writer's writer,"[14] an "author's author,"[15] or a "poet's poet."[16] Walser's more recent discovery by a broader audience in the English-speaking world indicates that readers are finally noticing. The popularity that Walser's work is currently enjoying can thus be seen as the end of a long process as well as the beginning of a new era in his reception.

Walser and the Visual Arts

The influence of Walser's work, however, is not confined to literature; he has also made an impact in other areas, especially in the visual arts. This is not surprising, given Walser's focus on the arts, painting in particular. Not only did he write several dozen prose pieces and poems about (or inspired by) paintings;[17] he was also deeply influenced by his brother, Karl, a painter and illustrator. Indeed, some of Karl's work was used on the covers and as illustrations for his books. Mostly notably, Karl's painting of the young Robert dressed up as a "robber" (from Schiller's play) is the inspiration for the late microscript novel of that name. Relatedly, Tamara Evans has written about the relation between Walser and his contemporary Paul Klee (1879–1940).[18] Picking up Susan Sontag's suggestion that Walser is a "Paul Klee in prose,"[19] Evans looks at how both the writer and the painter respond to the crisis of modernity by spatializing time. One might also find a structural similarity in each Swiss artist's concentration on the miniature, which places them at odds with the maximalist aesthetics of much of modernism, its striving to encompass the whole. Walser and Klee instead seek out the inconspicuous, the overlooked, the tiny detail.

Walser's work has also left its mark on the visual arts in the English-speaking world.[20] American artist Joan Nelson (1958–) painted a series of miniatures titled *Fragments of Imaginary Landscapes*, which were displayed at a 1994 conference on Robert Walser and the visual arts held at the Swiss Institute in New York.[21] English musician-painter-writer Billy Childish (1959–), leader of the low-fi garage band Thee Headcoats, among other groups, included paintings of the police photographs of Walser's death in his 2010 Basel exhibition *I Am Their Damaged Megaphone*. Most notably, prominent gallerists

Donald Young and Christine Burgin created an entire exhibition called *A Little Ramble* around Walser's work. Running for almost a year, from 2011 to 2012, the exhibition included facsimiles of the microscripts along with pieces commissioned by Young and Burgin as responses to Walser's life and work. Artists displayed at this exhibition included Mark Wallinger (1959–), Josiah McElheny (1966–), Rodney Graham (1949–), and Moyra Davey (1958–), among others.[22] Walser's microscripts have even been treated as objects of art themselves, most notably when they were brought together with Emily Dickinson's penciled poems (Dickinson, like Walser, composed on scraps of paper, backs of envelopes, and torn stationery) for the exhibition *Dickinson/Walser: Pencil Sketches*, curated by Claire Gilman for New York's Drawing Center in 2013/2014.[23]

In the work of the Quay Brothers (1947–), American artists based in London who are primarily known for their work with puppet animation, we find one of the most remarkable and abiding explorations of Walser's world in images. The Quays' medium of choice is film, primarily animated, but also live-action. Over the course of four cinematic works spanning about seven years the Quays practiced an esoteric mode of adapting Walser's writings that does not visualize specific stories so much as create a cinematic world in the mood of his work, along with oblique allusions to his life. Their first Walser-inspired film is *Stille Nacht I: Dramolet* (1988), roughly two minutes long, whose title contains both a reference to Walser's Christmas Day death and the genre designation he used for his early dramas. A title card dedicates the film to "R.W. in Herisau," the mental institution where Walser would spend the last twenty-three years of his life. The film itself shows a tiny room in which a cracked and chipped doll is sitting at a table; in the adjoining room a magnet summons moving slivers of fine steel wool, which multiply and infiltrate the space. Spoons shoot out from the wall where the doll sits, and tiny bits of the steel wool begin to appear in its bowl. In the final two shots a minute sliver of silvery stuff makes its way to the spoon by the doll's bowl, and then the doll appears to reach for that spoon. Swift fade to black. Credits. End of film. Like the Quays' later Walser films *The Comb: From the Museums of Sleep* (1990) and *Stille Nacht III: Tales from Vienna Woods* (1993), this short imagines a surrealistic dream world (the shreds of steel wool on bowl and spoon seem to allude to another Swiss artist's work, Méret Oppenheim's *Object* [1936]), in which the small, forgotten, broken-down, and disappearing things of everyday life are made animate, interacting with people who have also been transformed into things, dolls, or puppets.[24] These works pick up Walser's obsession with the minute and with household objects, using them as players in a staged, silent, and secret commentary. The resulting works are astonishing.

The Quays would later go on to film a live-action and feature film–length version of *Jakob von Gunten* with the title *Institute Benjamenta, or This Dream People Call Human Life* (1995). While this film appears on the surface to be a more conventional adaptation in that it provides the main characters, setting, and occurrences from the novel, it nonetheless carries on the tradition established by the earlier Walser-inspired shorts in opting for atmosphere over story structure. Here, too, objects dominate: pinecones, forks, antlers, and so on. The Quays also brilliantly mobilize the novel's thematically central zero (see Peter Utz's contribution to this volume for an extended treatment of this theme)[25] as a visual leitmotif that echoes through the film's décor, and they overlay the story with elements from the same fairy-tale traditions that Walser himself adapted in his early plays. Thus, for instance, stag antlers appear throughout the film, and the butler-in-training Jakob soon emerges as a master-of-animals crossed with Christ figure, a reluctant redeemer, his antlers doubling as a crown—another figure of the "zero," of course. The Quays do not aim for anything like a faithful rendering of Walser's texts, if by "faithful" one expects correspondence to the original work; but in their daring creativity the Quays' cinematic reimaginings of Walser come closer to anything outside the realm of actual scholarship to being true interpretations.[26]

Another cinematic Walser adaptation of sorts, equally nonconventional, is the experimental film *All This Can Happen* (2013), created by British choreographer Siobhan Davies and filmmaker David Hilton. Ostensibly a version of "The Walk," the film consists solely of archival stills and film from the 1910s, primarily in split screen, over which a narrator reads passages from Walser's story. This work, too, attests to the remarkably enduring influence of Walser's work on the experimental arts.

Walser and the Canon

Despite rave reviews by important and influential writers in German and English, and despite his lasting influence on the visual artists, there is no doubt that Walser was for a long time completely absent from the Anglo-American reception of German-language modernism. He was not alone. That reception had long been limited both to and by the dominance of the same small group of writers: Franz Kafka, Thomas Mann, Bertolt Brecht, and Rainer Maria Rilke. This is a pantheon few would dispute, on grounds of either literary quality or influence. It is also a pantheon whose apparent inviolability has been well maintained by a steady flow of scholarly works and translations, the latter of which frequently appear on college (and even high school) curricula. It furthermore helps consolidate the singular influence of these four writers that each is master of a different literary genre: short prose, the novel, drama, and lyric poetry, respectively. We would seem to have the modernist era covered, then. Any other writers will have to wait on the sidelines.

Indeed, for a good half-century they did. Other important modernists who wrote in German had their day, to be sure. But one thing or another kept them from attaining the prominence of the "big four." Stefan George, Ernst Jünger, and Gottfried Benn, for instance, had problematic ties to National Socialism that kept their brilliant work from finding broader acceptance. Hermann Hesse, while wildly popular, is still considered a bit saccharine and shallow by comparison with his contemporaries. Other writers suffered from poor and/or piecemeal translations of their work: Else Lasker-Schüler, Hugo von Hofmannsthal, Arthur Schnitzler, Karl Kraus, Frank Wedekind. The list goes on. New translations of Thomas Mann continue to appear—and continue to sell. But it has taken almost eighty-five years for a new translation of Alfred Döblin's best-known work, *Berlin Alexanderplatz*, to materialize. Döblin's dozen-plus other novels, though equally important, remain untranslated. Willa and Edwin Muir's universally criticized translations of Kafka, moreover, have been superseded by countless newer ones; yet their translation of Hermann Broch's masterpiece *The Sleepwalkers* is the only one available—and is now over seventy years old.

None of these modernists has succeeded in usurping or even just expanding the German-language literary pantheon beyond Kafka, Mann, Brecht, and Rilke in terms of critical and popular visibility. Two authors, however, have in the past few decades risen above the rest, and while they haven't eclipsed the "big four," they have slowly begun to elbow their way to broader visibility. One is Robert Musil; the other is the writer Musil so greatly admired: Robert Walser. This is not the place to reflect on these writers' similarities. It is, however, worth considering how Walser's wily and mercurial modernism has taken foot in the realm well trodden by the discourse surrounding the "big four." With the exception of Musil, and of course the established canon, Walser is the only other German-language author of the first half of the twentieth century to attract so much critical acclaim outside Germany, Austria, and Switzerland; the only author to be celebrated so widely by other prominent global authors and to inspire so many works of art beyond the realm of literature. The number of Walser translations alone attests to the rapid growth of his importance and popularity. Thanks in great part to the efforts of Christopher Middleton and more recently of Susan Bernofsky, Walser counts among the most widely translated of German-language modernists. We maintain that part of this success has precisely to do with Walser's resolute outsider status, his refusal to be easily categorized, and his tenacious marginality in the face of a dominant and largely unchanging discourse.

Robert Walser's work presents us with a different face of German-language modernism—indeed, it's not just one face, but a face with multiple masks. Walser's narrators—so often mistaken for the writer himself—are a strange hybrid of ironist and sentimentalist. They skirt the edges of his texts like jesters, infatuated with the world that they seem at the same time to be laughing at, somehow both cunning and naive, jubilant and forlorn. Walser's experimentalism is stubbornly idiosyncratic. Indeed, its governing characteristic is a rampant instability, staged with such poise that the apparent disorder that ensues is as beguiling as it is bewildering. Constitutive of this delightful disorder is that his work is playful and inviting, guileless and simplistic, yet also overwhelmingly erratic, exceedingly self-reflexive, and intricately labyrinthine. Walser's formal innovations lie in the linguistic prestidigitations by which he maneuvers these often conflicting tones and impulses. His texts are virtuosic performances of stylistic excess, complete with an arsenal of popular discourse, topical references, and literary allusion. They are, moreover, usually helmed by narrators who appeal to the reader directly and even seductively. In the end, Walser's readers are invited—typically cordially—to revel in his stylistic flourishes, his narrators' mercurial trains of thought, and to share in their multiply irreconcilable expressions of affect. Yet this style, like his narrative personas, at once welcomes the reader and—ever politely—denies her complete access. Since Walser prefers to play the outsider, the reader is usually kept tangled up on the inside, lost in a delightful outpouring of language, while the mysterious narrative voice surrounds her, unlocatable, unknowable. The playful exuberance of Walser's prose, its extravagant excesses and its roguish self-reflexivity, the very characteristics that often led to the writer's rejection by editors and readers, have also doubtless contributed to his recognition by other authors as one of the great writers of the twentieth century.

Walser's Reception in Academia

As noted in the previous section, Walser's recent academic and critical reception in the English-speaking work has been facilitated greatly by the publication of a number of high-quality translations. In fact, the first English translations of Walser's work (indeed, the first translations of his work into any language) began during the writer's lifetime, when the "young English poet Christopher Middleton," as Carl Seelig referred to him when he told Walser the news, began to translate Walser's "Der Spaziergang" ("The Walk") into English.[27] This story was published in 1957 by the English publisher Calder and Boyars as part of a collection titled *The Walk and Other Stories*.[28] Middleton continued on his quest to make Walser accessible to an English-speaking public with a translation of *Jakob von Gunten*, which was published in 1969.[29] The fact that one of its reviewers praised the novel as "one of the wittiest, wackiest, most charming and most civilized satires I have ever read" can be taken as evidence of the quality of Middleton's translation and his sensitivity to Walser's eccentric style.[30] That this volume is still considered the authoritative translation of what is probably Walser's most famous novel furthermore demonstrates Middleton's lasting influence in communicating Walser's work to the English-speaking world. As a point of contrast, an early translation by Michael Bullock of Walser's second novel—*Der Gehülfe*, which was published as *The Assistant* by Calder and Boyars, also in 1969, the same year as *Jakob von Gunten*—has been superseded by a more recent translation.[31]

Susan Bernofsky and Lucas Marco Gisi note that the 1982 publication of another collection of short prose translated by Middleton, *Selected Stories*, sparked a new phase of interest in Robert Walser in the Anglo-American world.[32] There was a crucial difference: whereas the earlier translations had all been published by small, relatively local presses, the new volume appeared with the much bigger New York–based press Farrar, Straus and Giroux and with a foreword by the established critic and public intellectual Susan Sontag. This book thus launched Walser onto an international stage.[33] So when Mark Harman published his anthology *Robert Walser Rediscovered* in 1985, including translations by five different translators, the reviewers were already beginning to see Robert Walser as "one of the important writers in the German language in the twentieth century"[34] and "an author well worth reading."[35]

Though Christopher Middleton continued to publish translations of Walser—in 2005 he published a selection of texts from the microscripts as *Speaking to the Rose*,[36] and his last translation before his death in 2015 was a volume of Walser's poetry, published in 2012 as *Thirty Poems*[37]—it seems fair to say that Susan Bernofsky's translations have done more than anything else in the English-speaking world of the past two decades to bring Walser broader recognition. Bernofsky's first volume of translations, *Masquerade and Other Stories*, appeared in 1990.[38] She is now known as one of the great translators of German literature: since the early 2000s, and supported by the interest of several high-profile publishing houses, she has produced seven more high-quality translations of Walser, including his novels *The Robber* (2000), *The Assistant* (2007), and *The Tanners* (2009); a collection of pencil drafts published as *Microscripts* (2010); a reworking of Middleton's translation *The Walk* (2012); the prose anthology *Berlin Stories* (2012); and, most recently, a collection of writings on art, *Looking at Pictures* (2015).[39] The interest of the reading public in these translations has also prompted the reprint of some of the older translations.

In more recent years, a number of new translators have also begun to engage with Walser's work. Of particular note among these are Damion Searls and Daniele Pantano. Searls is responsible for the publication of *Fritz Kochers Aufsätze* (*Fritz Kocher's Essays*) and other early works, collected in *A Schoolboy's Diary and Other Stories* (2013), and has also translated a number of Walser's late poems;[40] Pantano has translated a selection of Walser's poetry under the title *Oppressive Light* and worked with James Reidel on a new translation of the fairy-tale dramolettes, which was published as *Fairy Tales* (2015).[41] A new collection of stories and prose sketches primarily from the Biel and Bern years, translated by Tom Whalen together with Nicole Köngeter and Annette Wiesner, was also recently published by New York Review Books.[42] These high-quality translations have gone a long way toward establishing Walser as one of the most important modernist writers in the German language. The enthusiasm of the translators, the encouragement of the publishers, and the interest of the reading public would also seem to suggest that Walser's star will continue to rise in the Anglo-American world for the foreseeable future.

Unusually, the academic reception of Walser in the Anglo-American world did not come late, as it so often does, but in fact inaugurated a new phase of interest in the writer's work. Indeed, the scholarly attention to Walser unfolded simultaneously in Germany and in the United States. An early essay from 1958 by Christopher Middleton celebrates the writer's marginality and argues that his position on the borderline gives him the freedom "to do other things with words." Middleton also draws attention to the musicality of Walser's language, asserting that it occupies a literary space beyond the verbal.[43] In 1959, the American scholar George Avery defended his doctoral thesis on Walser,[44] one year before the first German-language dissertation was submitted by Jochen Greven, then a pioneering Walser scholar who would later go on to become the editor of the first scholarly edition of the writer's collected works.[45] Bernofsky and Gisi see Avery's work as part of a "first wave" of the reception of Walser in the English-speaking world,[46] and they also note two other unpublished dissertations from this period.[47]

The "second wave" of interest in Walser in the Anglo-American world followed the 1982 publication of Middleton's translation *Selected Stories*.[48] Of particular note in this regard is the previously noted endorsement of Susan Sontag, who in her foreword to the volume called Walser "a cross between Stevie Smith and Beckett" and "a Paul Klee in prose" and proclaimed him "a truly wonderful, heartbreaking writer."[49] The fact that Mark Harman's 1985 anthology *Robert Walser Rediscovered* included a number of critical essays clearly aimed at an academic readership indicates its dual purpose of reaching out to a broad readership (with the translations) as well as a specialized audience. Bernofsky and Gisi also make particular mention of a special issue of the literary journal *Review of Contemporary Fiction*, which included contributions from established Walser scholars such as Werner Morlang, Bernhard Echte, and Tamara Evans as well as the prominent writers Martin Walser and Adolf Muschg.[50]

The proliferation of new translations of Walser since the early 2000s has made Walser's work accessible to a new generation of readers. This, combined with the efforts of Walser scholars in the English-speaking countries to embed Walser's work in the university curriculum, has finally begun to establish Walser as a canonical writer in the German language. In recent years, a number of new English-language monographs[51] and doctoral dissertations[52] have sought to locate Walser's work within broader literary traditions or to use contemporary theory to shed new light on his work. Many of this new generation of Walser scholars are represented in the present volume, which aims both to build on and add to this growing body of academic work.

Overview of the *Companion*

This book presents for the very first time in an English-language volume new scholarship on Robert Walser spanning his life and work.[53] Its aims are to offer a sampling of new approaches to Walser as well as an overview of his writings and their contexts that will be of use to established scholars and to those coming to the literature on Walser for the first time. This volume celebrates Walser as a modernist wanderer through overlooked and peripheral spaces. The contributions here present him not as a master of these marginal realms, however, but as a humble observer. Part of the aim of the present volume is to inquire into Walser's idiosyncratic modernism and to offer new readings of his life and work that demonstrate why he matters so much—especially now.

To this end we have commissioned pieces that deal with aspects of Walser's biography (the chapters by Bernofsky, Siegel, and Medin) along with pieces that focus on Walser's main periods of production: the early, pre-Berlin years (Bernofsky, Schwarz, Frederick); the Berlin years (Buchholz, Utz, Malkmus); the time he spent in Biel (Malkmus, Heffernan, Kreienbrock); and the later Bern years, during which he wrote the microscripts (Frederick, Heffernan, Evers, Fuchs). Alongside these we have strived to include discussions of each of the different genres in which Walser wrote: the novel (Buchholz, Utz, Fuchs), short prose (Malkmus, Kreienbrock, Evers), drama (Heffernan), poetry (Frederick, Bernofsky), and even his letters (Siegel, Bernofsky). We have also tried to aim for coverage of Walser's best-known works. All four surviving novels are treated at length, the first two—*The Tanners* and *The Assistant*—together in one chapter (Buchholz), with *Jakob von Gunten* and *The Robber* each accorded its own essay (Utz and Fuchs, respectively). Additionally, the early book *Fritz Kocher's Essays* is discussed in Schwarz's chapter; Walser's longest and best-known story, "The Walk," is treated in the chapters by Malkmus and Kreienbrock; and his early short masterpiece "Kleist in Thun" is analyzed in Malkmus's chapter.

The essays in this volume represent a wide array of approaches to Walser's work. Some of the contributors are established scholars in Walser studies with an international reputation. Foremost among these is Peter Utz, one of the world's leading Walser critics and author of the remarkable book *Tanz auf den Rändern: Robert Walsers "Jetztzeitstil"* (*Dance on the Edges: Robert Walser's "Style of Now"*),[54] as well as several dozen articles, book chapters, and other pieces on Walser. His contribution, which zeroes in—in the most literal sense—on Walser's best-known novel, *Jakob von Gunten*, was originally published in German in 2000.[55] Our inclusion of its translation here enables its wider distribution and accessibility to readers without German. Susan Bernofsky's central position on the Walser scene has already been elucidated above; her essay in this volume, "The Young Poet," is taken from her forthcoming critical biography of Walser, *Clairvoyant of the Small* (Yale

University Press). We are delighted to be able to offer this foretaste from the biography, which promises to be the definitive work on Walser's life, superseding the previous and somewhat problematic German and French biographies (neither of which has been translated into English).[56]

Several contributors to this volume have published monographs on different aspects of Walser's writing that have been well received by the scholarly community; their contributions build on their previous publications and extend them in new and fruitful ways. Anne Fuchs's book *Dramaturgie des Narrentums* was the first to draw attention to the humor of the Walser text;[57] her essay in this volume takes her reading of the playful transgressions of Walser's prose a step further and offers a sustained reading of *The Robber* as an example of "camp" narration, which appropriates the conventions of the romance genre as it deliberately undermines them. Whereas Elke Siegel's monograph, *Aufträge aus dem Bleistiftgebiet*, considered how the material circumstances of the writer's unique method of textual production are written into the content of his texts, her essay here employs a similar approach to raise critical questions about the "epistolary-culinary poetics" at work in his body of correspondence, in which letters are exchanged along with all kinds of other "pieces": prose pieces, food pieces, (imagined and eroticized) body parts, and other gifts.[58] Valerie Heffernan's analysis in this volume of the power structures at play in two of Walser's dramatic scenes builds on her sustained engagement with Walser's performances of authority and power in her monograph, *Provocation from the Periphery*. Jörg Kreienbrock's exploration of the process of walking, writing, and particularly reading that is imagined by and through Walser's writing reflects the in-depth analysis of textual rhythm and progression—or lack thereof—in his *Kleiner. Feiner. Leichter: Nuancierungen zum Werk Robert Walsers*.[59]

Other contributors to this volume have examined Walser's work in relation to questions of narrative and genre experimentation, and their publications reveal those aspects of the writer's work that make him eminently modern. Samuel Frederick leaves behind the inquiry into digression that motivated his first readings of Walser (including those in his monograph *Narratives Unsettled*) in order to pursue questions about "unknowing" that have guided his more recent work on Walser,[60] here in the context of his lyric production. Bernhard Malkmus similarly moves away from his work on Walser and the picaresque tradition (developed in his book *The German Picaro and Modernity*)[61] in a piece that engages with Walser's experimentalism by way of the phenomenology of space and body. Anette Schwarz's reading of *Fritz Kocher's Essays* emerges from many of the same concerns with affect and language that animated the Walser chapter in her book,[62] but shifts focus to consider the dialectic of guileless innocence and (schoolmasterly/editorial) control at work in the "schoolboy's" essays. Paul Buchholz's contribution to this volume, an analysis of two of Walser's Berlin novels, stems in part from his dissertation research on monologue on Kafka, Walser, and Bernhard, but is also deeply informed by his interest in the figure of the social outsider and the language of refusal, which he explores in his new book *Private Anarchy*.[63] Kai Evers's interpretation in this anthology of the particular forms of violence represented in Walser's microscripts leans on his expertise on the aesthetics of violence and destruction in German modernism.[64] In a similar vein, Daniel Medin's discussion of Walser's various relationships with prominent Jewish intellectuals, including publishers, politicians, and art dealers, during his years in Berlin is informed by his scholarly interest in the intellectual culture of Berlin and Vienna more broadly.

The essays in this companion volume represent the breadth of existing and emerging scholarship on Robert Walser. They offer some useful new approaches to his work and relate it to established trends, tropes, and tendencies of literary modernism, particularly but not exclusively in the German-speaking world. They point to further publications in German and English for readers new to Walser's work—or for readers seeking to engage with it in more depth. And they open up some new avenues for further exploration, new ideas for how readers, students, and researchers might fruitfully engage with the vagaries of Walser's whimsical writing.

Modernist at the Margins

While it is true that during his life Walser was greatly admired by such figures as Franz Kafka, Robert Musil, and Walter Benjamin, he nevertheless remained a "minor" author—even more so after his disappearance from public life and publishing following his institutionalization in 1933. After his death in 1956 his work slipped into relative obscurity, only to slowly reemerge with the publication of *Das Gesamtwerk* (*The Complete Works*, 1966–75), edited by Jochen Greven, which was later reissued by the major German publishing house Suhrkamp in a paperback edition in 1978, Walser's centennial. It is at this point, especially with the appearance of a new edition of Greven's edition in 1985/86 (*Sämtliche Werke in Einzelausgaben* [*Collected Works in Individual Volumes*]), which coincided with the publication of the first two volumes of *Aus dem Bleistiftgebiet* (*From the Domain of the Pencil*), transcriptions of previously unavailable microscripts, that a Walser rediscovery proper begins. This rediscovery has in the past couple of decades in particular come to astounding fruition, with the completion of the microscript transcriptions in 2000 (now comprising six full volumes), abundant academic publications and conferences, translations in now over thirty languages, and a broader public reception, including that of prominent contemporary authors worldwide. Additionally, two new editions of Walser's work are currently under way: the *Kritische Robert Walser-Ausgabe* (*Critical Robert Walser Edition*) and the *Kommentierte Berner Ausgabe* (*Annotated Bernese Edition*). The former, overseen by Wolfram Groddeck and Barbara von Reibnitz and published by Stroemfeld, has already begun to appear. It is an exhaustive scholarly edition based on and including facsimiles of handwritten manuscripts, typescripts, first editions, and newspaper publications, and is anticipated to be about forty-five volumes when complete. The *Bernese Edition* will replace Greven's edition, subsuming all the microscripts, letters, and other scattered texts, to become the new standard annotated reader's edition.

But Walser's rediscovery and recognition does not mean that we should have to relinquish his marginality, that his work must now take a spot at the center, representative of some normative understanding of modernist literature. On the contrary: Walser persistently, even obstinately, maintains his place at the margins. His work resists assimilation to any particular style or movement or, for that matter, nation. It eschews any such centering in its celebration of the edges, limits, thresholds, fringes, spaces of playful experimentation, parodic performance, and fluid identity. If Walser is now finally receiving proper recognition, it is not because room has been made for him at the center, but because readers and critics have slowly shifted their gaze from that center to the periphery.[65] The distinction is a critical one. Walser's time has come because we have arrived at new ways of thinking about the literature of modernism—not because he has somehow been discovered to fit into an existing canon. Once modernist practices began to be seen in their inherent multiplicity, as modes of keeping heterogeneous spheres in tension or at play; as modes of constructing or exploring the decentered, the marginal, the neglected, the anomalous; as inextricable from popular culture and print media—only then could Walser's position at the periphery be seen as partaking in these practices in an essential way that is nonetheless irreducible to any one of them. Walser may be getting attention, finally; but that is because we have caught up with him. He may now be more prominent than ever as a key figure of German-language literary modernism; but his place is still, resolutely, at the margins.

Notes

1. For further details, see Roman Bucheli, "Deutschsprachige Literatur," in *Robert Walser-Handbuch: Leben—Werk—Wirkung*, ed. Lucas Marco Gisi (Stuttgart: Metzler, 2015), 371–80.

2. William H. Gass, introduction to *Masquerade and Other Stories*, by Robert Walser (Baltimore: Johns Hopkins University Press, 1990), ix–xix.

3. Ibid., xii.

4. Ibid., x.

5. W. G. Sebald, "Le promeneur solitaire," in *Logis in einem Landhaus: Über Gottfried Keller, Johann Peter Hebel, Robert Walser und andere* (Munich: Hanser, 1998), 127–68; W. G. Sebald, "Le promeneur solitaire," in *A Place in the Country*, trans. Jo Catling (New York: Random House, 2014), 117–54.

6. W. G. Sebald, "Le Promeneur Solitaire: W. G. Sebald on Robert Walser," *New Yorker*, February 6, 2014.

7. Sebald, *A Place in the Country*, 130.

8. Ibid., 139.

9. Ibid., 142.

10. Ibid., 159.

11. J. M. Coetzee, "The Genius of Robert Walser," *New York Review of Books* 47, no. 17, November 2, 2000, reprinted in J. M. Coetzee, *Inner Workings: Literary Essays, 2000–2005* (New York: Penguin, 2007).

12. Ibid., 17.

13. Ibid., 23.

14. Susan Bernofsky and Lucas Marco Gisi, "USA, England," in Gisi, *Robert Walser-Handbuch*, 396.

15. Irene Weber Henking, "Überblick," in Gisi, *Robert Walser-Handbuch*, 394–95.

16. Anna Fattori, "Forschungsgeschichte," in Gisi, *Robert Walser-Handbuch*, 417–30; quotation on 418.

17. A selection was collected along with reproductions as Robert Walser, *Vor Bildern: Geschichten und Gedichte*, ed. Bernhard Echte (Frankfurt am Main: Suhrkamp, 2006). See also the translated volume Robert Walser, *Looking at Pictures*, trans. Susan Bernofsky et al. (New York: New Directions / Christine Burgin, 2016); and Dominik Müller, "Text und Bild," in Gisi, *Robert Walser-Handbuch*, 283–89.

18. Tamara S. Evans, "'A Paul Klee in Prose': Design, Space, and Time in the Work of Robert Walser," *German Quarterly* 75, no. 1 (1984): 27–41; Evans, *Robert Walsers Moderne* (Bern: Francke, 1989), 81–115; and Evans, "'Ein Künstler ist hier gezwungen aufzuhorchen': Zu Robert Walsers Kunstrezeption in der Berliner Zeit," in *Bildersprache, Klangfiguren: Spielformen der Intermedialität bei Robert Walser* (Munich: Wilhelm Fink, 2008), 107–16.

19. Susan Sontag, "Walser's Voice," in *SS*, vii.

20. For a thorough discussion of Walser's influence on the visual arts not limited to the United States and England, see Lucia Ruprecht, "Film," in Gisi, *Robert Walser-Handbuch*, 385–87, and Konrad Tobler, "Gegenwartskunst," ibid., 387–90. For music adapted from and influenced by Walser, see Roman Brotbeck, "Musik," in Gisi, *Robert Walser-Handbuch*, 391–94. For discussions of Walser's work in relation to the arts (not necessarily in terms of influence), see Tamara S. Evans, ed., *Robert Walser and the Visual Arts* (New York: CUNY Press, 1996).

21. *Fragments of Imaginary Landscapes: Joan Nelson and Robert Walser* (art exhibition), Swiss Institute, New York, N.Y., 1994.

22. See Robert Walser, *A Little Ramble: In the Spirit of Robert Walser* (New York: New Directions / Christine Burgin, 2013).

23. *Pencil Sketches: Dickinson/Walser* (art exhibition), Drawing Center, New York, N.Y., 2014.

24. On the importance of dolls and puppets in Walser, see Samuel Frederick, "A Bursting Zero of Unknowing: Overcoming the Paradox of Infinite Knowledge in Heinrich von Kleist's 'Über das Marionettentheater' and Robert Walser's *Jakob von Gunten*," *Germanic Review* 88, no. 4 (2013): 375–90.

25. On the zero, see also Frederick, "A Bursting Zero of Unknowing."

26. For more on the Quays, see Suzanne Buchan's monograph *The Quay Brothers: Into a Metaphysical Playroom* (Minneapolis: University of Minnesota Press, 2011), and her article "The Quay Brothers: Choreographed Chiaroscuro, Enigmatic and Sublime," *Film Quarterly* 51, no. 3 (1998): 2–15. For analyses of the Quays' Walser films, see Samuel Frederick, "Redemption of the Miniature: The Quay Brothers and Robert Walser," in booklet for *Institute Benjamenta, or This Dream People Call Human Life*, directed by the Quay Brothers (DVD/Blu-ray, British Film Institute, 2010), 1–6; Samuel Frederick, "An Antlered Adaptation: Stag Iconography and Animal-Human Hybridity in the Quay Brothers' *Institute Benjamenta*," *Literature/Film Quarterly* 43, no. 3 (2015): 202–16; Laura Marks, "The Quays' *Institute Benjamenta*: An Olfactory View," *Afterimage* 25, no. 2 (September/October 1997): 11–13; David Sorfa, "The Illusory Architext of the *Institute Benjamenta*," *Adaptation* 5, no. 1 (2011): 88–101; and, most recently, the fourth chapter in Jan Plug, *They Have All Been Healed: Reading Robert Walser* (Evanston, Ill.: Northwestern University Press, 2016).

27. It is worth noting that Middleton uses the 1917 version of Walser's short story as the basis for his translation and not the later, reworked version that appeared in *Seeland* (1920).

28. Robert Walser, *The Walk and Other Stories*, trans. Christopher Middleton (London: Calder and Boyars, 1957).

29. Robert Walser, *Jakob von Gunten*, trans. Christopher Middleton (Austin: University of Texas Press, 1969). Note that our contributors cite the 1999 New York Review Books reprint of this translation, not the long out-of-print first edition, which has a different pagination.

30. J. Mitchell Morse, "Fiction Chronicle," *Hudson Review* 23, no. 2 (1970): 331.

31. Robert Walser, *The Assistant*, trans. Michael Bullock (London: Calder and Boyars, 1969).

32. Robert Walser, *Selected Stories*, trans. Christopher Middleton (New York: Farrar, Straus and Giroux, 1982). Note that our contributors cite the 2012 reprint of this edition throughout the book, which is identical to the 1982 printing. It is worth noting that this collection includes all four stories from Middleton's original translation, *The Walk and Other Stories*.

33. Cf. Bernofsky and Gisi, "USA, England." This handbook entry provides an excellent overview of the reception of Walser in the Anglo-American world. In the same volume, Anna Fattori provides an equally detailed and extremely helpful summary of the history of Walser reception, which is accompanied by an extensive bibliography. Fattori, "Forschungsgeschichte."

34. Ruth B. Bottigheimer, "Review of *Robert Walser Rediscovered*," *German Quarterly* 60, no. 2 (1987): 306.

35. Amy Stapleton, "Review of *Robert Walser Rediscovered*," *South Atlantic Review* 53, no. 4 (1998): 161.

36. Robert Walser, *Speaking to the Rose: Writings 1912–1932*, trans. Christopher Middleton (Lincoln: University of Nebraska Press, 2005).

37. Robert Walser, *Thirty Poems*, trans. Christopher Middleton (New York: New Directions, 2012).

38. Robert Walser, *Masquerade and Other Stories*, trans. Susan Bernofsky (Baltimore: Johns Hopkins University Press, 1990).

39. See Works Cited for details on these translations. It is worth noting that Bernofsky's translation of *Der Spaziergang* (*The Walk*) is a reworking of Middleton's 1957 translation using the 1920 revised version of the story.

40. These can be found in Thomas Schütte, *Watercolors for Robert Walser and Donald Young* (Paris: Editions Cahiers d'art, 2014).

41. See Works Cited for details on these translations, which are used throughout this volume.

42. Robert Walser, *Girlfriends, Ghosts, and Other Stories*, trans. Tom Whalen with Nicole Köngeter and Annette Wiesner (New York: New York Review Books, 2016).

43. Christopher Middleton, "The Picture of Nobody: Some Remarks on Robert Walser with a Note on Walser and Kafka," *Revue des langues vivantes* 24 (1958): 405.

44. George C. Avery, "Focus on Reality in the Novels of Robert Walser" (Ph.D. diss., University of Pennsylvania, 1959). A revised version of Avery's thesis was published as George C. Avery, *Inquiry and Testament: A Study of the Novels and Short Prose of Robert Walser* (Philadelphia: University of Pennsylvania Press, 1968).

45. Jochen Greven, "Existenz, Welt und reines Sein im Werk Robert Walsers: Versuch zur Bestimmung von Grundstrukturen" (Ph.D. diss., Universität Köln, 1960). Greven's dissertation was published in 1960 as *Existenz, Welt und reines Sein im Werk Robert Walsers* (Cologne: Kleikamp, 1960), and reprinted with a foreword by Reto Sorg as *Existenz, Welt und reines Sein im Werk Robert Walsers* (Munich: Fink, 2009).

46. Bernofsky and Gisi, "USA, England," 396.

47. Herbert L. Kaufmann, "The Narrative Structure in Robert Walser's *Geschwister Tanner*, *Der Gehülfe*, *Jakob von Gunten*" (Ph.D. diss., New York University, 1969), and Constance Colwell, "Robert Walser, *Der Räuber*: A Study of the Narrative Structure" (Ph.D. diss., Cornell University, 1977).

48. Bernofsky and Gisi, "USA, England," 396.

49. Susan Sontag, "Walser's Voice," in *SS*, vii, ix.

50. Susan Bernofsky and Tom Whalen, eds., *Review of Contemporary Fiction* 12, no. 1 (1992).

51. These include Valerie Heffernan's *Provocation from the Periphery: Robert Walser Re-examined* (Würzburg: Königshausen & Neumann, 2007); Samuel Frederick, *Narratives Unsettled: Digression in Robert Walser, Thomas Bernhard, and Adalbert Stifter* (Evanston, Ill.: Northwestern University Press, 2012); Erica Weitzmann, *Irony's Antics: Walser, Kafka, Roth, and the German Comic Tradition* (Evanston, Ill.: Northwestern University Press, 2014); and Plug, *They Have All Been Healed*.

52. These include Alexandra Huster, "Going One's Own Way: The Literary Construction of the Oddball in German Literature (Jean Paul, Franz Grillparzer, Robert Walser)" (Ph.D. diss., New York University, 2007); Paul Buchholz, "Monologue Overgrown: Revising the World with Speech in Franz Kafka, Robert Walser, and Thomas Bernhard" (Ph.D. diss., Cornell University, 2010); and Charles M. Vannette, "'Wir pröbeln und schneidern mit Dingen, die in der Brust anderer Menschen gesund und geheimnisvoll und unangetastet ruhen . . .': Narrative Observation and Hyperreflexivity in the Works of Robert Walser" (Ph.D. diss., Ohio State University, 2011).

53. We acknowledge two important precursors: Mark Harman, ed., *Robert Walser Rediscovered: Stories, Fairy-Tale Plays, and Critical Responses* (Hanover, N.H.: University Press of New England, 1985), and Evans, *Robert Walser and the Visual Arts*. The former collects six short conference proceedings, but consists primarily of translations of previously unavailable texts by and about Walser. The latter publication of conference proceedings is excellent, but is limited in thematic scope, and in number of contributions (there are only seven presentations printed, along with one translation of a Walser text, and a panel discussion).

54. Peter Utz, *Tanz auf den Rändern: Robert Walsers "Jetztzeitstil"* (Frankfurt am Main: Suhrkamp, 1998).

55. Peter Utz, "Robert Walsers Jakob von Gunten: Eine 'Null'-Stelle der deutschen Literatur," *Deutsche Vierteljahrsschrift für Literaturwissenschaft und Geistesgeschichte* 74, no. 3 (2000): 488–512.

56. Robert Mächler, *Das Leben Robert Walsers: Eine dokumentarische Biographie*, 2nd ed. (Frankfurt am Main: Suhrkamp, 2003 [first published 1966]) and Catherine Sauvat, *Vergessene Weiten: Eine Robert Walser-Biographie* (Frankfurt am Main: Suhrkamp, 1995). Bernhard Echte's excellent documentary biography, *Robert Walser: Sein Leben in Bildern und Texten* (Frankfurt am Main: Suhrkamp, 2008) represents a far more useful resource than these two more conventional biographies.

57. Annette Fuchs, *Dramaturgie des Narrentums: Das Komische in der Prosa Robert Walsers* (Munich: Wilhelm Fink, 1993).

58. Elke Siegel, *Aufträge aus dem Bleistiftgebiet: Zur Dichtung Robert Walsers* (Würzburg: Königshausen & Neumann, 2001).

59. Jörg Kreienbrock, *Kleiner. Feiner. Leichter: Nunancierungen zum Werk Robert Walsers* (Zurich: Diaphanes, 2010).

60. E.g., in Frederick, "A Bursting Zero of Unknowing."

61. Bernhard F. Malkmus, *The German Picaro and Modernity: Between Underdog and Shape-Shifter* (New York: Continuum, 2011).

62. Anette Schwarz, *Melancholie: Figuren und Orte einer Stimmung* (Vienna: Passagen Verlag, 1996).

63. Buchholz, "Monologue Overgrown"; and Paul Buchholz, *Private Anarchy: Impossible Community and the Outsider's Monologue in German Experimental Fiction* (Evanston, Ill.: Northwestern University Press, 2018).

64. Kai Evers, *Violent Modernists: The Aesthetics of Destruction in Twentieth-Century German Literature* (Evanston, Ill.: Northwestern University Press, 2013).

65. The importance of the margin, edge, periphery for Walser is attested to in the titles (and of course contents) of two major works of criticism from the past couple decades: Peter Utz's *Tanz auf den Rändern* and Heffernan's *Provocation from the Periphery*. Cf. Deleuze and Guattari's notion of "minor literature," in their *Kafka: Toward a Minor Literature*, trans. Dana Polan (Minneapolis: University of Minnesota Press, 1986). See also Michael Böhler, "Dichten aus der Peripherie des Schreibens: Überlegungen zu Robert Walsers kulturpolitischem Ort im deutschsprachigen Raum," in *"Wärmende Fremde": Robert Walser und seine Übersetzer*, ed. Walter Lenschen and Peter Utz (Bern: Peter Lang, 1994), 31–44.

The Young Poet (1896–1899)

Susan Bernofsky

For a poet to chafe against the necessity of a day job is nothing new. For the young Robert Walser, just exiting his teens, to decide at the very moment he was embracing his new artistic calling that regular employment was incompatible with his aspirations—wasn't that just flirting with foolhardiness? After all, he had experienced firsthand as a child what precarious finances could do to the well-being of a family. He had watched his own future prospects dwindle along with the fortunes of his parents' business. And even though his father had done his best by Robert, apprenticing him in a field chosen for its promise of security, Robert appeared hell-bent on making the accidental precariousness he had experienced in childhood his chosen way of life—not because he was interested in poverty for its own sake, but because he had fallen in love with art in all its many incarnations and was dreaming of a life devoted to creative pursuits. He was fantasizing not of struggle and impecuniousness but of acclaim and honor, the just rewards of the successful artist. He would claim this success in exchange for honest work and artistic achievement. Watching his older brother reject a career in architecture to pursue his painting inspired and encouraged him. He was filled with optimism and faith in his own talent, though also somewhat apprehensive.

The transitional years that began when Robert struck out on his own in 1896, parting from Karl and taking up residence in Zurich, the commercial and artistic capital of German-speaking Switzerland, were crucial in young Robert's development, the period when he set the goals and standards for his artistic production that he would adhere to for the rest of his career. Describing this period in retrospect in a biographical note written in 1920 to accompany a selection of his work printed in the journal *Der Lesezirkel*,[1] Walser reports that the young man he had been in those days worked

> now in the insurance business, now in banking, living both in the Aussersihl district [of Zurich] and on the Zürichberg, and wrote poems, whereby it must be stated that he did not do this on the side but instead always first rendered himself jobless for the purpose, apparently in the belief that art was a noble thing. Indeed he considered poetry almost sacred.[2]

When he first arrived in town, though, gainful employment was still a priority for him, and he was hired by the cargo insurance firm Schweiz to work in its bookkeeping division for an annual salary of 1,500 francs—three times the profit his father had reported to the Biel tax office from his business the year before.[3] To eighteen-year-old Robert, it must have seemed a fortune. The detail of this generous salary remained lodged in his mind; seventeen years later, writing a story based on his experiences in Zurich that year ("Johanna," 1913), Walser recalls that princely sum: "I was, I recall, nineteen years old, still wore no proper collar, ran around in the snow and rain, always arose early in the morning, read Lenau, considered an overcoat a superfluous item, received a monthly salary of one hundred twenty-five francs, and did not know what I should do with all that money."[4]

The narrator of this story rents a room from "package man Senn," who took in several lodgers in the rooms of his vast apartment not occupied by his cowering wife and his two sons, "Theodor and Emil Senn, [whom] he thrashed."[5] Zurich Registry Office records from this period show that Robert Walser did indeed rent a room from a post office employee by the name of Caspar Senn (with three sons: Heinrich, Emil, and Theodor) at Zeughausstrasse 3 for several months beginning October 1, 1896,[6] though Robert's age at the time was not nineteen but eighteen. The records also document a second tenant who moved in around the same time: Johanna Lüthy, twenty years old and born in Biel; she lists her profession as "shopgirl."[7] Walser's fictionalized reminiscence describes just the sort of flirtation a very young man holding down his first job in a new city might wish for:

> Johanna was indescribably dear and as gentle as moonlight. I wrote a poem in her album, a bold, extravagant firstborn—she showed it to her mother, and the mother warned her little daughter about me, how heartily this made us laugh. Oh how sweet I found these gracious knightly duties. We lived four flights up. Should Johanna, standing downstairs at the front door, have forgotten her umbrella or handkerchief or something else, I would receive the commission to dash upstairs and fetch the forgotten item. How happy that made me, and how sweetly, how beautifully, how tenderly she would smile to see it. Her hands were voluptuous and soft and as white as snow, and kissing them—how it intoxicated and enchanted me. Senn was furious with us, because we would study English together until deep into the night in Johanna's room. He no doubt heard through the wall what a caressing, amusing sort of English we were up to. Lovely, unforgettable language lesson, dear unforgettable fair creature.[8]

So did eighteen-year-old Robert enjoy a real-life romance with the young lady? Two years his elder, she was likely more experienced than he in city life. As his fellow Bieler, she no doubt shared his sense of being an outsider here in this much larger and more cosmopolitan city, where an unfamiliar dialect was spoken and people inclined to snobbishness. Perhaps he did creep into her room at night, taking care that the floorboards of the corridor beneath his feet—thickly padded in wool socks, since these attic bedrooms were unheated—not reveal too much about his destination, and perhaps they did then giggle together over a language textbook like a modern Paolo and Francesca. The awkwardness of the foreign tongue, poorly spoken, mitigated the awkwardness of the conversation itself. Robert no doubt wrote to Karl, his confidant in all things, about this pretty girl-next-door, but no letters from these months survive, and later ones make no mention of young ladies and their knights, nor of shopgirls and the assistant bookkeepers who kiss their hands. A photograph of Johanna Lüthy shows a happy-looking, healthy-looking girl with a glowing complexion and thick hair tied back in a loose chignon, smiling with a mischievous air.[9]

Robert's official position at the Transport Insurance Company Schweiz was assistant bookkeeper, a job that involved the keeping of ledgers on pages preprinted with grids. The clerk's responsibilities were graphic as well as mathematical: using a straightedge aligned exactly parallel or perpendicular to the edge of the page, he inked in lines at the appropriate points, lines of various sorts: dotted, plain, double, extra thick. In an era before typewriters were widely in use, companies of all sorts relied on clerks or scriveners to keep their records and copy out their correspondence in a regular, impeccably legible script. The clerk was a craftsman, a calligraphic adding machine, his product page after flawlessly uniform page.

Even as a schoolboy, Robert had been praised for his penmanship. He wrote an immaculate copperplate hand, mastering a variety of styles from the plainest script to the most dramatic flourishes. He wrote a textbook *Kurrent*, the sharply slanting old form of German handwriting that corresponded to blackletter or Gothic type (*Fraktur*) in printing and remained widely in use through World War II. He also excelled in the newfangled roman script used for English and French. A day at the office typically included a whole stack of documents to process and copy, probably at a high desk where the clerk stood rather than sat, in a large room containing several other desks as well.

Clerks were at the bottom of the insurance company's administrative hierarchy. The only place for a promising young man of Robert's discipline and intelligence to go was up. Although he could never advance to the sort of position Franz Kafka, with his doctorate in law, would hold at the Workers' Accident Insurance Institute in Prague, there were still levels of advancement accessible to him. The main problem, it turned out, was that he hated the work. A life devoted to money and its management could hardly bring fulfillment to a soul still resonating with the passionate, revolutionary words of Karl Moor, the protagonist of Robert's favorite play (Friedrich Schiller's *The Robbers*).

Five months after moving to Zurich and taking up the post in the Schweiz offices, Robert found himself so unfulfilled by his labors that decisive measures were in order. The particular measure he chose reveals that the discrepancies in the standard of living of people of different social classes had made a profound impression on him. He decided he wanted to work to support the cause of workers, the eternally laboring underclass, and to this end sought employment in an organ of the Socialist Party.

On March 3, 1897, Robert sent a letter to Robert Seidel, the German-born journalist, poet, and teacher who also happened to be editor-in-chief of the Swiss socialist weekly newspaper *Arbeiterstimme* (*Voice of the Worker*), which was published in Zurich. "Highly revered sir," Robert wrote,

> Might you possibly require an employee in your esteemed offices as a copyist or something of the sort? If so, I would like herewith to offer my utterly devoted services and should consider it a stroke of good fortune and be grateful if you would make use of my offering.
>
> I am 19 years old, have completed a commercial apprenticeship and been active in various trades, as you will be so good as to confirm in the attached letters of reference. At present I am working here in an insurance firm, but I don't like it, I feel a powerful urge to leave. Please understand, this work simply does not interest me, it leaves me cold; I have no idea what I am working for, but I do have a fairly clear notion that I am of little, terribly little use here. It seems to me that if I came to work for you, even in the most trifling capacity, I should nonetheless know that these labors had a value and merit. In short, I should so dearly love to serve a Party to which my entire heart belongs, and should most certainly succeed in gaining your approval through my loyalty and industry and zeal. My expectations are modest, and I know 2 foreign languages, one of them more or less perfectly, the other fairly well.
>
> Please be so good as to accept the assurance of my utmost esteem.
>
> Your devoted Robert Walser
>
> Zeltweg 64^{II} Hottingen[10]

This high-flown epistle—the earliest of Walser's letters to survive—fell on sympathetic ears. Seidel responded with a friendly if businesslike letter ten days later, regretting that he was unable to offer Robert employment but saying that he admired his youthful enthusiasm ("You are full of drive and want to be of use to the world") and inviting him to pay a visit during his daily office hours. He would be happy, he said, to assist Robert in his search for "a sphere of activity that will bring you satisfaction and be of service to mankind."[11] The visit took place and must have been inspiring, because when Robert next wrote to Seidel, on the eve of May 1, wishing him a happy International Day of Labor, he sounded both encouraged and grateful:

> I shall never forget how amicably you received me and how kindly you advised me, and I intend to work following the path you have shown me. This, however, requires a great deal of endurance and strength; well, I shall strive to achieve everything that lies in my power to achieve, and you, most revered Herr Seidel, will always be present to me as a noble exemplar or splendidly clear beacon.[12]

Six weeks later, Robert wrote again, this time to submit a poem, asking Seidel to consider publishing it in *Arbeiterstimme*. In the accompanying letter, he reports that he is continuing in his efforts:

> In my work I am making progress very slowly, but still it is steady progress. I accomplish what I can. Now I want to read a great deal more than I used to—to read good books and read them slowly, isn't that right, esteemed sir?
>
> I take pleasure in immersing myself as deeply as possible in some matter, and getting properly to the bottom of things, and I can't help laughing—madcap laughter—when the bottom proves to be rotten, or when it gleams like the clearest sky.
>
> Above all I am making an effort to always fully and completely grasp and use each moment. This is the golden kernel of reason. It's just that my heart keeps ringing out overpoweringly.[13]

Robert's three letters to Seidel are revealing even in their handwriting. The first letter, written as a self-introduction, is penned in a flawless, regular *Kurrent* script. The second letter with the May 1 greeting is written in the more modern roman script—perhaps Robert decided that the copperplate formality of *Kurrent* was too office-dusty for an exchange between fellow lovers of progress and verse. He wasn't necessarily imitating Seidel's handwriting—Seidel had written to him using a typewriter—though Seidel probably favored roman script in general.[14] Robert's third letter to Seidel was written in a much looser hand, a more fanciful version of roman script, giving an even more informal impression (the same handwriting he used later that year writing to his sister Lisa).

Whether it was before or after meeting Seidel, Robert probably read his book of poems that had appeared two years before: *Aus Kampfgewühl und Einsamkeit* (*From the Frenzy of Battle and Loneliness*), a work that sold enough copies to go through a good half-dozen subsequent printings, though Seidel is now remembered only for his work as a journalist and editor, not as a poet.[15] These works are the rhyme-and-meter representation of revolutionary strivings, full of lines like "My belief is Progress's messenger" and "Only in freedom can I love my homeland." Seidel was working in a poetic idiom in which political slogans rhymed with the passionately inflamed hearts of young men striving for a cause.

Robert's own revolutionary poem that he sent to Seidel for consideration, "Future!" (the exclamation point is part of the title), displays a similar fervor.

Zukunft!

Es kommt die wunderschöne Zeit
Da in den Königshallen
Der Freiheit neuer Glaube wird
Am Marmor wiederschallen.

Wo sich in Lieb' ein Volk ergeht
Alleen auf und nieder;
Wo ungebundner Fortschritt blüht
Und blühen tausend Lieder!

Wo Menschen nur noch Menschen sind
Und sich unendlich lieben,
Und wo die Arbeit, die jetzt weint
Zur höchsten Lust getrieben.—

Wo Leidenschaft und edles Thun
Sind inniglich verbunden.
Es wird der freien Zeiten Glück
Ein frei Geschlecht bekunden!

Es kommt die wunderschöne Zeit
Wovon wir Lieder singen.——
Den Königsadler "Geist" hör ich
Schon kühn die Flügel schwingen. (*SW*, 13:48)

Future!

The wonderfully fair age is nigh
When in the royal halls
Freedom's new faith will resound
Against the marble walls.

Where people, loving, stroll upon
the avenues, up and down;
Where unfettered progress blooms—
And a thousand songs bloom too!

Where men are nothing more than men
and love each other infinitely,
and where Labor, which now is weeping,
will be raised to highest joy.—

Where passion and where noble deeds
are intimately conjoined.
The happiness of this free age
portends a free race of men!

The wonderfully fair age is nigh
of which we sing our songs.——
Already I hear the royal eagle "Spirit"
boldly spread its wings.

Just as "bold" and "extravagant" as the "firstborn" Robert and/or his fictional doppelganger penned in Johanna's album, this poem has little about it to suggest that its author might be destined for greatness. Conventional in imagery and sentiment, and alternating between clichés and awkward locutions, "Future!" speaks of a coming age in language cribbed from days of yore. Its one moment of appealing oddity—appealing despite the hopeless clunkiness of the lines—comes at the end of the final stanza, with the conceptually complex image of the spirit appearing in the guise of an eagle flapping its wings loudly enough to be audible to the poem's speaker. The poem shows the influence of Seidel's work, down to the overuse of exclamation points. The notion of *Zukunft* (future) might have stuck in Robert's head after reading one of the oddest and most striking poems in Seidel's book, a poem about miners titled "Deep in the Earth's Womb!," which ends on the image of a giant, identified as "the destiny of the future," emerging from the depths of the mine to stamp out injustice with mighty feet.

Robert's poem isn't much worse than one of Seidel's, so it's a shame Seidel declined to print it. But even unpublished, the poem was a breakthrough for him: it was the first time he'd submitted work of any sort for publication, and it is clear from his third letter to Seidel that writing poems and thinking about literature had begun to be what he referred to as his "work." In other words, his encounter with the older, engaged poet had given him both the permission and inspiration to set out on his own path of exploring the revolutions that could be wrought with words. Actual political fervor, on the other hand, proved to have a far less sustained impact on him—though, as we will see, the basic principles of socialism would play a significant thematic role in his work later on. The thought that it was in the interest of some for others to live in poverty continued to gnaw at him.

In a fictionalized account of the Seidel episode Walser published in 1917 in a story titled "Luise," the letter Robert received from Seidel (now described only as "a respected journalistic personality") appears in dramatically inflated form:

> "Youthful and tempestuous admirer," the man wrote back to me quite soberly, "it is not so easy as you apparently believe to perform duties and render sacrifices in a place where Meyer's *Encyclopedia* no doubt enjoys a foremost and also finalmost significance. That you look up to me meets with my understanding and approval, for you have every cause to consider me a great man."[16]

An impressionable youth no longer, the author looking back at the young clerk's admiration for Seidel found humor in his own erstwhile reverence for a man whose literary accomplishments Walser the writer had long since outstripped. The narrator also notes that his former passion for the socialist cause proved short-lived as well: "'This noble repudiator of all things selfish, this representative of all that is altruistic and modest must surely be a quite odd individual,' I said to myself, and my desire to champion and exert myself for the lofty goals and causes of mankind dwindled with remarkable speed."[17] The narrator's reporting on Robert's interactions with Seidel is no more accurate than his account of other parts of the young man's trajectory. For example, the narrator writes that in response to his disappointing exchange with the "respected journalistic personality," he decided it was time to "infiltrate the educated and elegant circles of society that until then I had merely admired, marveled at and worshipped from afar," describing a move to a furnished room in the apartment of a professor's widow in swanky surrounds that prompts him to think of the story's title character Luise, his once-admired friend, as "proletarian."[18] In truth, nineteen-year-old Robert relocated to a fancy neighborhood some weeks *before* writing his first letter to Seidel: the return address on the letter (Zeltweg 64) shows he was already living in Hottingen, an elegant district of upper-middle-class villas built on a hill overlooking the heart of town. So if it wasn't in reaction against Seidel, why did Robert decide to move there from his comfortable Aussersihl perch, where he was enjoying the company of the "unforgettable fair creature" down the hall?

Perhaps the real-life Johanna (who remained a lodger in Caspar Senn's apartment for another eight months) was not so well disposed toward Robert as her fictional counterpart. Or perhaps Senn, tired of the carryings-on under his roof that set so awkward an example for his young sons, sent him packing. Or perhaps Johanna, initially receptive, tired of her young neighbor's affections—or he of hers. In any case, when Robert left the apartment to move across town and across the Limmat River, he left behind more than simply a flopped or merely fantasized-about romance; it was a dramatic change of milieu.

The elegance of Robert's new Hottingen abode is difficult to imagine in retrospect, since the building at Zeltweg 64 no longer stands. Directly next door, though, is the imposing edifice built in 1877 as the home and studio of celebrated sculptor Louis Wethli, its stately façade adorned with decorative arched windows with sculptural insets and a Juliet balcony. Robert's landlady, whose name is unknown (her fictional counterpart in the story "Luise" is named Frau Professor Krähenbühl), had an apartment on the third floor, so Robert may have occupied a maid's dormer-windowed attic room, affording him a view between houses of the lake and city center at the bottom of the hill. Although this refined neighborhood lay outside the bustle of the center, it was still conveniently accessible, with the city's brand-new theater, the Schauspielhaus, which opened in 1892, just a short walk away, and Paradeplatz less than a twenty-minute walk from his front door. Although Robert was still just a subtenant—a "furnished gentleman," as the expression went—this was the fanciest place he'd ever lived, given that Zurich professorial grandeur trumped the mercantile middle-class elegance Biel had offered even at the most prosperous height of his early childhood.

The young poet held out in these elite surrounds for about a month before looking for change again. As the narrator of "Luise" reports, life in the elegant villa district soon seems unbearable to him ("all that refined behavior and all those lovely, witty turns of phrase and conversations fortunately soon filled me with apprehension and fear"), prompting him to petition his landlady for permission to depart. After he secures new lodgings in the "workers district," he reports feeling right at home among his largely indigent neighbors. His new landlord, he relates, is a carpenter;[19] no details about Robert's real-life landlord at Zurlindenstrasse 49 are known beyond the family name, Held, and we have no firm indication of what circumstances prompted this move. He was to remain here for half a year.

The first surviving personal letters by Robert we have—written to his sister Lisa on July 30 and August 3, 1897—were sent from Zurlindenstrasse, and in one of them he remarks that he likes living there and plans to remain another two months. These letters are remarkable in that they show Robert beginning to develop that characteristic voice that will later enliven his narrative prose. In the first of these two letters he declares that he is hungry and that this hunger is prompting his desire for letter-writing, since when his belly is full, he thinks only of himself and not of distant others. This association ("It is certainly not happiness to long for something far away!")[20] launches him into an entire mini-essay on the subject of longing:

> Where longing is concerned, it is first off superfluous, secondly comprehensible, and thirdly incomprehensible!—It's superfluous because it merely burdens one; comprehensible the way an illness is comprehensible, or a sin; but incomprehensible because so many people are unable to live without this superfluous thing, because so many people engage in longing, wasting away in longing and finding themselves unable to extricate themselves from it, indeed they even find a certain

> sweetness in longing. That people so often, so willingly engage in something so burdensome, something so longing as longing itself—that's the pathological condition afflicting us. Christianity is the religion of longing! For this reason alone, this religion is so unnatural, so unworthy of human beings! A person who has shaken off longing has done better than another who has written 100 very nicely rhymed but also longing-ridden songs. Songs of this sort should not even be printed. The police should most definitely intervene in such cases. O Uhland and his ilk! But enough for today![21]

This brief lecture embedded in this early letter by Robert Walser to his sister Lisa displays several key features that will later characterize the speeches delivered by the characters in many of his stories and novels. In other words, his true beginnings as a writer, I would argue, lie not so much in the stiff, cribbed lines of tendentious verse he was thinking of as his "work" but in this friendlier, playful, communicative mode of writing intended to give pleasure (both to himself as he wrote and to his sister, whom he loved). The generosity of spirit in these lines far outshines the grandeur of the "royal eagle Spirit" boldly spreading his wings in "Future!" Young Robert is far more philosophical when he allows himself to don the mask of unseriousness.

So what about this letter is "Walserian"? First there's the overall irony of his central conceit: his argument against longing belies the fact that he himself is filled with it, and indeed has begun this very letter by noting how receiving a letter from his sister made him sigh and even asking her to consider moving to Zurich rather than Bern to continue her studies. Then there is the juxtaposition of opposites (longing is simultaneously superfluous, comprehensible, and incomprehensible) without any acknowledgment of the contradiction, which has a humorous effect. Then there is the mock-philosophical musing ("That people so often, so willingly engage in something so burdensome, something so longing as longing itself—that's the pathological condition afflicting us") that soon gives way to a straight-faced and surprising observation: "Christianity is the religion of longing," which he says marks this religion as "unnatural" and "unworthy of human beings." If this religion is unnatural, does it mean that other religions are natural, or indeed that naturalness is a natural human expectation? Would a "natural" religion be worthy of humans? Immediately these two sentences open up a maze of questions and suppositions, which Robert leaves serenely unanswered, moving on to praise the person who has "shaken off longing." He himself, though, is clearly in its thrall, as was the German poet he cites a few lines later, Ludwig Uhland (possibly recommended by Seidel), a poet of the early nineteenth century who was revered for his passionate devotion to democracy as well as for his patriotic verse.

By the end of the letter, Robert is promising to speak the next time he writes of something more useful: "the deed." And indeed, the next time he writes to Lisa four days later, he does recall this promise, but instead of the expected discourse notes only that addressing the topic would require "an essay of many pages, which I prefer to leave unwritten for the moment," though he does add: "This much I can remark in any case: the world is practically suffocating beneath a lack of deeds. And so a single person can achieve an enormous amount with a deed!"[22] What sorts of deeds he has in mind he doesn't say, though it's quite certain from his correspondence with Seidel that sitting day after day in an insurance office copying out ledgers isn't what he has in mind. He may be thinking of Goethe's *Faust*, in which "die That" (deed) features prominently as one of the possible translations for *logos* in the first sentence of the Bible. Or perhaps he's already dipped into the letters of Heinrich von Kleist—we know he read them before 1898, in any case—and happened on the one in which Kleist famously reports to his sister Ulrike (on May 1, 1802) that he has "no other wish than to die after having produced three things: a child, a beautiful poem, and a great deed."[23]

Even in his memory of this period years later, Walser would remember this sense of longing for some meaningful activity that so powerfully moved him in these days. In "Luise," he has his narrator exclaim with impatience, "Nineteen years old, and still you haven't done a thing for posterity!"[24] So while Robert might have started the year thinking that the contribution he needed to make was a political one, his goals soon shifted to the realm of art; it was only a question, then, of how he would achieve this just-nascent dream of becoming a writer.

His employment at the insurance company was no help. While it paid well, at least for a young man's budgetary expectations, it was a drag on him emotionally and spiritually, and he sensed that year after year of bending his back in the service of other people's wealth would get him nowhere. He needed to get away from this world. But how would he live? All around him in Wiedikon, he saw his working-class neighbors struggling to make ends meet; were they any freer than he was? Was living among them an inspiration? Out at the edge of town, no one he met seemed particularly interested in literature, ideas, or art.

Fortunately inspiration soon arrived in the form of his brother Karl. In his August 3 letter to Lisa, Robert had mentioned that he would be spending his vacation with Karl in Stuttgart and that Karl would then be coming to Zurich. Karl had been studying for the past year at the Kunstgewerbeschule (School of Applied Arts) in Strasburg, where he had distinguished himself as one of the most talented students and had been chosen by the painting teacher to assist him in creating stage sets for a performance at Strasburg's Municipal Theater.[25] His studies there complete, he chose Zurich as his next way station, arriving on October 17.

In preparation for Karl's visit, Robert gave up his room at the edge of town and moved to quarters in a more urban setting. His new quarters, at Neumarkt 3, were situated in the very heart of the Niederdorf neighborhood in the city center, just east of the Limmat River. In contrast to the region west of the river—the location of Bahnhofstrasse and Paradeplatz—the Limmat's east bank was decidedly less prosperous, featuring tiny crooked alleyways snaking up the hill away from the river. The buildings in these alleys didn't get much light. Craftsmen lived here, and families who couldn't afford the glamour of Zurich's brighter streets. Still, the room he rented here was much more expensive than the one he'd been inhabiting in Wiedikon. Neumarkt was one of the grander streets of this relatively ungrand district, broader than most, with a fountain he heard burbling through his open window at night. It was also only a short walk from his Paradeplatz workplace, his first experience with living actually in the heart of the city where he'd made his home for the past year. Of the various Zurich neighborhoods he'd now lived in, whether lofty or lowly, this was his first chance to experience a fully metropolitan lifestyle.

Karl's arrival in Zurich meant a great deal to Robert. It brought him a conversation partner who truly understood his artistic strivings and had followed them since their earliest stirrings several years before. As much confrere as frère, Karl was able to respond meaningfully to Robert's early poems, to critique and encourage. And serving as host to Karl in this city in which Robert had lived and worked for a year now—where Robert moreover earned a salary that allowed him to pick up the tab when the brothers went drinking in the dive bars of Niederdorf—for once reversed the balance of power between the brothers, at least for the moment. (Karl, as an art student, was on such a tight budget that one of his fellow students said he lived "mainly on water, bread, and apples.")[26] For once, Robert was in a position to show his older brother around and to introduce him to the circle of his Zurich friends. Introducing Karl into this circle instantly produced complications, however—complications of a romantic nature.

We know, thanks to research done by Walser scholar Bernhard Echte, that Robert's associates in Zurich included two women whose portraits Walser repeatedly sketches in various works of fiction: Rosa Schätzle and Louisa Schweizer.[27] The two were close friends—they sometimes even lived together in Louisa's Aussersihl apartment at Badenerstrasse 257—and a fair bit older than Robert, by seven and eight years, respectively. Both of them had complicated romantic histories that they shared with young Robert, who was as eager to hear the stories told by these far more experienced women as they were to unburden themselves to their rapt, charmingly inexperienced listener.

Robert met Louisa Schweizer not long after this strikingly beautiful woman, who worked as a bookkeeper and photographic retoucher, had been seduced and impregnated by her married, adulterous boss. After giving birth (on September 5, 1897), she resolved to raise her son without the help of the child's father. The story "Luise" describes this episode, as does the novel *Der Gehülfe* (*The Assistant*), in which Louisa's story is attributed to a character named Klara), and several other texts as well.[28] The strength and determination of this woman who, though in a socially weak position, rejected the wealthy man who might have supported her made a powerful impression on Robert. In *The Assistant*, the young protagonist, Joseph Marti, credits Klara with introducing him to the ideas of freethinking nineteenth-century writers like Heinrich Heine and Ludwig Börne; she shares his enthusiasm for socialism.[29] In "Luise," the narrator repeatedly mentions Luise's self-identification as a proletarian and says that eventually, "living as a proletarian among proletarians," she became the "Queen of the Poor," an inspiration to her struggling neighbors.[30] The real-life Louisa was no doubt delighted to hear of young Robert's correspondence and meeting with Robert Seidel.

Rosa Schätzle had a more direct connection to Robert; like him, she was born in Biel and was the daughter of a stationery shop owner, and they had a Biel friend in common: the photographer Paul Hans Renfer, who introduced them.[31] Like Louisa Schweizer, Rosa Schätzle served as a model (often under the name Rosa) for characters in a number of Walser works, including the novel *Geschwister Tanner* (*The Tanners*) as well as several stories.[32] Walser's fictionalized portraits of Schätzle show her as passionate, temperamental, impulsive, and inclined to melancholy. Her romantic relationship with the handsome, younger Renfer (seven years her junior, one year older than Robert) eventually soured, but Robert maintained his friendships with both of them. Photographs from the time show Schätzle with an intense, almost hungry gaze, eyes bright in her open face, and with a flair for dramatic outfits and theatrical hats. In one fictional portrait, Walser says she liked to dance around her room with castanets.

Schätzle was a translator with literary aspirations and ties to the avant-garde literary scene in Zurich. In a letter thirty years later, Walser recalls witnessing a scene that displayed her characteristic spunk in a confrontation with Maurice Reinhold von Stern, editor of the journal *Stern's literarisches Bulletin* (*Stern's Literary Bulletin*), in which he published young authors such as Richard Dehmel, Karl Henckell, Ludwig Jakobowsky, Emanuel von Bodmann, and Rainer Maria Rilke. As Walser tells it, Stern once made the mistake of addressing Schätzle as "dear Fräulein," prompting her to reply indignantly, "I'm not your dear Fräulein."[33] In another story, Walser has his narrator claim Bodmann (at the time a young student in Zurich but later a respected German author) as an acquaintance, so it's likely he met at least some of Schätzle's literary pals, including two—the young art dealer Otto Ackermann and his girlfriend, the painter Maria Slavona—whom he mentions in a conversation many years later with Carl Seelig.[34]

By introducing Robert to her art- and literature-loving friends, Schätzle did him quite a service. He reciprocated by introducing her to Karl, with whom she promptly fell in love. Karl in those days was dashing: tall and slender, with a bright shock of red hair crowning eyes that looked perpetually sleepy or like those of a daydreamer. He wore an artfully curved thin moustache to set off his sensual lips and carried himself with the aplomb of one already convinced as a young man that he is destined for greatness. It isn't known to what extent he reciprocated Schätzle's feelings, but he did present her with one of his pictures, a landscape done in pastels. A mutual friend, Flora Ackeret (who will play a more significant role in this story later on), wrote about their relationship in a letter to Hermann Hesse (!), reporting that Karl's behavior toward Rosa was generally inconsistent and sometimes even insulting, as when he gave her a volume of letters by the painter Stauffer-Bern as a gift and later demanded its return.[35] Schätzle seemed disastrously attracted to handsome younger men who treated her dismissively; even her lover Paul Renfer, if Walser's fictional portrait of him can be believed, betrayed her trust and also had a serious drinking problem—he also died tragically young, at the age of twenty-six.[36]

Karl remained in Zurich until January 4, 1898, living first with Robert at Neumarkt 3 and then moving to quarters of his own at Aemtlerstrasse 106, in a section of Aussersihl far more distant from the city center than any of Robert's addresses, but no doubt in keeping with his budgetary limitations. Meanwhile Robert made a far more dramatic move. Prompted perhaps by the same desire for meaningful change that had caused him to write to Seidel half a year before, and now inspired as well by his brother's own artistic strivings, he gave notice at his insurance agency. An internal memo dated November 19, 1897, gives instructions for the hiring of his replacement (at a maximal salary 33 percent higher than Robert had been paid).[37] The memo notes specifically that Robert resigned from his position, so we know he wasn't fired. The letter of reference provided to him the following day affirms that the assistant bookkeeper "is leaving us today of his own volition" and that "Herr Walser has proven himself a capable, hard-working, and reliable employee & we sincerely wish him all the best for his future career."[38] It isn't clear what sort of "career" the writer of this reference letter had in mind, but for Robert it must have been clear enough, because just a few days later he set off for Berlin.

Then as now, Berlin was an important destination for young German-speaking artists and writers, already enough of a metropolis to make Zurich seem more a town than a city. It wasn't the sort of place you went to because you wanted to further your training as a copy clerk. For Robert, traveling to the German capital was a grand gesture, a great adventure—he was visiting the locus of art and culture, leaving his own homeland behind—and also something of an experiment, a testing of the waters to see whether he might find a place for himself there. He'd probably been encouraged in this venture by Renfer; a fictionalized account of the journey he wrote a quarter of a century later reports, "At the age of nineteen, I traveled to Berlin on the advice of a photographer and learned there what it meant to be homesick."[39] What exactly Robert did and saw on this journey is not recorded, though more than one Walser story set in this period refers to "a disappointment" experienced in Berlin.[40] He must have been expecting to stay for a while, since he applied before leaving for a deferment of the military service he would have been expected to do after his twentieth birthday the following spring.[41] What happened to him in the German capital? Had he been expecting to be welcomed into Berlin's circles of young writers, as had happened in Zurich, and had he instead found the Berlin intelligentsia unreceptive to him, his strong Swiss accent, and his utter lack of formal education? In any case, twenty days later, he was back in Zurich, where he moved in with Karl, sharing the room at Aemtlerstrasse 106 until Karl left for Sursee.

But even though the plan to become a Berlin poet had apparently come to naught, Robert had made a decisive step, one that would establish a pattern that would persist throughout his professional life: "rendering himself jobless" (as he put it in that 1920 bio note) for the purpose of writing poems. Although the assistant bookkeeper's salary he received could have permitted him to rent a small apartment and live alone—eventually resulting in an ever higher standard of living if he were promoted to positions of higher responsibility—he went on living in furnished rooms and taking his meals in inexpensive restaurants, just as his father as an impoverished widower was doing back in Biel. For Robert, cultivating this parsimonious standard of living meant that holding a job even for a relatively short period would allow him to save enough to live for a time without gainful employment and devote himself to writing. The most important thing he was earning each time was a period of freedom. This meant a completely different approach to working and work than he had been raised to pursue. Professional advancement as a clerk or accountant was no longer his objective. He had resolved to define these activities strictly as day jobs, unconnected to his true aspirations. This took a great deal of courage. Without professional advancement in the worlds of banking or insurance, he would be starting each new job at the bottom of the office hierarchy. He was betting on art by condemning himself otherwise to life as a clerical underdog. Or maybe he hoped, each time he left one of these jobs, that it would be he last one he would ever need. He was also thinking of his life as a writer as a *professional* form of existence. He didn't want to be a hobbyist. Just as his brother drew and painted all day long, thereby developing his skill, Robert meant to pursue his writing with all his energies, to give himself space for contemplation, for dreaming, for composing lines as ecstatic as the "first-born" in Johanna's album.

On the other hand, this triumphant narrative isn't the only version of the becoming-a-writer story Walser tells. He has a number of tales about aspiring young poets, one of which in particular—"Die Gedichte (II)" ("The Poems") from 1919—displays far less swagger. The narrator of this story has backed himself into a corner by impulsively giving up his job to run off to Berlin:

> I gave up a quite acceptable position and set out to make the acquaintance of Life; but what goes by the name of Life frightened me, and I experienced a disappointment; I wept on foreign soil about my error

> and returned home. Here at first I was in difficult straits, finding myself unemployed, yet at the same time I was unspeakably courageous and had the feeling that things would go well for me.
>
> I myself don't quite know how I started writing poetry. I read poems, and this gave me the idea to write some of my own. [. . .] I wrote poems out of a mixture of bright-golden prospects and anxious prospectlessness, constantly half fearful, half almost bubbling over with exultation.[42]

According to this account, long-term intentional unemployment-for-the-sake-of-art, which is so romantically described in his bio note years later, isn't exactly how things looked for him at the time: "Since I was jobless, I wrote letters of application to commercial firms and took a secret pleasure in this as well. Everything gave me pleasure." And he held more jobs than we now have records of. In a letter to his sister Lisa written on May 5, 1898, he writes: "As for me, I am valiantly studying French, I go to the office every morning, return home insane, expect letters, don't write any but nonetheless expect every evening to find at least three letters."[43] We don't know what office he was going to, but no more than half a year can have passed between when he left the insurance firm and went looking for his next day job.

Meanwhile he had spent the better part of the winter writing, and by the spring had assembled something on the order of forty poems that he carefully copied over into a notebook that he placed in an envelope and mailed off to Joseph Viktor Widmann, the literary editor of the important newspaper *Der Bund*, published in Bern. Widmann had been publishing short texts (essays on geography and travelogues) written by Robert's older brother Hermann—at this point a geography teacher who had just (in 1896) completed his Ph.D.[44] Not so much is known about Robert's relationship to this brother, eight years his senior, whose teaching income had helped support Robert and his siblings during their financially tight childhood.[45] There is no evidence that Robert was helped in any way by Hermann in establishing the contact to Widmann; he appears to have sent in his work blind. So why did he pick Widmann to send his work to? For one thing, ever since Widmann had taken over the feuilleton section and literary supplement of *Der Bund*, it had become an extremely prestigious place to publish. Widmann was considered a literary authority in Switzerland, an eloquent critic who himself wrote in several genres, a personal friend of Carl Spitteler, Gottfried Keller, and Johannes Brahms. Ferdinand Hodler painted his portrait. There were also curious overlaps in the Widmann and Walser family histories: Widmann's father, Joseph Otto Widmann, had taken over the pastor's post in Liestal several years after it had been vacated by Robert's grandfather. And Widmann's son Max, then twenty-eight years old, had run the amateur theater club in Biel that young Robert had joined.[46] Finally, Robert's parents probably subscribed to *Der Bund*: one photograph of his father shows him reading it.

In his May 5 letter to Lisa announcing the publication of his poems the following Sunday, Robert saves the big news for last, first scolding Lisa for the melancholy tone of one of her recent letters, rhapsodizing about letters he'd like to receive, and then apologizing for an unspecified incident that took place over Easter: "You no doubt were a little bit disappointed in me, along with the other Bielers, at Easter, I mean. You mustn't go on introducing me as an extraordinary artistic beast [*Kunsttier*] for, you see, it's always a quite ordinary beast that comes home at Easter and Christmastime: me."[47] Maybe he'd told her he'd been writing poems, and that he'd been sending them out, and then she bragged about it. Maybe she'd even asked him to recite one of his poems in front of the family and friends gathered for the holiday, and given his native stiffness and awkwardness, that probably didn't go so well. He might well have embarrassed her as much as himself.

But then he goes on in the letter to crow a little bit himself, in a way that suggests he's confirming news she's heard elsewhere (from Hermann or Karl):

> Yes, it's me who sent Widmann the poems, and it's my poems that will soon be served up for dessert in the Sunday supplement of *Der Bund*. I wonder if I'll hear many flattering things with regard to the delicacy of my effervescent culinary art? Karl's going to Berlin! Haven't heard anything. I'll soon be moving to new quarters.[48]

The six poems whose publication would launch Robert's literary career were carefully selected by Widmann from among the forty-odd poems Robert sent him, published (by whose choice is unclear) with only the initials *R.W.* identifying the poet, and prefaced with an account of how the poems came into the hands of their editor: "A twenty-year-old commercial employee in Zurich, R.W., who left school for the office at the age of fourteen and so had no opportunity to pursue a course of higher education, recently sent the editor of this supplement a notebook containing approximately forty lyric poems, his 'firstborns.'" Widmann goes on to discuss the poems' strengths and weaknesses as he sees them, singling out certain lines for particular praise. He writes how pleased he was by the absence of "banal love poetry" in the selection, finding instead "something elemental and authentic and at the same time something very delicate" in the moods summoned up by the poems, along with a "strange sureness of foot, almost that of a sleepwalker," allowing the poet to move "at the outermost borders where one can so easily tumble from the standpoint of the sublime into the abyss of the ridiculous."[49]

The six poems Robert published in *Der Bund* were titled "Helle" ("Brightness"), "Trüber Nachbar" ("Gloomy Neighbor"), "Vor Schlafengehen" ("Before Bedtime"), "Ein Landschäftchen" ("A Little Landscape"), "Kein Ausweg" ("No Way Out"), and "Immer am Fenster" ("Always at the Window"). Two of the six invoke the "Sehnsucht" (longing) Robert had written about so extensively to his sister the previous July. All six show how much Robert had learned about poetry since writing "Future!" the previous spring. Gone was the fatal combination of solemnity and clichéd rhymes. He was still using rhymes, but now they were quirkier and lighter. One of the poems—"Trüber Nachbar," on the subject of poverty—still shows a concern with social justice, but it is the weakest of the batch, marred by inconsistent rhythms and a formal unsureness of hand; it is the only one of the six Robert would later discard when assembling his first book of poems. Others are quite strong. He later referred to "Ein Landschäftchen" as his first poem worthy of the name;[50] it sketches its landscape using a strategy of strict repetition, creating formal expectations that are surprisingly shifted in the last two couplets:

Ein Landschäftchen

Dort steht ein Bäumlein im Wiesengrund
und noch viel artige Bäumlein dazu.
Es friert ein Blättlein im frostigen Wind
und noch viel einzelne Blättlein dazu.
Ein Häuflein Schnee schimmert am Baches Rand
und noch viel weiße Häuflein dazu.
Ein Spitzlein Berg lacht in den Grund hinein
und noch viel schuftige Spitze dazu.
Und in dem allem der Teufel steht
und noch viel arme Teufel dazu.
Ein Englein kehrt ab sein weinend Gesicht
und alle Engel des Himmels dazu. (*SW*, 13:20)

A Little Landscape

There stands a little tree in the meadow's ground
and many more nice little trees as well.
A little leaf freezes in the frosty wind
and many more single little leaves as well.
A little snow heap shimmers on the bank of a brook
and many more white little heaps as well.
A pointy little mountain peak laughs down into the depths
and many more rascally peaks as well.
And in all these things the devil lies
and many more poor devils as well.
A little angel averts his weeping face
and all the angels of heaven as well.

Although written before the end of the nineteenth century, this poem seems like a work of early expressionism with its landscape abstracted into discrete features of the natural world, each of them presented in isolation from their context and then curiously multiplied. The sudden shift to devils and angels takes this poem unexpectedly into the religious realm, particularly when it turns out the angels are horrified at the hidden devilry of all these seemingly harmless natural phenomena (trees standing, leaves freezing, snow shimmering, mountain peaks laughing). The strange psychological animation of this landscape must have caught Widmann's attention—most of the landscape poetry crossing his desk must have been far tamer.

The strongest poems in the group, "Helle" and "Immer am Fenster"—two more landscape poems—are thickly lyrical, with musically integrated rhymes and slightly disjoined imagery that lends them interest. The second of these (from whose title Walser later dropped the "Immer" [always]) repeats the atomizing strategy from "Ein Landschäftchen," breaking down the landscape into isolated elements:

Immer am Fenster

Das herzwarme Braun der Erde,
das kindliche Weiß darauf,
die silbergrüne Wiese jetzt
haben einen Traum in die Welt gesetzt,
den Traum des Lächelns.

Es streichelt meine Wangen
die Hand eines guten Menschen;
mein Auge ist seelig blind,
ich würde sonst sagen können,
wessen Hände so zärtlich sind.

Den Traum des glücklichen Lächelns
haben die frauenhaft feinen,
zustimmend nickenden Farben
in die weite Welt gesetzt:
Ich steh am Fenster jetzt. (*SW*, 13:22)

Always at the Window

The heart-warm brown of the earth,
the childish white on top,
the silver-green meadow now
have sent a dream into the world,
the dream of smiling.

My cheeks are being stroked,
stroked by the hand of a good person;
my eye is blissfully blind,
otherwise I might have said
whose so tender hands these are.

The dream of a happy smile
was sent by femininely dainty,
assentingly nodding colors
out into this wide world:
I stand at the window now.

This charming poem has the landscape—whose colors have become animated, psychological—conjuring up a dream that is then experienced by the speaker in the second stanza. The only real action described in the poem comes in the last line: the speaker standing at the window. The smile—and the caressing mysterious hands stroking the speaker's cheeks to summon it forth—is just a dream produced by colors, colors that in the first stanza are described as "heart-warm" and "childish." These adjectives create the impression that the world described is a welcoming, friendly place with all its colors that "assentingly nod" in a feminine way, inviting us to gender the hand stroking the speaker's cheek. This playful poem with its lightheartedly skipping rhythms (particularly successful in the middle stanza) and sparing use of rhyme shows a mastery of the form that is a far cry from the forced and lumbering lines Robert was writing just one year before. He had now surpassed Robert Seidel in aesthetic accomplishment, and quite rightly decided the time had come to present himself to the world at large—at least the Swiss world at large—as a poet.

Imagine Robert's pride. Since the poems were signed only with his initials, it was his choice whether or not to identify himself as their author to the others in his workplace who knew him merely as a totter up and copier of ledgers and no doubt also as someone who read over his lunch break and always had a book in the pocket of his none-too-elegant jacket. The honor of having his work accorded praise in one of the most important newspapers in the country must have changed how they looked at him, assuming he admitted the poems were his. The publication was no doubt also good for his relationship with his brother Karl. Now that Robert too was being recognized for his art, the two stood on a more equal footing.

The publication of Robert's poems also brought him a connection to another powerful literary figure who was to play an even more important role than Widmann in launching his career: Franz Blei. Blei was only seven years older than Robert but had already published two plays and a number of essays when they met. Born into a wealthy Viennese family, he had come to Zurich to complete his studies of political economy and literature, publishing as his dissertation a translation of Ferdinand Galiani's 1770 *Dialogues on the Grain Trade* with a critical introduction (1895). He had connections to Zurich's literary world as well, counting among his acquaintances a number of young North German writers who had settled in Zurich, including that Maurice Reinhold von Stern who locked horns with Rosa Schätzle. Among his literary friends was a German student of psychiatry and literature, Otto Hinrichsen, who read the poems by Widmann's latest discovery in *Der Bund* and brought them to Blei's attention, whereupon the ever-resourceful Blei wrote to Widmann requesting the young poet's name and address and dropped Robert a note inviting him to call on him.

In a portrait written decades later, Blei provides the most complete physical description of young Robert we have:

> A few days later, he stood there in my room and said, "I'm Walser." A tall, rather gangly fellow with a bony, reddish-brown face, over which fell a thick blond shock of hair that had successfully resisted the comb, gray-blue dreamy eyes and well-fashioned hands that stuck out from the too-short sleeves of his jacket and did not know where to go and would have liked best to have hidden out in his trouser pockets so as not to be there at all. That was Walser, half itinerant journeyman, half pageboy, and all poet.[51]

Blei, who was self-possessed and quite the man of the world already in his late twenties, must have appeared an impressive figure to the socially insecure Robert. Blei was well educated, well spoken, and decidedly natty, comfortable in the nicely tailored suits that came with his social position. He had an open, friendly face adorned with a pince-nez on top and a pointy little beard below. He also enjoyed playing the host. Walser himself described his visit to Blei's home and the circumstances leading up to it in a 1917 text titled "Doctor Franz Blei":

> One evening [I received a letter from] Doctor Franz Blei, who asked me to be so good as to visit him, since he wished to make my acquaintance. The next day, at six in the afternoon, I went to see him. [. . .]
>
> Carefully I stepped into the house—I was setting foot for the first time in my life in a refined, elegant household. He gave an extremely friendly smile when he caught sight of me, and with visible courtesy and graciousness ushered into his home a young person who had as yet in no way acquired the art of presenting himself in a self-assured manner.[52]

Blei, the narrator tells us, goes on to draw his attention to the work of several writers, including Jakob Michael Reinhold Lenz, Georg Büchner, Clemens Brentano, and Novalis. There's no obvious trace of irony in the narrator's description of this interaction, so these may in fact be writers Robert was unacquainted with beforehand. Blei gives him several books as well, and then invites him to a party at his house that the narrator attends. All of this is related with a similar narrative inflation to what we see in Walser's account of his visit to Robert Seidel also written the same year (1917) in a period when he was thinking back on and mining his experiences in Zurich for narrative material. Unlike in the case of the Seidel story, we can't check Walser's account of the conversation against an actual document, but the main discussion points included here sound plausible, even if the language they are couched in is not. In the story, Blei asks the narrator twice about his future plans. At first the young man affirms that he intends to continue to work as a clerk as he pursues his writing—a response Blei is said to accept respectfully and without a trace of arrogance. But then they meet a second time, and the narrator tells a different tale. Blei asks if he wouldn't like to travel to Munich, and the narrator says he doesn't want to, explaining that he is capable of being his best only if he stays in Zurich. When asked to elaborate, he replies:

> I said: "When speaking with an intelligent person who is gentle in his thoughts one gladly communicates all sorts of things with the greatest contentment and with definite trust. So hear something that will perhaps appear to you quite foolish. This coming fall, I shall resign from the position I currently hold and as a result shall be without employment and work, whereupon it is my intention to go into seclusion. I shall lock myself away in the remoteness of some room on the outskirts of town and there continue to write poems. This is a quite simple plan that—if I am not terribly mistaken—I can definitely carry out, realize, and bring to life. When I have then written a few acceptable things, I shall look for and find a new suitable position, shall return to an office and be the same sensibly and purposefully working individual as before."[53]

Assuming that Walser's later account of the conversation is correct in its substance, Blei was the first member of the literary establishment to whom young Robert confided his plan to quit his job to write.

Robert's acquaintance with Blei proved crucial in the advancement of his nascent career. An entry in Blei's diary from June 24, 1898, shows how impressed he was with Robert right from the start: "Robert Walser, a young man from Bern who is working as a clerk here, recently paid me a visit. He will achieve extraordinary things." And on July 1, Blei wrote, "Walser brought me his poems, of which I am copying these"—he then copied out between five to eight poems; the exact number is unclear, since he later tore out one of the pages from the diary. These are the only poems copied out in this two-hundred-page diary, so they really must have meant something to him.[54] These were probably more or less the same poems Robert had showed to Widmann, since two of them are poems either printed by Widmann or mentioned in his introduction.

Franz Blei's prophecy that Robert would "achieve extraordinary things" was self-fulfilling, to the extent that Blei not only encouraged the younger writer but also helped him continue to publish. The following spring, he suggested that Robert send his work to Peter Altenberg, the master feuilletonist and key figure in Vienna's bohemian coffee house scene, who was also an editor at the respected bimonthly journal *Wiener Rundschau*. Robert did as he was told, accompanying the poems with a letter dated April 15, 1899, and the magazine published eight of the poems in its August 1, 1899, issue, this time using Robert's full name.[55] These poems are similar to the ones Robert had sent Widmann and Blei; one of them ("Helle" [Brightness]) was even among the first group published in *Der Bund*. The last and shortest of them, the rhyming quatrain "Spruch" ("Adage"), has gone on to become—under the revised title "Beiseit" (off to the side, in seclusion, discarded, shelved)—one of the most beloved of Walser's short poems:

Spruch

Ich mache meinen Gang;
Der führt ein Stückchen weit
Und heim. Dann ohne Klang
Und Wort bin ich beiseit. (*SW*, 13:22)

Adage

I go out on my walk;
It leads me a little way
And home. Then without sound
Or word, I am put aside.

The editors' note published in the *Wiener Rundschau* along with the poems praises their author's "honest talent" and "utterly autonomous feeling for nature" despite a certain "awkwardness." The note also quotes from Robert's letter to Altenberg that he sent to accompany the poems he was submitting:

> While I do hope that this delivery does not come as a surprise to you, might I also at the same time hope that no disturbance lies herein. If this should nonetheless be the case, I should like to ask your forgiveness. I should like to leave all directives regarding this matter entirely to your benevolence, to which I most thankfully and calmly bow.[56]

As letters of submission go, this one is remarkable. While the editor's note cites these lines as evidence that the poet is "free of all posing," I would argue that the opposite is the case. These lines in their highly mannered humility are in fact *performing* modesty rather than exemplifying it. They are markedly different from the writing in the genuinely humble letter Robert wrote to Robert Seidel just two years before. There is in fact nothing remotely modest about the playfully overblown delivery of this letter to a respected older writer that Robert sent on the date of his final birthday in the nineteenth century, the day he turned twenty-one. The difference in approach between the two letters is clear; this one is written by a young man in the bloom of early adulthood who is now convinced of his own talent, assured that he is now in fact a writer. And as a writer, it is his job to send his work out for publication, as he is herewith doing.

Few of Robert's letters from this period survive, but we can see from those that do—particularly those he wrote to Lisa, which are already playfully essayistic as early as 1897—that he is developing a particular way of speaking in them: a voice characterized by playful mock solemnity, rhetorically strategic repetitions, a strategy of discussing serious topics with a humor understood not to belie the seriousness of the matter under discussion, whether his sister's loneliness or the respect in which he holds writer Peter Altenberg. At the same time as Robert is working hard to develop his craft as a writer of poetry, he is also "playing hard" as the author of letters written in such a way as to provide entertainment both to him and to the letters' recipients. All those who praise his early poetry emphasize that these works show talent while being interesting, quirky, and a little awkward. No one says they are great, and in fact they aren't. If poems of this sort are all Robert Walser ever wrote, he would be forgotten as a writer today. He didn't realize it, but it was as the author of letters that young Robert was teaching himself to write.

Notes

1. *Der Lesezirkel* in Zurich printed a selection of poems and a prose piece, accompanied by a biographical note. This was the journal of the literary club Lesezirkel Hottingen, which invited Walser to give a reading on November 8, 1920. *SW*, 20:457.

2. "Lebenslauf (I)," in *SW*, 20:433.

3. Bernhard Echte, *Robert Walser: Sein Leben in Bildern und Texten* (Frankfurt am Main: Suhrkamp, 2008), 32, 58.

4. *SW*, 4:29. The salary of 125 Swiss francs per month is also assigned to the narrator of the somewhat later (1917) story "Luise," whose story overlaps with the one related in "Johanna," in *SW*, 5:193.

5. *SW*, 4:29.

6. Echte, *Robert Walser*, 61; and Bernhard Echte and Andreas Meier, eds., *Die Brüder Karl und Robert Walser: Maler und Dichter* (Stäfa: Rothenhäusler Verlag, 1990), 160.

7. Echte and Meier, *Die Brüder*, 160. Echte gives the Einwohnerkontrolle Zürich as the source of this information.

8. *SW*, 4:30.

9. Echte, *Robert Walser*, 61.

10. Elio Fröhlich and Robert Mächler, eds., *Robert Walser zum Gedenken* (Frankfurt am Main: Suhrkamp, 1976), 14.

11. Ibid., 17.

12. Ibid., 18.

13. Ibid., 20.

14. Seidel used roman script for the dedication he wrote in a copy of his book of poems *Aus Kampfgewühl und Einsamkeit* to fellow socialist Julius Vahlteich By the time this copy of the book was signed in 1903, Julius Vahlteich had been in the United States for over twenty years, having emigrated after laws passed in 1881 in Germany made all activities in support of Social Democracy in Germany illegal. Vahlteich eventually became the editor of the anarchist German-language *Arbeiter-Zeitung* (Workers' Newspaper) in Chicago, which is no doubt why his signed copy of Seidel's book wound up in the collections of the University of Chicago's library.

15. Robert Seidel, *Aus Kampfgewühl und Einsamkeit: Gedichte* (Stuttgart: J. H. W. Dietz, 1895).

16. *SW*, 5:194–95. "Luise" first appeared in 1917 as part of the collection *Kleine Prosa*.

17. Ibid., 195.

18. Ibid.

19. Ibid., 195–96.

20. Letter to Lisa Walser, July 30, 1897. *Briefe*, 7.

21. Ibid., 8.

22. Letter to Lisa Walser, August 3, 1897. Ibid., 9.

23. Heinrich von Kleist, letter to Ulrike von Kleist, *Sämtliche Werke und Briefe*, 9th ed., ed. Helmut Sembdner (Munich: Carl Hanser, 1993), 725.

24. *SW*, 5:194.

25. Echte and Meier, *Die Brüder*, 159.

26. Ibid., 158.

27. Ibid., 160–62.

28. Among others, Echte cites the stories (not yet translated into English) "Weihnachtsgeschichte I," and "Der Gute schrieb" as well as the poem "Der fünfzigste Geburtstag" (Echte and Meier, *Die Brüder*, 160). The character Luise also makes a cameo in "Festzug."

29. *TA*, 133–35.

30. *SW*, 5:206.

31. Echte, *Robert Walser*, 61.

32. Including "Rosa," "Luise," "Weihnachtsgeschichte I" and "Ich weiß zur Stunde nicht recht." Echte and Meier, *Die Brüder*, 161.

33. Letter to Therese Breitbach, late February/March 1926 (*Briefe*, 263).

34. Carl Seelig, *Wanderungen mit Robert Walser* (Frankfurt am Main: Suhrkamp, 1981), 59.

35. Quoted in Echte and Meier, *Die Brüder*, 197n60.

36. Echte, *Robert Walser*, 66.

37. Ibid., 59.

38. Ibid., 61.

39. "Fidelio," in *SW*, 17:212.

40. For example, "Die Gedichte (II)," *SW*, 16:254.

41. Robert Mächler, *Das Leben Robert Walsers: Eine dokumentarische Biographie*, 2nd ed. (Frankfurt am Main: Suhrkamp, 2003), 53.

42. "Die Gedichte (II)," in *SW*, 16:254.

43. Letter to Lisa Walser, May 5, 1898. *Briefe*, 9.

44. Fritz Nußbaum, "Professor Hermann Walser," *Geographische Zeitschrift* 26, no. 3 (1920): 65–67.

45. Katja Zellweger, "Familie Walser," in *Robert Walser Handbuch*, ed. Lucas Marco Gisi (Stuttgart: Metzler, 2015), 16.

46. Werner Morlang, *Robert Walser in Bern: Auf den Spuren eines Stadtnomaden*, afterword by Reto Sorg (Oberhofen: Zytglogge, 2009), 160–61.

47. Letter to Lisa Walser, May 5, 1898. *Briefe*, 10.

48. Ibid.

49. Echte, *Robert Walser*, 75.

50. Morlang, *Robert Walser in Bern*, 164.

51. Franz Blei, "Robert Walser," *Prager Presse*, April 21, 1935. This is one of a series of portraits Blei wrote of Walser, always recycling the same anecdotes. This particular description recalls a photograph of Walser taken in 1899, which Blei may be using to prompt his memory. The final version of this sketch appeared in 1940 in Blei's book *Zeitgenössische Bildnisse*. See Anne Gabrisch, "Robert Walser und Franz Blei—Oder: vom Elend des literarischen Betriebs," presentation at the annual gathering of the Robert Walser-Gesellschaft, Berlin 1999, accessed January 6, 2016, http://www.robertWalser.ch/fileadmin/redaktion/dokumente/jahrestagungen/vortraege/gabrisch99.pdf, 12.

52. "Doktor Franz Blei," in *SW*, 5:213–14.

53. Ibid., 219.

54. Echte, *Robert Walser*, 78–81. Credit for discovering these poems in Blei's diary goes to Bernhard Echte—a particularly valuable find, since some of the poems Blei copied are otherwise unrecorded.

55. Ibid., 90.

56. Ibid.

To Pieces

Robert Walser's Correspondence with Frieda Mermet

Elke Siegel

> For in gluttony two things coincide: the boundlessness of desire and the uniformity of the food that sates it.
>
> —Walter Benjamin, "Fresh Figs"

In 1975, Jörg Schäfer and Robert Mächler selected about four hundred of Robert Walser's letters and postcards from a much larger epistolary corpus and published them under the title *Briefe* (*Letters*). This volume has long been out of print.[1] The forthcoming *Kommentierte Berner Ausgabe* (*Annotated Bern Edition*) of Walser's works and letters will soon make available for the first time Walser's complete epistolary oeuvre from the archive: 750 documents, from 1897 to the final years in Herisau.[2] The prospect of this important body of letters and cards becoming public is reason to recall the question Peter von Matt has posed so succinctly: "Who wrote Robert Walser's letters?"[3]

Walser, as a professional clerk well versed in epistolary conventions, was also an excellent clerk of his own writing industry: negotiating, pressuring editors, struggling for his honoraria in elegant, sometimes outrageous, willfully unprofessional or utterly professional business letters.[4] In these, but even more so in his personal letters, Walser experiments with language, style, forms of address, and signatures in ways not easily distinguishable from his short prose, which itself often takes the form of the letter. Indeed, Stephan Kammer has recently shown that Walser's "letter writing games" exceed the model of self-positioning that still adheres to a "subject-centered communicative pragmatics."[5] Walser's epistolary performances, Kammer argues, subvert any notion of the representation of a self or of a role taken on by a presupposed self.[6] The first person in Walser's letters, as in his short prose, is, as Peter Utz emphasizes, first of all a pronoun: Walser's "first pseudonym."[7] In other words, the letters are further pieces of Walser's "mannigfaltig zerschnittenes oder zertrenntes Ich-Buch" (multiply cut-up or torn-apart book of the self).[8] Both his letters and his prose are marked by a peculiar and singular performance of first-person speech that makes his writing eminently recognizable but, at the same time, never entirely accessible.

Walser's epistolary work comprises what Vincent Kaufmann calls a "writer's correspondence." Such a body of work is "brought about by his [the letter writer's] existence as a writer" and "exists only where it can form a link between life and work."[9] The epistolary thus shows (and performs) a life that has always already been "lived in letters." It is also, as Kaufmann notes, characterized by "a taste for distance and perversion."[10] This latter observation holds especially true for Walser's correspondence, particularly for the personal letters he exchanged with female addressees, which reveal a desire to endow distance and writing quite literally—as we will see—with as much taste as possible. Indeed, as I argue in this essay, Walser succeeds in creating an epistolary configuration of hunger, desire, and gourmandizing, a configuration that lies at the heart of his metabolic experiments with a writerly life and, thus, with literature. Walser used the medium of the letter to play with language and to construct a self in writing, both of which were essential to his nomadic existence in and at the limit of (literary) society as an unbound, unmarried man. Indeed, a large portion of Walser's private correspondence is with women. His sisters Lisa and Fanny; Flora Ackeret (his and his father's married landlady); Therese Breitbach (a young woman from Germany who started writing to him on behalf of her brother, an aspiring writer): these are just some of Walser's female addressees. In Peter Utz's words: "Walser cannot write without women."[11] His most important addressee, however, is without doubt Frieda Mermet. Walser's correspondence with her constitutes, for Utz, an "author's correspondence" that forms a late "highpoint of bourgeois epistolary culture."[12]

The intimate entwinement of the epistolary and the literary, or the birth of literature out of the correspondence between a male author and female readers, seems reminiscent of what Bernhard Siegert has posited as the conditions for the emergence of modern literature around 1800. If the modern novel develops from the epistolary novel, the latter has as its condition the new possibility of individuals to send private letters. The act of folding up a piece of paper and putting it in an envelope creates interiority.[13] Moreover, the modern author evolves in his correspondence with female readers, creating feedback loops that allow him to gauge the effect of his writing in order to then feed this knowledge of "woman" (which supposedly couldn't be conveyed in the form of discourse)[14] into his work. Thus around 1800, according to Siegert, the "media status of poetry [. . .] corresponded to supplementary letters such as this: a printed text without an address, which was meant to be understood as a private letter addressed to each individual feminine reader."[15] In other words, printed literature, growing out of the new medium of the private letter, accomplished the feat of speaking to each reader as if she were the addressee of a letter. This epoch of literature closed, Siegert argues, around 1900, when the specific coupling of male author and female reader dissolved and women became media experts themselves. At that point, the correspondence between Franz Kafka and Felice Bauer—Kafka writing amorous epistles on his office typewriter—will belatedly reveal that the post was always already the condition of possibility of love letters.[16]

Walser's correspondences with women seem to be strangely at odds with his time and with the history of literature, technology, and media. He insisted, for instance, on writing by hand, and he wrote to and about women using the outdated discourse of gallantry such as "maid," "madam," "lady," and "girl."[17] The modernity of Walser's texts—both that of his prose and his letters—thus paradoxically manifests itself in seemingly anachronistic modes of address and in figurations of the literary that reach back beyond the Age of Goethe. In this way his work creates an alienation effect that on the one hand sheds light on the commodification of literature and the precariousness of the writer's existence in modernity, and on the other hand allows for depictions of roles and power structures governing social existence and desire.[18]

Walser starts constructing a culinary-epistolary poetics[19] in his letters to his sister Lisa that seems to describe a dynamic at the heart of his writing *tout court*; he discovers and uses the postal system as an essential feature of life and writing in the Ackeret house; and with Frieda Mermet, Walser creates a system of circulation in which prose pieces, pieces of food, in short a metonymic love for "pieces" of the other, come—by post—into contiguous relation in the service of a life that needs first of all enlivening through writing. Furthermore, what emerges in the latter correspondence is a post-publication parallel world of (textual) circulation that reconfigures and genders the feuilleton publication process according to Walser's need for the writerly, motherly care for his texts and their legacy.

Hunger, Games

One of the first surviving letters written by Walser is dated July 30, 1897. In it the nineteen-year-old assistant accountant in Zurich, addressing his oldest sister Lisa Walser (1875–1944),[20] announces the "exposition" for an "epistolary concept."[21] After thanking Lisa for her last letter and inquiring about her life, Walser exclaims, with gusto:

> Ich habe Hunger! Und immer, wenn ich Hunger habe, gelüstet es mich, einen Brief zu schreiben! An irgend jemand! Das ist doch begreiflich! Mit gefülltem Magen denke ich nur an mich, nie an jemand anders! Mit gefülltem Magen bin ich also glücklicher! Denn das ist doch kein Glück, sich nach etwas Fernem zu sehnen! Nun bin ich an dem Punkt, worüber ich in diesem grünen Brief mit dir reden möchte, sehr gern, wenn ich nur könnte. Aber ich versuche es: Also, was die Sehnsucht betrifft, so ist sie erstens etwas Ueberflüssiges, zweitens etwas Begreifliches und drittens etwas Unbegreifliches! [. . .] Ein Mensch, der sich

> die Sehnsucht abgeschüttelt hat, hat besser gethan, als ein anderer, der 100 sehr gut gereimte aber sehnsüchtige Lieder geschrieben hat. Solche Lieder sollten überhaupt gar nicht gedruckt werden. Hier sollte die Polizei entschieden eingreifen! O Uhland und dergleichen! Aber für heute ist genug! Ach, was soll ich zu Nacht essen? Schwierige Frage in solch traurigen Fressverhältnissen. Siehe, da nützt einem die Sehnsucht auch nichts. Oder verhilft mir die Sehnsucht nach einem saftigen Braten und einem Glas Veltliner zu beiden? Macht die Sehnsucht etwa, daß ich nicht so langweiliges Zeug zu fressen kriege, wie es der Fall ist? Die *That* allein kann hier helfen! Und das nächste Mal spreche ich über die That! (*Briefe*, 7–8)

> I am hungry! And every time I am hungry I crave to write a letter! To anybody! That's understandable! With a full stomach, I only think of myself, never anybody else! With a full stomach, I am thus happier! It is certainly not happiness to long for something far away! Now I have reached the point that I want to talk with you about in this green letter, very much so, if only I could. But I'll try: Where longing is concerned, it is first off superfluous, secondly comprehensible, and thirdly incomprehensible! [. . .] A person who has shaken off longing has done better than another who has written 100 very nicely rhymed but also longing-ridden songs. Songs of this sort should not even be printed. The police should most definitely intervene in such cases. O Uhland and his ilk! But enough for today! Oh, what should I eat for dinner? Difficult question under such sad food conditions. See, all longing doesn't help in this. Or will longing for a juicy roast and a glass of Veltliner get me these two things? Does longing ensure that I don't get such boring stuff to eat as it is the case? *Action* alone can help here! And next time I'll speak about action![22]

The young Walser, Utz writes, already practices the formula for turning unhappiness, associated with a longing for what or who is absent, into the happiness of writing (in)to the distance.[23] Starting out with hunger, the text moves on to the craving to write letters, on to a reflection on longing and literature, further on to thoughts of food and the ineffectiveness of longing, then to the need for action, and finally back to the writing of letters.[24] Encircled and partly sublimated is the initial hunger; discarded is the imagined transcendence through romantic longing; invoked is the pathos of action—all this to arrive at the projection of the next letter in the series. This gliding and spiraling textual movement draws the circle of a mouth, crying out from hunger, expressing its desire to be filled, and yet not wanting to close down on words. Longing is superfluous, Walser writes; and the letter—as performance of ongoing "talk"—makes manifest the paradox of this utterance: longing is superfluous *and* overflowing (the German for "superfluous," *überflüssig*, literally means "overflowing").[25] Just as volatile as the chain of words and sentences streaming out of that exclamation—"I am hungry"—is the addressee of the letter, who is and is not specifically addressed: this letter is written to Lisa as if she were "anybody." The logic of excess also can be seen in the fact that this letter is not just one, but comes with a further appended letter penned days later. Hunger, oscillating between material need and a principal lack of the subject, spills over in a desire ("gelüstet") to write—but also to receive—letters.

It is, again, a letter to Lisa, from May 5, 1898, that spells out the urgency of Walser's desire to find a letter waiting when he returns home:

> Was mich betrifft, so lerne ich tapfer französisch, gehe jeden Morgen ins Geschäft, komme Abends verrückt nach Haus, erwarte Briefe, schreibe keine, erwarte aber dessenungeachtet jeden Abend mindestens drei Briefe. Da sollten sie so liegen, wenn ich die Thür aufmache, weiss, blendend weiss, die liebe Marke drauf, der süsse Poststempel und all das andere. Und wenn nun keiner daliegt, so werd ich ganz dumm und kann nicht arbeiten und sage mir darauf sehr vernünftig: du schreibst ja keine Briefe, und erwartest welche! Ei du Schafskopf.
>
> Es ist nicht gerade, dass ich Briefe erwarte, aber ich erwarte jetzt immer etwas ebenso liebes, zartes, als ein Brief ist. Es sollte jeden Abend hier für mich eine kleine erhebende Ueberraschung aufliegen, gerade wie so ein Brief. (*Briefe*, 9)

> As for myself, I industriously study French, go to the office every morning, return in the evening as a madman, expect letters, write none, but nonetheless expect every evening at least three letters. There they should lie waiting when I open the door, white, blindingly white, the dear stamp on it, the sweet postmark and everything else. And when then none lies there I become completely stupid and can't work and then tell myself very reasonably: well, you're not writing any letters, and still expect some! Ah, you blockhead.
>
> It's not as if I am expecting letters, but I now always expect something just as dear, tender, as a letter. Every evening a small uplifting surprise should await me, just like such a letter.

A letter has been written; an envelope has been addressed and postmarked; the letter has arrived and awaits the addressee as a promise. Receiving a letter is tied to a pleasure of seeing an awaiting envelope, blinding in its paper-whiteness. The personal side of the letter, its sender or content, recedes in that decisive moment behind the sheer materiality and facticity of the epistolary and postal system. While in the first letter to Lisa words spill out of a mouth that lacks nourishment and still hungers, Walser's babbling here works at filling a void in the absence of letters addressed to him by her, or anybody. Writing a letter takes the place of reading one when the missing letter is made into a reason to write. The "hunger" of the first letter to some degree can be read as a boredom hungering for stimulation, which leads to letter-writing. Here poetic talent lies at the heart of the need for excitement: "Aber es lässt sich ganz gut auch ohne Erregungen leben, nicht wahr, man sollte nur mit etwas weniger Poesie und dergleichen begabt sein, nicht wahr, nicht wahr. Was bin ich für ein Schwäzer [*sic*], nicht wahr, nicht wahr?" (But one can also live very well without excitement, isn't that right? One should only be gifted with a bit less poetry and the like, don't you think, don't you think. What a babbler I am, don't you think, don't you think?) (*Briefe*, 9). The poetic gift pushes against the limits of everyday life, and the excitement that promises freedom from the quotidian is tied to letters awaiting him (or the waiting for the letter): a message that has passed posts, stations, and hands into his space and life. In other words: Walser's epistolary poetics grows out of his poetic gift, which expresses itself first of all as the experience of the lack of experience in everyday life. Walser's letters, then, are not about experiences; rather, they grow out of the absence of lived experience.

Excitement, desire, and poetic talent are evoked in the post. Where there are letters, there is distance, absence, and deferral; a titillating "epistolary secret" is contained in folded paper that creates a space for experiencing something different in the everyday. A strategy aimed at the possibility for such pleasure can be clearly seen in a letter from March 1905 that Walser wrote to Flora Ackeret, the wife of a postal clerk, landlady of Walser's father and Walser himself, and one-time lover of his brother Karl.[26] This letter, made available in print thirty-six years after the *Letters* volume first appeared, is written by Walser from the second story of the house, adorned with the sketch of a stamp, and addressed to Ackeret "in der Untern Welt" (in the Nether World). Claiming the letter "kommt von so weit her" (comes from so far away), Walser writes that, after having put on an old pair of pants, he feels entitled to write letters to the whole world, as he repeats twice. He continues: "Zwischen mir und Ihnen liegt eine Welt" (Between me and you there lies a world).[27] Getting up, getting dressed, and stepping into the world means writing letters to the whole world; and if those closest are not to fall outside this world, they should be integrated into the great postal universe that relates all, allowing for desire and writing as a perpetual writing *to*. Should there be no postal system for posting letters in-house, Walser invents a miniature post office where he occupies all positions, including that of the mailman.[28] The letter system is in place, and hunger feeds the writing. But how not to let hunger and the particulars of the world be absorbed, how to keep feeding the hunger, how to use the mouth to eat, kiss, taste, speak—all at the same time?

Eating (as a social ritual) or not-eating,[29] desire, appetite, deferral, momentary gluttony—these all form important aspects of Walser's letters, novels, and short prose, creating an intense sense of taste as a corporeal phenomenon. The culinary nature of Walser's writing therefore extends from the level of representation to the way language and texts should exist, how they are to be fed into life. Concepts such as the culinary or the gastronomic evoke a sense of the tactility and physicality of writing,[30] which can tickle the taste buds and be relished like delicious food, letting us taste language as something that is vital, real, material. The prose pieces in particular, given their designation as "Stücke" (pieces), should be imagined as not only existing in print, but being enjoyed as, say, a piece of cheese or cake, instead of wasting away as art.

Mermet's Company

Robert Walser met Frieda Mermet, a friend of his sister Lisa, when he returned to Switzerland from Berlin in 1913, "shipwrecked," as Mermet once said.[31] Before settling for the next few years in his hometown Biel, he spent time with his sister in Bellelay, a village in the Jura Mountains, where she worked as a teacher. Her friend Frieda made a living for herself and her son as the *lingère* (head of the laundry) at the psychiatric hospital located there.

The friendship with Mermet, lived primarily in what is the most regular and copious of Walser's correspondences, came at a decisive moment in Walser's life and work. The war would soon, for a time, cut Walser off from the German literary market, forcing him to refashion and reorient himself as an author.[32] As Utz shows convincingly, writing to Mermet played a central role in this transformation, but would last well beyond this critical moment up to 1942. Mermet as a figure co-organizes Walser's life and work for decades; the correspondence with her forms the "backbone"[33] of all his correspondences and of his literary existence. It is here that Walser (together with Mermet) creates and performs an epistolary poetics where eating, speaking, and sensing meet across a distance that allows for relationality. This is even more striking since letters were sent by two people who did not live very far apart—a fact that, as Utz points out, is easily forgotten when reading Walser's letters, which never seem to increase in intimacy.[34]

Walser and Mermet would occasionally take walks around Bellelay, or in Biel, where she visited a few times, and they traveled together twice. The topic of marriage was talked about, but they didn't become husband and wife and never shared a home.[35] The nature of their relationship was changeable and vague: Walser's letters address her as friend, mother, mistress, sometimes all at the same time. Here is the beginning of the first preserved letter to Mermet, sent from Biel, dated December 13, 1913:

> Liebe Frau Mermet.
>
> Meine Schwester, Sie und ich haben uns am vorletzten Sonntag gut unterhalten zusammen. Uebrigens hat das Stück Käse, wozu Sie so freundlich gewesen sind mir das Papier zu geben, gut geschmeckt. Wie geht es Ihnen? (*Briefe*, 67)

> Dear Frau Mermet.
>
> My sister, you and I had a good time together the Sunday before last. By the way, the piece of cheese for which you were friendly enough to give me the paper tasted good. How are you?

These first sentences—in which a correspondence is instigated by way of the movement from "my sister" to addressee to letter-writer to a piece of cheese—are literally (about) forging connections. Walser's sister Lisa, who introduced them, will keep appearing in the ensuing correspondence between Mermet and Walser, who occasionally asks about Lisa or asks Mermet to get a book for him from her. Mermet, as it were, relates to those who are related. She stands between and connects "my sister" and "I," creating a social entity out of a brother and a sister. It is thus, I would argue, no coincidence that three times in this brief letter Walser uses the word "Gesellschaft" (society/company) in relation to Mermet: once for her "company," which he enjoyed; then for her life in the "company" of her son Louis; lastly, for her friendship with Lisa, whom she keeps "company." What emerges, as epistolary product, is a parallel society or sociability, in which Mermet is connected to all members: a texture where man, woman, sister, boy, mother, and friend are woven together in and through her figure, who, on the other hand, is contiguously related to her friend, his sister Lisa. Thus, when Walser writes to Mermet, he does not write to one addressee: "Mermet," rather, denotes a net of relations. In addressing her, Walser is able to address her alternately as lover, as mother, as friend; through her he speaks to her son (including the eroticized role of the boy) or to his sister.[36] It might seem that Walser displaces the (prohibited) love to his sister or to Louis onto Mermet; but such a logic of substitution does not account for the much more pervasive sense of enjoyment that Walser gains, with and through Mermet, from a whole "company" of people standing in familial and nonfamilial relations with each other. Mermet, in other words, is his partner in a correspondence that grants Walser a family life without the conventional family structures; she takes on the chores of a wife without them being married and stands in for the stability of place without him having to settle down for good. She *has* and can offer a place (and company). It might be precisely Mermet's motherhood, Utz argues, that allows for the more transgressive erotic fantasies Walser voices in some letters, which he can always rein in by addressing her as mother.[37]

What gets to the heart of the matter (of the connection to Mermet) is the possibility of short-circuiting the epistolary exchange and the circulation of "pieces." The letter performs and creates "connections" (before there is a connection, as it were) between three people; but it also connects a piece of cheese, a piece of paper, and a woman. This is nowhere more clear than in Walser's reference to the good cheese he brought back from the first encounter. In a laborious relative clause ("the piece of cheese for which you were friendly enough to give me the paper tasted good") he connects the good cheese to her through the paper she provided for the transport of the cheese. The strained formulation might serve as a veiled request for more enjoyable food to be sent. But what is more important is that the piece of cheese becomes pleasurable not least because it can be tied to her. Moreover, it is as if with the wrapping paper for the cheese Mermet has already sent the first (wrapped) package, has already started their correspondence. This correspondence thus appears to be backdated: Walser might lure Mermet into it, but her paper, folded around cheese, has lured him, and has set the precedent for the form of exchange that will remain the most important aspect of their epistolary relationship. The food and the paper provided by her, touched by her: this provides the bare form for the fulfillment of the wish that writing, as a culinary art, succeed in feeding sense to life, and life to the senses.

This quasi-domestic exchange system built around writing and food appears, then, as the unlikely realization of that epistolary-culinary poetics already suggested in the first letter to Lisa. It is as if Walser, writing to Mermet (and through her, to everyone in the world), is allowed to call out—in as many ways as conceivable—"I am hungry," and will receive, in return, words and food that are never intended or expected to still this hunger. Starting with the letter to his sister, Walser manages, with time, to dissociate desire from lack, suggesting, as Samuel Frederick argues, that "there is a certain satisfaction in this proliferation of desire."[38] In other words, one could look at the self-perpetuating feeding- and writing-ritual enacted between Walser and Mermet as an ongoing celebration of the ever-present, never-to-be-stilled hunger at the heart of their exchange.

Pieces

The most striking aspect of the correspondence between Walser and Mermet is that it is a poetic endeavor, one which weaves a texture out of pieces of writing and other kinds of pieces that writing never quite seems to detach from: prose pieces; pieces of clothing that need mending; new pieces of clothing as gifts; pieces of food that were especially important in times of wartime rationing (cheese, butter, bread); a coin sent by Walser for Mermet's son Louis's savings; or books from Lisa's library that Walser requested through Mermet. All these pieces are "fed" into writing and feed writing.

The correspondence between Walser and Mermet has therefore famously been described by Peter von Matt as a continuous "feeding ritual" whose gendered erotic structure hinges on the various meanings of its "pieces" (of writing, of food, and related to erotic fantasies).[39] For von Matt, it is Walser who composes, directs, and regulates a game from the distance, which seems to leave no agency to Mermet, but installs a procedure of gift- and word-exchange as a system, in which appetites are stilled temporarily, over and over. Walser hereby constructs a household without the danger of producing a proximity that could domesticate the more anarchic energies vital for his writerly existence.

Von Matt's reading of the correspondence captures the "hard and dangerous Walser"[40] and points to the uncomfortable sense that a man here is asserting power over a woman, demanding reproductive work without taking responsibility. Such an interpretation, however, does not capture Walser's idiosyncratic ways, well known from his prose, of playing with power and dominance while at the same time subverting these forms of relation. Thus Marianne Schuller shows how in the context of this correspondence, while it does function as a well-oiled "writing-machine," fantasies of pieces from and of Mermet (her feet, fingers, nose) should also be considered as expressions of a love that withstands the "greedy desire of so-called love" (Nietzsche), which appropriates the other whole.[41]

"Pieces" in the Walser-Mermet correspondence come to function, I would argue, primarily as synecdoche: as pieces *of* (something or somebody). Rhetorically, as a trope based on metonymic contiguity, these pieces sustain a relationship to a whole. Furthermore, due to their transportability a metonymic movement is created and fed in which pieces of radically dissimilar nature touch: prose pieces, pieces of clothing, pieces of cheese, pieces of the body. Thus a sentence written by Walser to Mermet in March 1914 is itself a further piece of his impossible epistolary poetics, which aims to give life to numb existence and to create, as it were, bread out of words: "Wenn man sich schreibt, so ist es, als rühre man sich zart und sorgsam an" (When one writes to one another, it is as if one touches one another tenderly and carefully) (*Briefe*, 74). For von Matt this "wonderful sentence about writing letters," in the context of the correspondence as a "feeding ritual" manufactured by Walser, merely feigns mutuality.[42] I would suggest a somewhat different reading. If writing letters is likened to a tender and careful touching ("anrühren"), it is implied that a touch not mediated by letters might not be "tender and careful." In turn, because writing is likened to touch with the verb *anrühren*, this comparison creates two meanings for "writing" ("sich schreiben"): it designates a letter as an object coming from the hands of the other, carrying touch; and it designates that which is written, words that affect ("rühren") the reader. Both senses are mobilized in this correspondence: a letter is message and medium. It transports meaning and traces, and is accompanied by things, including itself as material object. What is envisioned in this correspondence, though, are letters where the "and" between material object and supposed immaterial meaning would vanish. What is more, though: in this sentence that appears to von Matt as performing a feigned mutuality, what becomes readable in the reflexive formulations is a double movement of writing. While the German uses the phrase *sich schreiben* for corresponding with somebody, it can also mean to write oneself or to write to oneself. Equally, *sich anrühren* might mean to touch each other or to touch oneself. In other words, Walser exposes that writing to another, in the sense of touching or affecting another, is not separable from auto-affection. Writing (letters) for Walser is writing, affecting, sensing oneself, but always at the same time in a relation to another. Tenderness and care reside in making this relationality—which goes beyond mutuality or balance—readable. Care and tenderness, in turn, are what is to be affected not only by but also for writing.

The Cares of Mothers

While the Walser-Mermet correspondence may seem merely to repeat the age-old gendered division of labor between man and woman, between male productive work and female reproductive work, this does not adequately capture the particularity of this relationship.[43] Walser's letters to Mermet, like all his writing, don't adhere to the model of the love letters—and yet they convey love. Although he is a man using up the gifts of a woman, it is not clear what "man" means or how the position of the male author is to be performed. As Patrick Eiden-Offe argues, it is precisely the male author figure in Walser's texts that displaces the (gendered) division of spheres and its concomitant division of labor.[44] After all, given Walser's limited literary successes and ongoing struggle to publish and get paid for them, the notion of productive male work comes under pressure: "Maybe literary writing is 'not a very manly behavior' *at all*."[45] The work of the writer finds itself lost "between-the-spheres," casting doubt on the classification of the author in terms of the gendered division of labor. Walser's correspondence with Mermet partly functions as a parallel world of writing and exchange where, speaking in an aside of his dealings with editors, he negotiates questions of power, submission, and sovereignty as they arise out of the so-called literary market and its implied ideas about male authorship.

On April 27, 1928, Walser writes to Otto Pick, editor at the *Prager Presse*: "Ich weiß nicht, ob es Stärke oder Schwäche bei einem Schriftsteller ist, wenn er mitunter ein Gedicht macht. Mir scheint die Frage, ob ein Dichter an sich Mann oder Weib sei, schwierig zu beantworten" (I don't know if it is a strength or weakness in a writer when he occasionally makes a poem. The question if a poet per se is a man or a woman seems to me hard to answer) (*Briefe*, 328).[46] While Walser operates here within gender stereotypes (strong/weak, man/woman), he moves these into the poet's zone of indeterminacy—his "in-between." If this question can be asked about a "poet per se," a gap seems to open which denaturalizes the poet's sex: s/he might be a man or a woman.

Walser does, as his letters show, at times feel the need to prove to himself and to society, and that means also to Mermet, that he is in fact working. Thus he claims that he sends her copies of printed prose pieces not merely for her entertainment, but as an "Arbeitsbeweis" (proof of work) (*Briefe*, 222; January 1925): proof to her of his status as *published* author, proof of his successful labors. This proof Mermet was to keep safe for possible further use. Thus, in November 1925, Walser writes to her: "Darf ich Sie bitten, alle diese Zeitungsauschnitte gut aufzuheben. Aber das versteht sich bei einer so sorgsamen Frau, wie Sie sind, von selber" (May I ask you to take good care of all these newspaper cuttings. But with such a diligent woman as you are, that goes without saying) (*Briefe*, 247). Mermet's reliability and carefulness, her *Sorge* (care), especially for her son, are traits he praises from the outset of their correspondence.[47] As a "diligent" woman, furthermore, who is taken care of ("gut aufgehoben") in Bellelay,[48] she has now to take care of ("gut aufheben") his prose pieces. In fact, in 1920, Walser enthusiastically adopts an analogy Mermet must have suggested regarding the relation between mother and child, on the one hand, and the poet and his work, on the other:

> Ihren netten kleinen Brief habe ich mit Vergnügen gelesen, und es hat mich gefreut, wie Sie mich mit ein paar Worten so gut verstehen, wie Sie sagen, daß es dem Dichter ähnlich gehe wie einer Mutter, die für's liebe Kind sorgt und in dieser Sorge freudig aufgeht und glücklich damit ist. (*Briefe*, 178; October 19, 1920)
>
> I read your nice little letter with pleasure, and it made me happy to see how with just a couple of words you understand me so well, how you say that the poet feels like a mother who cares for the dear child and is joyfully absorbed in this care and is happy with it.

While reminiscent of the "bachelor machine," with the male poet creating an apparatus of perpetual writing (desire)[49] that allows for procreation without women, this comment is not preoccupied with birth, but rather with motherhood as a feeling and practice of care to be shown his "children" in prose. Due to an unsteady lifestyle and numerous venues for publication, Walser, however, cannot take care of his pieces, even if he cares. He therefore delegates this task to Mermet, from mother to mother so to speak, who will in this way create the first Walser archive. This as it were double caring that is at work in the preservation of Walser's complicated oeuvre cannot be overestimated. After all, when assembling his collections of prose pieces starting in 1913, Walser often reused previously published texts.

However, when in June 1927 Walser wanted to draw texts from Mermet's archive—because a "lady" wished to read some of his work—Mermet seems not to have sent what he asked for. Walser is not amused and takes a somewhat unusual tone:

> Aber, aber, Frau Mermet, Sie erfüllten ja meine Bitte nur sehr unvollkommen. Wie soll ich das verstehen? [. . .] Ich bat Sie ja, das alles sorgsam aufzubewahren, um es mir zur Verfügung zu halten. Diese Sachen gehören Ihnen nicht, mir im Grund auch nicht, obschon ich der Autor davon bin, sondern Sie gehören dem gebildeten Teil der deutschsprechenden Menschheit. [. . .] Wollen Sie dies bedenken und wollen Sie dafür sorgen, daß ich jedes Stück, das hinterste, das letzte, zurückbekomme? [. . .] Aber, aber, liebe Frau Mermet, ich hätte nie geglaubt, daß Sie mir auf so auffallend lückenhafte Art ergeben wären. (*Briefe*, 279–80; June 7 and 26, 1927)

> Now now, Frau Mermet, you fulfilled my request only very incompletely. How am I to understand that? [. . .] Didn't I ask you to preserve everything carefully in order to keep it at my disposal? These things don't belong to you, essentially also not to me, although I am the author of them; they belong rather to the educated part of German-speaking people. [. . .] Would you consider this and take care that I receive back every piece, even the one all the way in the back, the last one? [. . .] Now, now, dear Frau Mermet, never would I have believed that you are devoted to me in such a conspicuously patchy way.

The "I" in this letter speaks from the position of the conventional (male) author who wants to posit himself as an artist and a man of interest to another woman—and ultimately to all German-speaking mankind. Given that Walser once wrote to Mermet that in their time—in the 1920s—success in the sexual and the cultural realm was difficult,[50] the scene that Walser makes here appears to result from a desire to create a success in both these realms at once. But then again, as we read in the next letter, this posture appears as a role taken on to run a test of Mermet's archive, possibly already with a view to the posthumous life of his writing. Quite aware of his still patronizing tone, he writes: "Ich bin jetzt, falls das nicht überheblich gesprochen ist, sehr zufrieden mit Ihrer in der Tat beinahe rührenden Zuvorkommenheit. Mir kam es bloß auf die neuere Zeitungsmitarbeit an, die Sie nun die Güte hatten, mir wieder einzuliefern" (I am now, if that is not spoken presumptuously, very satisfied with your indeed nearly moving obligingness. For me it was only about the newer newspaper collaborations, which you now had the kindness to send) (*Briefe*, 282; June 29, 1926). The use of the verb *einliefern* for Mermet's act of sending his pieces to him gives the scene yet another sense: *liefern* denotes the delivery of supplies or commodities, and it is the word Walser uses tongue-in-cheek in some letters to describe his dealings with newspapers over the publication of prose pieces.[51] If Mermet now delivers texts to him per mail, she is put into *his* position vis-à-vis the world of publishing, becoming his outwardly projected double. With Mermet, Walser works on creating a postpublication parallel world of textual circulation. Indeed, he had already playfully set up this analogous but distinct world of sending and receiving when he wrote, in April/May 1925, "Und nun teile ich Ihnen furchtbar ernsthaft mit, daß ich Ihnen für die gütige Einsendung nicht von Manuscripten sondern von gestopften und geflickten Strümpfen innig danke" (and now I am imparting to you horribly seriously that I thank you cordially for the submission not of manuscripts but of darned and mended socks) (*Briefe*, 230). Walser usually applies the verb *einsenden* for submitting prose pieces to editors with the request for publication.[52] In a process of analogy and wild circulation, manuscripts now become mended socks, and these, in turn, manuscripts.[53] While the sequence of letters discussed seems to put Mermet "in her place," I would argue that she ends up in a position of submitting texts similar to the way Walser submits them ("einsenden").

In December 1936 Walser writes to Mermet from Herisau that he is proud "eine so gute Freundin, wie Sie es sind, in Ihnen zu haben oder wenigstens gehabt zu haben" (to have or to at least have had such a good friend as you are) (*Briefe*, 353). He thereby acknowledges that theirs was a relationship in which the wish for the other's well-being has priority over the desire to merge two into one.[54] Not only should Walser's letters to Mermet, as von Matt writes, be considered among the famous love correspondences, such as the one between Franz Kafka and Felice Bauer, they should also be regarded as letters of friendship. Mermet, Walser once observes gratefully, would rather see him "in der Ferne fröhlich und schaffenslustig als in der nächsten Nähe verdrießlich und untüchtig [. . .]. Es zeugt dieser kluge Satz von Ihrer richtigen Auffassung. Menschen sollen sich nie den Lebensweg verschließen sondern einander helfen, denselben zu finden" (cheerful and eager to create in the distance than sullen and inept in closest proximity. This wise sentence bespeaks your correct opinion. People should never block the road of life, but help each other to find it) (*Briefe*, 182; December 13, 1920). Walser's letters to Mermet engage issues of authorship, work, masculinity, and precarious living conditions as central concerns of the literary in a way that won't allow for the stabilization of the borders separating public and private, man and woman, literary and supposedly nonliterary. The "taste for distance and perversion" (Kaufmann) at the heart of Walser's life (and) writing makes itself felt—and, if only as a hint, tasted—particularly in his writings to Mermet. Ultimately, however, all of his letters to women give a sense of the epistolary-culinary underpinnings of Walser's experiments with writing and with a writerly life, wherein hunger and desire, without lack or despair, are sustained through the mutual gifting of "pieces."

Notes

Chapter epigraph: Walter Benjamin, *Selected Writings*, vol. 2., ed. Michael W. Jennings, Howard Eiland, and Gary Smith (Cambridge, Mass.: Harvard University Press, 1999), 358.

1. The archive from which these selections were taken includes letters and cards mainly by Walser, who did not store much of the mail he received.

2. As Peter Stocker details, about two-thirds of Walser's letters were written after his return to Switzerland in 1913, with a concentration in the years 1917–19. Of the letters, 200 are addressed to various publishing houses (Insel, Rascher, Huber), and about 140 to editors of the feuilleton sections at twenty different papers in Germany and Switzerland as well as in Prague. See Peter Stocker, "Korpus, Brieftypen, Deutungsaspekte," in *Robert Walser-Handbuch: Leben—Werk—Wirkung*, ed. Lucas Marco Gisi (Stuttgart: Metzler, 2015), 217–24, and "Adressaten und Adressierungen in Robert Walsers Briefen und ihre editorische Behandlung in der Kommentierten Berner Ausgabe (KBA)," *Germanistik in der Schweiz* 9 (2012): 57–78. I want to thank Peter Stocker for the correspondence about letters in the archive that have not yet been published.

3. Peter von Matt, "Wer hat Robert Walsers Briefe geschrieben?," in *"Immer dicht vor dem Sturze . . .": Zum Werk Robert Walsers*, ed. Paolo Chiarini and Hans Dieter Zimmermann (Frankfurt am Main: Athenäum, 1987), 98–105.

4. See Teresa Vinardell Puig, "'In unaufrichtigster, dafür aber schimmerndster Hochachtung': Überlegungen zu Robert Walsers Briefen an Verleger und Redakteure," in *WortKulturen TonWelten: Festschrift für Alfonsina Janés zum 70. Geburtstag*, ed. Marisa Siguan, M. Loreto Vilar, and Rosa Pérez Zancas (Marburg: Tectum, 2014), 101–14.

5. Stephan Kammer, "Gestörte Kommunikation: Robert Walsers Briefschreibspiele," in *"Ich an Dich": Edition, Konzeption und Kommentierung von Briefen*, ed. Werner M. Bauer and Wolfgang Wiesmüller (Innsbruck: Universität Innsbruck, 2001), 229.

6. Ibid., 230.

7. Peter Utz, "Ausgeplauderte Geheimnisse: Die Verwandtschaft von Brief und Feuilleton am Beispiel Robert Walsers," in *Briefkultur: Transformationen epistolaren Schreibens in der deutschen Literatur*, ed. Isolde Schiffermüller and Chiara Conterno (Würzburg: Königshausen & Neumann, 2015), 192.

8. *SW*, 20:322.

9. Vincent Kaufmann, *Post Scripts: The Writer's Workshop*, trans. Deborah Treisman (Cambridge, Mass.: Harvard University Press, 1994), 10.

10. Ibid., 6, 10.

11. Peter Utz, "La fringale épistolaire de Robert Walser," in Robert Walser, *Lettres de 1897 à 1949*, trans. Marion Graf (Geneva: Éditions Zoé, 2012), 8.

12. Utz, "Ausgeplauderte Geheimnisse," 184.

13. Bernhard Siegert, *Relays: Literature as an Epoch of the Postal System*, trans. Kevin Repp (Stanford, Calif.: Stanford University Press, 1999), 30.

14. Ibid., 77.

15. Ibid., 91.

16. Ibid., 83.

17. Pia Reinacher, *Die Sprache der Kleider im literarischen Text: Untersuchungen zu Gottfried Keller und Robert Walser* (Frankfurt am Main: Peter Lang, 1988); Marion Gees, "Robert Walsers galante Damen: Fragmente einer Sprache der höfischen Geste," in *Text und Kritik: Robert Walser*, vol. 12/12a, ed. Heinz Ludwig Arnold (Munich: Edition Text + Kritik, 2004), 142–54.

18. On Walser's questioning and subversion of the literary establishment as well as a reading of sexual relations in Walser's texts as figurations of the Hegelian dialectic of master and servant see Valerie Heffernan, *Provocation from the Periphery: Robert Walser Re-examined* (Würzburg: Königshausen & Neumann, 2007), 76–87, 103–14.

19. See Dieter Roser, who draws on Walter Benjamin's notion of "gastronomic prose" to discuss the connection between eating and writing in Walser in his *Fingierte Mündlichkeit und reine Schrift: Zur Sprachproblematik in Robert Walsers späten Texten* (Würzburg: Königshausen & Neumann, 1994), 80. This also entails the emphasis on the mouth as the place of language and of incorporation (ibid., 96). For Walser's "culinary poetology" see Iris Denneler, "'Erzähle ich eine Geschichte, so denke ich ans Essen': Zur kulinarischen Poetologie Robert Walsers," *Wirkendes Wort* 49 (1999): 167–295.

20. Lisa, the oldest daughter of the Walser family, took care of her younger siblings after their mother's death in 1894. She later worked as a teacher in and close to their hometown Biel, as well as in Italy and Bern, before settling in Bellelay, where she taught until her retirement in 1940. Walser at times found shelter with Lisa, who would later take over his guardianship after having him committed first to the mental institution Waldau (1929) and afterward Herisau (1933). At least in part, she was the model for Hedwig in *Geschwister Tanner* (*The Tanners*) and for the enigmatic Fräulein Benjamenta in *Jakob von Gunten.*

21. Silvia Henke, "Eigensinnige Briefe: Zwischen Literatur- und Medienwissenschaft," in *Weiterlesen: Literatur und Wissen*, ed. Ulrike Bergermann and Elisabeth Strowick (Bielefeld: Transcript, 2007), 174–98. For further important discussion of this decisive letter see Utz, "La fringale épistolaire," 8; Utz, "Ausgeplauderte Geheimnisse," 185; and Marianne Schuller, "Briefe an Frieda Mermet," in *Robert Walser-Handbuch: Leben—Werk—Wirkung,* ed. Lucas Marco Gisi (Stuttgart: Metzler, 2015), 224–30.

22. Parts of this translation are by Susan Bernofsky, taken from her essay in this volume.

23. Utz, "La fringale épistolaire," 8.

24. Henke, "Eigensinnige Briefe," 190.

25. Schuller, "Briefe an Frieda Mermet," 227.

26. See Erich Unglaub, "Flora Ackeret und Robert Walser: Poetisierung oder Poetologisierung einer Beziehung?" in "*Immer dicht vor dem Sturze . . . ,*" ed. Chiarini and Zimmermann, 106–21. Walser's letters to Ackeret will become accessible in print for the first time with the new edition of Walser's letters.

27. Bernhard Echte, *Robert Walser: Sein Leben in Bildern und Texten* (Frankfurt am Main: Suhrkamp, 2008), 169. See also Utz, "Ausgeplauderte Geheimnisse," 185. See, for a literarized version of this scene, Walser's piece "Marie" (*SW*, 6:61–83).

28. This scene in the house Ackeret seems reminiscent to some degree of the bachelor machines of Duchamp or Kafka, albeit inverted. See also Walser's prose piece "Der andere Junggeselle" (*SW*, 5:118–20).

29. See Denneler, "'Erzähle ich,'" 54; Samuel Frederick, *Narratives Unsettled: Digression in Robert Walser, Thomas Bernhard, and Adalbert Stifter* (Evanston, Ill.: Northwestern University Press, 2012), 32–36.

30. A case in point is a letter from January 1924 to Frieda Mermet about Jeremias Gotthelf, whose sentences, Walser writes, "taste like meat" (*Briefe*, 211). See Roser, *Fingierte Mündlichkeit*, 89–97.

31. Frieda Mermet, "Frau Frieda Mermet erzählt," *Neutralität* 5, no. 3 (1967): 16.

32. Utz, "La fringale épistolaire," 10. Utz maintains that around 1913, on his return to his hometown Biel at the border between French- and German-speaking Switzerland, Walser experimented increasingly with dialect and French in his writing and particularly in his letters to Mermet (ibid., 13).

33. Ibid., 10.

34. Ibid., 8; Schuller, "Briefe an Frieda Mermet," 227.

35. For Walser's phantasies and thoughts about a possible marriage see *Briefe*, 137 (July 10, 1918) and 154 (December 6, 1918). Regarding Walser's explicitly masochistic phantasies see Wolfram Groddeck, "Masochismus," in *Robert Walser-Handbuch: Leben—Werk—Wirkung*, ed. Lucas Marco Gisi (Stuttgart: Metzler, 2015), 332–36, and Jens Hobus, *Poetik der Umschreibung: Figurationen der Liebe im Werk Robert Walsers* (Würzburg: Königshausen & Neumann, 2011), 185–201.

36. In one letter he even imagines a marriage with Mermet in which they would live together with Lisa (*Briefe*, 159).

37. Utz, "La fringale épistolaire," 11.

38. Thus, Walser writes in the prose piece "Auflauf" ("Casserole"): "Sollte ich nicht den Beweis erbracht haben, daß der Hunger in gewisser Hinsicht vollständiger sättigt, als es das kompletteste Essen imstande ist?" (Haven't I proven that hunger in a certain respect satiates more completely than the most complete meal can?) (*SW*, 20:44). See Frederick, *Narratives Unsettled*, 33.

39. Von Matt, "Wer hat Robert Walsers Briefe geschrieben?," 101.

40. Ibid.

41. Schuller, "Briefe an Frieda Mermet," 226–29. See *Briefe*, 73 (probably March 1914), 82 (Winter 1914/1915), 85 (probably January/February 1915), 100 (probably February 1917), 139 (August 7, 1918), 153 (December 6, 1918), and 171 (November 1919); Friedrich Nietzsche, *The Gay Science: With a Prelude in German Rhymes and an Appendix of Songs*, ed. Bernard Williams, trans. Josefine Nauckhoff (Cambridge: Cambridge University Press, 2001), 39–40.

42. Von Matt, "Wer hat Robert Walsers Briefe geschrieben?," 101.

43. Ibid.

44. Patrick Eiden-Offe, "Männlichkeitsvertreter: Figurationen von Männlichkeit in der späten Prosa Robert Walsers. Eine exemplarische Lektüre des Prosastücks 'Es war einmal,'" paper presented at the "2. Tagung AIM Gender" (2002), 8. https://www.fk12.tu-dortmund.de/cms/ISO/de/arbeitsbereiche/soziologie_der_geschlechterverhaeltnisse/Medienpool/AIM-Beitraege_zweite_Tagung/eiden.pdf. Accessed October 1, 2015.

45. Ibid.

46. See also *AdB*, 5:273.

47. See *Briefe*, 128; after April 17, 1918.

48. See, for example, *Briefe*, 124 (March 21, 1918), 135 (June 30, 1918), 142 (June 9, 1918), 166 (April 12, 1919), 172 (November 1919), 293 (April 13, 1927).

49. See note 28, and Frederick, *Narratives Unsettled*, 33–34.

50. *Briefe*, 290 (December 7, 1926).

51. See *Briefe*, 222 (January 1925), 290 (January 3, 1927).

52. See, for example, *Briefe*, 10 (May 2, 1899), 40 (June 26, 1905), 74 (March 1914), 113 (September 11, 1917), 141 (September 6, 1918).

53. When Walser writes once that in the German-speaking literary world authors must fill "laundry baskets" (*Wäschekörbe*) with writing and then die to gain recognition, this is yet another moment of an intersection between their respective work (*Briefe*, 232; April/May 1925).

54. For the literary afterlife of the relationship between Walser and Mermet, see Daniel de Roulet, "Wandern, Schreiben, Lieben," trans. Marion Gees, in *Text und Kritik: Robert Walser*, vol. 12/12a, ed. Heinz Ludwig Arnold (Munich: Edition Text + Kritik, 2004), 44–51; Jürg Amann, "Liebe Frau Mermet: Eine Art Liebesbrief nach Briefen von Robert Walser," in Jürg Amann, *Pornographische Novelle* (Cologne: Tisch 7, 2005), 67–98, and Gert Hofmann's audioplay *Die Brautschau des Dichters Robert Walser im Hof der Anstaltswäscherei von Bellelay* (1982).

Robert Walser as Lyric Poet

Samuel Frederick

Robert Walser's earliest literary production and publication consisted almost exclusively of lyric poetry, and much of his early writing was dominated by verse forms of various kinds, including verse dramas. Although he took a brief hiatus from writing poetry when he moved to Berlin in 1905, and produced very little verse during the subsequent Biel years (1914–21), Walser wrote and published poetry almost as steadily as prose during the extremely productive dozen years he spent in Bern (1921–33). Indeed, there is nearly as much verse as there are prose pieces in the microscripts.[1] Walser's poetry nonetheless continues to be seen as marginal to, and qualitatively lesser than, his novels, short prose, and even dramatic works. While it is not true that poetry was marginal to Walser's productivity, the question of quality is more complicated, particularly when considered in terms of reception history, for although Walser's early verse was mostly very well received at the time, his later verse was initially completely dismissed.[2] Today the situation is almost the reverse; but unlike Walser's contemporaries, we are the grandchildren of modernism. The more experimental later verse, which often completely flouts and sometimes even mocks convention, is much closer to our aesthetic sensibilities than the quite formal and apparently conventional early verse, which is deeply steeped in the traditions of late nineteenth-century song forms.

The present essay is guided by the conviction that these two periods of Walser's lyric productivity are not so dissimilar after all, that despite their surface differences they share some of the same formal idiosyncrasies, and that these idiosyncrasies have similar consequences for the kinds of sense these poems make—as well as for the kind of sense they make *as* poems. The essay as a whole aims to offer an overview of Walser's lyric works, and it does so in two parts: one devoted to the early poems, the other to the late poems.[3] In both sections I trace a dialectic of convention and experimentation, of normative form and strategic disruption. This pattern is, in itself, nothing new (one might even say it defines how literature functions). The difference is that in each case the initial phase of this dialectic differs. In the early poems convention precedes the disruptions of experimentation; in the later poems experimentation is the dominant mode and is countered, even restrained, by the paradoxically antithetical forms of convention. In both cases Walser's poetry tends toward a playful reduction of semantic content in the face of the more conspicuous elements of form and technique.

I look in particular to the role of repetition in the early verse as a means of poetic erasure and to the role of rhyme in the later verse as a symptom of the poem's "inanity" (*Blödigkeit*)—a term Walser used to describe his own poetic modus. My contention is that in Walser's lyric output in general erasure and inanity are opposite sides of the same coin. His poems from both periods are engaged in a performance of inanity—as both silliness and lack of sense or signification—that participates in evacuating content and erasing stable points of orientation, be they the things of this world or our intellect. Ultimately the poems celebrate inanity as a mode of self-erasure that has the potential to inaugurate a privileged mode of nonthinking, a kind of escape from the burden of self and consciousness.

I. Early Poems (1897–1901): Repetition and Erasure

In the few years between Walser's first serious attempts at writing verse in early 1897 to around 1900 he wrote more than a hundred poems,[4] dozens of which were published in the feuilleton section of various newspapers and in literary magazines, and many of which would later be collected in the volume *Gedichte* (*Poems*), which appeared in March 1909. This collection of verse included no new poetry, Walser having dedicated the prior half-decade to prose and novels. His desire to collect together and publish these poems nonetheless indicates that he by no means disowned his early lyric work as mere juvenilia. Indeed, the 1909 collection would be published in a second edition a full decade later, with only minor stylistic changes and with no additions, which testifies to Walser's continued conviction in the quality of his early lyric output, even during a time when he published almost no poems at all.

The verses collected in *Poems*, as well as those found in the unpublished (and uncirculated) handwritten manuscript *Saite und Sehnsucht* (*Chord and Longing*; ca. 1900),[5] are characterized by a surface simplicity and naïveté made possible only by a strong sense of artificiality and knowing mannerism. Their at times inflexible regularity suggests a feigned artlessness, drawing the reader's attention away from ostensible content to manner and form. Take, for instance, one of the six poems that together comprised Walser's very first publication (in a May 1898 Sunday edition of *Der Bund*):[6]

Wie immer

Die Lampe ist noch da,
der Tisch ist auch noch da,
und ich bin noch im Zimmer,
und meine Sehnsucht, ah,
seufzt noch wie immer.

Feigheit, bist du noch da?
und, Lüge, auch du?
Ich hör' ein dunkles Ja:
das Unglück ist noch da,
und ich bin noch im Zimmer,
wie immer. (*SW*, 13:14)

As Ever

The lamp is still here,
the table, too, is still here,
and I'm still in the chamber,
and my longing, ah,
still sighs, as ever.

Cowardice, are you still here?
and, lies, you too?
I hear a dark Yes:
misfortune is still here,
and I'm still in the chamber,
as ever.[7]

This is a poem about lethargy and monotony, which succeeds in evoking the speaker's melancholic unease by way of the form of the list. The poem catalogues what "is still here," as if to demonstrate that this matters only insofar as the things catalogued testify to the speaker's stagnancy and inability to escape.[8] The inventory enumerates, and in thus adding one thing paratactically to the next, it levels differences. Even the speaker is by virtue of this enumeration reduced to the same level as the objects in the room.[9] This leveling is also carried out by the repetition of the same. While the poem rhymes ("da"/"ah"/"Ja" and "Zimmer"/"immer"), it first offers us repetition without difference in the form of "here," which ends the first two lines and reappears twice in the second stanza. These four instances of "here," together with the repeated "still" and the poem's syntactic (paratactic) repetition ("and" is the only conjunction used), lend it the performative power of the "always the same," that gives recurring time the "character of yawning, dead emptiness," as Thomas Binder puts it.[10]

Running counter to this performance of languor and emptiness is the voice of affect ("my longing, ah")[11] and the second stanza's shift from concrete objects to abstractions: cowardice, lies, misfortune. These phenomena, folded into the list of things, we take to be the origin of the speaker's condition. The catalogue becomes a litany, a supplicatory call that even receives a mock-ceremonial response in a "dark Yes." The abstractions, that is, are personified—but they are at the same time divested of the presence one might expect from this substantiation. For not only are cowardice and lies negations (lack of courage and truth, respectively), both are also immaterial. Their personification, in other words, is nothing but a rhetorical device incapable of granting actual substantiality. Furthermore, the "presence" of cowardice and lies is the apparent cause of the speaker's fundamental "misfortune," his perpetual "longing" for something *not here*. Their presence, in other words, marks an absence, an absence paradoxically reinforced at the poem's end in the repetition of line 3 ("and I'm still in the chamber") followed by the final words (and title of the poem): "as ever." Here, even more forcefully than in the first stanza, repetition instantiates "the same" in the form of invariable recurrence, which becomes both a temporal and a spatial problem. The speaker is "still here," just as the lines "and I'm still in the chamber" and "as ever" are *still here*. We may have moved on from the previous appearance of these phrases, but we haven't arrived anywhere. And although time has elapsed, the lack of change gives us no sense of this temporal advance. By means of repetition we follow the speaker into an abstract place where time and space seem to have come to a standstill.[12] Yet while this stagnancy and confinement seems above all to be the source of the speaker's melancholic condition, repetition also generates the sense that this standstill might, in the end, coincide with an escape from time and space, altogether, and as such entail an overcoming of their inherent burdens.

These are not isolated examples of the repetition of word or phrase in Walser's early verse. He uses the technique frequently. At times it appears to function as a strategy of intensification, as in the poem "Schnee (II)" ("Snow [II]"), which begins:

> Jetzt seh ich von der Welt
> von Himmel und von Erd
> nichts als den weißen Schnee.
> Hier Schnee und wieder Schnee,
> dort Schnee und wieder Schnee. (*SW*, 13:35)
>
> I now see of the world
> of sky and of the earth
> nothing but the white snow.
> Here snow and again snow,
> there snow and again snow.

These lines' description of a buildup of snow corresponds to the buildup of the word for snow, which here appears six times within two and a half lines of the poem. The word "snow" thus does not just signify the meteorological phenomenon; its repetition imitates—both graphically and as sound within the economy of the metrical pattern—the activity of the phenomenon signified: the piling-up of snow. The word's repetition also functions structurally as a form of negation: it whites out the things that preceded it. If the first two lines balance speaker and world, heaven and earth (a balance reinforced by the regular iambic trimeter), the next three systematically erase these stable points of orientation, until there is indeed "nothing" left but (the word) "snow."[13] This erasure is further stressed metrically. Once the first "snow" falls at the end of the third line, the strict iambic meter shifts, the subsequent lines beginning with spondees: "Here snow [. . .] / there snow [. . .]." These two stressed syllables participate in announcing rhythmically the snow's heavy, muffling fall.

Walser is fond of mimicking the activity signified by his words using repetition, particularly forms of epistrophe, repetition of the same word at the end of successive lines. In the poem "Winterregen" ("Winter Rain") he combines epistrophe with anaphora (repetition of a word at the start of the line)—a technique known as symploce—to evoke the falling of rain:

> Ich sehe weichen Regen
> auf harte Wiesen fallen,
> auf böse Bäume fallen,
> auf dunkle Häuser fallen (*SW*, 13:37)

> I see the soft rain
> on hard meadows falling
> on angry trees falling
> on dark houses falling

Here the regularity of three consecutive lines that are bookended by "on" at the start and "falling" at the end, together with these lines' regular iambic meter, imitates the steady drumming of the rain as it falls. Repetition, in other words, is itself—independent of signification—mimetic.[14]

The same cannot be said of how Walser makes use of repetition (specifically, symploce) in the poem "Wiesengrün" ("Meadow Green"), which starts:

> Hervorgetreten ist
> aus hingegangnem Schnee
> ein schönes Wiesengrün,
> ein Grün, ein dunkles Grün.
> Dasselbe scheint der Welt
> als milde Sonne jetzt,
> als wilde Sonne jetzt,
> als warme Sonne jetzt.
> Die rechte scheint ja nicht,
> die rechte wärmt ja nicht. (*SW*, 13:32)

From the melted snow
has emerged
a lovely meadow green,
a green, a dark green.
The same appears to the world
now as the mild sun,
now as the wild sun,
now as the warm sun.
The real one doesn't shine,
the real one doesn't warm.[15]

This poem continues with nearly as many repetitions, which preclude any rhyme in the face of the reappearance of the same. Of course the poem is precisely about mistaking difference for identity. Green "appears" to "shine" (both meanings of the German verb *scheinen*) like the sun—but the meadow's green is not the sun, which as the poem goes on to explain is hiding behind thick clouds. The three repetitions of "green" in close succession (lines 3–4) correlate to the three appearances of "sun" in lines 6–8. In fact, these latter lines are nearly word-for-word identical; only the adjective modifying "sun" shifts slightly from "mild" to "wild" (requiring, in English as in the original German, only the first letter to be flipped upside down) to "warm." Yet these lines refer to a misperception, a failure to see the sun in any of these guises, for "the real one" neither shines nor warms, since it is covered over. Repetition of the same therefore does not intensify, but rather fills a void where the thing invoked should be.

Before returning to this peculiar effect of repetition, I want briefly to consider the "jetzt" (now) that ends each of these lines (in Daniele Pantano's English translation the "now" comes at the start of the lines), because it brings us back to the problem of temporality broached by the analysis of "As Ever" above, as well as—relatedly—to the question of rhyme, specifically the absence of rhyme inaugurated by this kind of repetition (epistrophe). One might read each "jetzt" that ends lines 6–8 as a different moment in time, so that the repetition of the word performs the similar repeated "moment of time" that is at once the same word and, by virtue of succession, a different one. The repetition of the same, however, attempts to cover over this difference. Indeed, it appears to insist on sameness in the face of difference. The sun is precisely *not* visible "now"—or "now" or "now." Something else—something different (the newly emerging "green" of the "meadow")—has replaced its glow so that the "world" does not notice its absence. Sameness is here asserted; indeed, in its threefold repetition we might even say it is *imposed*.[16] What at first appears to announce joy at the emergence of vernal life after a dead winter in fact carries with it a forceful forgetting. Change has arrived, a profound change that marks the most determinate, because collectively experienced, shift in time: one season has given way to the next.

And yet "now" does not (appear to) change. The repeated "now" marks stasis in the face of movement. It stubbornly pronounces sameness against all evidence to the contrary.

The problem of time and repetition comes to a peak in the following poem, dating from the same period as "Meadow Green" (both were found in the unpublished manuscript *Chord and Longing*):

Zeit

Ich liege hier, ich hab ja Zeit,
ich sinne hier, ich hab ja Zeit.
Der Tag ist dunkel, er hat Zeit,
mehr Zeit, als ich mir wünsche, Zeit
hab ich zu messen, lange Zeit.
Das Maß wird größer mit der Zeit.
Nur etwas übersteigt die Zeit,
das ist die Sehnsucht, keine Zeit
ist zeitig mit der Sehnsucht Zeit. (*SW*, 13:31–32)

Time

I lie here, I've got the time,
I ponder here, I've got the time.
The day is dark, it has time,
more time than I wish for, time
that I have to measure, long time.
The measure gets bigger with time.
Only one thing rises above time,
that is longing, no time
is ripe with longing's time.

The nine lines of this poem contain the word "Zeit" (time) ten times, not counting the poem's title and the adjective "zeitig" (ripe), which would raise that number to twelve. What compounds the apparent intensity of this repetition is its relentless epistrophic form: each line ends with the same word. When employed in verse, such that the repeated end of the clause corresponds to the end of the poetic line, epistrophe urges us to consider how, precisely, it differs from rhyme, and in turn what makes rhyme distinctive as a poetic form. In one sense, epistrophe is an instance of *perfect* rhyme—so perfect that the words repeated cannot be distinguished from one another. Rhyme, however, is necessarily imperfect. It demands repetition *with* difference. Rhyme may depend on the repetition of (a similar) sound, but it requires a distinction in sense.[17] Giorgio Agamben writes that rhyme precipitates a "disjunction between a semiotic event (the repetition of a sound) and a semantic event."[18] Where the similarity in sound (the semiotic level of the word) leads us to expect a similarity in sense (the semantic level of the word), we instead experience a discontinuity. This "antagonism between sound and sense by virtue of the noncorrespondence between homophony and meaning"[19] simply does not obtain in Walser's repeated "time," because the semantic thrust of each word remains, in every instance, the same. Paradoxically, the identity of the words cancels out their rhyme, even though it is this appeal to identity that makes rhyme possible in the first place. Yet in each identical recurrence of "time" there *is* a difference—though only in its repetition. The very reason for this difference in repetition is, precisely, *time*. Each reappearance of the word is in fact a separate and distinct instance of that word. Thus the paradox of time is instantiated by means of the repetition of the word "time," which—similar to the way "now" functioned in "Meadow Green"—enacts the way time itself is both always the same and fundamentally unrepeatable.

The question remains, however, whether these repetitions in fact lead to some sort of intensification or heightening, as intimated above. Hans-Jost Frey describes how repetition in poetry is usually understood as a means of strengthening or amplification: "Repetition as intensification [*Verstärkung*] is based on the quantitative notion that twice is more than once. Increase [*Steigerung*] is achieved through the summation of words. The weight of meaning of a single word is doubled by means of repetition."[20] Yet Frey goes on to question whether this intensification is always the impulse and effect of repetition, and he suggests that it might instead be a sign of weakness, not of strength: "It could thus be that the need to repeat is also the admission of a weakness that makes persistence necessary in the first place."[21] I have already suggested that repetition without difference in Walser's early verse corresponds to something similar to what Frey describes here. In the two poems from *Chord and Longing*, "Meadow Green" and "Time," the repeated words do not so much build in intensity as parade their inefficacy. Because the sun in "Meadow Green" is still covered over by clouds, the speaker covers over this absence with repetitions of the word "sun." In "Time," the repeated title word attests to the speaker's own experience of the paradox of time.

In this regard it is important to note that weakness and lowliness and lack are precisely those qualities that Walser embraces as positive and even productive in his later writings. The ambivalence voiced in these poems with respect to privation and powerlessness, which often appear alongside expressions of joy and wonder, already points to the peculiar mixture of tones that characterizes Walser's idiosyncratic ironic mode. I would like to end my discussion of the early verse by considering three lines from "Snow (II)," the poem discussed briefly above, in which the speaker displays this jumble of affects in announcing the successful erasure of the visible world by the colorless snow:

Ganz weiß ist nun die Welt.
Erloschen ist die Welt.
Vergangen ist die Welt.

The world is now completely white.
The world has disappeared.
The world has slipped away.

As in the poems from *Chord and Longing*, here too epistrophic repetition (anaphoric in my translation) expresses a loss of the thing signified by the recurring word. That thing, however, is more than just an object here; it is "the world" as space of orientation and meaning. To appeal to Frey again, by repeating "the world" Walser intensifies neither the significance of that word nor that of its referent; rather, he voices the condition of such meaning's dissolution. Frey notes that "in the realm of language repetitions easily bring about a withdrawal of what is said [*des Gesagten*] behind the movement of saying [*des Sagens*], so that repetition in general pulls our attention away from what is repeated and diverts it onto the act of repetition itself."[22] In this way, the repeated word becomes "entdeutet," Frey's neologism for "divested of meaning."[23] It is the first step in turning the language of poetry into the language of mere sound—or of sound poetry.[24] In its repetition, the word's semiotic properties are brought into perfect alignment with a second, and then a third, copy of itself, so that its semantic properties begin to fade. Yet it is only *because* the repeated word, perfectly identical in sound and appearance, appears to mean the exact same thing as its copies that this same semantic content is threatened. According to Agamben, since poetry is only possible because of difference, such "exact coincidence of sound and sense" would be tantamount to the "end of the poem"—its outright impossibility *as* poem.[25]

Walser's early verse is hardly so radical as to participate in this "end of the poem." Nor is it sound poetry, however much it seems to gesture in this direction. But neither is his early verse as conventional at it appears to be on the surface. Its playful yet tradition-bound structures come up against an impulse to disrupt these same structures, an impulse frequently tied to forms of repetition. Through these forms (e.g., anaphora, epistrophe, symploce) Walser flirts with language's abilities to drain itself of meaning, allowing sense to withdraw—though not disappear entirely—as sound assumes prominence. In the lines from "Snow (II)" that describe the disappearance of things under a sheet of snow—white nothingness reverting everything to a blank, dimensionless space—repetition participates in the depicted erasure of the world by participating in the attempted erasure of "the world," as semantic unit. It hints at that erasure by announcing the world and then helping it cease to be by helping the word "world" abandon its signifying function. But this is all a prelude to the world's rebirth—inside the speaker.

For these lines mark a caesura in the poem, after which, now that the world outside has fully vanished, the speaker can build up a new one. The colors drowned in the snow now reemerge in the speaker's self: the world (now distinct, though never entirely independent of, "the world") is doubled, repeated—again.

II. Late Poems (1924–1933): Rhyme and Inanity

Let us now turn to Walser's late verse, with an eye to his near-obsessive use of rhyme—another form of repetition. It is with this ostensibly more conventional formal technique that Walser carries out some of his most daring lyrical experimentation. Herein lies an essential element of Walser's late-period irony, in which adhering to poetic manners and discipline exposes something of the absurdity of these established practices—while at the same time celebrating them. In this section I argue that rhyme becomes a kind of artificial, self-imposed restraint—a form of what Walser himself called "Blödigkeit" (inanity)[26]—under which he can push his poems to a new lyrical territory where parody abuts nonsense.

A significant majority of Walser's late lyric work not only makes use of end rhymes, but does so to a high degree of ostentation. Walser rhymes, to provide only a few of many outrageous examples, "Ibsen" with "beschwipsen" (*AdB*, 6:447); "Mädchen" with "Frühmorgengebetchen" (*AdB*, 2:301); "Chaisen" with "gewesen" (*SW*, 13:94); "personifizierte" with "umfrisierte" (*AdB*, 2:397); "Paradieren" with "Friedologieren" (*AdB*, 2:392); and "Meer" with an abbreviated "Europä'r" (*AdB*, 4:311). (Since these and some of the subsequent examples are meant to illustrate rhyme, I will only provide the original text, with nonrhymed translations relegated to the notes.)[27] Rhyme so governs some of these poems that Walser even resorts to malapropism to maintain it, as when he rhymes "idillisch" and "billisch" (should be *billig*) or "Kunst" and "umsunst" (should be *umsonst*) (*AdB*, 6:481).[28] These idiosyncratic rhymes are meant to sound highly affected. When the rhymes are less unusual, Walser often accentuates them by employing strong forms of enjambment. In these cases a line is cut short, often splitting an adjective away from the noun it modifies, in order to assure an end rhyme:

in welch wehen
Beziehungen er sich sah stehen (*AdB*, 6:466)

als mit überaus frommen
Schüchternheiten vor die Türe mir zu kommen (*AdB*, 4:282)[29]

In a number of poems Walser takes this method one step further, using morphological enjambment to impose end rhyme:

Manchem ist, ihm müsse wochen-
lang das Herz beruhigt sein.
. . . .
Man erzählt oft seine Betroffen-
heit ganz offen. (*AdB*, 2:379)

Das kreiden-
weiß angefärbte Leiden,
und ihn darf sein seiden-
weiches Mitleid so herrlich kleiden? (*SW*, 13:135)[30]

In these poems content begins to look extremely arbitrary. Yet Walser apparently has no intention of concealing this fact. In the microscripts we even find a poem in which the speaker admits to using a woman's name solely because it rhymes (which I have taken as license to change that name so as to create a rhyme in English):

[. . .] Stunden, Tag' und ganze lange Wochen
vereinigen sich wie zu einem Bilde,
die schönste im Damenkreise hieß Mathilde,
die ich natürlich nur des Reimes wegen
so nenne. (*AdB*, 6:434)

[. . .] Hours, days and whole long weeks
unite as into one image together,
the most beautiful woman in the group, Heather,
whom naturally only in order to rhyme I give
this name.

In another poem from the microscripts we see the inverse of this technique. In ostensibly translating a poem by Paul Verlaine (*AdB*, 2:355), Walser repeatedly uses the French poet's name in the end-rhyme position. This begins well enough, so that "Verlaine" rhymes, as when properly pronounced it should, with the river "Seine." To allow for variation, however, the poet's name must be mispronounced in order to maintain the rhyme scheme. In subsequent stanzas, therefore, the poem forces the reader to Teutonize the name "Verlaine" so as to make it properly rhyme with such words as "sehne" and "träne."[31]

On the one hand, the excessive, indeed at times obsessive, rhyme of these poems slips over into parody.[32] On the other, it seems deeply bound up with how Walser understands the relation between compulsion and creativity. As he announces in another poem, "Der Wille zu Reim / legt zum eben Gesagten den Keim" (The will to rhyme / lays the seed for what was just said) (*AdB*, 4:298). Rhyme determines not just the shape of the poem, but also the actual objects that are picked up and transformed by the lyrical persona.

Rhyme thus generates not only the sound of the poem, but also its sense. In another poem from the microscripts the speaker advises all poets to submit to "rhyme's compulsion":

> Den Lyrikern empfehl' ich dringend,
> sich dem Zwang des Reims zu unterziehen,
> weil sie, auf den Pegasus sich schwingend,
> gern der Sittsamkeit entfliehen. (*AdB*, 6:423)
>
> All poets I urgently advise
> to subject themselves to rhyme's compulsion,
> because in mounting onto Pegasus they
> wish to escape from modesty and manners.

Rhyme is here figured as a limitation or restraint on poetic "flight," the desire of the poet for fame (represented by the mythic flying horse Pegasus) without regard to conventions or "good manners." Creating formal regularity with rhyme is a "modest" means, one opposed to artistic vainglory, for producing "mannered," proper poetry. Except that such is precisely *not* the kind of poetry Walser writes. His rhymes, as we have seen, are frequently over-the-top. Indeed, we might say that in so stubbornly, almost absurdly, maintaining rhyme he ends up breaking with the "manners" of convention—and thus could hardly be said to be following the advice voiced by this poem. Walser's subversion in the late poems consists of employing the conventional, measured, and modest form of rhyme both as a means of conforming to lyrical tradition and, simultaneously, as a means to break with this tradition. It is both despite and by virtue of playing the servant to rhyme's domination, of presenting himself as bound to rhyme's formal demands, that Walser gains a necessary freedom from form.[33]

This paradoxical notion of submission and subservience as a means of attaining autonomy and creativity can be found throughout Walser's work, where it is usually linked to a positive or productive notion of stupidity, unknowing, or foolishness. From the lowly servant who reduces himself to a mere nothing or zero to the clerk who submits himself to the will of others, Walser's figures often act according to their desire to be without desire, their striving for a state in which the loss of individuality signals the attainment of some mysterious condition of blissful unknowing.[34] The late poems express this sloughing-off of personality in terms of a cultivation of not-knowing. "Zu viel Vernünftigkeit ist unvernünftig" (Too much rationality is irrational) (*AdB*, 2:306), we read in one poem. Walser's lyrical subjects sometimes appeal to "Nichtwissen" (not-knowing) as a source of their verse (e.g., *AdB*, 2:336), expressing their wish to be "im Schutze der Gedankenlosigkeit" (in the refuge of thoughtlessness) (*AdB*, 2:319). Indeed, thoughts have the potential to be frightening: "mir ist oft, was ich denke, / fürchterlich" (what I think is often / horrible to me) (*AdB*, 2:338).

Yet fear is not what lies behind these impulses. In one poem the speaker suggests that seeking not-knowing is an ethical stance:

> Sich selber nicht spüren, nicht fühlen, nicht wissen,
> wer und was man ist und wessen man bedarf,
> ist Sittlichkeit. (*AdB*, 2:330)
>
> Not to sense, to feel, to know
> who and what one is and whom one needs
> is morality.

The complete withdrawal of the self expressed here includes deprivation of senses and consciousness, as well as dissociation from others, suggesting a cloistering of the self, as though self-awareness (both sensuous and conscious) were a transgression. Usually, however, Walser's tone is playful with regard to the ideal of not-thinking: "Kluge beneiden oft die Dummen, / denn es ist was Schönes um die Einfalt" (Smart people often envy the dumb ones, / because there is something beautiful about simplemindedness) (*AdB*, 2:317). Not to be burdened with an overly active intellect is, according to the speaker, a blessing; it makes possible an innocent view of the world in all its simple beauty. To be silly and simple of mind, then, is nothing less than a creative mode, a way of letting go of the constraints imposed by self-consciousness to allow for the power of language (as the will or compulsion to rhyme) to assume control:

> Kaum weiß ich, was ich sage,
> die Worte springen mir wie Löwen
> aus dem Käfigmund heraus,
> blicken und staunen,
> legen sich der Bändigerin zu Füßen,
> vom Zittern bewältigt,
> und scheuen die Scheu, und es kommt einmal dahin,
> daß die Unbehülflichkeit und das Fragwürdige
> geehrt wird (*AdB*, 2:320)
>
> I hardly know what I'm saying,
> the words leap out of my cage-mouth
> like lions,
> gaze about astonished,
> lay themselves at the feet of the lady tamer,
> mastered by their trembling,
> and eschew timidity; and then it happens
> that helplessness and what's questionable
> are revered

The metaphor of language set loose here complicates how Walser conceives of the dialectic of creativity and control. He figures the poet's lack of control over his words in terms of a lack of "knowing": "I hardly know what I'm saying." This does not mean that the content of his poem is opaque to him; rather, it describes how the poem seems to take shape without his conscious effort. And yet the result is not nonsense verse. This is a poem consisting for the most part of standard German words that fall within a conventional—if slightly protracted—syntactic structure. These words-as-lions thus do not in fact escape captivity. They may no longer be locked in the cage of the poet's mouth, but they remain in the circus ring, under the control of the female lion tamer. That means that their "leaping out" is sanctioned by—indeed, necessary to—the entertaining spectacle. Perhaps it is "questionable" that they be "mastered" by their own fear; but their fundamental "helplessness" is, ultimately, a sight in and of itself. The subdued words-as-lions are accorded value *as* the potentially free-roaming creatures who are now incapable of helping themselves overcome their predicament.

I read the two agencies of restraint at play in this metaphor as providing insight into the way Walser relinquishes control of his poetic language while at the same time making sure that control is reasserted elsewhere—or in another way. Recall the ironic advice of the poet on rhyme: writers must "subject themselves to rhyme's compulsion," let go of their own control over language in order to allow language itself to assume control. We are dealing with the compulsion *of* rhyme, after all, not the compulsion *to* rhyme. Poetic agency is no longer entirely located in the writer, but in his tools, which now dictate what he must write. In the above lines, because the speaker is no longer able to restrain his words, a new "tamer" must take over. Who is this tamer, exactly? The woman with a whip alludes to Leopold von Sacher-Masoch's *Venus in Furs*, a novel whose figures and themes appear frequently in Walser's work.[35] The masochistic pleasure of submission to domination central to that book intersects with Walser's inversion of servant and master, his privileging of the position of servitude and lowliness. The "knowing" poet figure, in ceasing to know what he is saying, takes pleasure in seeing his words submit to another's domination. He (in his unknowing) and his words (in their wild unpredictability) are in fact participating in a larger show—a carnival stage act.

Let us look briefly at one virtuoso, dizzying performance from this stage, complete with whips and animals:

> Schildkrötelein
> schien nicht besonders aufgeweckt zu sein,
> doch dafür mundete der Wein
> überaus vortrefflich, doch wie fein
> strahlt heute zarter Sonnenschein,
> zum Reitpeitschengewitterlein,

das gestern herrschte, spricht das heut'ge schöne Wetter niedlich nein.
Freundliches Lichtelein
lächelt zum Fenster herein.
Glücklicherweise war das Peitschelein nur klein.
Ich bin nicht mein und bin nicht dein,
sondern sehe als ein Freier drein.
Ein Dichter names Heym
sank eines Abends in die ihn umschling'nde Tiefe ein.
Reizend fand ich, so dem Plauderstündchen mich zu weih'n,
das schweigsam sich verhielt und nicht bestand aus Pein.
Du wirst mir sicher verzeih'n,
daß mich Pistölelein und Dölchelein
in keiner Art und Weise hinderten, nach jeder Richtung hin vergnügt zu sein. (*AdB*, 4:277)

Little turtle thine
seems still to be on cloud nine,
at least we get some tasty wine,
indeed superb, yet how fine
the rays of today's soft sunshine,
the riding-whip-inclement-clime
that yesterday reigned today's nice weather cutely declines.
Friendly little light ashine
into the window smilingly inclines.
Luckily the little whip was small and not malign.
I'm not yours and I'm not mine,
but rather a suitor and voyeur combined.
A poet named Heym
sank one evening into the depths that him entwined.
I found it fetching to devote myself to the wee hour of chatter so divine
that kept so silent and did not pine.
You'll surely forgive me: benign
are the little dagger and tiny carbine.
They won't stop me from being amused all of the time.

This poem—quoted here in full—enacts "rhyme's compulsion" with (nearly) unrelenting consistency. Unlike my imperfect translation, Walser's text only once breaks away from its otherwise strict adherence to rhyming on the phoneme *-ein*.[36] Marking that break is the German expressionist poet Georg Heym, as if in acknowledgment that the singularity of an individual—especially someone who writes verse—is irreducible to the same. Yet even his name hardly disrupts the poem's rhyme scheme, since its only difference from the *-ein* phoneme is the almost inaudible shift of the final consonant from *n* to *m*. What of this rhyme scheme? It reminds us that while rhyme may rely on the repetition of sound that does not correspond to a repetition of sense, a rhyme scheme relies on the variation of that repetition of sound. When two or three lines rhyme within a poem, we situate them within the larger rhyme scheme. But when all nineteen lines of a poem rhyme, we are at a loss to designate any scheme at all.

Rhyme in this late poem thus returns us to the problem of repetition encountered in the early poems: recurrence of the same creates stagnancy. This poem never goes anywhere; it doesn't even get off the ground. Its rhyme leaves us stuck waiting for a resolution to the next phoneme—which doesn't come. Sameness thus ends up creating dissonance. The fact that the phoneme repeatedly rhymed here ("-ein") is also the word for "one" serves to drive this effect home. The poem is reduced to a singular, monotonously repeated rhyme. It does not advance to the next number. Important in this regard is that the only repeated end-rhyme syllable besides "sein" (which appears twice) is the diminutive "-lein," repeated four times. Smallness is of great importance to Walser—diminutive forms appear in the poem seven times—and here it seems to refer back to the smallness of the rhyme scheme: you can't reduce rhyme to anything lower than "one" ("-ein").

The consistency of the poem's rhyme scheme contrasts with its lack of consistency in theme and content. The poem is highly desultory. The words-as-lions have here been let loose, no doubt. Their erratic movement (as semantic units conveying "content") is even made visible in the poem's highly variable line lengths. One might say the poem lacks not just a cohesive content, but a coherent one. Its anaculothic shifts betray its reliance on that unruly principle of disorder: the non sequitur. Yet if the lions have been freed, the "whip" (6, 10) is still cracking. The poem's apparently free associations are actually not so free at all. We see the principle of restraint most plainly in the highly mechanical regularity of the rhyme. Yet conventional formal structures are also at work in the poem's metrics. Many of the lines adhere to an iambic pattern. In lines 7, 14, and 15 Walser even drops a syllable (in the words "heut'ge," "umschling'nde," and "weih'n," respectively) in order to maintain the iambic meter. Are these—rhyme and meter—our "lion tamers," making the words tremble in fear? The speaker seems to side with the words. He aims to resist any "anguish" ("Pein"), and refuses to let anything potentially harmful (the poet Heym's death is described in line 14; the "whip" of storms is mentioned twice; and weapons appear in the penultimate line) to prevent him from being constantly joyful. In fact, the poem links his joyfulness to these threats. The "little riding whip" of bad weather was nothing but a small distraction, and besides, "riding whips" are for pleasure, whether equestrian or otherwise (just think of *Venus in Furs*). A similar fascination with the "little dagger and tiny carbine" lead us to believe that, like the whips, they haven't prevented the speaker's constant amusement, but have—*by virtue* of their threat of violence or force—somehow made it possible.

How the potential for violence makes amusement and pleasure possible is related to the inextricability of compulsion and creativity, restraint and freedom, joy and loss that have been variously discussed in this essay. We see these themes broached in one of Walser's own poetological pronouncements on the lyric poem, in which the relation of poetic value (as "beauty" and "goodness") to submission and servitude plays a central role. Here is a longer excerpt from the source of these comments, Walser's letter to Max Rychner of March 18, 1926:

> Im Begriff Blödsein liegt eben etwas Strahlendschönes- und Gutes, etwas unsäglich Feinwertiges, etwas, das gerade die Inteligentesten sehnsüchtig gesucht haben und fernhin sich zu eigen zu machen suchen. [. . .] Das schöne Gedicht hat meiner Ansicht nach ein schöner Leib zu sein, der aus den gemessenen, vergeßlich, fast ideenlos auf's Papier gesetzten Worten hervorzublühen habe. Die Worte bilden die Haut, die sich straff um den Inhalt, d.h. den Körper spannt. Die Kunst besteht darin, nicht Worte zu sagen sondern einen Gedicht-Körper zu formen, d.h. dafür zu sorgen, daß die Worte nur das Mittel bilden zur Gedichtkörperbildung, d.h. die Verblödetheit *Kerr*'s liegt darin, daß der Gedichtelidichter es versteht, Inteligentika's in Menge nach links und nach rechts, zu Gunsten des Gedichtbildes zu verdrängen. Sich dümmer, unwissender zu benehmen, als man ist, ist eben eine Kunst, ein Raffinement, das und die wenigen gelingt. [. . .] In der Dichtkunst aller Schattierungen ist der Intelektualismus "nur" der Diener, und derjenige Dichter dichtet am besten, dem dieser Diener am besten, d.h. so gehorcht, wie es der Bildende, Schaffende braucht, und die Kerr'sche Frage bezüglich der Blödigkeit ist nach der Brauchbarkeit, Geschmeidigkeit jenes Dieners hin zu übersetzen. Beim Gedicht muß sich eben dieser Diener gelernt haben, besonders fein, vorsichtig, bescheiden, taktvoll aufzuführen. Das Gedicht entspringt aus der Lust des Intelektbesitzers, auf eine große Portion hievon zu verzichten. Beim Gedicht hat also dieser Diener ganz einfach am aufopferungsvollsten zu dienen. (*Briefe*, 266–67)

> In the concept "being inane" there is something radiantly beautiful and good, something subtly significant that cannot be expressed, something that the most intelligent people longingly have sought and that they furthermore try to make their own. [. . .] For me the most beautiful poem has to be a beautiful body that must blossom forth out of measured words that have been set to paper obliviously, nearly without ideas. The words constitute the skin that stretches taut over the content, i.e., the body. Artistry consists not in saying words, but rather in forming a poem-body, i.e., making sure that words only constitute the means for constructing poem-bodies, i.e., *Kerr*'s

> becoming-inane means that the poet-of-tiny-verses understands how to displace to the left and right Intelligenticas in droves for the benefit of the poetic image. To act like one is dumber, more unknowing than one is constitutes an art, a refinement, which succeeds for few. [. . .] In literary arts of all kinds intellectualism is "only" the servant, and that writer writes best who obeys this servant best, i.e., obeys him the way the one constructing, creating requires, and Kerr's question with regard to inanity is to be translated in terms of the usefulness and flexibility of that servant. With a poem this servant simply needs to have learned to perform especially subtly, carefully, unassumingly, and tactfully. The poem originates from the pleasure of the one who possesses intellect in doing without a large portion of it. For with the poem this servant must quite simply serve in the most sacrificial manner possible.

Walser constructs a strange relationship here between form and content. The latter does not precede the former. There is not some content that is then *formed* into the poem; rather, form allows for content to emerge from it. Walser figures the relation as one between "body" and "skin." The skin does not just give shape to the otherwise unformed body; it allows for this body to come into existence at all. This skin is language, "words," which is stretched over the body, "content." The exact nature of this content, however, remains unspecified. Although Walser's metaphor appears to privilege it—words should only be "the means for constructing poem-bodies"—it does not divulge what it is beyond appealing to form: content is that-which-has-been-formed. More strangely, the words themselves, Walser insists, should not "be said," but should rather only serve as means for the "image" of the poem to be made visible. Words must be divested of their own content so as not to obscure the body (content) of the poem. Furthermore, words should be "set to paper" without much thought: "obliviously" and "without ideas." In the end, words (as form) should become not just a container, but an empty one, lacking significance and lacking sense.

The condition of the possibility of the poem, then, and what makes it "good" and "beautiful" *as* a poem, is that the poet ceases "saying words" and instead uses them as a "means." But if the "poem-body" which these empty words now participate in forming is itself nothing more than something-that-has-been-formed, then we seem to have entered a peculiar feedback loop. Indeed, that seems to be Walser's point in this letter. As he puts it, in order to construct a poem the writer must cultivate "inanity." This involves suppressing the intellect, since it is the intellect that provides (or rather demands) content. Inanity, contrarily, is a principle of formation, "constructing, creating," without the imperative of "saying" something. By indenturing intellect to the task of crafting the poem-body or "poetic image"—which, after all, are nonlinguistic figures[37]—the poem can assume its shape *as* mere shape. It is thus ultimately the intellect (which governs content) that must withdraw in order for inanity (as the principle of pure form) to take over. Form does not disappear behind content; rather, content becomes irrelevant in form's celebration of itself. For Walser, the poetic process is, in the end, a matter of form(ation).[38]

Conclusion

To submit to this principle of form is to relinquish the intellect's domination. And that, in turn, is to submit to a new compulsion. In Walser's lyric poetry that compulsion seems to come from language itself, and to submit to it is to allow—or to pretend to allow—the generative force of words to assume control. As we have seen, Walser stages this takeover with and as repetition and rhyme. Each formal technique becomes simultaneously symptom and cause of the poem's—and thus also the speaker's—inanity.

Walser's friend and later literary executor Carl Seelig was somewhat embarrassed by Walser's later poems; he wrote that they are "actually weak, indeed often childish."[39] I would like in closing to suggest that we actually agree with Seelig—not with his evaluation, but with his description. For weakness and childishness are indeed fundamental to the "inanity" of Walser's poems, which display weakness in the profound fragility of the lyric voice, the longing for smallness, and the (celebration of a) lack of knowing or of sense; and childishness in their child*likeness*, their simplemindedness, and their proclivity for play and silliness. These characteristics find their formal correlates in the kinds of extreme repetition and extravagant rhyme I have analyzed in this essay. In the hands of Robert Walser these techniques reconfigure how we think of the relation between form and meaning in a poem, where the former does not simply convey the latter, but resists it—and in doing so transforms it. The self-reflexivity of Walser's poems, then, not only proliferates meaning but also, simultaneously, works toward canceling it out. The resulting dialectic of sense and nonsense is both means and end in Walser's lyric work, and its failed resolution the condition of its success.

Notes

1. In a letter to Frieda Mermet from December 23, 1929, Walser said that he was writing mostly poetry and relatively little prose. *Briefe*, 341.

2. Max Brod and Carl Seelig, for instance, were both embarrassed by Walser's late poems. Brod said that although he printed many of them in the *Prager Presse*, he received complaints from readers. Cited and discussed in Werner Morlang, "Gelegenheits- oder Verlegenheitslyrik? Anmerkungen zu den späten Gedichten Robert Walsers," in *Robert Walser*, ed. Klaus-Michael Hinz and Thomas Horst (Frankfurt am Main: Suhrkamp, 1991), 115–19. A more contemporary example:

in his afterword to the volume *Gedichte und Dramolette* (*Poems and Dramolets*) in the first collected edition of Walser's work (and reprinted in volume 13 of the standard *Sämtliche Werke in Einzelausgaben*) Robert Mächler writes that Walser's late poems "are often nothing but Walserian prose pieces outfitted with the exterior features of versification" (*SW*, 13:274).

3. I will skip the roughly two decades between these two periods of high productivity, primarily because, as noted, Walser's lyrical output during this time was relatively low.

4. The exact number of poems can only be conjectured. Over eighty poems from this period have been identified (*SW*, 13:7–54), but it is speculated that an even larger number were lost or destroyed (*SW*, 13:270).

5. Daniele Pantano translates *Saite und Sehnsucht* as *String and Desire*. Robert Walser, *Oppressive Light: Selected Poems by Robert Walser*, trans. Daniele Pantano (Pittsburgh: Black Lawrence, 2012), 5.

6. This poem appeared under the title "Kein Ausweg" ("No Way Out"); Walser renamed it for its appearance in *Poems*.

7. Cf. Pantano's translation: Walser, *Oppressive Light*, 17.

8. The setting appears to be the clerk's office. Walser's work as a *commis* during this period found its way into a number of his works.

9. Thomas Binder, *Zu Robert Walsers frühen Gedichten: Eine Konstellation von Einzelanalysen* (Bonn: Bouvier Verlag Herbert Grundmann, 1976), 99.

10. Ibid., 98.

11. For Binder this longing, too, is leveled along with the speaker to the same status as the things in the room. Ibid., 99.

12. Cf. ibid.

13. On the color white in Walser's early poems, its alignment with "nothingness," and the German word's play on "to know," see Uve Fischer, "Armut und Schnee in den frühen Gedichten Robert Walsers," in *"Immer dicht vor dem Sturze . . .": Zum Werk Robert Walsers*, ed. Paolo Chiarini and Hans Dieter Zimmermann (Frankfurt am Main: Athenäum, 1987), 74–76.

14. This is not the same as onomatopoeia, which "auf . . . fallen" is not. The distinction between this type of repetition and onomatopoeia comes down to that between rhythm and sound.

15. Walser, *Oppressive Light*, 45 (translation modified).

16. "The same" from the immediately preceding fifth line is meant to refer to the repeated "green" of lines 3–4, but might also be read as expressing the very problem of change and sameness.

17. It also usually requires a distinction between the sounds. Rhyming perfect homonyms (e.g., "here" and "hear") is considered a weak form of rhyme.

18. Giorgio Agamben, *The End of the Poem: Studies in Poetics*, trans. Daniel Heller-Roazen (Stanford, Calif.: Stanford University Press, 1999), 110.

19. Ibid., 111.

20. Hans-Jost Frey, *Lesen und Schreiben* (Basel: Urs Engeler, 1998), 70.

21. Ibid., 70–71.

22. Ibid., 61. Frey's formulation almost exactly echoes Walter Benjamin's on Walser: "The How of his work is so far from irrelevant to Walser that everything he has to say fully withdraws into the background in the face of the importance of the process of writing. One might say, that it ["everything he has to say"] goes to

naught in the act of writing." Walter Benjamin, "Robert Walser," in *Gesammelte Schriften*, vol. 2, ed. Rolf Tiedemann and Hermann Schweppenhäuser (Frankfurt am Main: Suhrkamp, 1977), 325.

23. Frey, *Lesen und Schreiben*, 72.

24. Urs Allemann reads "As Ever," discussed above, as in effect anticipating Dadaist sound poetry. In Robert Walser, *Der Schnee fällt nicht hinauf: Dreiunddreißig Gedichte ausgewählt und kommentiert von Urs Allemann* (Frankfurt am Main: Insel, 2009), 31. Christian Walt makes a similar claim, but for the poetry from the microscripts. Christian Walt, "'Den Lyrikern empfehl' ich dringend, / sich dem Zwang des Reims zu unterziehen . . .': Zur Übererfüllung von Gattungsnormen in Robert Walsers späten Gedichten," in *"Ich beendige dieses Gedicht lieber in Prosa": Robert Walser als Grenzgänger der Gattungen*, ed. Anna Fattori and Kerstin Gräfin von Schwerin (Heidelberg: Universitätsverlag Winter, 2011), 167.

25. Agamben, *The End of the Poem*, 113–14.

26. *Briefe*, 267.

27. "Ibsen"/"getting-tipsy"; "girl"/"little early-morning prayer"; "chaises"/ "been"; "personified"/"coifed"; "to parade"/"to lodge-in-peace"; "ocean"/ "European."

28. English: "idyllic"/"cheap" and "art"/"for nothing."

29. The first couplet: "in what woeful / relations he saw himself standing." The second couplet: "as to come with exceedingly pious / shynesses to me at the door."

30. Although the adjectives "kreidenweiß" (chalk-white) and seidenweich (silk-soft) are hyphenated in the English translation below, they never would be in German:

> For some it appears, he would need a week-
> long rest for his heart.
> . . . .
> One often tells of his constern-
> ation, quite openly.
>
> The chalk-
> white colored sorrow,
> and his silk-
> soft pity may clothe him so well?

31. English: "long" (the verb); "cry tears." See, on the Verlaine poem in particular, Stephan Kammer, "'Sorgsam übersetzt'? Robert Walser als 'Verdeutscher von Verlaine,'" in *Edition und Übersetzung: Zur wissenschaftlichen Dokumentation des interkulturellen Texttransfers*, ed. Bodo Plachta and Winfried Woesler (Tübingen: Max Niemeyer, 2002), 154–55. For an excellent English rendering of the poem, see Damion Searls, "That Old Goat! Robert Walser's Scrupulous Art of Translation," *Paris Review* blog, September 30, 2015, https://www.theparisreview.org/blog/2015/09/30/that-old-goat/.

32. On parody in Walser more generally, see Annette Fuchs, *Dramaturgie des Narrentums: Das Komische in der Prosa Robert Walsers* (Munich: Wilhelm Fink, 1993), 25–30.

33. The importance of limitations and restraints for experimentalism has since Walser been shown most successfully by the Oulipo movement. Walt incisively claims that "Walser's repetitive fulfillment of generic norms" can be read (via Deleuze) "as a subversive act for attaining sovereignty." Walt, "'Den Lyrikern empfehl' ich dringend,'" 166. See also Walt's discussion of this poem (ibid., 169–72). On how Walser's rhymes and homophonies create discontinuity despite being moments of accord, see Bernhard Böschenstein, "Sprechen als Wandern: Robert Walsers *Aus dem Bleistiftgebiet*," in Chiarini and Zimmermann, "*Immer dicht vor dem Sturze . . .* ," 19–23.

34. See Samuel Frederick, *Narratives Unsettled: Digression in Robert Walser, Thomas Bernhard, and Adalbert Stifter* (Evanston, Ill.: Northwestern University Press, 2012), 58–60, and "A Bursting Zero of Unknowing: Overcoming the Paradox of Infinite Knowledge in Heinrich von Kleist's 'Über das Marionettentheater' and Robert Walser's *Jakob von Gunten*," *Germanic Review* 88, no. 4 (2013): 375–90.

35. See Jens Hobus, *Poetik der Umschreibung: Figurationen der Liebe im Werk Robert Walsers* (Würzburg: Königshausen & Neumann, 2011), 185–94.

36. My translation can only approximate this effect by rhyming "-ine," "-ime," "-ined," and "-ines" endings.

37. See Walt, "'Den Lyrikern empfehl' ich dringend,'" 168–69.

38. Walt makes a similar claim (ibid., 169), which is also Benjamin's observation (see n. 22). On these questions, see Hendrik Stiemer, *Über scheinbar naïve und dilettantische Dichtung: Text- und Kontextstudien zu Robert Walser* (Würzburg: Königshausen & Neumann, 2013), in relation to Walser's work as a whole, in relation to the late poetry (192–244), and in relation to the "inanity" letter (201–3); and Peter Gronau, "*Ich schreibe hier dekorativ*": *Essays zu Robert Walser* (Würzburg: Königshausen & Neumann, 2006), 153–64.

39. In the afterword to the 1958 publication *Unbekannte Gedichte* (*Unknown Poems*). Cited in Morlang, "Gelegenheits- oder Verlegenheitslyrik?," 116.

Antechambers of Life

School and Living-On in *Fritz Kocher's Essays*

Anette Schwarz

When Robert Walser appeared on the literary scene at the end of the nineteenth century, the critics reacted with mixed reviews, but they were united in their judgment of his style as one of profound modernity, uniqueness, and innovation. Fourteen books later, critics are still fascinated and confounded by the forceful and mysterious effects of his stylistic artistry. In a way that is perhaps comparable only to the critical attention given to Franz Kafka's style, contemporary readers and scholars alike are still attempting to demarcate the intricacies of Walser's "linguistic fireworks."[1] Just as each brilliant spark lights up the sky only for a moment to be extinguished and followed by yet another short-lived explosion, so is Walser's style devoted to the instant of a "now" in its fleeting existence.[2] Each moment, each observation, each impression, and each encounter becomes the occasion for Walser's undivided but quickly passing focus. This focus is one of care, one might say, because each attentive moment will produce another word, another sentence, and another phrase. Walser's care is less for his themes than for his language, not for the meaning of things but for the writing of things. His prose pieces move the reader to join the author on his stroll through the landscapes of a life in which each step resembles another dance with words.[3]

Throughout his work, both Walser and his language remain at play, and the author will never relinquish the role he played in his first book publication: a pupil at heart. *Fritz Kochers Aufsätze* (*Fritz Kocher's Essays*) extend this invitation to the reader to join the dance with words and to take on the role of pupil in order to arrive at one of Walser's most valued states of existence: the state of childhood as the realm of learning and discovery. The role of pupil affords Walser the opportunity to stay within a state of transition and process without an end or destination in sight. This playful movement of hovering prior to settling in the world of fixed meanings and conventions represents for Walser nothing less than the only resource for authentic expression. This essay proposes to show how Walser, as the self-declared editor of *Fritz Kocher's Essays*, appropriates this resource to serve as his writerly practice ground. Taking on the voice of a schoolboy engaged in his daily homework assignments, Walser can find his own authorial voice and signature style in a language that is still developing, at play, experimenting and inventing. Walser's schooldays will not end with these essays, but they set the tone for his entire work.

Walser's first book publication came in November 1904, when Insel Verlag published a collection of stories titled *Fritz Kocher's Aufsätze: Mitgeteilt von Robert Walser* (*Fritz Kocher's Essays: Conveyed by Robert Walser*), which included eleven illustrations by his brother Karl; the four prose sketches it contained had already appeared in the Sunday literary supplement of the Bern daily newspaper *Der Bund* two years earlier, after Walser sent some of his texts to the paper's editor, Joseph Viktor Widmann.[4] The collection includes a foreword signed with the initials *R.W.* explaining the origins of the essays: they are ostensibly a collection of twenty school essays written by a young boy, Fritz Kocher, before his premature death. The author—or putative editor—further explains that the essays were passed on to him by Fritz Kocher's mother on the condition that they be published only in their original, untouched form:

> Der Knabe, der diese Aufsätze geschrieben hat, ist kurz nach seinem Austritt aus der Schule gestorben. Ich hatte einige Mühe, seine Mutter, eine verehrenswürdige, liebe Dame, zu bewegen, mir die Stücke zur Veröffentlichung zu überlassen. Sie hing begreiflicherweise sehr an den Blättern, die ihr eine wehmütig-süsse Erinnerung an den Sohn sein mussten. Nur die Versicherung meinerseits, dass ich die Aufsätze ganz unverändert, so wie ihr Fritz sie geschrieben, drucken lassen wolle, gab sie mir endlich in die Hände. Sie mögen vielen an vielen Stellen unknabenhaft und an vielen andern Stellen zu knabenhaft erscheinen. Aber, ich bitte zu bedenken, dass meine Hand daran nichts geändert hat. Ein Knabe kann sehr weise und sehr töricht fast im selben Moment reden: so die Aufsätze. (*SW*, 1:7)

> The boy who wrote these essays passed away not long after he left school. I had some difficulty convincing his mother, a dear and honorable lady, to allow me to publish them. She was understandably very attached to these pages, which must have been a bittersweet reminder of her son. Only after I promised to have the essays published unchanged, just as her little Fritz had written them, did she finally agree. The essays may seem unboyish in many places, and all too boyish in others. But please keep in mind that my hand has not altered them anywhere. A boy can speak words of great wisdom and words of great foolishness at practically the same moment: that is how these essays are too. (*ASD*, 3)[5]

Any editorial intervention would not only violate the memory of a deceased son and the hope for his living on in the unaltered documents of his life, but such intervention would also inhibit the unfolding of the uniqueness of this pupil's "reden" (speech, speaking), which is characterized by the simultaneity of contradictions. Editorial intervention might introduce the rules of style according to which the simultaneity of "unboyish" and "boyish," or "foolishness" and "wisdom" would be perceived as senseless, incoherent, or simply as absurd.

Writing in December 1904, just after the appearance of Walser's book, Widmann looks back on the initial publication of *Fritz Kocher's Essays* in *Der Bund*:

> When the then very young Swiss poet Robert Walser published his sketches in our Sunday paper, many readers shook their heads in disbelief because he had feigned to imitate the style of a precocious schoolboy who supposedly had left those essays after his early death. The readers could forgive the inclusion of these works in our paper only when assured that the editor also believed in the actual existence of this so early deceased "Fritz Kocher," and that he had felt obliged out of piety not to exclude these scribblings by a doubtlessly talented boy, but to publish them as documents of pedagogical and psychological interest.[6]

The leisurely Sunday reading pleasure seems disturbed when suspicion of trickery and deceit arise in the reader; a sense of unease and disbelief emerge when the identity of the author and the authenticity of the subject matter seem in question. Might the reader be falling for the artistry of a swindler, a con artist who managed to successfully place his work in a well-respected literary magazine by falsely appealing to the editor's and reading public's sense of piety? Only the firm belief that this schoolboy actually once existed before dying at a very young age can grant legitimacy to the publication. Only when his status as factual is proven can his "scribblings" gain acceptance and attain generic classification as documents of "pedagogical and psychological interest." However, Widmann is not interested in appeasing the literary taste of his readership by labeling what he appreciates as "poetic production" a document. Instead, he exposes and identifies those stylistic characteristics of Walser's writing that meet resistance and doubtful head shakes. For him, Walser practices in the field of poetics what has been practiced in painting and the visual arts, namely the return to "primitive art." But while this return was positively received by viewers of paintings ("immediately understood and appreciated"), it was unwelcome in readers of literature (13). What readers dismiss as "absurd" (14) is exactly what Widmann celebrates in Walser: "weariness of pathos," which replaces "immodest exuberance" with a profound "simplicity" of style (15). The simplicity has its ground in what Widmann calls Walser's "authentic, inartificial naivety" and "his great joy at living and everything that exists" (14). The qualifier "primitive" thus stands for an ever-fresh and innocent sense of perceiving the world in astonishment at its sheer existence: "The fact that there exist people and animals and grasses and flowers and stars and clouds—, this fills the tender poetic heart daily with exuberant happiness, and it feels as if the world were created anew just for him" (14). In order to capture appropriately the affective force that drives Walser's sense of abhorrence against any linguistic attempt to assign a determining meaning to this only just "created world," Widmann utilizes (or reactivates) the emotive force of the tragic. In Widmann's view, were Walser to grasp these seedlings of ever newly repeated acts of creation with cognition, phrasing, and naming, it would be equal to an act of "desecration" and profanity:

> What am I saying: aversion! "Horror" it is. His maturation as a poet may have developed otherwise quite strongly,—his emotional modesty, however, shudders away from linguistic acts of desecration. This modesty is deeply embedded and belongs to his soul, just as much as the protective curling up of its leaves belongs to the mimosa when touched by grasping hands. This fear and horror of rhetorical pathos has led the poet by necessity to the use of the least adorned language and towards the attempt to express noble and beautiful sentiments and intimate and tender feelings with the diction of a pupil. (15)

The emotive force of "horror" here leads to a necessary insight and hence to a linguistic necessity: if "noble and beautiful sentiments" as well as "very intimate and tender feelings" withdraw and resist "grasping hands" of "rhetorical pathos," then the poet needs to experiment with a different "Zugriff" (grasping approach) (15), one perhaps that needs to be put into hands with a different touch. Thus Walser lays the capture of these emotive states into the hands of a pupil and his honest diction. Only a schoolboy's language ushers in a state of fundamental simplicity and honesty, in contrast to the supposed dishonesty of the conceptual grasp or "Zugriff" of "pathos." The pupil stands in awe before the sheer factuality of all that exists and expresses his plain astonishment in a language that is prior to any dishonesty, adornment, or artificiality: his is "die schlichteste Sprache" (the most unadorned language) (15). For Walser, only the pupil occupies this linguistic territory prior to these distinctions and qualifications.

It is not by accident that Widmann uses the word *Blätter*—"leaves" or "pages"—to describe *Fritz Kocher's Essays*, since they represent nothing but a compilation of "leaves" put into the hands of yet another editor on the condition of restraint from any act of editing. As editors, both Widmann and Walser feel an obligation to protect the fragile linguistic nature of these "leaves"; in both cases the editorial charge is to protect a "mimosa" (Widmann, 15) from withdrawing its leaves when handled. Thus both editors are intensely concerned with the question into whose hands these "leaves" can be entrusted. In Widmann's case, it is the editorial decision to publish Walser's *Fritz Kocher's*

Essays that protects the style of the "mimosa": it is both validated and protected from nonexistence by its circulation in his "Sonntags*blatte*" ("Sunday paper/leaf"). This editorial decision is due not to piety before death, but to a sense of piety for the "innocence of the soul" and to the horror of "linguistic desecration" (Widmann, 15). What these editors also leave untouched is the "primitive" style of childhood that captures a world before any conceptual "Zugriff" or intervention. Again, it is not by accident that Widmann so easily compares—almost conflates—Walser's prose style with the "primitive" painterly style of his brother Karl, whose drawings accompany the essays: "Those eleven drawings which adorn the book are so like the text that one could assume that they also stem from Robert Walser, if it were not for the fact that his brother's name, Karl, is noted" (15). What the brothers share, according to Widmann, is an "ironic stance towards obtrusive, importunate practices of art" (16). Widmann returns here to the obtrusive, importunate, and overwhelming grasp of "rhetorical pathos" from which the "mimosa" withdraws in horror. To the rescue comes an artistic practice that with "honesty," "simplicity," and "modesty" returns "things" to an original state of "innocence." The artistic practice of "primitive" style in prose or painting becomes an artistic "method" (15) in which "natural simplicity" is paired with an "intentional naïveté." This method, in its proximity to romantic irony or Brechtian estrangement, leads to the unmasking of the dishonest face of things:

> Also during the exhibitions of the Berlin "Secession," Karl Walser's small paintings garnered attention. And everything written by Alfred Gold regarding the manner of this young Swiss artist can be applied, with few changes, to Robert Walser. For example: "K. Walser, just like every romantic artist, unmasks things and lifts up their sober outer surface so to reveal them in their ideal picturesque appearance. This they only have for us in those original, highly emotional moments when they seem 'strange' to us." (16)

Things appear in their original strangeness, otherness, and honesty at the moment of their first perception; at a moment without conceptual registration or classification; at the moment of astonishment in the face of their emergence as sheer existence. This existence, however, is "fleeting" and escapes a firm "intervention" in form and formulas. Walser's "method" never presents the reader or viewer with "things"; these are offered only as "suggestive" glimpses of a passing moment:

> What was most annoying to some readers was the fact that they felt compelled to finish reading these things although they deemed them "absurd." There was something suggestive in the way Walser let his curious thoughts unfold without any haste or pressure—like

> balls rolling on the green cloth of a billiard table. And, as if wrapped within the magic of a dream, the reader gets a glimpse of something very beautiful floating by really closely. (14)

For a passing instant Walser's reader feels the proximity of the ephemeral existence not just of things but also of people. Walser's thoughts pass by fleetingly, and their opening movement of "rolling" is not only related to the closing movement of the "mimosa" ("rolling up of the mimosa leaves"); it is, rather—and more importantly—the one movement that exclusively lets what would otherwise withdraw emerge in the first place, though it can only be experienced as a dreamlike hovering. The opening and closing movement of the "leaves" of the "mimosa" is mirrored in those "leaves/pages" (*Blätter*) handed over to Walser by a grieving mother. At the cusp of life, the young pupil is taken by an early death; but it is as if he were resurrected in the unfolding *Blätter* of his essays. Like the play between life and death, the movement of folding and unfolding describes the other side of the experience of fleeting beauty: it floats or hovers by as if in a dream, but this dream is also suspended at the edge of an abyss.

The ever newly created experience of the world in Walser—what Widmann calls Walser's "great joy at living and everything that exists" (14)—is intimately linked to the ever-present threat of death and loss. To recognize "things" as curiously strange, one needs to encounter them without the "mask" of "pathos" and "phrase" (15): "things" are "strange" when we see them anew after or at the moment of their death. To let these "things" then unroll as "strange" corresponds to an act of resurrection during and after which all can be renewed and viewed, touched and read as if for the first time. Readers who cannot share these "moments of original, deep emotion" (16) should not, according to Widmann's advice, read *Fritz Kocher's Essays*:

> "All is mine," and raptured, tender eyes see an infinite series of gloriously beautiful things in all that appears: in the play of infernal flames, and in the grey haze of rain dripping from the fir tree in a forest, as well as in the muddled hubbub of trumpets and organs you hear at a fair, and also on a lonely hillside. The fact that there exist people and animals and grasses and flowers and stars and clouds—, this fills the tender poetic heart with exuberant happiness, and it feels as if the world were created anew just for him. With this we can at least allude to the true content of Walser's little book. Readers, however, who have never felt compelled to caress a green branch of a fir tree should better disregard the book. (14–15)

This caressing hand touches the "fir tree" in the awe-inspiring recognition that it belongs to a nature never seen before, or never seen before in its curious ("strange") particularity as this "fir tree"—and, furthermore, in the equally awe-inspiring recognition of its limited existence and possible disappearance at any point. This caressing hand is also that of our "editors." Neither Widmann's nor Walser's editorial hand seizes with a firm grip what only responds to the gentle touch of "simplicity" and "honesty." Both find that gentle touch in "the honest diction of a pupil" (Widmann, 15). In the course of the unfolding of his "essays," Kocher can live on and live anew: in a curious state of suspension, a state after death but before life. Kocher calls school "den Vorsaal, [. . .] das Wartezimmer zum Leben" (the antechamber, the waiting room of life) (*SW*, 1:19).[7] He knows full well, however, that it is also a waiting room for dying.

What do you speak about while waiting in this "antechamber of life," especially after you have supposedly just died? When your "Austritt aus der Schule" (leaving school) curiously coincides with your death and your "Eintritt" (entrance) into "die Schule des Lebens" (the school of life)?[8] When every "Adieu, mein Kleiner!" (Farewell, my little friend!) (*SW*, 1:8; *ASD*, 3) also means a "hello"? This anteroom points to the ghostly existence in a suspended state between a "not yet" and a "no longer," and Walser will call this state of suspension a state of learning: learning to live at the cusp of dying, or learning to live in an ever newly repeated state of resurrection after which every experience can begin afresh, as if for the first time, again and again. We meet Fritz Kocher in this state of living on in his "essays," and in Walser who communicates and "shares" Kocher's existence by means of his editorial signature: "mitgeteilt von Robert Walser" (conveyed by Robert Walser). Because of this shared existence it is no wonder that in the course of one short paragraph Widmann raises doubts concerning the validity of Kocher's "existence," which seems to be divided ("geteilt," "mitgeteilt") into various roles: "a talented schoolboy," "the prematurely deceased boy," "the prematurely deceased 'Fritz Kocher,'" or "the truly talented boy" (13). Who is this "boy"? Walser, the "very young Swiss poet," or Kocher?

Widmann seems almost to be haunted by the fact that he is unable to assure us with certainty that Walser is just pretending to communicate Kocher's writings. For Widmann, Walser's split between the roles of author, editor, and double cannot easily be resolved, especially since Widmann adds Walser's brother to this riddle of missed identities, copyright, and authorship. Whose "mouth" is speaking in these essays?

> And this fear and abhorrence of rhetorical pathos has led the poet by necessity to the most unadorned language, and towards the attempt to express noble and beautiful feelings with the diction of a pupil. Where he got it from is not easily found out—maybe this diction was still close to the "tongue" of this young man whose schooldays were not yet that far off. Or, maybe, he had to search far for it, or had to study it in a rather artificial manner. (15)

It is not easily found out—and neither is it easily said or read. The question about authorship strangely gains more urgency and clarity once an uncanny correspondence between the nature of the text and the confusion about its author emerges. Both text and author represent an intermingled web of personas and topics that Walser/Kocher very appropriately calls "ein krauses Zeug" (muddled stuff), "süsser Wirrwarr" (too sweet a muddle), or "Mischmasch" (mishmash) (*SW*, 1:11, 19; *ASD*, 6, 13). It is up to the reader to decipher those "scribbles." In order to do so, however, the reader would, like Fritz Kocher, first need to die and be released into a state of living on. Only when the reader relinquishes his or her conventional expectation to find sense and coherent meaning in a text will he or she be released into a state of suspension between comprehension and incomprehension. Thus hovering, having forsaken any desire for clarity, the reader can appreciate these "scribbles" as both nonsensical and meaningful. Accordingly, the introduction to *Fritz Kocher's Essays* ends with "Adieu, mein Kleiner! Adieu, Leser!" (Farewell, my little friend! Farewell, reader!) (*SW*, 1:8; *ASD*, 3). Both Kocher and the reader have been relegated to the "antechamber," the "waiting room of life." Here reigns a different "diction," authored, edited, and spoken by the mixture of Walser and Kocher; here the poet awakens in the schoolboy and both begin anew, as a "pupil of life" who "learns by beginning like a child" (*SW*, 16:257).[9] As Walser writes in a piece from the Biel years, where he reflects back on his early writing:

> Wo ich als Dichter begann [. . .] fing ich auch als Mensch an und war wie neugeboren. Täglich war die Welt neu, als sei sie über Nacht gestorben und erwache frühmorgens aus dem Tode. Frei wie nie vorher war ich und wie nie mehr nachher wieder. (*SW*, 16:256)
>
> Where I began as a poet [. . .] I also began anew as a human and I was as if newly born. Daily, the world appeared as new, as if it had died overnight and had awakened at dawn from death. I was free as never before and never again.

The freedom associated with the daily opportunity of experiencing the world as if resurrected is linked to the resurrection of the human in the poet. And both are linked by Walser to a profound experience of finitude. Walser situates the child at the cusp of these opportunities, between death and birth and living on, in and as learning.

Walser scholars have long noted the great importance of the topic of childhood in his writings, the way he transforms the denigrated attributes of the child into positive resources for a different "Zugriff,"[10] a different approach toward life and living. While Widmann calls the style of this approach "primitive," other readers of Walser still defer to Benjamin's poignant term "Sprachverwilderung" (linguistic wilderness).[11] By connecting this famous attribute to other writings by Benjamin, Davide Giuriato has shown how productive the relationship between Benjamin's notions of the "wild," the "barbaric," and "childhood" is for a reading of Walser's representation of childhood as a state of "having-not-yet-arrived-in language," that is, the speaking being in its infancy. Giuriato refers to Benjamin's essay "Experience and Poverty" and his remarks on Klee, where Benjamin undertakes a major reevaluation of the term "barbaric" by connecting it to the potential of an always- and ever-repeatable opportunity to begin again: "But where does poverty of experience take the barbarian? Poverty of experience causes him to begin again anew, to begin again from the start."[12] Benjamin's notion of the "barbaric" should not be understood in terms of a theory of cultural socialization that leads from an inferior state of nature to an advanced state of civilization, but rather as the state of a nonteleological "not yet." As Giuriato writes, "Walser's poetics of childhood is neither a poetics of development and transience, nor one of dissolution and disappearance. It is rather a poetics of fragile becoming, a poetics of a not-(yet) in language."[13]

This "not yet" is essential to Walser's poetics: it is the pupil (but others, such as the poet, could take on that role) who, as the one still learning, points to the experience of language when first encountered as curiously "strange," and it is this experience that fuels the so-called childlike "mishmash" and the necessarily nonnarrative structure of Kocher's essays: "The child's relationship to language in Walser's work can be put thus: the child is not naturally situated in language, but comes toward language from nonlanguage, and can occasionally disrupt language."[14] Nothing about Fritz Kocher's existence in language is simply given, or can be taken for granted, for the simple reason that he does not yet exist in it; rather, he exists in a state of not-yet-language. Kocher's approach to the world, his "Zugriff," is indeed prelinguistic and often preverbal: he does not yet grasp the world either in concepts or in rhetorical "phrases"; instead, his is an almost synesthetic approach responding only to colors, sounds, dreams, and feelings. The term "mishmash" is the appropriate expression of a still undifferentiated conglomerate of impressions that are not yet fastened in definitions or meanings. In this realm, impressions are still interchangeable and can replace each other in a nonsignifying manner. In this vein, Fritz Kocher's "Zugriff" is utterly sensory and allows him a playful approach to things and words. Thus, under the heading "Herbst" (Autumn), Kocher can quickly move from the absence of birdsong to the color white (*weiß*), indicating both the absence of color and the presence of knowledge (*weiß*, the conjugated form of *wissen*, "to know"):

> Man hört keine Vögel mehr singen. Die Natur ist doch herrlich. Wie sie die Farben ändert, das Gewand wechselt, Masken aufsetzt und wieder abnimmt! Es ist wunderschön. Wenn ich ein Maler wäre, und es ist nicht ausgeschlossen, daß ich einer werde [. . .] so würde ich am leidenschaftlichsten ein Herbstmaler. Ich fürchte nur, daß alsdann

meine Farben nicht ausreichen werden [. . .]. Es wird bald Winter werden, Schnee wird wirbeln, ach, wie ich mich darauf freue! Wenn alles so weiß ist, weiß man alles viel besser in der Stunde. Farben erfüllen zu sehr das Gedächtnis mit allerlei krausem Zeug. Farben sind ein zu süsser Wirrwarr. Ich liebe das Einfarbige, Eintönige. Schnee ist so ein recht eintöniger Gesang. Warum sollte eine Farbe nicht den Eindruck des Singens machen können! Weiß ist wie ein Murmeln, Flüstern, Beten. Feurige, zum Beispiel Herbstfarben, sind ein Geschrei. Das Grün im Hochsommer ist ein vielstimmiges Singen in den höchsten Tönen. Ist das wahr? Ich weiß nicht, ob das zutrifft. Nun, der Lehrer wird so freundlich sein und es korrigieren. (*SW*, 1:11)

You don't hear any birds singing anymore. Nature really is great. The way it shifts colors, changes robes, puts on masks and takes them off again! It's very beautiful. If I was a painter, and it's not out of the question that I'll become one someday [. . .] I would be most fervently an Autumn painter. I'm only afraid that my colors wouldn't be up to it [. . .]. It will be Winter soon, the snow will swirl, oh how I'm looking forward to that! When everything outside is so white, everything in class is so right.[15] Colors fill up your mind too much with all sorts of muddled stuff. Colors are too sweet a muddle, nothing more. I love things in one color, monotonous things. Snow is such a monotonous song. Why shouldn't a color be able to make the same impression as singing? White is like a murmuring, whispering, praying. Fiery colors, like for instance Autumn colors, are a shriek. Green in midsummer is a many-voiced song with all the highest notes. Is that true? I don't know if that's right. Well, the teacher will surely be so kind as to correct it. (*ASD*, 6)

A masquerade has an annihilating effect on any signifying system: when everything is equal and each part can function as the other's placeholder, then the world dissolves into an allegory. Its emblem is precisely the pictorial and tonal qualities of words (such as the beautiful analogy, unfortunately lost in translation, between "weiß" [white] and "weiß" [know]), which combine image and sound to make what Martin Roussel calls a "sound picture,"[16] at times hardly audible as "murmuring" and "whispering," at others a vehement "shriek" that forestalls any listener's comprehension. While these degrees in tone mark the limit and threshold that lets language vacillate between "still-speaking" and "mere noise" (or even undifferentiated screaming), as Roussel suggests,[17] the conflation of "eintönig" (monotonous) and "einfarbig" (monochrome) in the color "weiß" points to the pictorial quality of writing and the limits of reading comprehension. When the color "weiß" is associated with both knowledge (*wissen*) and nonknowledge ("I don't know [*ich weiß nicht*] if that's right"), then this oscillation at the cusp of comprehension echoes and projects these limits from the realm of sound to the realm of writing and reading. The whiteness of a page, then, might sound like a "whispering," and create a "sound picture" ("Klangbild") whose "notation" as "print" or "typeface" ("Schriftbild") is no longer legible with certainty.

Fritz Kocher's essays are by necessity off-topic because this pupil's approach to the world is neither one of conceptual "Zugriff" nor even of correct linguistic agreement between word and thing. His writing is thus in need of "correction" by the teacher who, after all, ought to know how to divide the world according to themes and topics, which he prescribes as homework. Kocher's understanding of the world, however, is utterly unthematic, and only attuned to the "sweet muddle" of sound and color; accordingly (and here in total agreement), his essays know only one theme, and that is the dissolution of topic-driven writing.[18] Kocher's assertion that he prefers "vorgeschriebenen Stoff" (a prescribed theme) when faced with the freedom of choice does not contradict the nonthematic directionality of his writing: the difference between a topic given or a topic freely chosen is of no importance when what is at stake is a fundamental nonrelation to a world divided and articulated by thematic references. Kocher's points of reference are only "vorgegaukelt" (feigned), playful opportunities for the next "jump"[19] from correspondences to coincidental resemblances in sound and color. Peter Utz, appropriately, calls the heading for each of Kocher's essays his "trampoline."[20]

> Diesmal, sagte der Lehrer, dürft ihr schreiben, was euch gerade einfällt. Ehrlich gesagt, mir will nichts einfallen. Ich liebe diese Art von Freiheit nicht. Ich bin gern an einen vorgeschriebenen Stoff gebunden. Ich bin zu faul, etwas zu ersinnen. Und was könnte das auch sein? Ich schreibe über alles gleich gern. Mich reizt nicht das Suchen eines bestimmten Stoffes, sondern das Aussuchen feiner, schöner Worte. Ich kann aus einer Idee zehn, ja hundert Ideen bilden, aber mir fällt keine Grundidee ein. Was weiss ich, ich schreibe, weil ich es hübsch finde, so die Zeilen mit zierlichen Buchstaben auszufüllen. Das "Was" ist mir vollständig gleichgültig. (*SW*, 1:24)

> This time, the teacher said, each of you can write whatever comes to mind. To be honest, nothing comes to mind. I don't like this kind of freedom. I am happy to be tied to a prescribed theme. I am too lazy to think of something myself. And what would it be? I'm equally happy to write about anything. I don't like hunting around for a topic. I like looking for beautiful, delicate words. I can come up with ten, even a hundred ideas from one idea, but the original idea never comes to me. What do I know. I write because it's nice to fill up the lines with pretty little letters like this. The "what" makes no difference to me at all. (*ASD*, 17)

Walser scholars have long appreciated this famous passage as an expression of the author's poetic program.[21] Not only does the passage emphasize Walser's profound disregard for content and his refusal to be guided by any fundamental idea; it also emphasizes his main poetic preoccupation, namely the selection of fine and beautiful words. Benjamin's equally famous coinage "Sprachgirlande" (linguistic garlands)[22] is an apt description for the continuous regeneration of one idea into an allegorical chain of hundreds, and finds its equivalent in Widmann's comparison of this movement to the unmotivated play of billiard balls: "There was something suggestive in the way Walser let unfold [*hervorrollen*] his curious thoughts without any haste or pressure—like balls rolling on the green cloth of a billiard table" (14). Again, we encounter the movement of opening and closing, unfolding and curling up ("hervorrollen" and "zusammenrollen") of "Blätter," either as those belonging to a "mimosa," or those made of paper. When open, both can be covered with beautiful words, but will close under the "Zugriff" of a "prescribed theme." Only indetermination of topic and free play allow "mishmash" to emerge on the white page, and that only as a "question," and not as "meaning": "Man kann allerlei plappern, ja; ob aber das Mischmasch (ich verzeihe mir die Ungezogenheit, womit ich meine Arbeit tituliere), das man schreibt, etwas spricht und bedeutet, ist eine Frage" (You can blabber all kinds of nonsense, but it's a real question whether the mishmash you write (I allow myself the bad manners of entitling my work in this way) actually says and means anything) (*SW*, 1:19; *ASD*, 13).[23] By deviating from the prescribed title and topic of his essay, Kocher/Walser literally "entitles" himself by putting every text bearing the title "mishmash" forever into "question." Peter Utz has shown—and Walser's admission to being forward with a wink speaks to this—that Kocher's essays underhandedly subvert the prescribed relationship between title and topic by flattening them out into a surface structure awaiting its playful inscriptions. It is not by accident that both Utz and Widmann use examples such as "trampoline," or "das grüne Tuch," the felt of a billiard table. The flatness of each indicates the movement of Walser's writerly hand: he springs forth, allows balls to roll, and uses his painterly brush. For Utz, the topic/title combination is flattened into the surface of a painterly canvas. It is here, on such a canvas, where, as Widmann puts it, "attempts at primitive art emerge on purpose" (13). "Mischmasch," as this other (primitive) combination of color and sound, literally surfaces ("auftauchen") when prescribed title and text separate:

> Also those texts dating from Bern, although they still carry these school-titles, increasingly liberate themselves from this pre-scription [*Vorschrift*]. [. . .] The text turns against the program of the title, rips open the canvas by painting over it. The "prescribed material" [*vorgeschriebener Stoff*] is a linguistic fabric of themes; it is the canvas that Walser covers with "beautiful words." Onto the pre-formatted

> "autumn" he paints his own autumn—not by accident are all of Fritz Kocher's essays of the same size. The title is not only the hook for the picture but also serves as the label for the canvas which Walser needs as an external directive in order to let his writing reign with an even freer hand.[24]

"Vorgeschriebener Stoff" (prescribed material) and "title" literally materialize here into the "Stoff," the fabric of a canvas. What we view, then, and not read, are evenly sized and hung paintings in a gallery pretending to be a collection of "essays" in a book. A process of transformation has occurred in which the textual "fabric" of "essay" as a generic form of writing gives way to the painterly "fabric" of a canvas. The essay as form is transfigured, and, as if by a "hands-on act" ("eigenhändig")[25] is formatted into the flat surface of a canvas. It is here where one can observe a double movement of liberation: Walser's painterly world emerges only at the moment when title and text, but also "Vorschrift" (prescription) and "Stoff" (theme/material) are separated from each other. Only then can "Autumn" emerge as colorful "shrieks"—not as topic or title, but in its nonthematic quality as "mishmash." The transformative process one witnesses in Kocher's essays is one from "Vorschrift," as prescribed or dictated task, to "Vor-schrift," (literally, "before-writing," with emphasis on the prefix "before"), indicating a realm of prelinguistic expression and "entitlement": a "prior-to-language." Paradoxically, an act of entitlement can only occur in this realm of indetermination: choosing "mishmash" as a title in fact entitles—in the other sense of the word—an emerging self to become, as Utz writes, "eigenhändig" (able to write with one's own hands), an authorial self with its own unique signature. The emergence of a writerly self occurs at the threshold of the thematic and the unthematic. It happens, however, by reversing the regular developmental direction of pedagogical instruction: in this "Vorschule" (preschool), one proceeds from the thematic to the unthematic state of "pre-." Here a pupil does not graduate but remains in a state of learning. Yet learning how to write ("schreiben lernen") implies a process neither of regression nor progression; it rather indicates an existence within a "not yet" and its poetic potential as "nonsense" and "a sweet muddle." Within the context of Kocher's classroom the question of how to read or how to correct this "hubbub" is still valid, since the essays are nonetheless addressed to a teacher who demands clarity of style. While the pupil is more interested in the beauty of letters and words, the teacher is still interested in legibility and content. But how does one read pictures of sound?

This question will remain urgent and will become even more prominent in the publications following *Fritz Kocher's Essays*. The liberation of the text from its title is only the first step toward a writerly existence within the realm of "mishmash"; the movement of "living on" in this realm will imply a more pronounced retreat from the public demands of reader or teacher toward a more arbitrary, independent, and private use of and play with "Stoff,"

"Vor-schrift," and formatting.[26] The separation between title and text as practiced in *Fritz Kocher's Essays* is only a step away from a more radical liberation of the writing process: Kocher's "preschool" and "antechamber to life" is also the antechamber to Walser's "Bleistiftgebiet" (domain of the pencil). It is here where titles are no longer dictated and the canvas is cut to a desired size.[27]

Walser's interest in the format, length, and size of his productions is already evident at this early stage and anticipates the beginning of his famous microscripts.[28] All of Kocher's essays are equal in size, and each piece represents the flat canvas-like surface onto which the next deviant writerly move can be projected, written, or painted; where the dictated topic ("Vorschrift") is erased by "Überschreibung" ("writing over" or "covering over").[29] Reminiscent of Freud's "mystic writing pad,"[30] the dictation is covered with new inscriptions that erase its legibility and add a new layer of markings. The previous dictation may still shine through the overlay and continue to exert effects, but a new text has replaced the surface. This two-step movement from "Vorschrift" to "Überschreibung" that was already active in Kocher's essays (as the playful separation of "title" and "text") will continue into the "Bleistiftgebiet," where Walser will first compose a text in pencil and only then copy—and often recompose—it in ink. The writerly movement between pencil and ink, from draft to final copy again resembles the rolling movement of "billiard balls" or the opening and closing of mimosa-"Blätter":

> The purpose of both movements of writing—the "writing into" the micrographic realm of script, and the "writing out" of this realm which, nonetheless, represents yet another "writing into"—this time, a writing into the realm of publication (a realm characterized by the spatial proximity of the most different themes and contents) [. . .] seems to be less about exerting control over the contexts but is more motivated by the interest in an experimental shifting of layers of these contexts, and the subsequent transitory movement of meaning that these changes and modulations cause.[31]

Here Christian Walt emphasizes the territorial and thus contextual changes implicit in Walser's compositional steps from private copy, or "Vor-schrift," to a final text aimed at publication. Widmann already emphasized the significance of publication venue when he remarked how much more pleasure he got from the book version of *Fritz Kocher's Essays* compared to its journal form: "Now, in this fine little book, and nicely arranged together, one can enjoy those zestful revelations of an indescribably sensitive soul. This enjoyment was not possible when published irregularly [*verzettelt*] over weeks in a newspaper" (14). Maybe unintentionally, Widmann has chosen one of the most fitting terms to characterize both Walser's preference for scraps of paper found by happenstance ("Zettel") and the formal content of his writing as "a muddle" ("Wirrwarr," a muddled collection of slips of paper, which can also be described as *verzettelt*). In both cases, the word *verzettelt* points to Walser's method of cutting paper to size, but also to the composition of "a muddle" as a poetic production that denies any dictated or "prescribed theme," either in the form of title or topic.[32] While in *Fritz Kocher's Essays* Walser undercuts any dictation by what Utz calls "Überschreibung" ("writing over" or "covering over"), in the microscripts he undercuts the "Vorschrift" (prescribed theme) by a "Vor-schrift," a first draft in pencil that neither carries a title nor always a coherent theme. "Verzettelt," in scraps of paper, also expresses quite powerfully the sense of multiplying ideas, and equally powerfully points to a profound state of disorientation and loss when both author and reader get lost in this multitude of ideas.

Continuity, changes in degree, but also radical innovations characterize the relationship between *Fritz Kocher's Essays* and the realm of the pencil and its microscripts. Both are concerned with the tension between private and public addressees; the tension, however productive, between prescribed theme and its deflation in unthematic chatter; and the description of a writerly self as emerging in a prelinguistic state of colors, touch, sound, and feelings. The step from Kocher's preoccupation with colors to Walser's preference for the grayness produced by a pencil does not represent a contradiction. In the end, whether as colorful "shrieking" or as minute grayish matter, both turn into inaudible, indecipherable markers of a poetic language only heard or read in its resistance and refusal. For Walser, the ability to hear or read this poetic potential in its retreat is a task to be learned—more specifically, a task that will never be fully achieved, but instead requires an ongoing, continuous learning process. It is this process of necessary, continuous learning that connects *Fritz Kocher's Essays* to Walser's "Pencil Realm": the authors of both do not grow up, but continue on as "boys" and pupils in school as the "Vorschule," the preschool of life. Both know that the lesson at hand is to learn how to hear and read language in its refusal; yet they also know that one first ought to learn how to write a language *as* refusal. This learning process is one without either regression or progression;[33] it is simply ongoing, repetitive, ever newly beginning, even after dramatic setbacks such as Walser's famous writerly breakdown with the pen. To remain "at play" with language, one has to remain in the role of "boy," and the task is always the same: "knabenhaft schreiben lernen" (to learn to write as a boy).[34]

Notes

1. Hans H. Hiebel, "Robert Walsers *Jakob von Gunten*: Die Zerstörung der Signifikanz im modernen Roman," in *Robert Walser*, ed. Klaus-Michael Hinz and Thomas Horst (Frankfurt am Main: Suhrkamp, 1991), 249.

2. Peter Utz, *Tanz auf den Rändern: Robert Walsers "Jetztzeitstil"* (Frankfurt am Main: Suhrkamp, 1998).

3. On the topic of the stroll in Walser's work, see, among many others, Peter von Matt, "Wie weise ist Walsers Weisheit?," in *Robert Walsers "Ferne Nähe": Neue Beiträge zur Forschung*, ed. Wolfram Groddeck et al. (Munich: Wilhelm Fink, 2007). On the motif of dance, see Utz, *Tanz auf den Rändern*, esp. 424–97.

4. The apostrophe in the title was dropped in posthumous editions of the book. For information on the publication history, see Paul Keckeis, "Fritz Kocher's Aufsätze," in *Robert Walser-Handbuch: Leben-Werk-Wirkung*, ed. Lucas Marco Gisi (Stuttgart: Metzler, 2015), 90–94.

5. Translation modified. For more information on Walser's use of *Blatt*, see Wolfram Groddeck, "Weiss das Blatt, wie schön es ist? Prosastück, Schriftbild und Poesie bei Robert Walser," *Text: Kritische Beiträge* 3 (1997): 23–41.

6. Joseph Viktor Widmann, "Gebrüder Walser," first published in *Der Bund*, December 9, 1904; reprinted in *Über Robert Walser*, ed. Katharina Kerr, vol. 1 (Frankfurt am Main: Suhrkamp, 1978), 13–16, here at 14. Hereafter cited parenthetically in the text; when the source is unclear, "Widmann" will precede the page number.

7. My translation.

8. "Die Arbeit muß ihren bestimmten Charakter und einen Zweck haben, zu dem sie führen soll. Um das zu erreichen, wählt man einen Beruf. Dies geschieht, wenn man aus der Schule tritt, und mit diesem Ereignisse ist man ein erwachsener Mensch, das heißt, nun hat man eine andere Schule vor sich: das Leben" (Work has to have a particular character and a goal it is aiming toward. To reach that goal, you choose a profession. This happens when a person leaves school, at which point that person is an adult, or in other words, he now has another school he has to attend: life) (*SW*, 1:28; *ASD*, 21).

9. Hartmut Vollmer, "Die erschriebene Kindheit: Erzähllust, Sprachzauber und Rollenspiel im Werk Robert Walsers," *Euphorion: Zeitschrift für Literaturgeschichte* 93, no. 1 (1999): 82. For more on the topic of childhood in Walser, see Davide Giuriato, "Kindheit, Naivität, Dilettantismus," in Gisi, *Robert Walser-Handbuch*, 337–40; Davide Giuriato, "Robert Walsers Kinder," in Groddeck et al., *Robert Walsers "Ferne Nähe,"* 125–32; Stephan Kammer, "'Lib/e/ri': Walsers poetologisch souveräne Kinder," in Groddeck et al., *Robert Walsers "Ferne Nähe,"* 133–40; Peter von Matt, "Wie weise ist Walsers Weisheit?," in Groddeck et al., *Robert Walsers "Ferne Nähe"*; Peter Utz, "Die Kalligrafie des 'Idioten,'" in *Text und Kritik: Robert Walser*, ed. Heinz Ludwig Arnold, vol. 12/12a, 4th ed. (Munich: Edition Text + Kritik, 2004), 106–18; Stephan Kammer, *Figurationen und Gesten des Schreibens: Zur Ästhetik der Produktion in Robert Walsers Prosa der Berner Zeit* (Tübingen: Max Niemeyer, 2003); Victor Zmegac, "Robert Walsers Poetik in der literarischen Konstellation der Jahrhundertwende," in *Robert Walser und die moderne Poetik*, ed. Dieter Borchmeyer (Frankfurt am Main: Suhrkamp, 1999), 21–36; Klaus-Michael Hinz, "Wo die bösen Kinder wohnen: Robert Walsers Melancholie. Mit einer Fussnote zu Franz Kafkas Spielsachen," in Hinz and Horst, *Robert Walser*, 310–22; Gerd Hammer, *Momente des Kindlichen im Werk Robert Walsers* (Frankfurt am Main: Griedel, 1989).

10. See Giuriato, "Robert Walsers Kinder," 129.

11. Walter Benjamin, *Selected Writings*, vol. 2, ed. Michael W. Jennings, Howard Eiland, and Gary Smith (Cambridge, Mass.: Harvard University Press, 1999), 257.

12. See Giuriato, "Robert Walsers Kinder," 129, for a comparison between Benjamin's notion of "barbarism" and Walser's "linguistic wilderness." On the notion of "barbarism" in Benjamin, see *Selected Writings*, 2:732. See Giuriato, "Robert Walsers Kinder," 131, for a discussion of children and language learning.

13. Ibid., 132.

14. Ibid., 131.

15. Searls attempts to capture the play of "weiß" and "weiß" here with rhyme ("white"/"right").

16. Martin Roussel, "Schreibszenen (Schreiben, Materialität, Schriftbild)," in Gisi, *Robert Walser-Handbuch*, 266.

17. Ibid.

18. See Vollmer, "Die erschriebene Kindheit," 75, for more on the relationship between writerly enjoyment and play.

19. "Gaukler sein wäre schön" (It would be great to join the circus) (*SW*, 1:30; *ASD*, 22). Walser uses variations of the verb *springen* (to jump) throughout the text.

20. Peter Utz, "Robert Walser: Stück ohne Titel," in Groddeck et al., *Robert Walsers "Ferne Nähe,"* 51.

21. Ibid.

22. Benjamin, *Selected Writings*, 2:258.

23. Translation modified.

24. Utz, "Robert Walser," 53, 51.

25. Ibid., 54.

26. Regarding Walser's preferences for formatting and other material concerns, see ibid. Regarding continuation of the topic of "Wirrwarr" (muddle) in the microscripts, see Kerstin Gräfin von Schwerin, "'Kolossal zierliche Zusammengeschrobenheiten von durchweg abenteuerlichem Charakter': In den Regionen des Bleistiftgebiets," in Arnold, *Text und Kritik*, 161–80; see esp. "In a microscript he describes his theme as 'a muddle, a mess, a confusion' " (176).

27. On Walser's different approach toward titles in the microscripts, see Utz, "Robert Walser," 54.

28. Ibid.

29. Ibid., 51: "The 'prescribed material,' linguistic textured fabric of themes, is a canvas that Walser writes over with his own 'beautiful words.' "

30. Sigmund Freud, "A Note upon the 'Mystic Writing-Pad,' " in *The Standard Edition of the Complete Psychological Works of Sigmund Freud*, 24 vols., trans. and ed. James Strachey (London: Hogarth, 1961), 19:225–32.

31. Christian Walt, "Schreibprozesse: Abschreiben, Überarbeiten," in Gisi, *Robert Walser-Handbuch*, 272.

32. "Verzettelt" in German can point to a state of mind: one dissipates one's energies, fritters it away. It also points to the organization of paper: a process of cataloguing. On "Zettel," see Adriano Aebli, "'Diese Art von belächelnswerten Sächelchen': Ein Vorschlag zur Lektüretechnik des Bleistiftgebiets," in Arnold, *Text und Kritik*, 181–91.

33. Giuriato, "Robert Walsers Kinder," 132.

34. *Briefe*, 322.

Robert Walser's Jewish Berlin

Daniel Medin

When Robert Walser first arrived in Berlin, his Swiss provincial origins were immediately apparent to all: he was not just a stranger to the imperial capital, but a foreign national. Moreover, he appears to have been at ease with his own marginalization. Between the years of 1906 and 1913, Walser mingled with dozens of Berlin's most influential writers, publishers, editors, and politicians, many of whom were assimilated Jews. He never speaks of a "Jewish Berlin," but his descriptions of these individuals reveal something of the social pressures they faced regularly. Walser's own position as outsider doubtlessly contributed to his perceptiveness concerning that community's leading lights. The purpose of this essay is to gather his sketches of these figures and to provide some context—biographical, historical, or textual—about their composition. Despite the prominence of individuals discussed, many of these documents are little known in German (and even less so in English). So another aim is to make the materials available to readers less familiar with the status of Walser's Jewish colleagues; hence my prioritization of the author's own words, whether from his published feuilletons or his correspondence and unpublished manuscripts.

Having quit the Silesian castle where he had worked as a servant for three months, Robert Walser reinstalled himself in his brother Karl's Charlottenburg apartment during the first weeks of 1906. Nearly a decade had passed since a disastrous audition in Stuttgart had convinced him to become a writer instead of an actor. Now twenty-seven, he was an author whose verse, playlets, and short prose had drawn acclaim from discriminating circles.

These modest successes, however, could not measure up to the accomplishments of his host. After years of toil, Karl was rapidly becoming one of the most sought-after artists in the city. Commissions poured in from several directions at once—from collectors (for his paintings), theaters (for his stage sets), and publishers (for his illustrations). Karl's activity in these different areas widened their social circles further, as Robert profited from his brother's renown.

Berlin's eminent theater critic, Alfred Kerr, admired Karl's designs for the stage. "I saw wonderful sets," he enthused about Max Reinhard's inauguration of the Deutsches Theater on October 19, 1905.[1] This appreciation remained undiminished when Kerr reviewed a premiere at the Komische Oper by calling attention not to the music but to Walser's design for the stage:

"*The Tales of Hoffmann*," he exclaimed: "A Walser Dream!"[2] Evidently, this affection did not spill over to Karl's younger sibling. In a show of characteristic cheek, Walser published an essay titled "Brief an Alfred Kerr" ("Letter to Alfred Kerr") in September 1927 in the *Prager Presse* (the cultural pages of which were edited by another German Jew, Otto Pick). "Ich hielt Dich für ein wenig mißtrauisch," recalls Walser's narrator:

> Eines Abends stellte ich mich Dir in den Räumen der Berliner Sezession freudig vor. Die Freudigkeit schien Dich in einem gewissen Grad zu stören. Immer sahest Du ebenso stattlich aus, wie Du schriftstellertest, und benahmest Dich stets ebenso knapp und kurzangebunden, wie Du Wahrheiten zu verbreiten suchtest. [. . .] Darf ich Dich außerdem an die Tatsache erinnern, daß ich Dich im Alter von vierundzwanzig Jahren fröhlich, d.h. sachlich anpumpte? Für mich war es belehrend, aufklärend, daß Du mein Gesuch unbeantwortet ließest. (*SW*, 19:26)

> I thought you were a little mistrustful. One evening in the rooms of the Berlin Secession I introduced myself to you exuberantly. The exuberance appeared to disturb you to a certain degree. Your appearance was always as stately as your writing, and you comported yourself exactly as curtly and coolly as the truths you sought to disseminate. [. . .] May I furthermore remind you of the fact that at the age of twenty-four I cheerfully, i.e. matter-of-factly touched you for a loan? For me it was telling, illuminating, that you left my appeal unanswered.

Walser had little patience for those surrounded by an aura of self-importance, even less so if the individual in question belonged to the intelligentsia. This is already visible in the ironic qualification that opens his "letter" to Kerr, where his narrator insists, in a parody of stately language, that everything to follow is ostensibly harmless.

Still, the indifferent Kerr was an exception to the rule, at least during the first few years of Walser's stay in Berlin. Many still saw the Swiss poet as a prodigy in search of his proper form—which is perhaps why publisher Bruno Cassirer, one of Karl Walser's most important patrons, encouraged Robert to try his hand at a novel. Karl had met Cassirer a few years earlier, when Bruno comanaged a gallery and printing press with his cousin Paul. On August 30, 1901, they went their separate ways, with Paul taking charge of the gallery and Bruno managing the press. Although this break was not amicable, Karl managed to sustain relations with both men, showing his work at Paul's Berlin Secession on the one hand and becoming the principal illustrator of Verlag Bruno Cassirer on the other.

During a long ramble in the countryside decades later, Walser discussed this period with a sympathetic journalist. In his record of their conversation, Carl Seelig notes:

> His brother, the painter Karl, introduced Robert to the publishers Samuel Fischer and Bruno Cassirer in Berlin; at the time Karl had become famous through [. . .] several of his theater sets. He painted often with Max Liebermann in Holland and at the Baltic Sea. Bruno Cassirer encouraged Robert to write a novel. The result was *The Tanners*, though Cassirer did not particularly like it.[3]

Cassirer's skepticism would never diminish. He rejected Walser's second novel (which Walser then destroyed), despite the strong case made for it by the press's principal editor, Christian Morgenstern.[4] Cassirer's support had been initially founded on the need to remain in Karl's good graces. He also became possessive when he discovered that fellow publisher Samuel Fischer wished to acquire work by his author. "Ich wurde einst," writes Walser of what appears to be the same episode in "Potpourri," "von einem übrigens anscheinend durchaus ehrlichen Verleger ernsthaft ersucht, nicht nebenbuhlerische Verleger gegen ihn auszuspielen. [The character based on Bruno Cassirer declares in a letter,] 'Ich setze mich für Sie ein, und darf nicht gestatten, daß sich die Konkurrenz für Sie interessiert' " (An allegedly—by the way—thoroughly trustworthy publisher once entreated me in all earnestness not to pit him against a rival publisher. "I represent your work, and cannot permit the competition to take an interest in you") (*SW*, 18:214).

Walser was nevertheless the first German-writing author to be published by the press. Before *The Tanners*, Cassirer had focused exclusively on art books and reliable staples of world literature like Flaubert and Dostoevsky; the fact that he printed three Walser novels in three years despite lackluster sales suggests at least a little faith in Morgenstern's opinion, and, no doubt, a desire to retain Karl's allegiance. In addition to publishing his books, Cassirer featured Walser's short prose frequently in his successful periodical, *Kunst und Künstler*, which is where "Leben eines Malers" ("A Painter's Life"), Robert's tribute to his brother, first appeared.

By this time, the younger sibling's feuilletons were visible regularly in scores of prestigious journals, many of them managed or edited by Berlin-based Germans of Jewish origin. In a 1907 letter to Morgenstern, Walser announced his submission of a text to *Die Zukunft*, the famous—and at times, notorious—brainchild of Maximilian Harden (*Briefe*, 49). Bernhard Echte attests to the significance of Walser's presence in these pages during those years:

> Harden's acceptance of a text for publication signified [. . .] a greater level of recognition. Among critics of the Wilhelmine period, Harden had one of the highest profiles, and he maintained an extensive range of contacts that spanned all of the leading political, economic, and cultural circles. His mainly politically oriented journal included few literary contributions, which lent an even greater significance to those

> [that were] selected. Walser was represented in *Zukunft* by longer texts on multiple occasions until the start of the First World War.[5]

On learning of Harden's death in 1927, Walser wrote an elegy of sorts and sent it to Otto Pick, who duly ran it in the *Prager Presse*:

> **Harden**
>
> [. . .] auf dem breiten
> Kurfürstendamm
> grüßt' ich ihn einmal riesig stramm,
> der einst die *Zukunft* redigierte,
> mit großer Fähigkeit in seinem Reich brillierte.
> Welch ein Erfolg war ihm beschieden
> bezüglich dessen, was er schrieb hienieden!
> Er trug sich, was Gewandung
> betrifft, höchst fein, und seine jetz'ge Landung
> dort, wo wir alle hingelangen, ließ mich, da sie zu Herzen mir gegangen,
> daran erinnern, daß mir sein Gesicht
> gefiel. [. . .] (*SW*, 13:185)[6]
>
> [. . .] on the broad
> Kurfürstendamm
> I once greeted big and strong,
> the former editor of *Die Zukunft*,
> who dazzled in his kingdom with his ability.
> What success was upon him bestowed
> apropos of his prose!
> He dressed, as far as his outfits
> are concerned, impeccably well, and his present arrival
> in that country where we all shall one day dwell
> recalled to mind, since it
> moved me so deeply,
> that I liked his
> face. [. . .]

Walser appreciated Harden for more than his elegant costumes. In a conversation with Carl Seelig shortly before the onset of the Second World War, he lauded the editor's "talent for capturing the character of his time in brilliant articles"; he even ranks Harden over Ludwig Börne—another politically oriented, and Jewish, author for whose melodious language Walser elsewhere expressed his high esteem.[7]

Harden's style also left an impression on the young Siegfried Jacobsohn, who at twenty-six—two years Walser's junior—founded the *Schaubühne*.

Of the thirty-nine feuilletons by Walser published in 1907, an astonishing twenty-six of them appeared in the pages of this editor's journal. Unlike Cassirer, Jacobsohn clearly recognized the singularity of his contributor's talent.

Walser eventually fell out with Jacobsohn, but not before the latter published dozens more of his texts. On December 3, 1926, Jacobsohn died of a stroke: a surprise to many, as he was only forty-five years old. The news must have moved Walser. "Gestorben ist soeben in Deutschland ein Freund von mir," he wrote in a letter to a (nonliterary) friend,

> dem ich gewissermaßen verdanke, daß ich mich, was schriftstellerischen Ausdruck betrifft, einigermaßen entwickelt habe, in dem er die Aufmerksamkeit hatte, mich gleichsam auf die Anforderungen hinzuweisen, die eine neuere Zeit mit Recht an den Schriftsteller stellt. Andere sinds, die die Quellen entdecken helfen, die in uns oft ohne unser Wissen vorhanden sind. (*Briefe*, 292)

> A friend of mine in Germany has just died, a person to whom I am to some measure indebted as far as the development of my literary expression is concerned, since he had the thoughtfulness to point out, correctly, the demands that a new age exacts from a writer. It is thanks to the assistance of others that we uncover sources within us which we often possess without our knowledge.

Walser, a consummate ironist, rarely expressed gratitude of this order. Nor did he apply the term *Freund* (friend) to many beside his brother. Only the suppression of Jacobsohn's name betrays a lingering ambivalence. Were it not for the painstaking effort of scholars to decipher Walser's microscripts, even this omission might seem of little import. But Bernhard Echte is probably right to suspect that Jacobsohn's brisk rejection of a submission by Walser during the 1920s—the text was returned with a form letter declining to publish—provoked an enduring resentment in the latter.[8] Scurrilous references to the editor thus surface in a microscript dated a year and a half after Jacobsohn's death.[9]

Walser also appears to target, in a 1928 poem, those he blamed for contributing to his reputation as a harmless, happy-go-lucky crank. In the first lines his speaker asserts that the serious content to follow has been provoked by those who have spread this reputation. After jabs at Hermann Hesse and Hugo von Hofmannsthal, Walser trains his sights on the deceased editor of the *Schau-* and then *Weltbühne*:

> Das Siegfried Jakobssöhnchen ist verreckt
> wie eine Kröte, o wie hat mich das gefreut, als ich's vernahm.
> Der Luscheib hat mich einmal frech geneckt,
> als ich nachts
> häufig spät nach Hause kam. (*AdB*, 6:490–91)

> Little Siegfried Jakobsohn has croaked
> like a toad, oh how delighted I was by the news.
> The scoundrel mocked me insolently once,
> when I often returned home
> late at night.

The collaboration between Jacobsohn and Walser nevertheless yielded many of the latter's most memorable texts, among them "Gebirgshallen" ("Mountain Halls"), the sketch that Franz Kafka recited enthusiastically to Max Brod—in all likelihood directly from his February 1908 copy of the *Schaubühne*.[10] Alongside Brod, Efraim Frisch, and a handful of others, Jacobsohn belonged to the handful of contemporaries who immediately recognized Walser's genius. Long after their collaboration had ceased, he would assert that he had never come across another writer of equal caliber.[11]

The same cannot be said for Bruno Cassirer. The turning point in his relationship with Walser occurred in 1909, after the tepid reception of *Jakob von Gunten*, the author's third novel in four years. Even in 1906, Cassirer had viewed Walser's work with suspicion, finding the writing undisciplined, garrulous, and dull.[12] To Cassirer's mind, the tepid reaction to *Jakob von Gunten* confirmed these fears. He thus went on the offensive, attempting to persuade Walser to write more commercially accessible stories—a request that betrays the publisher's ignorance of his author's gifts.[13] Moreover, Cassirer appears to have rejoiced in the news that Walser's first collection of short prose, published only a few years before by Insel Verlag, had sold poorly. "You see, Walser," he reportedly taunted, "the Wertheim warehouse is offering your magnificent *Fritz Kocher's Essays* at a discount. You see? Ha-ha!"[14]

Curiously, Walser seems to have been in partial agreement with the publisher. It comes as a surprise that he never quite unloaded his rage at Cassirer—at least not in the letters and microscripts that have been preserved. And on one occasion in Seelig's account, Walser identifies with the verdict:

> Robert tells of how Max Slevogt made fun of Walser's failures one day when they were seated together with Count Leopold von Kalckreuth and Bruno Cassirer. Robert simply needed to become more like Stendhal. His books were too boring for the public. "How was I supposed to reply? I sat there in my total lack of success and had to concede that he was right."[15]

Nevertheless, *Jakob von Gunten* did not go completely unnoticed. The astute critic, editor, and dramatic adviser Efraim Frisch read the pulse of his time much better than Cassirer and other contemporaries. In a long review published in *Die neue Rundschau*, Frisch marveled at the poetic construction—indeed, the overall achievement—of Walser's latest novel.[16] This article appeared in 1911.

Frisch was a close friend of Christian Morgenstern. In a letter to Morgenstern written at the time of *Jakob von Gunten*'s publication, Frisch laments that the collaboration between author and publisher has amounted to "nothing but a great misfortune" for the former. "He has curious ideas about the practice of publishing," says Frisch of Bruno Cassirer:[17]

> (1.) every transaction must from the outset be profitable; his vision reaches no further. (2.) The author is granted a favor, indeed, is shown benevolence, if his work is printed at all. (3.) one should be dependent upon him [the publisher], without any obligation by the latter to provide some kind of service in return.

He goes on to declare Walser's treatment terrifying. Indeed, Bruno Cassirer's decision to release *Jakob von Gunten* in March—an all but dead season for bookselling—appears to confirm Frisch in his assertion that Walser's writing would have been better served by Samuel Fischer.

Frisch's wife Fega is another interesting character from this period, and not only because of Walser's ongoing flirtation with her. Carl Seelig's record of a conversation between the two from October 1944 remains an essential document for all biographers. Fega must have known Walser well, for she speaks with confidence about his childhood here, as well as of the growing tensions between the brothers (once inseparable, the two began to drift apart after Karl's marriage in 1910). The only line of Walser's that hints at this nearness appears in *Wanderungen mit Robert Walser* (*Walks with Robert Walser*). After identifying Fega as "the subtle translator of nearly fifty masterpieces from Russian," Seelig records that Robert once met her for tea while her husband was away. "When they were about to go out together after tea," he reports, "he offered to help her put her shoes on. 'But she declined my proposition with enchanting delicacy.' "[18] Both Frisches stayed in touch with Walser after his return to Switzerland in 1913, and Efraim would continue to print his feuilletons as editor of the *Neue Merkur* more than a decade later.

Oddly enough, Walser's relationship with Paul Cassirer was among the most complicated of those discussed thus far—"oddly" because it was *Bruno* Cassirer, and not his cousin Paul, who severed Walser's monthly stipend in 1912, effectively abandoning him to penury. The fact is that Paul Cassirer had a more developed literary sensibility than his cousin, and this sympathy brought with it greater intimacy between the writer and his distinguished patrons—a familiarity evinced in Walser's always unflinching portraits. Cassirer was also considerably more powerful as a cultural figure. During the first two decades of the new century, his was the most important gallery in town; it was he who introduced seminal French impressionist (Monet, Renoir) and postimpressionist (Cézanne, Van Gogh) painting to the city. He also helped nourish native talent, as the Berlin Secession featured modern artists such as Max Slevgot, Lovis Corinth, and Max Liebermann, all of whom endeavored to renew German painting.

Cassirer enjoyed performing the role of noble benefactor. As the lettered brother of one of his leading artists, Walser was a frequent beneficiary of the gallerist's enthusiasms and whims (such as the time Paul Cassirer invited him on a balloon trip, all expenses paid). For a short period during the spring of 1907, Walser acted as official secretary of the Berlin Secession. In a feuilleton titled "Der Sekretär" ("The Secretary"), Walser's narrator recounts his hiring:

> Der kommerzielle Leiter einer Vereinigung bildender Künstler forderte mich eines Tages wohlgewogenermaßen auf, sein Sekretär zu werden. "Ich hoffe," sprach er, "daß Sie ebensogut Bilder zu verkaufen wie Bücher zu veröffentlichen imstande sind!" Das Anerbieten war zu liebenswürdig, als daß es sorglos hätte abgelehnt werden können. (*SW*, 16:272)
>
> The commercial head of an association for practitioners of the fine arts one day invited me, after appropriate deliberation, to become his secretary. "I hope," he said, "that you will prove just as capable of selling pictures as you are of publishing books!" The offer was too kind to be dismissed out of hand.[19]

In another sketch from the same period, Walser represents a similar dynamic between a capricious millionaire and his bemused servant.

> "Kommen Sie, wir fahren zu Frau Bähni," sagte der Gewalthaber Bösiger zu mir. Ich war damals etwas wie Bösigers bevorzugter Günstling. Der Umgang mit mir mochte ihm angenehm sein, weil ich unerfahren war. Meine Harmlosigkeit bereitete ihm eine Art Vergnügen, und die Ungeschicktheiten, die ich dann und wann sehen ließ, machten ihn lachen. Es ist bekannt, daß große und einflußreiche Herren gern in Gesellschaft von Leute sind, die keinerlei Gewicht haben. Ich spielte damals in den Kreisen, die den Ton angeben, d.h. in der Welt der Bildung, Intelligenz und Eleganz die Rolle eines jugendlichen Anfängers. (*SW*, 16:277)
>
> "Come with me, we'll go visit Frau Bähni," the potentate Bösiger said to me. At the time I was something resembling Bösiger's favored protégé. He no doubt found it agreeable to consort with me because I was inexperienced. My innocuousness gave him a sort of pleasure, and the infelicities I now and then displayed made him laugh. It's well known that powerful, influential gentlemen like to spend time in the company of people who have no importance at all. In those days, I was playing the role of youthful novice in the circles that set the tone, i.e., the world of culture, intellect, and elegance.[20]

"Frau Bähni" depicts the employer's brutish attempts to conquer the heart of an already-married beauty. Indications in the text would lead the reader to recognize Bösiger as a caricature of Cassirer, and Frau Bähni as a barely disguised substitute for Cassirer's second wife, the celebrated actress Tilla Durieux.[21]

When it appeared in *Die neue Rundschau* in 1909, "Die kleine Berlinerin" ("The Little Berliner") caused a stir. The story reads like the kind of essay that Fritz Kocher—or any of the other mischievous pranksters who narrate Walser's fiction—might have written if he had been a girl. For those in the know, it was a delicious send-up of Paul Cassirer, the mighty art dealer, as seen through the eyes of Suzanne Aimée, Cassirer's young daughter from a previous marriage. One can easily imagine the delight of the Secession crowd on encountering the following passage:

> Papa unterstützt die Kunst und die Künstler. Es ist Handel, was er treibt. Nun, Fürsten treiben ebenfalls oft Handel, und dann sind die Geschäfte Papas vor einer absoluten Vornehmheit. [. . .] Die Sache mit Vaters Geschäften, glaube ich, ist so: die Künstler verstehen in der Regel nichts von Geschäften, oder sie dürfen aus irgendwelchen Gründen nichts davon verstehen. [. . .] Papa verachtet oft seine Käufer. Aber er verachtet oft auch die Künstler. Es kommt da ganz darauf an. (*SW*, 3:91–92)

> Papa supports art and the artists. What he engages in is business. Well, lords often engage in business, too, and then Papa's dealings are of absolute refinement. [. . .] The point of Father's business, I think, is this: the artists, as a rule, understand nothing about business, or, for some reason or other, they aren't allowed to understand anything about it. [. . .] Father often looks down upon his buyers. But he often looks down upon the artists, too. It all depends.[22]

Yet in this and other parodies Walser suggests that Cassirer's Napoleonic demeanor is just a façade. His "Porträt eines Kaufmannes" ("Portrait of a Businessman") was triggered by the art dealer's dramatic suicide and appeared in the *Prager Presse* one month later, in February 1926.[23] There Walser makes the following observations about his former employer:

> [Daß] es ihm beliebte, sich immer ein bißchen kräftiger zu gebärden, als er in Wirklichkeit sein mochte. Nicht, daß ich behaupten möchte, er habe geprahlt. Keineswegs! Aber er berauschte sich an der Vorstellung einer Macht und einer Gesundheitsfülle, die leider zum Teil Illusion blieb; Geduld und Ausdauer in der Geschäftsführung schienen ihm versagt zu sein. (*SW*, 18:25–26)

> He always took pleasure in making himself appear a little more robust than he might in reality have been. I am not trying to claim that he swaggered: by no means! But he was intoxicated by an idea of power and vigorous good health, which sadly remained an illusion in part; patience and resilience were apparently missing from his business dealings.

Walser then proceeds to mercilessly expose Cassirer's discomfort about his origins. The symptoms conveyed are readily recognizable as manifestations of Jewish self-hatred:[24]

> War er ein genialer Mensch? Ich verneine diese Frage. Für kolossal klug hielt ich ihn. Mit seinem Betragen wußte er mitunter zu bezaubern, also sehr für sich einzunehmen, aber bei allem dem schien er nur beständig mit einem Degout vor sich und vor allem andern kämpfen zu müssen. Die Genialität zeichnet sich aber dadurch aus, daß sie nichts von Ekel weiß und nie an der eigenen Person Sentimentalität wahrzunehmen in die unappetitliche Lage kommt. Wenn bedeutende Menschen sentimental sind verringert das natürlich ihre Bedeutendheit. (*SW*, 18:26–27)

> Was he a brilliant man? I would answer this question in the negative. I considered him colossally clever. He knew how to enchant [people] by his conduct from time to time, and how to win favor with them, but constantly present was a sense of self-revulsion and the need to compete with everyone else. Whereas brilliance is marked by its complete ignorance of disgust, and never arrives at the unsavory position of regarding itself with sentimentality. When distinguished people are sentimental, that naturally diminishes their distinction.

"Vielleicht gelang es diesem Großbürger nie," the narrator pointedly concludes, "mit dem Kleinbürger in ihm gänzlich fertig zu werden, den Kreis zu überschreiten, zu überwinden, dem er entsprang" (Perhaps this outstanding citizen never succeeded in altogether surmounting the petty bourgeois in him, in stepping out of, overcoming the circle from which he had sprung) (*SW*, 18:28).

The premature death of Paul Cassirer elicited in Walser feelings not unlike those generated earlier by Siegfried Jacobsohn. In both cases, he veers from expressions of perceptive sympathy to others of outright abuse. Walser had a long memory for unkind slights. He never forgot how Cassirer, although a frequent patron, once declined his request for a commission at a dire moment. That refusal surfaces in a microscript written during the mid-1920s (*AdB*, 1:232) and in Walser's 1926 letter to Therese Breitbach, a teenage fan. The section on Cassirer in the latter is extensive, and suffused with a complex irony that obligates a minimal number of omissions:

> Sie wissen ja [. . .] was Wuchtigkeit bedeutet, mit welcher viele Männer oft ihre Schwäche verkleiden, was vielleicht, um gerecht über mich zu urteilen, bei mir auch schon vorkam. Und nun ist da in Berlin der berüchtigte Räuberhauptmann, pardon, ich wollte sagen, berühmte Kunsthändler Paul Cassirer gestorben, obwohl man allerdings über Gestorbene nie spötteln sollte. Dieses Herrn Paul Cassirer's Bild brachte letzthin die *Literarische Welt* und in derselben Woche erschießt sich aus einer Menge über ihn herfallender Alltagssorgen dieser selbe gewiß sehr bedeutende Mann, den ich persönlich sehr gut kannte. Wer hat ihn nicht gekannt? Er war ja in so hohem [Maße] gesellschaftlich. Junge Mädchen kamen zu ihm, Künstler, Prinzen (ächte), Kaufleute, alles, einfach alles. Mich nannte er eines Nachts in einer Weinstube am Kurfürstendamm einen Witzbold, und eines Abends im Theater Kroll im Tiergarten imponiert ihm mein hoher weißer Stehkragen mächtig. . . . Man nennt die Art und Weise, mit der ich hier über Herrn Cassirer rede, karikieren. Sie wissen ja, daß es große und berühmte Karikaturisten gegeben hat, wie etwa in Frankreich, Zeichner vom Schlage eines *Daumier* oder Dichter wie z.B. Heinrich Heine, von dem Ihnen das Loreleilied bekannt sein dürfte. [Breitbach, this letter's recipient, came from Koblenz on the Rhein.] Heine war der Lieblingsschriftsteller eures unvergesslichen und teilweise genialen Bismark [*sic*], und er stammte vom Rhein und war in gewisser Hinsicht ein Lausbub, ein sehr talentvoller Schlingel, der sich über charaktervolle, ernsthaftstrebende Männer, wie etwa über Börne, fürchterlich lustig machte, der aber dabei eine glänzende Prosa schrieb, von der Sie vielleicht schon die Gnade hatten, einiges zu lesen. Er war ein auserlesener Sprachmusiker. (*Briefe*, 255–56)

> You already know [. . .] what vehemence means, many men often disguise their weaknesses in it, myself perhaps included, which I mention so that you may judge me fairly. And just now in Berlin the notorious bandit chief, sorry, I meant to say illustrious art dealer Paul Cassirer, has died, although one should not speak ill of the dead. Just recently the *Literarische Welt* brought out a picture of Mister Paul Cassirer and in the very same week this no doubt very important man, whom I knew personally very well, shoots himself over a host of quotidian cares that had been raining down on him. Who did not know him? He was social to the highest degree. Young girls came to him, artists, princes (real ones), businessmen—everyone, simply everyone. One night in a Kurfürstendamm wine bar he called me a joker, and one evening at the Kroll Theater in Tiergarten my white high standing collar impressed him mightily. [. . .] One calls the manner in which I speak here of Mister Cassirer caricature. Of course you know that there have been great and famous caricaturists such as, in France, the

> first-class draftsmen *Daumier*, or poets, for instance, Heinrich Heine, whose song about the Lorelei you may have heard of. Heine was the favorite author of your unforgettable and partly brilliant Bismark, and he came from the Rhein and was in a certain respect a scallywag, a very talented rogue who made terrific fun of serious, striving men full of character such as Börne, but writing thereby a sparkling prose, of which you have perhaps already had the grace to read. He was an exquisite musician of words.

This appreciation of Heine reveals many of Walser's own predispositions as a writer. And the feuilletons quoted earlier suggest that Walser regarded Cassirer as "serious" as well as "striving"—hence, a target worthy of ridicule. Moreover, a private resentment is also at work. Walser continues,

> Er pflegte zu meinem Bruder Karl zu sagen: "Kommen Sie heute Abend zu mir zu Tisch. Bringen Sie Ihren Bruder mit, aber nur unter der Bedingung, daß er keinen allzu starken Hunger hat." Ich teile Ihnen das alles selbstverständlich im Vertrauen mit und fahre beruhigt in der Indiskretion fort und melde Ihnen folgendes: Paul Cassirer weigerte sich im Jahre 1913, Aufsätze von mir zu verlegen und mir einen Vorschuss von M. 300.- in die Hand zu drücken. (*Briefe*, 257)

> He used to say to my brother Karl: "Join us tonight for supper. Bring your brother along, but only on the condition that his appetite is not too great." I tell you this of course in discretion and proceed, relieved, with my indiscretions further by informing you of the following: In 1913, Paul Cassirer refused to publish essays that I had written and to press an advance of 300 marks in my hand.

Before abandoning the subject, Walser speculates that Cassirer's demeanor might be ascribed to his uneasy relation to Judaism.

> Paul Cassirer hat sich vielleicht, wer kann es wissen, entleibt im Sinne, daß er sich, sein Leben züchtigen, strafen wollte. Ich bin von ihm überzeugt, daß er das denkbar feinste, zarteste Gewissen besaß, dessen Vorhandensein ihm sehr lästig war. Als Israelit neigte er zur Wehmut, Melancholie, zugleich aber zu allem Lebensgenuß. (*Briefe*, 257)

> Perhaps Paul Cassirer has, who can know, committed suicide because he wanted to chastise, to punish, himself and his life. I am convinced that he possessed the finest, most tender conscience imaginable, whose presence was a tremendous burden to him. As an Israelite he was inclined to dejection, to melancholy, yet at the same time to every pleasure of living.

The parallels between what Walser observes in Cassirer and what he sees in Walther Rathenau are striking. But before moving on to an examination of the author's preoccupation with the latter, I want to consider some relevant remarks by South African novelist J. M. Coetzee about one of Walser's best-known characters. In a much-cited piece for the *New York Review of Books* in 2000, the soon-to-be Nobel laureate asserted that *Jakob von Gunten*'s protagonist harbors several resentments which, "in a time of greater social confusion," would ultimately attract many men of his class—the lower middle class—to Hitler's Brownshirts.[25] This link is tenuous, pivoting as it does on the assumption that Jakob is an entirely cynical character—an assumption that underplays his childishness and only partly feigned innocence. I mention it here because Coetzee has nevertheless put his finger on something that is readily apparent in the most aggressive of Walser's parodies: namely, the distinct traces of a class-based *ressentiment*. We see it surface now and again in some of Walser's sketches from the 1920s, particularly those inspired by Walther Rathenau, who was prominent in Wilhelmine Germany as a business man and intellectual before becoming one of the Weimar Republic's most important statesmen.

The 1918 story "Zwei Männer" ("Two Men") begins by drawing a sharp contrast between two men who will go on to become writers. The first is a vagabond bank clerk who, like Walser, comes from a ruined family and learns to fend for himself as a teenager. Not that he sees this is a cause for pity: endowed with a gift for reverie and wonder, this man gives himself over wholeheartedly to the poetic vocation. The second figure can be none other than Walther Rathenau. Sire of a prominent industrialist, he enjoys a first-class education and every possible advantage for making his way in the business world.[26] In little time, he is named director of a global financial institute. Yet despite this success, his achievement proves unsatisfactory; the man is dogged by inner demons:

> Gedanken plagten ihn zeitweise arg. Allerhand schlichte Wahrheit war für ihn durchaus unbehaglich. Er fühlte aufrichtig, daß es unrichtig sei, materiell tausendmal besser zu stehen wie Tausende seine Mitbürger. Sein Reichtum befriedigte ihn absolut nicht; dazu besaß er allzuviel Sinn für Brüderlichkeit und Gleichheit. (*SW*, 16:199)

> He was plagued by nagging considerations. Every kind of simple truth discomfited him thoroughly. He sincerely felt that it was wrong to be a thousand times materially better off than thousands of his fellow citizens. His affluence offered him no consolation whatsoever; for that he possessed too strong a feeling of fraternity and equality.

Such concerns are conspicuously absent from the mind of the story's unprivileged vagabond, who has in the meantime moved to a big city and dashed off a novel. The two writers eventually cross paths at a *Klubabend* (in real life, almost certainly the Secession gallery on Kurfürstenstrasse), where the distinguished but persistently unhappy celebrity informs his confrère: "Ich habe Ihr Buch, das mich ungewöhnlich fesselte, einer schönen Frau zu lessen gegeben, die etwas Proletarisches stark vertreten fand" (I gave your book, which captivated me extraordinarily, to a beautiful woman, who found a strongly proletarian element represented there) (*SW*, 16:201). A few years later they encounter one another again at the distinguished man's estate in the countryside, where the poet spurns an offer for material aid.

From this and other texts, we can infer that Walser met Rathenau in 1907 after the publication of *The Tanners*, in all likelihood when he was still working as factotum for Paul Cassirer. (The possibility that they may have met while Walser was serving refreshments at a vernissage is intriguing, although—sadly—impossible to prove.) Something about the future minister's conduct must have struck Walser as laughable, for it is hard not to marvel at the cheek of Walser's appeal to Rathenau that May on behalf of the Berlin Secession. Almost immediately after his formal opening ("Lieber, sehr geehrter Herr Doctor"), Walser asks the patron whether he might

> uns mitteilen wollen, wann es Ihnen möglich sein wird, uns einmal zu besuchen, um uns etwas abzukaufen. Wir bitten Sie, das zu tun, und hoffen, Sie werden nicht böse sein, daß wir Sie an das Versprechen erinnern, einen E. R. Weiß zu kaufen. Mit den Prozenten, die die Sezession davon bekommt, haben wir bereits gerechnet, das heißt, der Gewinn ist bereits verbraucht (vertrunken) worden. Ist das nicht fabelhaft schönes Wetter jetzt?[27]

> be so good as to let us know when it would be possible for you to drop by so as to purchase something from us. Won't you please do this? We hope you won't be angry with us for reminding you of your promise to buy an E. R. Weiß. We've already taken the Sezession's percentage into account, i.e., the profit has already been used up (drunk). Isn't this fabulous weather we're having?[28]

On the basis of this letter, it is easy to understand why Walser did not last long as the association's secretary.

In any case, "Two Men" remains the most neutral of Walser's texts about Rathenau. The others date from 1925 or later: that is, *after* Rathenau's assassination on June 24, 1922. Nearly all of them remained in draft form, unrevised and presumably deemed unsuitable for publication. In *Der Räuber* (*The Robber*), the sole novel among these texts, Walser has his protagonist, an unmistakable alter ego of the author, come across a notice announcing Rathenau's murder on his return from a walk in the mountains. "Und was tat der wundervolle, seltsame Fötzel" (And what did this marvelous, weird scoundrel do now), asks the narrator, who has already anticipated the reader's surprise at what is to come:

> Er klatschte in die Hände, anstatt daß er vor Schreck und Trauer umgesunken wäre bei solcher niederschmetternden Benachrichtigung. Suche eine uns nur das Händeklatschen zu erklären. [. . .] Diese Gottesluft auf dem Berg, die Atemübungen im Tannenwald, und dann noch dieser Extragenuß, lesen zu können, ein Großer sei von einigen Unbedeutenden überwältigt worden. [. . .] "Bravo," hat er da sogar noch extra ausgerufen und hat sich nachher in's Café verfügt. Wie ist dieses rohe "Bravo" zu erklären? Eine schwierige Nuß. (*AdB*, 3:21)

> He clapped his hands, when he ought to have sunk to the ground in horror and grief at this shattering announcement. I'd like to see someone explain this hand-clapping to us. [. . .] This heavenly air on the mountain, the deep-breathing exercises in the fir forest, and then the additional pleasure of being able to read of a great man's downfall at the hands of a few insignificant persons. [. . .] "Bravo!" he even shouted, on top of everything else, and hereafter betook himself to a café. How can this uncouth "bravo" be accounted for? A difficult nut. (*TR*, 11)

A difficult nut to crack indeed, one the narrator comes closest to explaining when he hints that he has suppressed something from his account of meeting Rathenau years earlier, at the great man's chateau in Mark Brandenburg—a meeting that must have taken place in 1910 or 1911.[29]

Whatever this was, writing the above scene was obviously not sufficient to purge it from his system. Within weeks of completing the novel, Walser generated two more sketches about Walther Rathenau. The first was withheld from Suhrkamp's edition of the microscripts, but published by Jochen Greven in a 1996 article. Untitled by the author, the editors have listed it after its opening line: "Rathenau war von etwas melancholischem Gemüt" (Rathenau was in a somewhat melancholy mood). After declaring Rathenau a lost soul who never could find his way to women (a reference to the minister's homosexuality), Walser launches into an unsparing and vicious analysis:

> Scheinbar war er ganz ein Mann, mit einem Verantwortungsgefühl ausgestattet, das an Umfang einem weitläufigen Park glich, wo die Buchen und Eichen des guten Willens hoch in eine verzweifelte Gränniatmosphäre emporragten. Er gab sich nach außen so elegant, wie er innerlich fortwährend pessimisselte.[30]

> Apparently he was quite a man, fitted out with a sense of responsibility whose compass was as extensive as an enormous park where the beech and oak trees of good will towered above a distraught crybaby atmosphere. He presented himself to the outside world as elegant, while inwardly pessimisticating without cease.

The assault gathers steam as Walser draws ruthlessly on his knowledge of Rathenau's personal history. He even invokes "Höre Israel" (Hear, O Israel), the statesman's notorious plea to fellow Jews—by this time already more than two decades old—"to accelerate their assimilation by consciously imitating Prussian manners":[31]

> Er brachte es nie weiter als vors Antlitz seiner Frau Mutter, an deren Rockzipfel er allerliebst klebte, und solch ein Zipfeler wollte ein Volk aus seinem Dilemma geleiten! [. . .] Rathenau war kaum viel anderes als ein Vertreter von seiner Zeitgenossen angelesener Bildung. Insofern er viel las, schrieb er auch sehr viel, und weil er viel schrieb, wird man so ziemlich bereits aufgehört haben, ihn zu lesen. [. . .] Rathenau war ein wahres Prachtexemplar des für brutale Kraft schwärmenden, zerstückelten, über und über von Bildung angegossenen, sentimentalen Industrialmenschen, der entzückt war, wenn unter den Fenstern seiner Achtzehnzimmerwohnung Kavallerie vorbeiritt. Blaue Augen verwirrten ihn, und sein Semitentum verachtete er aufs Unvorsichtigste. [. . .] Ein typischer Sohn einer geringen Epoche. Eine seufzende Literaturpflanze, tugendhafter Sumpf. [. . .] Er war unoriginal, wie es alle lediglich Gebildeten sind. Er litt an einer unglaublich starken Sehnsucht, Schaf zu sein. Und so einer wollte den Hirten spielen? Elendigliche Komödie![32]

> He never made it far from his mother, to whose apron strings he liked best to cling, and such an apron-stringer wanted to lead the people out of its predicament! [. . .] Rathenau amounted to little more than the representative of his educated middlebrow contemporaries. In this respect he read extensively, and because he wrote extensively, you will have pretty much have already ceased to read him. [. . .] Rathenau was a true exemplar of the sentimental industrialist who, formed entirely by higher learning, rhapsodizes about brute strength and is captivated whenever the cavalry parades beneath the window of his eighteen-room residence. Blue eyes confused him, and he disdained his Semitism in the most reckless fashion. [. . .] The typical son of a banal age. A sighing literature-plant, a virtuous swamp. [. . .] He was unoriginal, like all those who are merely educated. He suffered from an incredibly powerful yearning to be a sheep. And this kind of person wanted to play the shepherd? What wretched theater!

Another microscript written around this time begins "Dieser Minister erhielt vielleicht gleichsam eine zu sorgfältige Erziehung" (This minister more or less probably had too meticulous an upbringing). Like "Two Men," it consists mainly of a short recapitulation of Rathenau's life. But the critiques here are private, and in most respects meaner. Once more, Walser savages Rathenau's artistic dilettantism, his sexuality, his shame of his Jewish origins, and his mannered behavior:

> Er malte auch ein wenig, ach ja, und las viel und eignete sich eine Sorte Weltanschauung an, die unter der Bezeichnung Pessimismus Ansehen bei den philosophischen Gilden genießt, wobei ich nicht zu untersuchen wage, ob pessimistisch denkende Männer bei den Frauen beliebt sind oder nicht. [. . .] Er besaß immer Geld, und er wusste, daß es Menschen gab, die durchaus nicht immer bei der Kasse sind. Wir sehen also, daß ihm die Scham, das Zartgefühl, das soziale Empfinden keine Fremdheit waren. [. . .] Er ging an den Hof, wo gerade in jenen Tagen glänzende Feierlichkeiten begannen wurden, doch seine Melancholie, sein Seelenschmerz, begleitete ihn, und kein noch so prächtiges Kostüm, keine schmeichelhafte, gewinnende Anrede vermochte ihn wirklich von seiner Umdüsterung zu befreien, ihm das Weh seiner sonderbaren Existenz auszureden. (*AdB*, 4:225–28)

> He dabbled in painting, too, oh yes, and he read a great deal and adopted a kind of worldview which, under the term *pessimism*, enjoys the esteem of philosophical guilds, although I would not wager to investigate whether pessimistically thinking persons are liked by women or not. [. . .] He always had money and he knew that there were people who were definitely not always rolling in it. We see thus that shame, sensitivity, and social perceptions were not foreign to him. [. . .] He went to the court, where in those very days glittering festivities were initiated, and yet his melancholy, the ache in his soul, accompanied him there, and ensured that no matter how magnificent his outfit, no flattering, amiable greeting could truly liberate him from his gloominess, could dissuade him of the anguish of his strange existence.

This was not the last appearance of Rathenau in Walser's writing, although the most virulent texts were written within a few weeks, perhaps days, of each other in 1925. It is worth mentioning that Walser never singled out Jews for this kind of criticism; he handled siblings and fellow gentiles equally when they elicited his scorn—one reason, no doubt, for his eventual estrangement from his brother Karl. Nor was he the only author to have replied in this manner to the conflicted statesman; Rathenau provoked disdain among many of his contemporaries, among them Walter Benjamin, Franz Blei, Hugo von Hofmannsthal, and Maximilian Harden—to say nothing of Robert Musil, who fictionalized him as a pompously solemn mystic in *The Man without Qualities*.[33]

The antipathy of these figures never prevented Rathenau from playing a prominent role in the cultural and intellectual life of turn-of-the-century Berlin. On the contrary, Rathenau was an important patron of the arts: he contributed, as did many of the Jewish figures mentioned in this essay, to the dissemination of modernist art. The individuals Walser interacted with in the capital were among the most influential of their time, whether in the theatrical world (Alfred Kerr was a key booster of Ibsen and Hauptmann, and Jacobsohn and Frisch contributed in this arena too); the visual arts (it is hard to imagine expressionism developing in Germany without Paul Cassirer's contributions as a curator and patron); publishing and belles letters (Samuel Fischer, Bruno Cassirer, and Fega Frisch all made lasting contributions); or political writing (Maximilian Harden, Walther Rathenau). They were all driven and prolific, their ambitions no doubt spurred by their standing within the empire as Jews.

What makes Walser's description of secular Jews in his writings especially fascinating is the attentiveness he brings to bear on their demeanor. Among his peers Walser's emotional intelligence was second to none, and I suspect that his understanding of their "melancholy" was very much informed by his own position at the margins of Berlin society. As the result of his nationality and language (Swiss), his socioeconomic background (more modest than many of those he worked with in Berlin), and his temperament (very much that of an outsider), Walser could recognize their dilemma in a way that few others could; degrees of difference in this particular milieu equipped him to view his contemporaries with greater sensitivity. And despite the scurrilousness, indeed pettiness, of personal attacks like those cited above, Walser's writings reveal an uncanny perceptiveness about these prominent Berliners, several of whom—as if to confirm the origin of the insecurities depicted by the author—met violent ends during the second decade of the twentieth century.

Notes

1. Bernhard Echte, *Robert Walser: Sein Leben in Bildern und Texten* (Frankfurt am Main: Suhrkamp, 2008), 175.
2. Robert Mächler, *Das Leben Robert Walsers: Eine dokumentarische Biographie* (Frankfurt am Main: Suhrkamp, 1978), 87–88.
3. Carl Seelig, *Wanderungen mit Robert Walser* (Frankfurt am Main: Suhrkamp, 1996), 18–19.
4. Echte, *Robert Walser*, 194.
5. Ibid., 202.
6. See also Walser, *Briefe*, 316.

7. Seelig, *Wanderungen mit Robert Walser*, 19.

8. See Echte, *Robert Walser*, 331.

9. "Eine feiste Sau," *AdB*, 5:60–61.

10. Max Brod, *Über Franz Kafka* (Frankfurt am Main: Fischer Taschenbuch, 1974), 294.

11. Echte, *Robert Walser*, 201.

12. Bernhard Echte and Andreas Meier, eds., *Die Brüder Karl und Robert Walser: Maler und Dichte* (Stäfa: Rothenhäusler, 1990), 182.

13. E. Frisch to C. Morgenstern, qtd. in Echte, *Robert Walser*, 252.

14. Ibid., 189.

15. Seelig, *Wanderungen mit Robert Walser*, 100.

16. Katharina Kerr, ed., *Über Robert Walser*, vol. 1 (Frankfurt am Main: Suhrkamp, 1978), 72.

17. Echte, *Robert Walser*, 252.

18. Seelig, *Wanderungen mit Robert Walser*, 95.

19. Robert Walser, *Berlin Stories*, trans. Susan Bernofsky (New York: New York Review Books, 2012), 103.

20. Ibid., 106.

21. Echte, *Robert Walser*, 208.

22. Walser, *Berlin Stories*, 71.

23. After signing divorce papers with his second wife—the woman that Walser had used as his model for "Frau Bähni"—Cassirer entered an adjoining room and shot himself.

24. For details concerning the internalization of anti-Semitic rhetoric and beliefs in Jews see Sander L. Gilman, *Jewish Self-Hatred: Anti-Semitism and the Hidden Language of the Jews* (Baltimore: Johns Hopkins University Press, 1986).

25. J. M. Coetzee, *Inner Workings: Literary Essays, 2000–2005* (New York: Penguin, 2007), 19–20.

26. Walther Rathenau's father, Emil Rathenau (1838–1915), was one of Germany's most prominent entrepreneurs and industrialists during the second half of the nineteenth century.

27. Echte, *Die Brüder Karl und Robert Walser*, 184.

28. Trans. Susan Bernofsky and Tom Whalen. In "Introduction," *Review of Contemporary Fiction* 12, no. 1 (1992): 11.

29. During the Robber's visit, the two reportedly go for a walk, where they discuss "islands, poets, etc." (ibid., 24). It remains unclear as to what, if anything, caused the vehemence of the later microscripts.

30. Jochen Greven, "Die beklatschte Tragödie: Robert Walser und Walther Rathenau—Versuche einer Rekonstruktion," *Allemande* 16, nos. 50/51 (1996): 20.

31. Amos Elon, *The Pity of It All: A Portrait of the Jewish-German Epoch, 1743–1933* (New York: Picador, 2002), 232. Walser may have read this article in the 1897 issue of Maximilian Harden's *Zukunft*.

32. Qtd. in Greven, "Die beklatschte Tragödie," 20–21.

33. Ibid., 22–23.

Out of a Job

Giving Notice in *The Tanners* and *The Assistant*

Paul Buchholz

Walser as a Novelist

Robert Walser's career as a published, publicly recognized novelist lasted roughly three years. In an intensely productive period between 1906 and 1909, Walser wrote with "record speed" three novels that would be published by the Cassirer Verlag in Berlin, along with two novel manuscripts that have been permanently lost.[1] *Geschwister Tanner* (*The Tanners*) appeared in 1907, *Der Gehülfe* (*The Assistant*) in 1908, followed by *Jakob von Gunten* in 1909. While the novels do not form a trilogy with a common cast of characters or storyline, all three of the novels are recognizable as fictionalized autobiography. The episodes of tenuous employment and vagabondage that provide the content of these three novels match the record of Walser's life from his teenage years up until his late twenties, from the moment in 1892 when his family's financial problems led him to leave school early up until around 1905 when Walser briefly became a servant in an aristocrat's castle in Upper Silesia.[2] Walser's Berlin-era novels are, among other things, fictionalized retrospectives on that period of relative nomadism in his life. As fruits of a short-lived but intense moment of literary output, the novels also serve as indications of a professional instability that mark not only the lives of Walser's fictional heroes, but also his own literary career. After the publication of *Jakob von Gunten* Walser effectively left his work as a novelist in any traditional sense of the term. Indeed, the act of *quitting work* has an existential significance both for Walser as an author as well as for his fictional characters, such that it has proved tempting to conflate his life with his literary prose.[3] Yet Walser's early novels do not simply reproduce the author's life; his prose also estranges the language of life through literary experimentation. In the novels *The Assistant* and *The Tanners*, the act of quitting one's job and refusing future work is a creative act. The speech in which the fictional hero "gives notice" becomes a kind of improvised artwork that posits an imaginative counter-reality to the routinized world of work around him. This estrangement of practical speech constitutes one of the creative achievements of Walser's early career.

Refusal, as the novelist Enrique Vila-Matas has noted, is a signature of Walser's work: Walser is a "writer of the No," and his work exhibits "an alarming tendency to negate the world."[4] In this essay, I will concentrate on a particular facet of Walser's tendency toward negation: the creative language employed by his characters in their *refusal of work*, which I call "the quitter's discourse."[5] As fashioned by Walser in his first two novels, the quitter's discourse is both a poetic experiment that disrupts the flow of realist narrative, and a political gesture that negates and redefines a particular, historically conditioned social relation (the bond of employee to employer).[6] The quitter's discourse in Walser's novels is a locus of linguistic creativity and affect. This discourse extends into an elaborate monologue that far exceeds the needs of practical communication. When Simon, the hero of Walser's first novel, *The Tanners*, quits his job at a bookseller, he "injects," in the words of critic George Avery, a "superfluous embroidery [. . .] into his leave-taking volley."[7] This linguistic "embroidery" grows out of a communication that could otherwise be accomplished in very few words. The phrase "I quit!," followed by a demand for back wages, would ostensibly be enough to "give notice" and sever the contract with the employer. Yet in *The Tanners*, the language in which the hero gives notice is a disruptive discourse, which attempts what should be impossible: to remake and revise the material social world already established by the novel's primary narrator. The quitter not only quits work, but also unsettles the reality given in the surrounding text by exhaustively and emphatically renarrating the past.

In this way, the quitter's discourse crystallizes that central comportment of refusal that defines Walser's verbal art. According to Tamara Evans, the modernity of Walser's prose consists in the "disruption of received contents of reality," by which she means the tendency of Walser's speakers to transform the real, natural, and social landscapes around them into "dream-scenarios."[8] In Walser's work, speech sometimes attains the capacity to annul the world. The "observed reality" in his narratives, as Markus Schwahl writes, is continually "flushed away" by the "subversive force of a free-floating imagination."[9] Likewise, the quitter's discourses in Walser's novels aim to duplicate and estrange the painful reality of the workplace imaginatively by seeking out new forms of freedom that are otherwise unavailable within the regulated world of office labor. In *The Tanners* and *The Assistant*, the quitter's discourse (spoken aloud in the first novel, and internally thought in the second) eclipses the given economic reality, governed as it is by laws of finance, with a social world that is constituted through an *affect* emanating from the hero and circulating around him. The hero, in the moment of severing ties with his employer, represents the hierarchy of social positions as a fleeting product of his own itinerant desires. The further existence of this socioeconomic hierarchy is, according to the quitting hero, contingent on his own emotional investment. Through the quitter's discourse, the asymmetrical tie between employer and the wage laborer is recast as a spontaneous emotional adventure, based first and foremost on the power of affect in all its fickleness, ambivalence, and intensity.

Walser's readers are thus provided with a double vision of the social world. While the primary narrator's discourse focuses on the external material facts of the hiring process, the quitting hero's discourse represents this process in audaciously affective terms. Rather than focusing on material necessity, Walser's quitters stress the constitutive role of their own anarchic desires in making and unmaking the employer-employee relation. They start and stop working because they don't *feel* like it—and construct a corresponding verbal picture of the world.

The quitter's discourse is one facet of an overarching theme of Walser's writing: the bureaucratized world of work that Walser's protagonist Simon Tanner himself succinctly dubs the "Arbeitssystem" (work-system) (*SW*, 9:43).[10] This system has given rise to the formation of a disposable proletariat of provisional white-collar paperwork laborers who live on the fine line between temporary employment and abject unemployment.[11] This recurring thematization of modern provisional employment, along with the institutions that manage unemployment, helps to locate Walser's novels as works of the twentieth century. It is particularly important to emphasize this historical specificity because, since the publication of *The Tanners*, Walser's work has often been identified as a continuation of a romantic tradition of vagabond literature, most clearly exemplified by Joseph von Eichendorff's 1826 novella *Life of a Good-for-Nothing*.[12] Walser's vagabonds, on the other hand, must navigate a vastly different landscape than that of their romantic predecessors.[13] Reveries in the forest alternate with trips to the employment office. *The Tanners* and *The Assistant* construct romances out of experiences of alternating employment and unemployment, in which the dire consequences of poverty (including starvation and exposure to the elements) remain fully within view. Walser's precarious protagonists are prone to temporary jobs, small debts, and a generally nomadic existence lived in small rented (or charitably provided) rooms.[14] In this sense, a thread of naturalistic social realism runs through both of these early novels. The attention to material necessities and economic inequalities in Walser's novels was praised by an early reviewer as a "serious grasp of real conditions."[15] The quitter's discourse is the anarchic counterpart of this social-realist tendency: it entertains the thought that these material "real conditions" are actually contingent on the circulation of desires. Walser's quitters "go on strike" by refusing to speak the language of economics, and speaking instead one of feeling.

An Introduction to *The Tanners* and *The Assistant*

The Tanners and *The Assistant* tell markedly different stories about precarious employment. *The Tanners* is primarily a story of *resistance* to the world of work: the protagonist Simon Tanner repeatedly refuses to allow himself to be domesticated as a proper worker. *The Assistant* is more a story of *compliance* within that same world of work: Joseph Marti tries hard to domesticate himself as a guest resident of his bourgeois employer's household. Simon Tanner of *The Tanners* perpetually and deliberately avoids commitment to employment; within the first few chapters, he quits several jobs. Joseph Marti, protagonist of *The Assistant*, just as vigorously strives to *maintain* his position with a single employer, against all the external circumstances that threaten his continued employment. Unlike Simon, Joseph only quits his job once, and then only at the very end of the novel. As a result, the temporal structure of these novels is very different. *The Tanners* contains a long series of separate episodes spanning several years, whereas *The Assistant* follows a single episode of employment lasting roughly six months. In what follows, I will provide a brief summary of these novels' stories of unemployment, paying special attention to how their respective protagonists' employment status also determines his position within a broader field of social ties, including friendship and kinship.

At the beginning of *The Tanners*, the young Simon Tanner is seen accepting and then leaving several jobs: first at a bookseller, then at a law office, then at a bank. The initial vagueness of the novel's setting (a city, presumably in Switzerland, but never named) reflects the unbound existence of the protagonist, who never settles in any one place for an extended period of time. After Simon is taken in as a house guest (paying no rent) by a married woman named Klara Aggapaia, he is joined in her forest villa by his brother Kaspar, a landscape painter, and their sister Hedwig. The siblinghood referred to in the novel's title appears in these early passages as a flexible form of kinship that permits free movement while offering a degree of emotional mooring. The Aggapaia villa serves briefly as a kind of complimentary artists' home for the Tanner siblings, as they take evening walks in the forest, rendezvousing with another traveling artist, the young poet Sebastian. This living arrangement does not last long, however, as Herr Aggapaia, Klara's husband, soon announces that he is leaving her to pursue a venture in the Far East. The eccentric trio of Simon, Kaspar, and Klara is left homeless, and scatters. As his family fades from view, wage labor again becomes necessary for Simon, who begins to feel the strain of material circumstances as he takes a job in a machine shop and rents a small garret.

From here on, Simon is increasingly isolated from any family ties. After an unhappy stay with his sister Hedwig in the winter months, Simon finds himself continually changing jobs and accommodations with no guarantee of help from anyone. He finds work as a house servant, then later shares accommodation with a male nurse who is romantically interested in him. Eventually he delivers himself to an institution that clearly establishes his status a member of an unemployed underclass: the pseudo-charitable "Schreibstube für Stellenlose" (Copyists Office for the Unemployed) (*SW*, 9:268; *TT*, 287). This institution provides Simon with temporary work while he searches for a more permanent position. Wandering the landscapes outside the city on his own, Simon's social encounters are now spontaneous and fleeting, offering little promise of any lasting bond. The novel ends with Simon walking alone, composing fairy tales in his head, then telling his life story to a stranger at a bar in a spa hotel where Klara's villa once stood. Simon's attempt to live completely freely, without material obligations, has culminated in a near-perfect isolation, as he is left with nothing but fragile hope for the kindness of strangers.

While *The Tanners* is a story of failed escape *from* economic dependency, *The Assistant* unfolds as a story of failed integration *into* a relation of economic dependency. Joseph Marti is hired as the sole assistant by the engineer and inventor Carl Tobler in the small town of Bärenswil, near the cantonal capital city (presumed to be Zurich).[16] Tobler has only recently set himself up as an independent inventor, having worked as an engineer in a larger machine shop until he inherited enough money to found his own firm, basing it in the same villa where he lives with his wife and four children. The Toblers' short history of employing outside help for their business and household has been turbulent. Wirsich, the previous assistant to the engineer, was fired for drunkenness and subsequent aggressive confrontations with his boss, in which he destroyed the fence of the Tobler villa. Thus, Joseph can present himself as an occasionally bumbling but nevertheless very earnest employee who badly wants to fit into the role of faithful and respectful servant. A stable routine emerges: Joseph converses daily with Frau Tobler, and assists in written work as the inventor Tobler attempts to attract the investment of venture capitalists for his key projects: a vending machine that dispenses rifle ammunition and a clock that displays advertisements. Tobler continually fails to pay any wages to Joseph. The mood in the house worsens as Tobler is increasingly pursued by lenders demanding money borrowed not only for Tobler's business expenditures, but also for the extravagance of the villa life. As Tobler's business and household verge on financial collapse, Joseph spends an increasing amount of time with his troubled predecessor Wirsich, whom he castigates for drunkenness and thievery, but also comes to more strongly identify with as a fellow worker. The two men begin to explore the pubs and streets of the nearby city, and Joseph begins to distance himself from Tobler's domestic workplace. In the novel's final scenes, Joseph comes to the realization that he deeply loves Tobler, but finally resolves to quit his job and demand one last time that he be paid his wages. Recognizing the immanent failure of Tobler's business, however, Joseph must abandon both his economic and emotional bonds to his employer, and he leaves the house with Tobler in a rage. Joseph finds himself again wandering the country roads with Wirsich: having become unmoored from his employer, he now enjoys fleeting solidarity with a fellow unemployed worker.

In the social worlds of *The Tanners* and *The Assistant* the protagonist continually faces the agony of material dependency, such that emotional bonds arise only under the shadow of financial need. Simon and Joseph are perpetually indebted, have no savings, and rarely own more than the clothes on their backs. Both Simon and Joseph tend to seek escape from this unending debt during their flights into nature, where they can experience a form of free existence beyond the confines of the social world. Yet natural spaces are not the only vantage point from which the given economic world is, as Roberto Calasso writes, "refused."[17] Even at moments where economic concerns come to the fore, Walser's heroes flee into a space of free thought, wherein relations of economic dependency can be radically negated. The moment of *quitting one's work*, like a walk into a forest, becomes an opportunity for the Walserian hero to derealize the material world presented by the primary narrator (who is in both novels a third-person, disembodied, extradiegetic narrator).

By turning attention to "the quitter's discourse," as a creative disruption of Simon's and Joseph's stories of dependency, I hope to bring together productively a number of the different critical approaches to *The Tanners* and *The Assistant* that have emerged since their publication. Early reviews of *The Tanners* praised the novel for establishing an artistic perspective that conquers fears of poverty,[18] and for injecting aesthetic joy into the monotony of everyday life.[19] *The Assistant* was likewise praised for its ability to find the beautiful in the mundane, in recording the minutiae of everyday Swiss existence.[20] *The Assistant* was praised, in parallel to *The Tanners*, for its sensitive observations of everyday reality, for a "dryness" that "makes beauty beautiful first through reality."[21] After Walser's postwar rediscovery, the aestheticist interpretations that cast Walser as a "poet of poverty" were replaced with existentialist readings that saw in these novels a particular bearing toward being. Such readings emphasized the ways in which the "freedom" of Walser's characters mandates a fundamentally rootless existence that is in tune with "pure existence" but remains alien to the world.[22] This freedom, moreover, carries with it the danger of psychological suffering.[23] Subsequent academic scholarship, taking into account Walser's institutionalization later in life, could interpret the escapist impulses of Walser's characters as the defense mechanisms of a disturbed personality,[24] and as symptoms of the alienation of human life within capitalist social structures.[25] A common thread in the reception of *The Tanners* and *The Assistant* has been to note an opposition between the wish-driven, artistic, or dreamlike subjectivity of the "idealist" protagonist (i.e., Simon and Joseph), and the harsh and threatening necessities of an unequal material reality.[26] In short, Walser's novels posit a fractured reality; this premise will guide my reading in what follows. By focusing on how one particular element of these works—the quitter's discourse—deliberately opens up gaps between idealism and materialism (and between fantasy and reality), I will show how this fracturing of reality cannot be read only as a symptom of a problematic attitude toward existence or of a troubled psychological state. Rather, the quitter's discourse, as a means of fracturing fictional reality, is a complex artistic gesture of Walser's prose itself, which reflects back on the reality-positing function of narrative discourse. A simple example: the first sentences of *The Assistant* establish the reality of material inequality between Joseph, with his cheap suitcase ("one of the very cheapest"), and the Toblers, with their "schmucken Haus" (attractive house) (*SW*, 10:7; *TA*, 7). However, when Joseph quits his work with the Toblers, he fashions a discourse of an emotional reality that opposes the initial, material reality: the poor assistant with his great reserves of "love" becomes the determining agent in the employer-employee relationship.

With *The Tanners* and *The Assistant*, Walser created fictions of heroic quitting, whereby the quitting hero vocally dissents from the facts of his existence. This heroism unsettles the ontology of the fictional world, such that the text itself becomes a site where objective, material economic reality is both posited and contested. In this way, both novels stress the contingency of the social world that their characters inhabit, and permit a deep divergence between the discourses of their primary narrators and the discourses of their protagonists. For this reason, Walser's novels invite a reading that is both formalist and historicist, in which the creative verbal strategies of refusal emerge as an idiosyncratic response to the problem of class struggle.

The Quitter's Affective Discourse

To write of *The Tanners* and *The Assistant* as narratives of *escape from* and *integration into* economic systems is to emphasize the objective material world posited by the novel's disembodied narrator over the peculiar subjectivity of the respective protagonists Simon and Joseph. Yet, as scholars have noted, Walser's novels are notable for their experimental perspectives in which established reality can be "flushed away" and transformed beyond recognition by a "hallucinatory" mode of writing.[27] Walser's novels do not (only) exhaust themselves in showcasing the workings of an economic system that is impossible to live in, and impossible to live outside of. The quitter's discourse breaks into the economic world, and confronts it with a radically different model of reality in which money matters less than the untamable force of affect, which ceases to be an immaterial feeling and instead takes on the power of a physical force within the social world.

The quitter's discourse is noticeable first of all for its distinct sound, which is heard in first pages of *The Tanners* as Simon loudly tenders his resignation to a timid bookseller who hired him in the novel's first scene, and again two chapters later when Simon takes leave of the bank director who has just fired him. A common feature of the excessive "linguistic embroidery" (Avery) of Simon's leave-taking speeches is their "heavy" tone, acknowledged by both the speaker and the listener (*SW*, 9:44; *TT*, 72). The authority of the speeches is not established by the speaker's position in the social framework (Simon enters the interaction as a subordinate employee, and ends as an unemployed outsider), but rather by their force of affect. This excessive heaviness consists not only in the sharpness of Simon's tone or the volume of his voice, but above all in a forceful exposition of affects ranging from disgust to love. From his own position of authority, grounded in affective heaviness, Simon's quitting speech retroactively inserts a dramatic backstory, which reframes the preceding episode of employment. Surprising causal links emerge, as he shows that he (the worker) was not the faceless instrument of the employer. Rather, as Simon now tells it in melodramatic terms, the employer has been the instrument of the worker.

The revisionary function of Simon's quitting discourse is illustrated by the contrast between the narrator's description of a bank where he works and the speech Simon delivers when he leaves the bank. The narrator introduces this bank, which "enjoyed international significance," as an enormous institution where coordinated labor is performed on a mass scale; workers are virtually indistinguishable from one another, as they constitute a "Rechnervolk" (calculating pack) (*SW*, 9:35; *TT*, 63). Individuals vanish into a collective subject: "Diese Leute schrieben alle mit emsigen Fingern, rechneten mit Rechnungsmaschinen, auch wohl bisweilen mit ihren Gedächtnissen, dachten mit ihren Gedanken und machten sich nützlich mit ihren Kenntnissen" (They all wrote with diligent fingers, made calculations using calculating machines and also sometimes their memories, thought using their thoughts and made themselves useful with their knowledge) (*SW*, 9:34–35; *TT*, 63). This relentless string of interrelated tasks engulfs both the body (fingers) and the mind (memory, knowledge), so that labor has properly colonized the entirety of these persons. When Simon quits the bank, however, he calls into question the automatized nature of this labor and declares instead that his involvement in this mass apparatus was guided by an entire unseen landscape of desires that underlies the reality of his employment. His speech includes a broad lexicon of emotional terms:

> Ich schreibe ganz *gern*, rechne ganz *gern*, betrage mich mit *Vorliebe* unter meinen Mitmenschen mit Anstand, bin *gern* fleißig und gehorche, wo es mein *Herz* nicht verletzt, mit *Leidenschaft*. Ich würde mich auch bestimmten Gesetzen zu unterwerfen wissen, wenn es darauf ankäme, aber es kommt mir hier seit einiger Zeit nicht mehr darauf an. Als ich mich heute morgen verspätete, wurde ich nur *zornig* und *ärgerlich*, war mit gar keiner ehrlichen, gewissenhaften Besorgnis erfüllt, machte mir keine Vorwürfe. (*SW*, 9:42; my emphasis)

> I *like* to write, I *like* doing calculations and find it *desirable* to behave in a decorous manner towards my fellow men, I *enjoy* being industrious, and as long as it does my *heart* no injury, I *passionately love* to obey. I'd also be perfectly capable of submitting to certain laws if this were important, but it's been some time now since such things

> had any importance for me here. When I found myself running late today, I merely felt *angry* and *annoyed*, I was by no means filled with honest conscientious concern, nor did I reproach myself. (*TT*, 70; my emphasis)

Elsewhere, Simon renarrates the routinized work he has done for his employers—which involves more solitary paperwork than social interaction—as a clash of wills between larger-than-life figures. As Simon tells it, it is not mechanized routines, but rather a drama of wills and desires, which make the machines of the work-system operate. The characters that Simon generates in his reproachful speeches are guided by aggressive passions, strong loves, conspiratorial impulses, and strong feelings about moral principles. It is in this dramatic, affectively charged language that Simon can display his "frei[e] Lust am Austreten" (the strength of my own desire to leave), that is, the undomesticatable desire that determines all his employment relationships (*SW*, 9:9; *TT*, 39).

Within the dramatic scenario that Simon constructs, the structure of expectations that conventionally characterizes the relationship between employer and employee is inverted. Quitting his job at the bookseller, Simon declares: "Sie haben mich enttäuscht" (You have disappointed me) (*SW*, 9:15; *TT*, 45). From this audacious opening, Simon proceeds to paint in broad strokes his own portrait of his addressee as an intentionally malicious, immoral, and vengeful old man. The bookseller, as Simon's rant suggests, has sought to insult Simon's youth by suffocating him, deliberately conspiring to disfigure Simon with a "hunchback" by procuring the worst possible desk for his written work. Simon interprets an uncomfortable feature of his work environment (which is presumably simply the result of cost-cutting on the part of the employer) as the result of a deliberate, intense vendetta against him, which he has narrowly escaped (*SW*, 9:16; *TT*, 46). The impersonal and institutional becomes intensely personal. In his ongoing construction of a melodramatic backstory, Simon also repaints his own prior expectations of his job with the bookseller in hyperbolically affective terms. He speaks of how he had initially expected his work to be a theater of exaggerated bourgeois formality, in which he could insert himself into the formalized position of the faithful servant, and "Bücher verkaufen, elegante Menschen bedienen, einen Bückling machen und adieu sagen zu Käufern, wenn sie im Begriffe sind, den Laden zu verlassen" (serve elegant people, taking a bow and saying *adieu* to the customers when they left the store) (*SW*, 9:16; *TT*, 45). Loudly severing his ties with these bourgeois caricatures, Simon voices his preference for the downtrodden (the have-nots and the "soldiers")—a declaration of solidarity that Simon himself later says is a "flüchtige Redensart" (a casual expression) that is important for the rhetorical integrity of his speeches (*SW*, 9:17, 19; *TT*, 45, 49). The quitter's discourse is a kind of art that establishes a wishful counter-reality, and Simon is himself aware of this.

As Simon announces his refusal to work, he reimagines everyday reality as a weighty character drama where routinized and economically driven operations of business play out according to affective charges, a character drama of love, hate, jealousy, excitement, and a desire for what is morally good. When taking leave from his work at a bank (not long after leaving the bookseller), Simon is able to level a critique against the "langsamen, trägen, trockenen, erbärmlichen Arbeitssystem" (slow, sluggish, dry, miserable work system) (*SW*, 9:43; *TT*, 71). With a parallel list of traits, he asserts his sovereignty within this economy of sensibility, in which the power of his own personality (his "Mut" [courage], "Geist" [wit], "Treue" [loyalty], "Fleiß" [industry], "Schaffenslust" [creative drive], "Begierde nach Anstrengungen" [desire for challenges]) serves as the most salient measure of value—rather than, as would be claimed from a materialist perspective, the accumulation of capital (*SW*, 9:43; *TT*, 71). Simon's own value system is strikingly *im*material, as if his personal will could intervene in social reality without the interference of any material or bodily constraints.

This quitter's discourse emerges in negative relation to the social framework around it, theatrically reassigning the roles of the individuals around him, and forcefully reinterpreting their speech. Simon (when leaving the bank) rhetorically transforms a situation where he is being fired (for showing up late), into a scene where he is *himself* the one telling off and taking leave of the employer. Hearing that he is being terminated, Simon provides a sprawling justification for why his own termination is justified, necessary, and desirable. He does not speak *against* the authority of the director, but rather purports to speak *for* the director (who has fallen speechless) in another sprawling rant. Leaving the bank, Simon again renarrates his employment at the bank as a character drama. In this case, he places himself on equal footing with the bank director: "Sie sind gewiß ein schätzenswerter, verdienstvoller, großer Mann, aber, sehen Sie, ich möchte auch so einer sein, und deshalb ist es gut, daß Sie mich fortschicken" (You are surely an admirable, commendable, great man, but, you see, I wish to be one too, and that's why it's good you're sending me away) (*SW*, 9:42; *TT*, 70). The implication of Simon's speech is that somewhere there is an alternative world of work that can accommodate Simon's "urge to become." This world arguably exists only in one place: in the imaginative counter-reality that Simon's speech creates over and against the reality of the business world.

In *The Assistant* Walser revisits the conceit of *The Tanners*. Again, quitting—the moment in which the social relation of employment is broken—holds a revelatory, transformative potential for the protagonist. Here once again, the scene of quitting provides a chance to renarrate and reframe economic relationships in a vocabulary that places affective attachment over material dependence. The single scene of quitting in *The Assistant* is ostensibly very different from Simon Tanner's leave-taking. Simon quits his work; he insists on it, because he *wants* to (*SW*, 9:9; *TT*, 39). Within the drama that

Simon weaves, he acts freely in accordance with the wild flows of his desire. By contrast, Joseph Marti quits his work because he *has* to; he is acting in accordance with forces over which he apparently has no control. Having been employed by Tobler for nearly half a year without being paid for his work, Joseph finds he has arrived at a point where he simply cannot work anymore. Having been verbally castigated by his boss one time too many, and without receiving his promised wages, he is overcome one winter morning by what the narrator calls a "Schluß-Bewußtsein" (which means literally "conclusion-consciousness" and is translated by Susan Bernofsky as "definitive sense of finality") (*SW*, 10:291; *TA*, 292). Suddenly Joseph's hands and mouth refuse to obey both his own will and the will of his superior: "Es wäre ihm unmöglich gewesen, die Feder in die Hand zu nehmen, so stark erzitterte er, deshalb sagte er unwillkürlich dasjenige, was die stärkste Möglichkeit darbot, zu Ende mit all diesen Dingen zu gelangen" (It would have been impossible for him to pick up his pen, he was trembling so violently, and for this reason he involuntarily said the thing most likely to put an end to all of this) (*SW*, 10:291–92; *TA*, 292). Thus, rather than delivering a long and playful speech (as Simon did), Joseph finds that he can end it all by uttering a single command: "Zahlen Sie mir den Rest des versprochenen Lohnes aus" (Pay me the rest of the salary as I was promised) (*SW*, 10:291; *TA*, 292). These words instantaneously drive his employer into an explosive storm of affect, which moves from rage to mournful lament. Unlike in *The Tanners*, quitting in *The Assistant* is a source of deep emotional pain. The speed and intensity of this exchange suggests an intimate connection between the two men, as if neither of them can consciously control his communications with or reactions to the other. In Joseph's own stream of thoughts this emotional intensity is revealed to have a secret source.

Pages earlier, in recounting Joseph's inner thoughts, the narrator had provided an explanation as to why Joseph's "conclusion-consciousness" precipitated this impassioned ending to Joseph's job (*SW*, 10:291; *TA*, 292). In his private thoughts, Joseph has already explained to himself why he has continued in the Tobler house despite not being paid. These thoughts form his quitter's discourse, now quietly and privately thought only to himself, yet also revealed to the reader by the narrator: "Er bemitleidete Tobler, er verachtete ihn, er fürchtete sich zugleich vor ihm" (He pitied Tobler, he felt contempt for him, and at the same time he feared him) (*SW*, 10:283; *TA*, 283). Joseph traces these three feelings to a primary emotion of love: "Er liebte aus dem Grund seines Herzens diesen Menschen" (He loved this man with all his heart) (*SW*, 10:283; *TA*, 284). Love has been the sustaining force in the relation of employment. This statement arrives as a surprising revelation, which reframes the entire story of *The Assistant*, demanding a reinterpretation. A careful reader of the novel might well have guessed that Joseph was staying with Tobler because of an infatuation with Tobler's wife, or because of the fine food he is served in the household. However, in Joseph's private declaration of love he suggests that the only reason he remained subordinate to this man was a strong yet ambivalent emotional bond.

The quiet, inward quitter's discourse in *The Assistant* reframes the exploitative relationship between the two main male characters. It is clear that Tobler has been exploiting Joseph throughout the novel, never paying him wages for his work. Joseph's employment with Tobler, and his induction into the hierarchy of the Tobler household, has been a financial dead end. Tobler also verbally abuses Joseph while not paying him. However, looking back from the moment of quitting, Joseph is not overjoyed when he is overcome with the "Gefühl des plötzlich notwendig gewordenen Abschiednehmens" (the spirit of the leave-taking that had suddenly become necessary) (*SW*, 10:293; *TA*, 294). Rather, on the verge of disavowing Tobler, Joseph unexpectedly *avows* his loyalty to him. This is the new story, introduced by the quitter's discourse: Joseph wants to love Tobler, but because of external circumstances (Tobler's failing business and unmanageable debts), he *cannot* love him. The determining factor in the employer-employee relationship has, according Joseph's inner thoughts, been a strong affective attachment and not a material dependence. In this way, Joseph's own unspoken language of emotion opposes a materialist conception of the employment relationship, where the *assistant* appears as the initiator and facilitator of the relationship. Unlike Simon in *The Tanners*, Joseph does *not* utter his quitting discourse aloud: outwardly, he engages in a pragmatic verbal exchange that underscores the transactional nature of his employment with Tobler. Only in an inner, mental realm does Joseph fashion a quitter's discourse that opposes and rejects the material workings of external reality. Perhaps more so than *The Tanners*, *The Assistant* emphasizes in its form the disjunction between the "inner" and the "outer" world: the quitter keeps his mouth shut and keeps his affective discourse to himself. It is the reader who is in a position to witness and reflect on the divergence of an external reality ruled by economic necessity and an internal reality governed by the heart.

Joseph's inward emotional reframing of the employment relationship adds a strong dose of irony to the engineer Tobler's quest to be a self-made man whose inventive ingenuity was supposed to assure a comfortable bourgeois existence for himself and his family. Considering the novel through the lens of Joseph's inner thoughts, it would now appear that Joseph loved Tobler *because he knew all along* that his superior was a precarious outcast, just like himself. All along Joseph has been perfecting his obedience to Tobler because he recognized in this aspiring inventor another would-be outsider whose existence is no more assured than his own. Before quitting, Joseph perfected his obedience to someone who turns out to be as socially null (because deeply indebted, publicly scorned, and so on) as himself. Again, as in Simon's quitter's discourse, we find a jarring inversion of economic hierarchy in the language that runs through Joseph's mind before he quits. Cause and effect are inverted: the sense of emotional dependency on one's employer is not the result of subordination; rather, subordination is the result of a secret emotional interdependence of the two men. Both Joseph and Tobler are equally "nothing," contrary to the initial appearance that it was the inventor Tobler who would make something of himself, while his assistant struggled to complete simple secretarial tasks. The inner language that Joseph develops, on the verge of quitting, suggests that all hierarchal positions are radically contingent, dependent above all on affective attachments that are beyond any one person's control. Joseph's quitter's discourse is democratizing, in the sense that it posits a vocabulary of emotion that neutralizes the material distinction between the positions of "employer" and "assistant." A similar process of democratization, elsewhere in the novel, is acknowledged as an objective historical process. Joseph noticed earlier that "die gegenwärtige Welt [sei daran,] die bestehenden gesellschaftlichen Rang- und Geburtsunterschiede allmählich, wenn auch nur nach außen, zu verwischen und aufzulösen" (today's world [was] in the process of gradually—if only to the outside observer—blurring and obliterating long-standing social distinctions of rank and birth) (*SW*, 10:120; *TA*, 120). Through his inward quitting discourse, Tobler participates in this very process of "blurring" and "obliterating."

Conclusion: Language of the Workers' Movement as a Parallel Discourse

Joseph Tobler's reflection on progressive democratization is one of the many moments that "date" Walser's novels, situating it within the sociopolitical world of Western Europe at the turn of the century. The quitter's discourse, after all, has not emerged in a vacuum. At key junctures in *The Tanners* and *The Assistant*, it is revealed that the protagonist is acquainted with the language of class struggle associated with the international socialist workers' movement. It is not that Walser's quitters are socialists in any straightforward sense: when Simon and Joseph quit, they are not striking for fair pay or better working conditions. What Simon and Joseph do share with the workers' movement, however, is the idea that refusing work provides a form of empowerment to the powerless. By forcefully asserting the emotional debt of employers to employees (i.e., Joseph's "loan" of love to Tobler, as it were), Walser's quitters recapitulate in an eccentric fashion a central gesture of the political Left—albeit without a Marxist, materialist framework that sees wage labor as a system for the agglomeration of capital at the expense of the dispossessed proletarians. The relationship of the quitter's discourse to the workers' movement could be described as one of *distant affinity*. It is telling that in both *The Tanners* and *The Assistant* socialism is associated with a long-estranged friend. On their lonesome journeys through the world, both protagonists have chance encounters with female friends from long ago, who are (in *The Tanners*) or used to be (in *The Assistant*) socialists. In each case, the protagonist is estranged from the socialist movement, but encounters it as an "old friend," with whom he unexpectedly crosses paths. Socialism is both familiar and distant.

In *The Tanners*, the surprise encounter with socialism occurs toward the end, as Simon is dangerously approaching a state of total destitution. One day he finds himself wandering into an outlying quarter of the city, through a development of mass housing for workers. At the sight of these large apartment buildings rising over meadows, Simon thinks to himself about how "das Ringen der armen Leute nach ein bißchen Frieden, ich meine die sogenannte Arbeiterfrage" (the struggle of the poor for bit of peace—I'm referring here to the so-called Workers' Question) (*SW*, 9:289; *TT*, 307) is as important as questions of art and aesthetics. Simon now explicitly sees himself as a social critic, who by material necessity must pay closer attention to economic relations than to beauty: "Ich bin kritisch und zugleich wehmütig, weil ich kein Geld habe" (I'm critical but at the same time feel quite melancholy because of my lack of money) (*SW*, 9:289; *TT*, 308). Here, for the first time in the novel, he seems to justify theft as a strategy for dealing with his poverty: "Ich muß zu Geld gelangen, das ist ganz einfach. Geliehenes Geld ist kein Geld, man muß es verdienen oder stehlen oder geschenkt bekommen" (I've got to get some money, it's quit simple. Borrowed money isn't money; money must be earned or stolen or received as a gift) (*SW*, 9:289–90; *TT*, 308). Simon places stealing alongside conventionally legitimate means of acquiring money; at this late moment of *The Tanners*, Simon's thinking comes close to a communist demand for expropriation of wealth.

Echoing this language of class consciousness, Simon meets his old friend Klara moments later in an apartment in the workers' quarter. She is now working for a photographer and performing charity among the working-class families around her, such that she now sees herself as the "Königin der Armen" (Queen of the Poor) (*SW*, 9:295; *TT*, 314). She speaks of how she grew to love the roughness of the workers and day laborers, and even remarks that they remind her in many ways of Simon and his brother Kaspar—establishing, for a moment, an overlap between proletarian laborers and the artistic Tanner siblings. Klara's approach to the working class is in any case maternalistic, and not exactly revolutionary; she speaks of how after discovering the hidden charms of the workers she resolved to make herself "Herrin und Bevormunderin dieser Menschen" (mistress and advocate for these people) (*SW*, 9:296; *TT*, 315). As an agent of social change, Klara sees herself as a charitable reformer motivated by her love of the working people. Klara's struggle for the workers is, however, introduced only as a point of comparison, and not as a possible path forward for Simon. Hearing that her jealous husband is approaching, Simon takes leave of Klara in solitude, not in solidarity.

Like *The Tanners*, *The Assistant* juxtaposes the social isolation of its protagonist with the language of solidarity furnished by leftist labor movements. When Joseph visits his old friend Klara (her name is the same as in *The*

Tanners) in the city while the Toblers are away for a weekend, the narrator recalls that Klara and Joseph had once been enthusiastic supporters of socialist movements:

> Unter dem Namen "Sozialismus" hatte sich, einer üppigen Schlingpflanze ähnlich, eine zugleich befremdende und anheimelnde Idee in die Köpfe und um die Körper der Menschen [. . .] geworfen [. . .]. Joseph und Klara waren damals ganz und gar von diesem vielleicht edlen und schönen Feuer ergriffen worden [. . .]. Sie liebten beide, wie es damals Mode war, die "Menschheit." (*SW*, 10:134–35)

> Under the label "socialism," a notion at once disconcerting and enticing had cast its tendrils, like those of a luxuriant vine, into the minds and about the bodies of [the people]. At the time, Joseph and Klara were utterly captivated by this perhaps noble and lovely blaze [. . .]. Both of them, as was the fashion in those days, were in love with "all mankind." (*TA*, 134–35)

The narrator speaks of this commitment without revealing any final judgment of the different strands of socialism (as suggested when the narrator mentions red and black, i.e., Internationalist Party–based and anarchist-spontaneist, flags) and its accompanying ideas of "humanity" as the de facto collectivity to which all working people belong. What is, however, made clear is that socialism has faded into the past as a youthful trend that both Klara and Joseph want to forget.[28] Since being abandoned by the politically engaged father of her child, Klara now "liebte nicht mehr die 'Menschheit,' sondern sie betete ihr Kind an" (ceased to love "mankind" and instead worshiped her child) (*SW*, 10:136; *TA*, 136). For both Joseph and Klara, socialism, along with "humanity," has the status of a nearly forgotten friend.

What is notable in the accounts of the "Klara" in *The Tanners* and the "Klara" of *The Assistant* is that their socialist commitment (present or past) is described as a "love." This *love* is, moreover, not supposed to be only Klara's peculiar subjective conception of what it would mean to fight in the workers' struggle, but rather represents a general feature of the turn-of-the-century labor movement. This movement's (reformist or revolutionary) calls for political and social transformation are supposed to be fueled first of all by a class solidarity that involves an affective attachment to humanity as a whole. In contrast to this socialist love of humanity, the quitter's discourse provides a model of the social world in which the primary category around which society coheres *is* love; but it is not an equalizing, undifferentiated love for the masses. The quitters' love will always lead to the construction of new hierarchies. Rather than offering up a solution for social suffering, or recommending an abolition of hierarchies, Walser's characters instead point to a perverse arbitrariness at the heart of all social hierarchies.

Having parted ways with their socialist friends, Walser's protagonists commit to a more diffuse, yet undeniably radical, form of refusal. This form of refusal is cogently illustrated in the quitting scene of *The Assistant*, as Joseph's hands and mouth refuse to obey not only his superior's will, but also his own (*SW*, 10:291–92; *TA*, 292). Whereas a striking worker refuses work as an act of self-preservation (for higher wages, or to stop an oppressive state from functioning), Walser's quitter refuses to be an acting, active subject. Walser's quitters are inclined, in the end, to be *nobodies*.

Notes

1. Walser himself destroyed one novel; Catherine Sauvat, *Vergessene Weiten: Eine Robert Walser-Biographie* (Frankfurt am Main: Suhrkamp, 1995), 88. Another novel manuscript was lost by a publisher. Peter Sprengel, *Geschichte der deutschsprachigen Literatur, 1900–1918: Von der Jahrhundertwende bis zum Ende des Ersten Weltkriegs* (Munich: C. H. Beck, 2004), 211.

2. Sprengel, *Geschichte der deutschsprachigen Literatur*, 212; Sauvat, *Vergessene Weiten*, 84.

3. On Walser's personality vis-à-vis his literary works, see W. G. Sebald, *A Place in the Country*, trans. Jo Catling (New York: Random House, 2014), 117–54. For a description of *The Tanners* as a "highly autobiographical" work, see Robert Mächler, *Das Leben Robert Walsers* (Frankfurt am Main: Suhrkamp, 1992), 91. For a juxtaposition of factual biographical documents with passages from Walser's fiction, see Jürg Amann, *Robert Walser* (Zurich: Arche, 1995).

4. Enrique Vila-Matas, *Bartleby & Co.*, trans. Jonathan Dunne (New York: New Directions, 2004), 4.

5. I am building here on Roland Barthes's conception of *The Lover's Discourse*, which, like the quitter's discourse, involves the inscription of affect. Roland Barthes, *A Lover's Discourse: Fragments*, trans. Richard Howard (New York: Hill and Wang, 1978).

6. For a canonical discussion of this relationship of dependency, in which worker becomes a commodity that can be purchased, see Karl Marx, "Wage Labor and Capital," in *The Marx-Engels Reader*, ed. Robert Tucker (New York: W. W. Norton, 1978), 205.

7. George C. Avery, "Focus on Reality in the Novels of Robert Walser" (Ph.D. diss., University of Pennsylvania, 1959), 26.

8. Tamara Evans, *Robert Walsers Moderne* (Bern: Francke, 1989), 31, 26.

9. Markus Schwahl, *Die Wirklichkeit und ihre Schwestern: Epistemologische Ideologiekritik und ihre ethischen Implikationen im Werk Robert Walsers* (Frankfurt am Main: Peter Lang, 2001), 33.

10. In the published English translation, the translation is simply "system," preceded by Simon's pejorative adjectives "slow, sluggish, dry, miserable." Robert Walser, *The Tanners*, trans. Susan Bernofsky (New York: New Directions, 2009), 71.

11. For a comparative discussion of Walser's texts alongside the social theories of Max Weber and Alfred Weber, see Reto Sorg and Lucas Marco Gisi, "'Er

gehorcht gern und widersetzt sich leicht': Zur Figur des Angestellten bei Robert Walser," in Robert Walser, *Im Bureau: Aus dem Leben der Angestellten* (Berlin: Insel, 2011), 130–31.

12. On the emphasis of Walser's romanticism by contemporary reviewers, see Barbara von Reibnitz and Wolfram Groddeck, "Editorisches Nachwort" in *Kritische Ausgabe sämtlicher Drucke und Manuskripte. Band I.2: Geschwister Tanner (Erstdruck)*, by Robert Walser (Basel: Stroemfeld, 2008), 309–32. For a discussion of Walser's resemblance of Eichendorff, see Sprengel, *Geschichte der deutschsprachigen Literatur*, 211. Perhaps the most famous connection of Walser's prose to the romantic tradition was drawn by Walter Benjamin, who saw that Walser was adding to a tradition in German letters of poetizing "windbags, wastrels, and thieves." Walter Benjamin, "Robert Walser," in *Selected Writings*, vol. 2, ed. Michael W. Jennings, Howard Eiland, and Gary Smith (Cambridge, Mass.: Harvard University Press, 1999), 259.

13. One early reviewer, Joseph Viktor Widmann, did note this crucial difference in Walser's world (as opposed to that of Eichendorff's). Joseph Viktor Widmann, "Geschwister Tanner: Roman von Robert Walser," in *Über Robert Walser*, ed. Katharina Kerr, vol. 1 (Frankfurt am Main: Suhrkamp, 1978), 17–23.

14. Jochen Greven, *Existenz, Welt und reines Sein im Werk Robert Walsers* (Munich: Wilhelm Fink, 2009), 55.

15. Widmann, "Geschwister Tanner," 18.

16. Karl Wagner, *Herr und Knecht: Robert Walsers Roman "Der Gehülfe"* (Vienna: Braumüller, 1980), 97.

17. Quoted from Vila-Matas, *Bartleby*, 4.

18. Widmann, "Geschwister Tanner," 17.

19. Auguste Hauschner, "Gebrüder Tanner," *Die Zukunft* 59 (1907): 100.

20. Joseph Viktor Widmann, "Robert Walsers Schweizerroman Der Gehülfe," in *Über Robert Walser*, vol. 1 (Frankfurt am Main: Suhrkamp, 1972), 27.

21. Albin Zollinger, "Robert Walsers Roman *Der Gehülfe*," in Kerr, *Über Robert Walser*, 1:133.

22. Greven, *Existenz, Welt und reines Sein*, 55.

23. Avery, *Focus on Reality*, 24.

24. Nagi Naguib, *Robert Walser: Entwurf einer Bewußtseinsstruktur* (Munich: W. Fink, 1970), 207.

25. See Lukas Rüsch, *Ironie und Herrschaft: Untersuchungen zum Verhältnis von Herr und Knecht in Robert Walsers Roman "Der Gehülfe"* (Königstein: Forum Academicum, 1983). See also Wagner, *Herr und Knecht*; Andreas Gößling, *Ein lächelndes Spiel: Kommentar zu Robert Walsers "Geschwister Tanner"* (Würzburg: Königshausen & Neumann, 1991).

26. See Gerhard Piniel, *Robert Walsers "Geschwister Tanner"* (Zurich: Juris, 1968).

27. Schwahl, *Die Wirklichkeit und ihre Schwestern*, 33.

28. As with the other narrative scenarios of *The Tanners* and *The Assistant*, Joseph's self-distancing from socialism is highly autobiographical. For an account of Walser's own short-lived, youthful enthusiasm for socialism, see Susan Bernofsky's essay in this volume.

Robert Walser's *Jakob von Gunten*

A "Zero" Point of German Literature

Peter Utz

I

Radically new books can be recognized by how they captivate their readers—or by how they shut them out. Robert Walser's third novel *Jakob von Gunten*, written during his Berlin years and published in 1909, gives readers exactly this choice: They either allow themselves to be drawn into the world of this "Tagebuch" (diary), entering the Benjamenta school for servants with its strange rituals along with Jakob von Gunten, or they circumvent the book entirely. Even the few reviews written when the book was first published are correspondingly divided: Efraim Frisch's long article in the *Neue Rundschau* is spellbound by the dreamlike "exhilarating, evocative and perturbing effect" the book emanates.[1] By contrast, Josef Hofmiller only had one sentence to say about it in the *Süddeutsche Monatsheften*: "Such rambling writing, void of any vigor or energy, is intolerable."[2] From today's perspective, Hofmiller made quite a blunder with his judgement. Yet even though Walser has been rediscovered in the last few decades and in the process *Jakob von Gunten* been commended for its modernity, the novel still remains Walser's most mysterious one. Between *Geschwister Tanner* (*The Tanners*) and *Der Gehülfe* (*The Assistant*), both of which appear more conventional in terms of theme and narrative style, and the highly reflective playfulness of the later novel *Der Räuber* (*The Robber*), which has attracted much attention in the era of postmodernism, the diary-novel *Jakob von Gunten* is the least accessible.

This resistance to being understood quickly, even when the reader gives in to it, characterizes the novel and its eponymous hero: "But who is Jakob von Gunten?" Efraim Frisch emphatically implores.[3] Jakob's diary only answers this question with one word, with a number: "zero." In the first entry the pupil Jakob announces: "Ich werde eine reizende, kugelrunde Null im späteren Leben sein" (In later life I shall be a charming, utterly spherical zero) (*SW*, 11:8; *JvG*, 5). He appears to have achieved this goal at the end of the text—in the concluding entry, just before his departure for the desert, Jakob declares: "Und wenn ich zerschelle und verderbe, was bricht und verdirbt dann? Eine Null. Ich einzelner Mensch bin nur eine Null" (And if I am smashed to pieces and go to ruin, what is being smashed and ruined? A zero. The individual me is only a zero) (*SW*, 11:163; *JvG*, 176). How can the reader interpret this "zero" without in turn merely going around in circles? How is the structure of the entire novel, which leads from the mysterious chambers of the Benjamenta Institute out into the desert, reflected in this zero? Finally, to what extent is the novel's aesthetic and literary-historical value inscribed into this zero?

The diary-novel assumes a circular form under the influence of the zero, and it is written by Jakob according to this leitmotif. In so doing, he embraces the educational goal of the Institute to become a "reizende, kugelrunde Null" (charming, utterly spherical zero). With this symbol he defines himself against the outside world, in opposition to his artist brother Johann, who lives in the city and who in many respects could be his alter ego. Jakob explains what differentiates them as follows:

> Was bin ich, und was ist er? Was ein Zögling des Instituts Benjamenta ist, das weiß ich, es liegt auf der Hand. Solch ein Zögling ist eine gute runde Null, weiter nichts. Aber was mein Bruder zur Stunde ist, das kann ich nicht wissen. (*SW*, 11:53)
>
> What am I, and what is he? I know what a pupil at the Benjamenta Institute is, it's obvious. Such a pupil is a good round zero, nothing more. But what my brother is at the moment I cannot know. (*JvG*, 54).

Using the "zero" as a point of comparison, Jakob can only define his brother's identity negatively; he can only say what his brother is "not." The zero sets a boundary of knowledge, a boundary that is just as clearly defined as the boundary between the Institute and the city that surrounds it. From the pupil's perspective, writing his diary on the school benches of the Institute, the city does not guarantee an identity.

Yet conversely, what is seemingly "obvious" to Jakob becomes a mystery to the reader. This reversal of perspective appears when the brothers actually meet. Johann says to Jakob:

> "Du bist jetzt sozusagen eine Null, bester Bruder. Aber wenn man jung ist, soll man auch eine Null sein, denn nichts ist so verderblich wie das frühe, das allzufrühe Irgendetwasbedeuten. Gewiß: dir bedeutest du etwas. Bravo. Vortrefflich. Aber der Welt bist du noch nichts, und das ist fast ebenso vortrefflich. Immer hoffe ich, du verstehst mich nicht ganz, denn wenn du mich vollkommen verstündest—." "Wäre ich ja gräßlich," fiel ich ihm ins Wort. (*SW*, 11:66)
>
> "You are now, so to speak, a zero, my good brother. But when one is young, one should be a zero, for nothing is more ruinous than being a

> bit important early on, too early on. Certainly: you're a bit important to yourself. That's fine. Excellent. But for the world you're still nothing, and that's almost just as excellent. I keep hoping you won't quite understand me, for if you understood me completely . . ." "I'd be a dreadful person," I broke in. (*JvG*, 68)

Through Johann, who to a certain extent shares the outside perspective with the reader, it becomes clearer what being a "zero" might entail. In the first instance being "bedeutungslos" is meant in the dual sense of the German word: at once "unimportant," that is, socially insignificant, as well as "meaningless," devoid of semantic content. Jakob, too, imagines himself as "unbedeutend" in this dual sense at an earlier point in the novel (*SW*, 11:54; *JvG*, 55). At the same time, however, Jakob is most certainly "a bit important" and meaningful to "himself": The "zero" constitutes a self-defining system of meaning that—from an outside perspective—includes its own meaning. Yet Johann and the reader, both outsiders, cannot and should not understand what exactly this "something" is that is contained in the "zero." This nonunderstanding is constitutive of the difference that distinguishes the self-defining "zero" from the "world," as Johann repeatedly emphasizes, and which Jakob for his part understands all too well.

In this way we learn a thing or two about the functionality of the "zero," and also about why we cannot and should not understand the essence of what it represents: semantic and social "Bedeutung," meaning and importance—"having any sense or significance at all" ("Irgendetwasbedeuten"; cf. Middleton's translation)—are linked. Those who wish to escape the social pressures of meaning and being important have to move beyond the realm of language. Therefore, in order to formulate this language-resistant potential for meaning and importance, something Jakob ascribes himself as his educational goal, he switches to the mathematical register: he reaches for the number "zero."

This frequent occurrence of the "zero" in the novel has already been noted in the secondary literature. Usually it is associated with the "disappearance" of the author, with the "self-minimization" of the "I" and—although much later—with the reduction in size of Walser's writing in the so-called "microscript" drafts.[4] Such interpretations, however, do not take the "zero" as both a number and a cipher seriously enough.

In order to understand the "zero" in terms of its resistance against the pressures of the "world" for meaning and social significance, one must bear in mind the mathematical dual function linked to its development by the Indians and the Arabs. On the one hand, the zero is essential for determining the position of the numbers; without the zero, for example, it would be impossible to determine the "place value" (*Stellenwert*) of other figures in the decimal system.[5] In this respect the zero is related to the algebraic letter symbols that can be used arbitrarily and which arrived in Europe via the Arabic world along with the zero. On the other hand, the zero references a non-value; in so doing it goes beyond a simple system of counting and calculating that is oriented toward visible realities and makes more complex operations possible in the first place. The zero's dual function as a placeholder and a character with "zero" value is evident in its etymology: the Arabs call this empty character *as-sifir*, meaning "emptiness." On the one hand, this results in "chiffre" and "cipher" (or number), on the other hand in "zéro." As an "empty space," the zero determines the place value of all other numbers. At the same time, the transition from the concrete unit of counting to the more abstract, mathematical "digits" is made tangible by the zero, which revolutionized the entire number system. The zero is the prototype of digits, a number without content. For this reason it is highly appropriate and obvious that it is at the center of "all" numbers, expanding the axis of "natural" numbers with the negative sequence of numbers. It is both the zero point and the central point of the number system: there is no negation without zero.

Therefore, the introduction of the "zero" during the Renaissance signals a turning point in Western thought. Brian Rotman has shown that the zero is inextricable from the introduction of one-point perspective in painting, the implementation of paper money, and a reemergence of autobiographical writing.[6] Just as the zero provides new orientation for the number system, the vanishing point reorients the semiotics of the picture: it directs the gaze to a point where the subject—both the painter and the observer—is virtually situated, however only in the form of an empty space. In parallel, the economic system that uses paper money is oriented toward a sign system that makes the absence of material monetary value calculable. And just as Vermeer or Velásquez place themselves absent-yet-present in scenes within their painter-portraits, Montaigne, too, develops in his *Essays* new possibilities for the formulation of subjectivity, which is aware of its semiotic character in the split between the subject who writes and the subject being described. The "I" constituted in this manner corresponds to the "zero": as a metasymbol it initially signifies the absence of other symbols, without having its own reference value. Yet at the same time the social space in this "I" contains a new vanishing point.

It is against this background and against these multiple dimensions of the "zero" that Jakob von Gunten's diary can be read anew and its literary-historical place can be determined. This is accomplished first of all in relation to both Jakob's identity and that of his fellow pupils, all of whom tend toward this empty point "zero" (*"Null"-Punkt*). Furthermore, it is accomplished by way of the figure of linguistic negation which, with the introduction of the empty "zero"-point, becomes constitutive for the novel. It can then be applied to a poetics of the periphery, which is inscribed into the novel. Taking it a step further, the "zero" can be related to the genre of the bildungsroman and contemporary novels that also make use of the mathematical register. Finally, the "zero" delineates the point of transition between civilization and desert, thereby locating the novel within a hidden tradition of literary modernity.

II

Just as the introduction of the zero in mathematics first made calculations with negative numbers possible, so too the appearance of the "zero" in the novel first makes the negativity both of the Institute and of Jakob's fellow pupils in their relationship to the outside world at all calculable to Jakob. In this respect Jakob is a zero, an "empty" figure. At the same time Jakob's "I" functions as the declarative subject—just like in an autobiography—and is thus the vanishing point that structures the diary-novel. As he writes, Jakob situates himself on the borderline between the inner world of the Institute and the outer world of the city, into which he repeatedly ventures. The city is embodied by his brother Johann, and when they meet it becomes visible as the antithesis to the world of the Institute: two worlds with different rules, so categorically separate from one another that any sort of understanding is very difficult, even though at the same time a symmetry between the two is evident just like the symmetry between the negative and positive numbers. The "zero" constitutes the borderline and transition point between the two, making this symmetry perceptible in the first place.

From this perspective of the zero as emptiness and mathematical threshold value the negativity of the Institute and of its pupils, but also of the entire diary-novel, can be newly interpreted. Hans H. Hiebel identifies the "destruction of signification" in this negativity, and derives from it the modernity of the novel.[7] He correctly points out that the "statically rotating and yet fugal structure of the novel" unravels the teleological plot of the bildungsroman. He also places Walser's novel close to modern painting, on the threshold to abstraction. From this he derives the "destruction of signification," the "annihilation of all things thematic." According to Hiebel all discourses in Walser's novel start to slip away; they are "decoded" in that they are exaggerated into the grotesque, linked to paradoxes, or immersed in a double irony. In this way, according to Hiebel, signification is destroyed in the novel.

Such a poststructuralist approach, however, overshoots the mark, and thereby misses the text as well. This is evident in how Hiebel also repeatedly includes "negation" itself among the ways in which signification is destroyed. Linguistic negation, however, is not simply "destruction" of signification. It merely crosses out established meanings, but still allows them to stand as such; indeed it emphasizes them exactly *as* what is crossed out. In this way negation concretely and critically refers to the discourses it negates. In so doing it adopts a particular position and itself creates new signification, even if this new signification cannot be formulated in a direct and positive way.

To begin with, this can be demonstrated by way of the pupils when they appear as the focus of Jakob's diary. Characteristic here is the buildup of linguistic forms of negation with which each is individually presented: Peter plays "den Unwissenden, Unbrauchbaren und Ungeratenen" (being ignorant, unusable, and unsuccessful) (*SW*, 11:41; *JvG*, 40); for Schacht every activity is "unziemlich, widernatürlich und unpassend" (improper, unnatural, and unsuitable) (*SW*, 11:123–24; *JvG*, 132); Fuchs behaves "wie eine große, zu Menschenform zusammengeknetete Unwahrscheinlichkeit. Alles an ihm ist unsympathisch, daher unbeherzigenswert" (like a big improbability pummeled into human shape. Everything about him is unpleasant, therefore unlovable) (*SW*, 11:43; *JvG*, 43); Hans is "nicht unhübsch" (not bad-looking) (*SW*, 11:40; *JvG*, 39); Jakob experiences an "unzarte" (indelicate) incident with Tremala (*SW*, 11:37; *JvG*, 36). As the prototype of the pupil, Kraus is the negative central figure: he is "unschön" (literally: "unbeautiful"), and there is nothing "Uneitleres, Unaufgeblaseneres" (more unvain, uninflated) than him (*SW*, 11:32; *JvG*, 31). The "ungraziöse" (un-graceful) Kraus with his "unverdorbenen" (unspoiled) heart is "ein echtes Gottes-Werk, ein Nichts, ein Diener" (a genuine work of God, a nothing, a servant) who seems "ungebildet" (uncultivated) to everyone (*SW*, 11:81; *JvG*, 85–86). "Dieser Mensch ist keiner Voreiligkeit, keiner Ungeduld fähig" (This person isn't capable of any overhastiness, or any impatience); "die Unscheinbarkeit seines Wesens hat etwas Unsichtbar-Herrscherartiges" (the unassumingness of his character has something of an invisible emperor about it) (*SW*, 11:124; *JvG*, 132–33).

This negativity is the lowest common denominator between the pupils who all come from different places and have different backgrounds, and will all venture in different directions when finished at the school. The prefix "un-" becomes an insignia that connects them—their un-iform, as it were. This does not mean, however, that the characteristics negated in each case by the prefix are canceled out. On the contrary, each pupil is disgusted by the instrumental rationality of the value-world that surrounds him, each in his own unpleasant way.[8] Jakob gathers all of these individual negative positions together in the "Unbürgerlichen" (unbourgeois), in the "Entgegengesetzt-Wohlanständigen" (utterly antithetical to well-being) (*SW*, 11:54; *JvG*, 55), which he embodies; he gathers them together in the word that brings negation full circle: a "zero."

Meaning is not annulled with this cascade of linguistic negation; rather, new meaning is created—which "ist Unsinn, aber dieser Unsinn hat einen hübschen Mund und lächelt" (is all very senseless, but this senselessness has a pretty mouth, and it smiles) (*SW*, 11:15; *JvG*, 12). This new meaning (or sense)—which the novel tries to communicate "smilingly," that is, ultimately, nonverbally—hides inside meaninglessness (or non-sense). Under the title "An Exercise in Nothing," Martin Walser described this new meaning using the category of irony.[9] Irony establishes an inverted relationship of representation between the outside world of the city and the world of the Institute. This is evident from the very first sentence, which places the Institute in a negative relationship to pedagogy and its optimism for progress: "Man lernt hier sehr wenig, es fehlt an Lehrkräften, und wir Knaben vom Institut Benjamenta werden es zu nichts bringen" (One learns very little here, there is a shortage of teachers, and none of us boys of the Benjamenta Institute will come to anything) (*SW*, 11:7; *JvG*, 3). In this negation, Jakob's diary develops that particular impetus which moves it forward, until by the end the difference between the Institute and the world has dissolved, along with the Institute itself, and the text thereby brings itself to an end in order to clear the way to freedom for Jakob.

From the very beginning the "zero" is put in place as the cipher and vanishing point of this negation. However, this negation is not a purely mathematical operation. The novel turns to the mathematical register, to the "cipher" par excellence, in order to set in motion a resistance against the pressures of "having any sense or significance at all" (*Irgendetwasbedeuten*). Yet the mathematical symbol is retranslated in the text back into language, written out as "zero." Correspondingly, the negation in the novel is not mathematical, but linguistic. Herein lies a fundamental difference. For unlike in the mathematical subtraction of "a – a = 0," in linguistic subtraction that which is negated remains, indeed, is at all posited in the first place.

This is evident in the "zero" itself, the central cipher of the diary and of Jakob's identity in the Institute. The "reizende kugelrunde Null" (charming, utterly spherical zero) that Jakob promises to become at the very beginning takes shape as a mathematical symbol, yet in linguistic form, charming and utterly spherical. Thus the "zero" as a symbol becomes conceivable in a tangible sense: a perfection that rounds itself out and comes full circle, and in this respect references only itself. As an absolute periphery around an undesignated center the zero encloses open space just as much as it closes off this space against the openness of the outside world. At the same time, it also becomes readable as a mathematical symbol in its multifarious signification, which results from the manifold functionalities of the mathematical zero. As a "digit" that obtains its position value only on the basis of its place within a number system, the "zero" represents the component of subjectivity that is determined from without. This is its social place value (*Stellenwert*), that "position" (*Stelle*) which all pupils except for Jakob assume. In these positions they will have to mean "something" (*irgendetwas*); they can be counted on and with. Jakob, on the other hand, insists until the very end that as "einzelner Mensch" (the individual me) he is a "zero" (*SW*, 11:164; *JvG*, 176). This also means that he will not contribute an absolute amount to the social balance sheet: in addition the zero has no added value. Yet the zero is indispensable for operations within the system because it determines the position—the place value—of the other digits. At the same time the zero has a function for all higher operations that is as important as it is risky: if one multiplies other numbers by zero, those numbers are nullified in the process. Textbooks simply forbid using zero as a divisor: one cannot divide a number by zero without jeopardizing the entirety of the system.[10] And if one tries to divide the "zero" itself, the quotient runs into infinity. In this sense zero is "indivisible," in a literal sense an *individuum*, "individual."

From this point of view Jakob's self-definition, taken at its numerical word, is of the utmost importance for the formulation of subjectivity. It shows that it cannot formulate its "meaning" or "significance" as "something" it contains if it does not want to surrender this meaning to the outside world straightaway. It must therefore close itself off and be self-contained, and it can only define itself from within itself. It thus remains resistant to determination by others from without; nevertheless, it insists on its function value within a complex system. In this regard it also affirms its social importance. For this reason it can, on the one hand, be interpreted positively as that particular "Souveränität" (self-assurance) that distinguishes all of Walser's heroes.[11] On the other hand, it can also be interpreted as the "skewed image of modern subjectivity that has been distorted into recognizability," and which is merely reflected in Jakob.[12] Characteristic for its function as a linguistic-mathematical "cipher" without an absolute "value" is precisely a multiplicity of meanings in which the leading signs are inverted depending on the system of coordinates according to which they are read. No matter how one applies the zero in interpretation, it remains a resistant riddle, spherical and charming. In this respect it is also the cipher for the manifold interpretations of the novel as a whole.

Jakob wants to be such a "zero" in the Institute. This function as an empty pivot point of social order is also inscribed into his own name. For on the one hand, "Jakob von Gunten" can be understood as a title of nobility, and Jakob's curriculum vitae also suggests this (*SW*, 11:50–52; *JvG*, 51–53). At the same time, Jakob declares himself the "modern" type who has disassociated himself from his aristocratic background. The fact that he can only breathe "in den unteren Regionen" (in the lower regions) (*SW*, 11:145; *JvG*, 155) is inscribed into his noble title by way of an anagram: "Jakob von Gunten" wants to begin "von ganz unten" (literally: "from all the way down") (*SW*, 11:117; *JvG*, 124). Thus this name itself becomes an intersection point of two social orders, a higher and a lower one. It is no accident that the "von" is in the middle of the name, which, as Efraim Frisch already noted in his review, should be pronounced "in a Swiss manner," with emphasis on the "von."[13] In this case the name becomes quite normal to the ears of those from Bern, with "Gunten" merely referring to a place on Lake Thun, not to noble origins. Just like an indicator of position, this "von" therefore determines the place value of the name. It is as unlikely as it is decisive. It is not for nothing that the central character of "von" is the *o*, that is, the sign for zero, though in linguistic form, around which the protagonist's name and that of the entire novel begin to revolve. In this way it becomes the linguistic cipher of Jakob's "nulled" identity. Walser included it at an elementary level in his text in such an obvious way that it has not occurred to anyone until now.

III

The Benjamenta Institute also has a "nulled" structure, just like its last pupil, Jakob. This is evident in the first instance at the level of content: the mysterious "inneren Gemächer" (inner chambers) which the text initially keeps circling around, turn out to be empty spaces that Jakob has merely filled with his dream fantasies.[14] Thus one night Fräulein Benjamenta leads him onto the fantastic-surreal ice rink of freedom. He then finds himself in an all too sumptuously decorated "Ungemach" (usually: "hardship"; literally: "un-chamber"; Middleton: "chamber of calamity"), that is, a negative "Gemach" (chamber) (*SW*, 11:102; *JvG*, 108). With this wordplay the empty space in the center of the Institute is bestowed with the same insignia of linguistic negation that also marks the pupils. Since this space is empty, Jakob can dreamily fill it from the circular periphery of his diary. After he has already ascertained that "keine [. . .] inneren Gemächer" (the [. . .] inner chambers [. . .] don't) exist (*SW*, 11:131–32; *JvG*, 139), he presents the reader with an image of how he had imagined the "inner chambers"—as an aristocratic world of castles and apartments. Then he states: "Nun, ich bereue tief, derart geträumt und gedichtet zu haben" (No, I deeply regret having dreamed up these fantasies) (*SW*, 11:132; *JvG*, 141). By way of contrast to the negative mathematical minus sign, this apparent revocation does not, in turn, cancel out what Jakob said and dreamed, but rather raises it to a poetological level: revocation grants the "inner chambers" the structure of linguistic negation, which allows that which is crossed out to remain, indeed even asserts it. "Träumen" and "Dichten" (dreaming and writing—conflated in Middleton's translation in "dreamed up") seem to make this happen. In symmetrical fashion, the outside world of the city, as Jakob puts it down on paper in one of the most elaborate city passages of his diary, appears "sehr dichterisch" (very poetic), even to himself (*SW*, 11:47; *JvG*, 47).

In this way inner space as well as outer space, the boundaries of which are outlined by Jakob's diary, appear as an open space of the poetic. At his school desk, Jakob all too gladly digresses into this space, writing and fantasizing in order to evade the austere "Vorschriften" (rules) (*SW*, 11:8; *JvG*, 5) that constitute the very essence of the Institute. In so doing Jakob frees himself from the fetters of time and space. His diary is thus not—or only very discreetly—chronologically structured, as a strict conception of the genre would dictate.[15] Rather, it has the appearance of a circumference. This is evident in the roundness with which Jakob, guided by the "zero," brings the end back to the beginning again, and then signals that this means the end of writing: "Ich einzelner Mensch bin nur eine Null. Aber weg jetzt mit der Feder" (The individual me is only a zero. But now I'll throw away my pen!) (*SW*, 11:164; *JvG*, 176). The empty circle which the pen has drawn by writing is complete, and the pen therefore superfluous. The diary has been written out—to its end.

A structural similarity links the diary, the Institute, and the title character. This is evident in how, on the one hand, the diary comes full circle to a close, yet on the other hand comes to nothing—along with the Benjamenta Institute. The Institute with its empty center of "inner chambers," the diary that constitutes this space in how it circles it, and Jakob himself are all "empty" figures of "zero." As the subject of his writing, Jakob writes *out of* this zero. Moreover, he writes himself *out of* the zero in that, even though he closes the circle by writing, he also ventures—using poetical gestures—into the dream-like interior world of the "inner chambers" and into the outside world of the city, until he is able to throw away the pen and leave for the open desert space, something he had initially only dreamed of. Out of the circling movement and along the periphery of the "zero"-figure, the departure for unknown dream-territories is made possible. The circling movement both delineates this periphery as empty space and also contains the empty space within it.

In this regard, the novel *Jakob von Gunten* anticipates a poetology of the periphery, as Walser would later formulate more explicitly in his short prose written during his time in Bern. This movement has often been described as a labyrinthine path that does not want to reach its center, like in the paradigmatic text "Minotauros" ("Minotaur").[16] Several references have also been made to the text with the programmatic title "Der heiße Brei" ("The Hot Porridge") as a figure for a writing that circles around the object.[17] The following self-reflexive sentence from this piece is often cited: "Besteht nicht Schriftstellern vielleicht vorwiegend darin, daß der Schreibende beständig um die Hauptsächlichkeit herumgeht oder -irrt, als sei es etwas Köstliches, um eine Art heißen Brei herumzugehen?" (Doesn't writing consist primarily in the writer constantly wandering or straying about that which is most important, as if it were something delicious to beat about the bush [literally: "to circle the hot porridge"]?) (*SW*, 19:91).[18] Indeed, the prose piece "The Hot Porridge" is related to *Jakob von Gunten* not only in this circular movement around an empty center. Similar to Jakob's dream of inner chambers, the first-person narrator of this prose piece dreams of a building as "etwas Vorübergehendes" (something transitory) that simultaneously "öffnet und schließt" (opens and closes), and in which the rooms are concentrically nested into one another. This is the space that induces the poetic circling movement with which the text reaches beyond the circular periphery into other territories, even if only in the form of linguistic negation. This is evident in the surprising territorial topoi that suddenly pop up in the text, the motivation for which is not elaborated upon. The text objects to its "Amerikanismusmangel" (lack of Americanisms), and it forbids inappropriate "Italianismen" (Italianianisms). By contrast it tries to "östreicheln" (Austrianize), which is nothing more than "ein gedankenloses Gedankenvollsein, ein stillstehendes Galoppieren, ein versteinertes über die Dinge, die man beschreibt, dahinfließen. Gewiß lassen sich solche beruflichen Finessen nur schwer definieren" (a thoughtless thoughtfulness, a stationary galloping, a petrified flow over the things one describes. Certainly such occupational finesses are very difficult to define) (*SW*, 19:90).

Such paradoxes do not dialectically resolve the contradiction constitutive to them; rather, they redirect it into a driving force that keeps the text moving horizontally.[19] But this movement does not take a set path; it can be neither "defined" nor enclosed. Walser's poetology of the periphery leads out into the open, which it encircles and into which it writes itself.

The openness of this circular movement is formulated even more radically in the prose piece "Cézannegedanken" ("Thoughts on Cézanne"):

> Er [Cézanne] erhielt mit der Zeit lauernde Augen vom vielen exakten Herumschweifen rund um Umrisse, die für ihn zu Grenzen von etwas Mysteriösem wurden. Sein ganzes stilles Leben lang kämpfte er den lautlosen, und, wie man versucht sein könnte, zu sagen, sehr vornehmen Kampf um die Gebirgigmachung, so dürfte vielleicht der umschreibende Ausdruck lauten, des Rahmens.[20]
>
> Der Sinn ist der, daß z.B. ein Gebiet durch Berge größer, reicher wird. (*SW*, 18:254)

> As time went by, his [Cézanne's] eyes became shifty from the repeated exact wandering around the edges, which for him became the boundaries to something mysterious. For his entire still life he fought the silent and, as one might be tempted to say, noble struggle to make the frame more visible and mountainous, that is to raise the flat frame to relief, as is perhaps the best way to define the circumlocutionary expression "making mountainous."
>
> The idea is that, for example, through mountains an area becomes bigger and more opulent.

By encircling the object, the defining frame that sets boundaries is opened up[21] and the "mysteriousness" beyond this horizon becomes perceptible. At the same time, however, the text comes up against the limitations of language and must itself resort to a "circumlocutionary expression." Yet even here the text finds territorial metaphors for the opening it seeks; these culminate in the assertion that as an artist Cézanne was "Asiat" (Asian), because according to the narrator, Asia is the "Heimat" (home) of art (*SW*, 18:255). The text therefore randomly and deliberately drifts into the realm of the exotic, just as Jakob will set out for the openness of the desert with Herr Benjamenta in his closing dream.

The circular structure of the "zero" contains this openness within it; indeed, it only manages to create the openness through exclusion and enclosure. It is for this reason that Walser's texts time and again set off in this circular motion. The circular movement is meant to lead beyond writing, to open the ears for that "etwas, was keinen Ton geben will" (something that doesn't want to make a sound) (*SW*, 11:50; *JvG*, 50), for which Jakob is listening long before he throws away his pen. This listening leads into an openness that is again envisaged topographically and thus anticipates the "Wüste" (desert): "Ja, wir warten, und wir horchen gleichsam ins Leben hinaus, in diese

Ebene hinaus, die man Welt nennt, aufs Meer mit seinen Stürmen hinaus" (Yes, we're waiting, and we are, as it were, listening to life, listening out into that plateau which people call the world, out across the sea with its storms) (*SW*, 11:93; *JvG*, 98). The diary opens itself up to the infinite, to an "anderswo" (somewhere else) beyond writing. Even before Fräulein Benjamenta's death, the diary notes: "Wir alle, Herrschaft sowohl als Elevenschaft, wir leben beinahe schon anderswo" (We're all, superiors and pupils, all nearly living somewhere else); and "Etwas wie treibende, schonungslose Energie schlägt hier rauschend die Flügel zusammen. Horchen wir alle hier auf das Spätere?" (There's something like a rushing, ruthless energy beating its wings and fluttering about the place. Are we all listening for what's to come?) (*SW*, 11:127; *JvG*, 135). Only by encircling the infinite over and over again, every time differently, can Jakob collect the energy in writing to enable him to set off for "what's to come," for this "plateau," this "sea," and this "desert." Jakob needs such linguistic ciphers for that which still evades language, and therefore experience. In this respect they are similar to the "zero," which as the perfect cipher encloses its meaning and content by encircling it, without directly describing it.

The diary keeps itself moving on this circular path by chatting, and at the same time it tries to separate itself from this movement as a "Vor-schrift" (pre-script or rule) by chatting. "Welch ein Geschwätz" (What a lot of talk), Jakob states in the diary in a self-critical manner (*SW*, 11:90; *JvG*, 95), only to subsequently keep on chatting. This is because the "feigned orality"[22] of his writing drives meaning outward in a centrifugal manner, away from the "single," "right" word that in the Western tradition stands at the origin of speech, indeed of creation: "Ich schwatze. Wie hasse ich all die treffenden Worte" (I'm just talking. How I hate all the right words) (*SW*, 11:50; *JvG*, 50). Thus that particular "Geschwätzigkeit" (talkativeness) which time and again has been attributed to Walser the feuilletonist is already staged in *Jakob von Gunten*. With its circular poetics of the periphery and the orality that serves as its driving force, *Jakob von Gunten* is structurally analogous to the small form of the feuilleton. Jakob even acts as if he were only filling out his diary for payment per line, like a feuilletonist: "Geb' es gern zu, daß ich schwatze, denn mit etwas müssen doch Zeilen ausgefüllt werden" (I admit that I'm gabbling, but the lines have got to be filled with something) (*SW*, 11:105; *JvG*, 111–12). In this regard Hofmiller's verdict of "rambling writing, void of any vigor or energy" is justified, as the diary writing is self-constituting and self-generates the tension at the surface of the text. This is the fundamental connection between the diary-novel, written in a "rambling" manner, and the feuilleton, which in a much more direct way is written for the "journal," that is, the newspaper, and therefore also for and in the moment.[23]

The feuilleton and the diary-novel are related in another way, too: a narrating "I" that constantly asserts the authenticity of its authorship is evident in both. This, however, is determined by readers' expectations and the conventions of the genre; that is, it is something external to the text. In this regard in both the feuilleton as well as in the literary diary the "I" is not located at the center of the text but on the linguistic periphery. As a pronoun, it indicates exactly the absence of the center, because it, the "I," has long since been missing such a thing as the "soul." Robert Musil wrote in his 1926 "Interview with Alfred Polgar" that Polgar, that doyen of the feuilleton, only dedicated various marginal notes to the "soul"—which he says would of course be badly missed by everyone—in his book *An den Rand geschrieben* (*Writing in the Margin*). Yet

> if one looks into the center where it [the soul] should be, everything is crossed out, and nothing is left there. However all of a sudden its lines appear in the corrections in the margins, in the footnotes, in the stab in the back practical observation issues to poetic observation, in this heterodoxy of reservations that keeps splitting deeper and deeper, therefore seemingly into an irreparable disintegration.[24]

In the crossed-out, negated center there is no "soul." The soul will appear, if at all, only in the margins. In Walser's feuilletons these are the insistent yet unstable first-person singular pronouns, which serve as placeholders marking the location of subjectivity. Walser already found a valid form in *Jakob von Gunten* for this placeholder function, which the subject ascribes to himself in the writing process: "I" is a cipher, a digit, a zero. As such it can take on a life of its own and become reified, without authorship becoming endangered in the process—an authorship without which there would be no writing. Instead of steering toward the convergence of the "I" who writes and the "I" being described, an inherent aspect of autobiographical writing since Montaigne, Jakob jettisons his "I" through writing, annuls it himself, and thereby becomes all the more a pure figure of writing: "Ich respektiere ja mein Ich gar nicht, ich sehe es bloß, und es läßt mich ganz kalt" (I don't respect my ego at all, I merely see it, and it leaves me cold) (*SW*, 11:144; *JvG*, 154).

IV

A common topos of Walser research is the idea that in *Jakob von Gunten* Walser nullified the *Entwicklungsroman*, the novel of development. This interpretation is based on passages such as the oft-cited sentence "Ich entwickle mich nicht" (I don't develop). But the relativizing sentence that follows—"Das ist ja nun so eine Behauptung" (At least, that's what I claim)—has mostly been overlooked (*SW*, 11:144; *JvG*, 154). This is all the more reason to view *Jakob von Gunten* as a "parody of the classic *Entwicklungsroman*."[25] Andreas Gößling even reads *Jakob von Gunten* as a poetic commentary on *Wilhelm Meister's Apprenticeship*, and, according to Gößling, Walser's achievement is also limited to this.[26] Yet the complex ciphering of individuality as "zero," in particular, does not merely arise from the tradition of the *Entwicklungsroman*, and it is also not its simple annulment. It is more so the continuation of the *Entwicklungsroman* in concrete negation. The dialectic of rounding and openness, with which the "zero" "circumscribes" both the "importance" and "meaning" of the individual as well as an entire aesthetic program, doing so in order to lead out into the open—this dialectic does, after all, belong to the basic structures of the genre: a self-contained development of subjectivity is fulfilled only at the end by setting off to face the contradictions of reality. Thus Goethe later appended the much more open *Journeyman Years* onto the indeed almost forcedly rounded *Apprenticeship*—incidentally it was the *Journeyman Years* that Albert Steffen saw lying open on Walser's desk in Charlottenburg in 1907.[27]

The move toward a mathematical ciphering of this dialectic is also to be found in the concept of education espoused by German classicism. In his letters *On the Aesthetic Education of Man* Schiller speaks about the perfect aesthetic determinability of a state of nothingness: "In the aesthetic state, then, man is *Nought*, if we are thinking of any particular result rather than of the totality of his powers, and considering the absence in him of any specific determination."[28] In one regard this "aesthetic disposition of the mind" is "*Nought*" when related to separate and concrete operations; yet it is also "a state of *supreme reality*" insofar as "all limitations" are absent.[29] In other words, in a state of unlimited openness in which the potential totality of man, which is Schiller's concern, can develop. In Schiller's case, "zero" or "nothingness" stands for this potential for perfection.

The other dimensions of the "zero," its self-referentiality, its resistance to the social pressures of carrying meaning and being important, and its quality as an abstract cipher, are, however, not developed further until Walser's diary-novel. This is not at all coincidental; rather it is determined to a large extent by the epoch in which Walser lived. In the direct literary surroundings of Walser's novel there are also other attempts to encipher subjectivity mathematically. For example, in Carl Spitteler's novel *Imago*, published in 1906, the hero finds himself confronted by the "zero" in a monologue:

> And what else are you capable of then, you thirty-year-old boy? You're not capable of a thing, not even of writing a correct sentence on a scrap of paper! You were, are, and will always remain nothing, a zero; somewhat like the others but at a lower level of nothingness. The others are humble, however, and are rewarded with a measure of happiness. Be humble and you too will be rewarded![30]

This may still be a relatively colloquial usage of the digit "zero," even if it is repeated conspicuously often in the novel,[31] and even if the hero with the programmatic name "Victor" develops a confident resistance to the demands of the world, which makes him akin to Walser's Jakob. The program of humble self-effacement that takes the form of the "zero" even has a tendency to change in both novels into ambitious dreams that reach for the infinite.

The novel *Hans Himmelhoch* by Jakob Schaffner prizes such ambitions, both rhetorically and mathematically. It appeared in the same year as *Jakob von Gunten*, was likewise published by a Berlin publishing house, and its author is similarly a highly respected and talented young Swiss man. With a mathematical potency that is exponential, the eponymous hero of the novel soars to those heights to which his subjectivity, up in arms against the heavens, appears to correspond. (Translator's note: Hans's family name means, literally, "High as the Heavens.") In chapter 8 he writes to his Hedwig, who as the addressee of the fiction keeps the text moving onward and upward throughout the entire book:

> No, dear Hedwig, no more ends. For all eternity no more ends. For where should yet another end come from? I have started to multiply, you see! The movement of fertile addition is underway with me! Look, the march of multiplication is already advancing and expanding, great as an army, from the marshal of my will; soon it will storm into the dark enemy land of time like a reconnaissance mission with swarms of flashing planes. [. . .] Are we too weak? Ha, who says we are too weak? Four times four is sixteen: are we still too weak? Yes? Oh please: sixteen times sixteen is so and so much. What? Be brave! be brave! We have the will to do it! And what we want is us. And what we are we can multiply by ourselves at any moment. We are always ourselves multiplied by ourselves. Who out there understands this and doesn't plunge into the chasms of joy?[32]

What is remarkable about this rhetoric of will, influenced by Nietzsche, is the use of mathematical metaphor, which seems to be in a better position to formulate the demands of this subjectivity than all linguistic superlatives. It counts—exponentially—only on itself. In this respect it is related to the "zero." However, an actual "zero" cannot creep into the rhetoric of multiplication of Schaffner's character because it would cause him to collapse immediately. In this regard both novels—published in the same year by competing publishing houses—are diametrically opposed attempts to encipher subjectivity through literature: while the one expansively exaggerates it and projects it upward, the other drives it toward zero, into the reflexive cipher of concentration.

Around the same time, Robert Musil was delving even more deeply into mathematics in his novel *The Confusions of Young Törless*. Walser was presumably acquainted with this novel, which was published in 1906 and has been discussed a few times in connection with *Geschwister Tanner* (*The Tanners*).[33] The outward parallels between *Jakob von Gunten* and *Törless* are hard to ignore: both novels lead their heroes into an educational institute in whose initiation rituals adolescence covertly or overtly runs amok. And both heroes leave the educational institute at the end of the novel in a state of mind that will no longer unquestioningly accept the truths of the adult world, because for both a world has opened up from the inner depths of the institute that no longer follows a simple rationality. For Jakob, this world opens up in the dreams with which he poetically fills the emptiness of the inner chambers and of daily life in the Institute. In Törless's case, this world opens up exactly in the middle of the text in the phenomenon of the "imaginary numbers."[34] That there can be no root of –1, yet one can still calculate with it, is the mathematical scandal that puts the decisive chink in Törless's worldview. For him the imaginary numbers are a sign "that our thinking doesn't walk on solid, secure, even ground, but rather that it walks over holes."[35] The "imaginary numbers" thus signify the empty spaces of the imagination. Törless reveals this realization to the disconcerted teachers in his visionary closing speech as he leaves the boarding school "in a moment of almost poetic inspiration."[36] While the "imaginary numbers" are not a cipher for the educational ideal, like the "zero" in Walser's novel, they are nevertheless the decisive catalyst for the subject's transformation in the sense that the subject learns to perceive the world no longer as consisting of one single thread of reality, but as an open field of incalculable possibilities.

Why is Walser's epoch so enamored by this literary number-acrobatics of subjectivity, this higher mathematics of the individual? At one time it was believed that numbers and figures could provide an alternative sign system, one that—in a much clearer manner than words—gets by without a relationship of similarity between sign and meaning. In his treatise *On the Spiritual in Art* Kandinsky, for instance, formulated the move toward abstraction by way of the abstractness of the "Zahl" (figure or number): "In any art the final abstract expression remains the number [*Zahl*]."[37] The "figure" becomes the point of convergence that is to bring the arts together in their epochal step beyond representation.

The critical discourse of the time also linked its cultural diagnosis to numbers, which were meant to impart the impression of exactness. Oswald Spengler mathematically derives the cultural state of his present day in *The Decline of the West*. In his introductory chapter, "The Meaning of Numbers," he places the individual "awakening of the ego" alongside the culturally determined awakening of number sense and language sense.[38] He thus attempts to deduce differences between cultures from their differing conceptions of mathematics: modern Western culture—and not the culture of classical antiquity—was the first to recognize the dimensions of the infinite and the problem of limit values. Evidence of this for Spengler is, among other things, calculating with negative numbers and the introduction of the zero as a number; this was then carried further with the introduction of irrational and imaginary numbers as well as the root of –1. In this Spengler sees the imprint of the foundations of Western culture, its thinking, but also its "style" and its "soul." According to Spengler's prophetic diagnosis, things would only go downhill from this peak.

In 1921 Musil criticized Spengler for exactly this diffuse juggling of mathematical terminology and his arbitrary conclusions about cultural epochs based on mathematical forms of knowledge. For Musil, it is typical of the era: "When one attacks Spengler, one attacks the era that has created him and that likes him, because his errors are its errors."[39] The paradigm of mathematics on which Spengler's cultural diagnosis is based, a mathematics as a logically well-formed rationality, had long been dubious to Musil. Even in his essay "The Mathematical Man" (1913), he shows how mathematicians—after they had established the mathematical principle of modern technology—realized that this fundamental principle "absolutely could not be put right." Today there is, therefore, "no other possibility of having such fantastic, visionary feelings as the mathematician does."[40] He is "an analogy for the intellectual of the future" because his way of thinking also has to be aimed at feelings and has to become "spirit" (*Geist*). The mathematician, however, is only a simile for this transformation—"taking this step is the task of writers."[41]

Musil takes this step, already prefigured in the "poetic" ending of *Törless*, in the essay "Sketch on What the Writer Knows" (1918). Here he unequivocally places himself on the side of the literary, because "the most basic principles of mathematics are logically unsecured."[42] Yet, while rational man "seeks the solid and fixed, and is content when he can establish for his computations as many equations as he finds unknowns," in the writer's "territory" there is "from the start no end of unknowns, of equations, and of possible solutions."[43] Using a mathematical metaphor, Musil gains access to exactly that area that no longer belongs to the mathematician. He only wants to calculate with these "unknowns" in his capacity as a writer.

It is not by chance that Ulrich, the "man without qualities," is a professional mathematician who, however, takes leave of his career.[44] Musil's massive unfinished novel thus answers the false expectations that the era attached to the exactness of mathematics by translating the "equations" and "unknowns" of mathematics into the poetic—as it were, converting these into similes. He also counters the mathematical ciphers of subjectivity as they appear in Spitteler's or Schaffner's novels. For what Törless only begins to realize becomes for Ulrich the formative insight gained from his continually unfolding experience, namely that reality, but also the subject that constitutes reality, has empty spaces and fissures. In these empty spaces there appear the dream territories of fantasy. In psychoanalysis these can only be tapped into conceptually from the edges of consciousness. However, in doing so, their edges begin to crumble away and become unstable. Musil therefore repeatedly attempts to build new bridges into the empty space of "qualitylessness," not through words and expressions, but through images. In the process, this space develops itself into an endless, novelistic text.

The "zero" paradox, as formulated in *Jakob von Gunten*, becomes in Musil a version of linguistic negation that strives toward the infinite. In the literary negation of "qualities," which the novel takes up in the title, these qualities are not annulled, but exponentially multiplied. "Zero" turns into "infinite." In this sense, *The Man without Qualities* is a continuation of *Jakob von Gunten* and its concept of annulled subjectivity. One sentence in *Jakob von Gunten* anticipates this relationship between the two works—once again, as a secret hidden on the linguistic surface—and even links the title of the novel in the visual and sonic pun "von ganz unten" (all the way down) with Musil's much later "ohne Eigenschaften" (without qualities): "Ich vergesse nie, daß ich ein Abkömmling bin, der nun von unten, *von ganz unten* anfängt, *ohne* doch die *Eigenschaften*, die nötig sind, emporzugelangen, zu besitzen" (I never forget that I'm descended beginning from *all the way down*, *without* having the *qualities* which one needs if one is going to rise to the top) (*SW*, 11:117; *JvG*, 124; emphasis added).

V

Jakob's diary opens up at its end point—its zero point—in his final desert dream. That's where he heads together with Herr Benjamenta—a desertion in the most literal sense. The desert and the zero have been associated with one another for centuries as symbols of nothingness, of empty space. In an Arabic poem from the eighth century, an Arab speaks of deserting when he says: "My name will be circled at the inspection." This is an early example of the occurrence of the zero in literature, which at the same time signifies, of all things, desertion. The example was contained in a 1926 article entitled "On the History of Zero" published in the *Schweizerischen Familien-Wochenblatt*, in which Walser also occasionally appeared.[45] At the end, when Jakob as an individual declares himself a "zero," he thus strikes himself off the crew lists for being drafted into reality. The zero he leaves behind before throwing away his pen is the symbol of his desertion. Furthermore, Jakob completes a circle with his dream-departure for the Orient, into the desert and then to India in the sense that he deserts into exactly the space from whence the "zéros"—the Arabic figures, the Indian empty character—originated.

This departure, however, is initially only realized in the novel as a dream. Jakob dreams it while he keeps the nightly vigil with Herr Benjamenta by the body of Fräulein Benjamenta. In this dream he finds himself in the middle of the desert together with Benjamenta:

> Wir wanderten und trieben mit den Wüstenbewohnern Handel, und wir waren ganz eigentümlich belebt von einer kühlen, ich möchte sagen, großartigen Zufriedenheit. Es sah so aus, als wenn wir beide

> dem, was man europäische Kultur nennt, für immer, oder wenigstens für sehr, sehr lange Zeit entschwunden gewesen seien. (*SW*, 11:162).
>
> We were traveling and doing business with the desert dwellers, and we were quite peculiarly animated by a cool, I might say splendid, contentment. It looked as if we had both escaped forever, or at least for a very long time, from what people call European culture. (*JvG*, 174)

The principal, who looked "wie ein Araber" (like an Arab), rides a camel, as does Jakob. They are "Ritter" (Knight) and "Knappe" (Squire), organizing a revolution together "in Indien" (in India) (*SW*, 11:163; *JvG*, 175). When he wakes up, Jakob agrees to go wherever Benjamenta wishes. In the final paragraph he only briefly explains: "Ich gehe mit Herrn Benjamenta in die Wüste. Will doch sehen, ob es sich in der Wildnis nicht auch leben, atmen, sein, aufrichtiges Gutes wollen und tun und nachts schlafen und träumen läßt" (I'm going with Herr Benjamenta into the desert. I just want to see if one can live and breathe and be in the wilderness too, willing good things and doing them, and sleeping and dreaming at night) (*SW*, 11:164; *JvG*, 176). Here the last word is also "Träumen" (dreaming), which not only occasions Jakob's departure but is also what he himself wants to take with him when he sets off—his most important piece of luggage. Thus Walser exponentiates the dreamlike quality of this departure. What lies ahead for Jakob is left open: perhaps a reality, perhaps a Fata Morgana. The only thing that is made irrevocably clear in the last sentence is what Jakob is leaving behind: "Nun den adieu, Institut Benjamenta" (So now adieu, Benjamenta Institute) (*SW*, 11:164; *JvG*, 176).

The interpretations of this departure have therefore remained just as controversial as those of the entire novel; in this respect, too, the ending appears as an "empty" space, a zero that has to be filled while reading. One can either interpret the departure for the desert as only an ostensible freedom, because with his departure Jakob once again falls back into the former dependency on Benjamenta.[46] Or one could postulate for this space the replacement of the old order of "fathers" with a new order of "brothers," the transformation of power into solidarity—even if this departure does not lead into society, it at least reflects Jakob's completed socialization, as one commentator puts it.[47] This new fraternity is previously signaled when Herr Benjamenta says to Jakob: "Manchmal ist mir, als seiest du mein junger Bruder" (Sometimes I feel that you're my young brother) (*SW*, 11:107; *JvG*, 113), and when Fräulein Benjamenta wishes to draw him into her "geschwisterliche, ins lächelnde Vertrauen" (sisterly and smiling confidence) (*SW*, 11:145; *JvG*, 155). The revaluation of the relationships of dependence is even contained within the names, because in the Bible Jakob is actually the father of his youngest and favorite son, Benjamin.[48] This reading of the end of the novel thus indicates a libertarian, egalitarian, fraternal society. Yet even if this is an echo of the French Revolution, as it were, then it is only, for the time being, a dream vision. Nevertheless, the novel also appears in this respect to reach a "zero" point, or point of "origin," a historical point of transition, a "plunge from what went before into what is to follow."[49] A new temporal coordinate system would now need to be introduced, just as the French Revolution had its own new calendar.

This ending is also a point of transition between two orders in terms of topography: the transition from the completely closed to the completely open structure, from the Institute into the desert. Jakob's dreams have prepared him for and also anticipated this. In the heart of the Institute, in the heart of its enclosed circle, Jakob creates empty spaces by dreaming, which, as the circle dissolves, he then hopes to find again on the outside. Thus "zero" here turns into the infinite.

The cipher for this is "desert," the operation that leads there is "desertion." On this point Hiebel makes the following claim—dubiously extending it to Walser's biography: "With the signifier 'desert' virtually a place *behind* signification is sought after; that is what is so 'crazy' about Jakob's decision. Was the clinic this place for Walser?"[50] Yet the "zero" no more than the "desert" simply means "nothing." Neither, in this respect, does the novel simply destroy signification, because the desert—the territory of this dream-departure—is densely packed with European phantasms in Walser's time, as well as with very real colonial claims to power. Walser was well aware of this. For example, in the prose piece "Abschied" ("Goodbye"), which was published in June 1909 in the *Neue Rundschau* and which is like a combined continuation of the dreams of power and the Orient from *Jakob von Gunten*, a very ironic sheen falls on the colonial exoticism of the time. The first-person narrator of the text stylizes himself as a Turkish-Oriental ruler, despotic and lecherous, who foresees the downfall of his empire:

> Mit dem Islam ist es zu Ende. Durch die Wüste, wo der Klang meines Namens die Hyänen zum Respekt zwang, werden die Eisenbahnen fahren. Die Türken werden Mützen aufsetzen und wie Deutsche aussehen. Man wird uns zwingen, Geschäfte zu machen, und wenn wir nicht fähig dazu sind, so erschießt man uns einfach. (*SW*, 15:103)

> Islam has seen its day. The trains will run through the desert where once the sound of my name forced respect from the hyenas. The Turks will put on caps and look like Germans. We will be forced to trade and do business, and if we are not capable of this we will simply be shot.

At a time when Germany was planning the Baghdad Railway in order to create economic and political ties with Turkey, one could hardly have more concretely and harshly formulated the idea that the European desert dreams instantly absorbed and thereby annihilated the "Other," which they sought in exotic lands overseas. In a dream-Orient that has actually been annexed, all Turkish people will look like Germans.

Walser thus emphasizes the precariousness of the real background of these desert dreams, which proliferated wildly in European literature beginning in the nineteenth century. Thus the desert is filled—and not only in the epoch-making novel series by Karl May—with a fixed inventory of images usually of European origin. Yet, it is more than just a place of escape for bored, Europe-weary Europeans. The desert also represents a fascinating openness without secured boundaries, a substructure in contrast to the superstructure of the cities, which have grown into labyrinths. It also becomes a space for mystical self-discovery, up to the brink of death, a space at the edge of silence into which one can only speak by way of monologue.

These are the elements of that particular desert dream of literary modernity that Rimbaud most effectively articulated. In *A Season in Hell* Rimbaud had sermonized on leaving the Western marshes behind and had simultaneously proclaimed: "One must be absolutely modern."[51] This Rimbaud paragon is reimagined in the dream of Jakob, who also labels himself "modern" (*SW*, 11:51; *JvG*, 52). The departure at the end of the novel, the "Adieu, Institut Benjamenta" (adieu, Benjamenta Institute), echoes the final section of Rimbaud's text, titled "Adieu." Walser directly refers to Rimbaud and modernity, without however subscribing to their exoticism as anything more than simply a dream. Walser revisits the "Afrika-Idee" (Africa idea) that supposedly drove Rimbaud "in die Wüste Sahara" (into the Saharan Desert) in "Studie (I)" ("Study (I)", 1926), in which Baudelaire, Verlaine, and Rimbaud appear (*SW*, 17:152–53). Walser himself, however, never set off for such faraway lands even though in 1906 he teased his editor Christian Morgenstern with the plan "nach Afrika zu gehen" (of going to Africa) (*Briefe*, 49). In the same year he also wrote the lost "zweiten Roman" (second novel) in which the hero really goes "nach Asien" (to Asia) "indem er sich einem tollen Gelehrten 'dem Teufel im Sommermantel' als Gehilfen anschließt" (by accompanying a great scholar, "the devil in a summer coat," as an assistant) (*Briefe*, 47). *Jakob von Gunten* is possibly a revised version of this second novel, which remains unidentified.[52] In this case Walser would have bracketed off the real departure to Asia in one of Jakob's dreams and placed this in analogy to the dream worlds of European exoticism. At the same time he would also have internalized this dream-territory—as an open surface inside the "zero."

In so doing, however, Walser would also have modernized the desert, because for literary modernity Africa lies within, and the desert becomes a cipher for inner desolation or desertization. Nietzsche leads the way in this reevaluation of exoticism when he includes the desert in his *Zarathustra*. Here European exoticism is brokenly reflected in the dramatic poem "Among Daughters of the Desert," which is recited by Zarathustra's shadow. The poem puts European clichés of the Orient on show in shrill form, and then concludes with this warning: "The desert grows: woe to him who harbours deserts within!"[53] In the *Dithyrambs of Dionysus* version, Nietzsche later adds: "Consumed by lust, O Man, do not forget: you—are the stone, the desert, you are death."[54] Thus Nietzsche inverts the desert, relating it to the inner topography of the subject. As such a cipher of inner emptiness it approaches Walser's "zero." And it is only as such a cipher that it grows into an extensive metaphorical system during the modern period. The following sentences from Kafka's unpublished fragments are exemplary of this: "The spiritual desert. The corpses of the caravans of your former and latter days."[55]

At the same time, literature of the twentieth century also explores real desert topographies. Friedrich Glauser, for example, does so in his legionnaire novel *Gourrama* from the 1930s, which incidentally also bears traces of Rimbaud.[56] It tells the story of desertion, meant in many senses: the flight from present-day Europe leads the foreign legionnaires into the Moroccan desert. However, the desert merely reflects back their inner emptiness—to which they can only react with aggression and self-aggression or with melancholic withdrawal. While the end of the novel leads its protagonist, named Lös, back into the urban world of Paris, this is not a resolution but a dissolution, or "Auflösung," as the last section of the novel is ambiguously titled: the destabilized subjectivity of the deserters fails to gain a foothold either in the desert or in its counterworld, the metropolis.[57]

Nevertheless, literature of the modern period ever more radically exposes itself to this emptiness. With its back to civilization, literature of the modern period calls monologically into the desert. This is evident with Glauser's legionnaires, and even more so in Wolfgang Hildesheimer's *Masante* (1973), in which the narrator with his "amor vacui" talks himself into the desert, like Beckett's figures in *Happy Days*. Hildesheimer's narrator eventually sets off for the desert—and this is where the text ends, where it sands up and peters out.[58] Ingeborg Bachmann searches even more persistently for points of transition from the power structures of civilization into a desert space, which she takes very seriously as both a fantasy of freedom and of fear. It is therefore telling that her project of a "Desert Book," which later became known as the fragment titled *The Book of Franza*, takes Berlin as its starting point, a city Bachmann called "A Place for Coincidences," in the Georg Büchner Prize speech of the same name (1964). For there the "Berlin sky" blends into the "desert sky,"[59] and she can be carried out of the city on imaginary camels into the desert, the "only landscape that says nothing, doesn't speak out, about which there is nothing to say."[60] Ingeborg Bachmann drives the desert into this form of negation as a real landscape, but also as an ultimate linguistic cipher in which language negates and annuls itself.

Walser already points in this direction in *Jakob von Gunten*. In Berlin, which is famously built on sand, he also makes the trek from the labyrinthine overcivilization of the city into the sands of the desert. In the prose piece

"Berlin und der Künstler" ("Berlin and the Artist," 1910) Walser shows how in the city the person from the province can, on the one hand, revel "wie in einem bezaubernden Morgenland-Traum" (as if in an enchanting Oriental dream). On the other hand, however, he can also experience "was es heißt, in Wüsten und Einöden zu leben" (what it means to live in deserts and wastes) (*SW*, 15:50).[61] It is for this reason that the passages describing the big city in *Jakob von Gunten* are replaced by the desert dream at the end. In this dream Walser draws on European exoticism, but places it in the inverted commas of a dream. Thus the desert dream displays its function as the antithesis of civilization and as its empty space. As one such "zero"-function Walser includes the desert in his novel of the big city. In this respect he is the "clever camel" that, as Jürg Laederach noted, carries "the desert on his back."[62]

In literary terms, Walser thus sets out for and breaks out into the modern period. With its charmingly inviting yet spherically repelling "zero"-form, the text of Jakob von Gunten's diary is only a shell that openly encloses that which is linguistically unreachable. It does not show any rhetorical consideration for the reader, but rather revolves around itself before the reader's eyes. It does not expect to be completely understood, as was already evident in the dialogue between Johann and Jakob. It also deserts the system of language for the system of numbers, tending toward the point of origin—zero—of the number sequence, which requires a very different reading. Herein lies a radical difference between *Jakob von Gunten* and Walser's earlier novels, which still greet the reader with the gestures of traditional narrative. In this regard *Jakob von Gunten* is also radically different from *The Robber*, which makes the reader a partner in a highly acrobatic game. *Jakob von Gunten* rather comes closer to that "writing degree zero" postulated by Roland Barthes. Barthes sees a final stage of literature in a "neutral writing," a form of negation of the traditional-rhetorical function of literature. For Barthes, its first realization is—as it happens—a novel that plays out under the sun of the Algerian desert: Camus's *The Stranger*. According to Barthes, this novel displays the minimalistic style of writing that brought literary modernism close to journalism.[63]

Setting off monologically for the desert, Jakob's diary-journal is likewise heading in this direction. For this reason one can recognize in Jakob's diary a point of origin of literary history—its "zero" point. Walser also located himself at such a point. In 1943 he remarked to Carl Seelig that he never took the bourgeois seriously, that he gave them the impression he was mocking them: "Darum blieb ich für sie immer eine dicke Null, ein Galgenstrick" (For this reason I always remained a plump zero, a rogue to them).[64] This "plump zero" is already inscribed into the "unbourgeois" Jakob von Gunten. It is the cipher for why this novel and Walser's work on the whole have for so long been forgotten. Now it can be interpreted as a cipher for how and why one nowadays has to count on and count with this "zero" in literary terms.

Translated by Leesa Wheatley

Notes

This chapter was originally published as "Robert Walsers *Jakob von Gunten*: Eine 'Null'-Stelle der deutschen Literatur" in *Deutsche Vierteljahrsschrift für Literaturwissenschaft und Geistesgeschichte* 74, no. 3 (2000): 488–512.

1. Efraim Frisch, "Ein Jüngling: Jakob von Gunten," in *Über Robert Walser*, ed. Katharina Kerr, vol. 1 (Frankfurt am Main: Suhrkamp, 1978), 71.

2. Josef Hofmiller, "Jakob von Gunten: Gedichte," in Kerr, *Über Robert Walser*, 51.

3. Frisch, "Ein Jüngling," 72.

4. See for example Dieter Borchmeyer, *Dienst und Herrschaft: Ein Versuch über Robert Walser* (Tübingen: de Gruyter, 1980), 36. See also Hans-Ulrich Treichel, "Über die Schrift hinaus: Franz Kafka, Robert Walser und die Grenzen der Literatur," in *Robert Walser*, ed. Klaus-Michael Hinz and Thomas Horst (Frankfurt am Main: Suhrkamp, 1991), 296–97.

5. Precursors for a number "zero" are evident in Mayan culture and in Babylonia. Cf. Georges Ifrah, *Histoire universelle des chiffres* (Paris: Robert Laffont, 1981), 453ff.

6. Brian Rotman, *Signifying Nothing: The Semiotics of Zero* (Basingstoke: Palgrave Macmillan 1987).

7. Hans H. Hiebel, "Robert Walsers *Jakob von Gunten*: Die Zerstörung der Signifikanz im modernen Roman," in Hinz and Horst, *Robert Walser*, 240–75.

8. Dagmar Grenz, *Die Romane Robert Walsers: Weltbezug und Wirklichkeitsdarstellung* (Munich: Wilhelm Fink, 1974). Although she recognizes the "structural principle of negation in *Jakob von Gunten*" (107–16), in so doing she overlooks exactly these explicit forms of negation that amass in the text.

9. Martin Walser, *Selbstbewußtsein und Ironie: Frankfurter Vorlesungen* (Frankfurt am Main: Suhrkamp, 1981), esp. 115–52.

10. Cf. the entry "Null," in *Meyers großes Konversations-Lexikon*, 6th ed. (Leipzig: Bibliographisches Institut, 1906): "On the other hand division by zero is impermissible. It can only be said that a quotient the divisor of which increasingly and incessantly approaches zero, will eventually exceed all limits."

11. Klaus-Michael Hinz, "Robert Walsers Souveränität," in *"Immer dicht vor dem Sturze . . .": Zum Werk Robert Walsers*, ed. Paolo Chiarini and Hans Dieter Zimmermann (Frankfurt am Main: Athenäum, 1987), 166.

12. Manfred Engel, "Außenwelt und Innenwelt: Subjektivitätsentwurf und moderne Romanpoetik in Robert Walsers *Jakob von Gunten* und Franz Kafkas *Der Verschollene*," *Jahrbuch der deutschen Schillergesellschaft* 30 (1986): 541.

13. Frisch, "Ein Jüngling," 72.

14. Cf. Henri Bloemen, "Durch die 'inneren Gemächer' geführt: Zur Lektüre von Robert Walsers *Jakob von Gunten*," in *Bild-Sprache: Texte zwischen Dichten und Denken*, ed. Luc Lambrechts and Johan Nové (Leuven: Universitaire Pers Leuven, 1990), 51–66.

15. Older secondary literature has argued this on numerous occasions: Nagi Naguib, *Robert Walser: Entwurf einer Bewußtseinsstruktur* (Munich: Wilhelm Fink, 1970), 61; Grenz, *Die Romane Robert Walsers*, 90–91. Likewise Hiebel, "Robert Walsers *Jakob von Gunten*," 249–50. Newer research demonstrates the necessity and possibility for differentiation, for example Urs Heiniger, "Ich

entwickle mich nicht: Das ist ja nun so eine Behauptung. Zur Tagebuchstruktur von 'Jakob von Gunten'" (M.A. thesis, University of Bern, 1996); Monika Lemmel, "Robert Walsers Poetik der Intertextualität," in *Robert Walser und die modern Poetik*, ed. Dieter Borchmeyer (Frankfurt am Main: Suhrkamp, 1999), 83–101.

16. Cf. Peter Utz, *Tanz auf den Rändern: Robert Walsers "Jetztzeitstil"* (Frankfurt am Main: Suhrkamp, 1998), 369–423.

17. Cf. Martin Jürgens, *Robert Walser: Die Krise der Darstellbarkeit*, 2nd ed. (Kronberg: Scriptor Verlag, 1973), 119–20.

18. Translation taken from Samuel Frederick, *Narratives Unsettled: Digression in Robert Walser, Thomas Bernhard, and Adalbert Stifter* (Evanston, Ill.: Northwestern University Press, 2012), 55.

19. Cf. Christoph Bungartz, *Zurückweichend vorwärtsschreiten: Die Ironie in Robert Walsers Berner Prosa* (Bern and Frankfurt am Main: Peter Lang, 1988), 162ff.

20. See Kreienbrock's contribution to this volume for a discussion of Walser's word "Gebirgigmachung."

21. Annette Fuchs, *Dramaturgie des Narrentums: Das Komische in der Prosa Robert Walsers* (Munich: Wilhelm Fink, 1993), 99: "a glossological poetics of marginality."

22. Cf. Dieter Roser, *Fingierte Mündlichkeit und reine Schrift: Zur Sprachproblematik in Robert Walsers späten Texten* (Würzburg: Königshausen & Neumann, 1994).

23. Cf. Utz, *Tanz auf den Rändern*, esp. chap. 9, 295–368.

24. Robert Musil, *Gesammelte Werke*, ed. Adolf Frisé, vol. 8 (Reinbek: Rowohlt, 1978), 1159.

25. Dierk Rodewald, *Robert Walsers Prosa: Versuch einer Strukturanalyse* (Bad Homburg: Gehlen, 1970), 104. Naguib (*Robert Walser*, 84) makes a similar point. Borchmeyer is somewhat more differentiated in his assessment: Walser's critique is aimed at demonstrating the impossibility of realizing the classical educational ideal in present-day society. Borchmeyer, *Dienst und Herrschaft*, 27ff.

26. With his often speculative and arbitrary collection of quotations from both novels, Gößling nevertheless falls well short of his ambitious goal: "If one systematically reconstructs the relationship between both texts there is hardly a 'puzzle' or 'mystery' that remains unsolved in either text." Andreas Gößling, *Abendstern und Zauberstab: Studien und Interpretationen zu Robert Walsers "Der Gehülfe" und "Jakob von Gunten"* (Würzburg: Königshausen & Neumann, 1992), 143.

27. Albert Steffen, "Robert Walser: Große kleine Welt," in Kerr, *Über Robert Walser*, 1:146.

28. Friedrich Schiller, *On the Aesthetic Education of Man in a Series of Letters*, trans. Elizabeth M. Wilkinson and L. A. Willoughby (Oxford: Clarendon, 1982), 145.

29. Schiller, *On the Aesthetic Education of Man*, 151 (translation modified).

30. Carl Spitteler, *Imago*, ed. Werner Stauffacher (Frankfurt am Main: Suhrkamp, 1990), 30.

31. Cf. ibid., 29, 95, 175.

32. Jakob Schaffner, *Hans Himmelhoch. Wanderbriefe an ein Weltkind*, ed. Christof Wamister (Berlin: Fischer, 1909; reprint, Zürich: Chronos, 2005), 70.

33. Anne Gabrisch, "Robert Walser in Berlin," in Hinz and Horst, *Robert Walser*, 30–35, 47–48.

34. Cf. Karlheinz Rossbacher, "Mathematik und Gefühl: Zu Robert Musils 'Die Verwirrungen des Zöglings Törless,'" in *Österreichische Literatur des 20. Jahrhunderts: Französische und österreichische Beiträge*, ed. Sigurd Paul Scheichel and Gerald Stieg (Innsbruck: Institut für Germanistik der Universität Innsbruck, 1986), 127–39.

35. Robert Musil, *The Confusions of Young Törless*, trans. Shaun Whiteside (London: Penguin, 2001), 132.

36. Ibid., 157.

37. Wassily Kandinsky, *On the Spiritual in Art*, trans. Hilla Rebay (New York: Solomon R. Guggenheim Foundation, 1946), 90.

38. Oswald Spengler, *The Decline of the West*, trans. Charles Francis Atkinson (New York: Knopf, 1927), 59.

39. Musil, *Gesammelte Werke*, 8:1048.

40. Robert Musil, "The Mathematical Man," in *Precision and Soul: Essays and Addresses*, ed. and trans. Burton Pike and David S. Luft (Chicago: University of Chicago Press, 1990), 42 (translation modified).

41. Ibid., 43.

42. Musil, "Sketch on What the Writer Knows," in Pike and Luft, *Precision and Soul*, 63.

43. Ibid., 64.

44. Robert Musil, *The Man without Qualities*, trans. Sophie Wilkins, vol. 1 (New York: Knopf, 1996), 36–37, 44.

45. "Zur Geschichte der Null," *Schweizerisches Familien-Wochenblatt*, vol. 45, February 6, 1926.

46. Klaus-Peter Philippi, "Robert Walsers 'Jakob von Gunten,'" in *Provokation und Idylle: Über Robert Walser*, ed. Jochen Greven (Stuttgart: Klett, 1971), 68. Similarly, Engel ("Außenwelt und Innenwelt," 541–42) also emphasizes the illusoriness of the departure at the end of the novel.

47. Peter von Matt, "Die Schwäche des Vaters und das Vergnügen des Sohnes: Voraussetzungen der Fröhlichkeit bei Robert Walser," in Hinz and Horst, *Robert Walser*, 197.

48. Nicole Pelletier, *Franz Kafka et Robert Walser: Étude d'une relation littéraire* (Stuttgart: Heinz, 1985), 122.

49. Martin Walser, *Selbstbewußtsein und Ironie*, 151. Grenz, *Die Romane Robert Walsers*, 158, similarly sees a transition from the "negation" into a "utopian new beginning."

50. Hiebel, "Robert Walsers *Jakob von Gunten*," 257 (emphasis in the original).

51. Arthur Rimbaud, *A Season in Hell and The Drunken Boat*, trans. Louise Varèse (New York: New Directions, 1961), 89. Tamara S. Evans refers to this too: *Robert Walsers Moderne* (Bern: Francke, 1989), 52. Marie-Louise Audiberti, on the other hand, sees "the desert in the sense of sterility" in the reference to Rimbaud. Audiberti, *Le vagabond immobile: Robert Walser* (Paris: Gallimard, 1996), 148.

52. Gabrisch makes this case. Gabrisch, "Robert Walser in Berlin," 47.

53. Friedrich Nietzsche, *Thus Spake Zarathustra: A Book for Everybody and Nobody*, trans. Graham Parkes (Oxford: Oxford University Press, 2005), 267.

54. Friedrich Nietzsche, *Dithyrambs of Dionysus*, trans. R. J. Hollingdale (London: Anvil Press Poetry, 1984), 37.
55. Franz Kafka, *Gesammelte Werke*, 12 vols., ed. Hans-Gerd Koch (Frankfurt am Main: Fischer, 1994), 7:172.
56. Friedrich Glauser, *Gourrama: Ein Roman aus der Fremdenlegion*, ed. Bernhard Echte (Zurich: Limmat, 1997), 290, 379.
57. Ibid., 233ff.
58. Wolfgang Hildesheimer, *Masante*, vol. 2 of *Gesammelte Werke*, ed. Christiaan L. Hart Nibbrig and Volker Jehle (Frankfurt am Main: Suhrkamp, 1991), 189.
59. Ingeborg Bachmann, *"Todesarten"-Projekt*, ed. Robert Pickl, vol. 1 of *Kritische Ausgabe*, ed. Monika Albrecht and Dirk Göttsche (Munich: Piper, 1995), 247.
60. Ibid., 37.
61. Robert Walser, *Berlin Stories*, trans. Susan Bernofsky (New York: NYRB, 2012), 62.
62. William H. Gass and Jürg Laederach, *Über Robert Walser: Zwei Essays* (Salzburg: Residenz, 1997), 20.
63. Roland Barthes, *Writing Degree Zero*, trans. Annette Lavers and Colin Smith (New York: Hill and Wang, 1998), 67. Thomas Horst already makes reference to this in "Robert Walser, Ein Forschungsbericht," in Hinz and Horst, *Robert Walser*, 433.
64. Carl Seelig, *Wanderungen mit Robert Walser* (Frankfurt am Main: Suhrkamp, 1977), 45.

Robert Walser's Sceneries

"Kleist in Thun" and "The Walk"

Bernhard F. Malkmus

A Diminutive Ramble

In one of the most powerful beginnings in the German narrative tradition, Georg Büchner's Lenz, in the eponymous novella, follows an invitation by the pastor Oberlin to convalesce in his parish in the Alsatian mountains: "Den 20. ging Lenz durch's Gebirg. Die Gipfel und hohen Bergflächen im Schnee, die Täler hinunter graues Gestein, grüne Flächen, Felsen und Tannen" (The 20th, Lenz walked through mountains. Snow on the peaks and upper slopes, gray rock down into the valley, swatches of green, boulders, and firs). The mountain faces are damp and cold, the fir trees sag "in the damp air," and the fog is "so sluggish." Everything feels narrow and claustrophobic: "Er ging gleichgültig weiter, es lag ihm nichts am Weg, bald auf- bald abwärts. Müdigkeit spürte er keine, nur war es ihm manchmal unangenehm, daß er nicht auf dem Kopf gehen konnte" (He walked onward, caring little one way or another, to him the path mattered not, now up, now down. He felt no fatigue, except sometimes it annoyed him that he could not walk on his head).[1] Lenz is suffering from a severe spell of schizophrenia during his stay with Oberlin.

In "Kleine Wanderung" ("A Little Ramble," 1914), Robert Walser uses most of the tropes Büchner employs in this sequence, but gently diverts them into something entirely different. Likewise, he modifies the deliberate edge in Lenz's narrated monologue by making the sentences breathe rather than gasp for air. His story is a sequence of finely wrought paratactic units. Its narrator may not have a specific goal, but he comes across as refreshingly determined, which is captured by the slight shift, difficult to render in English, from the verb *gehen* to *laufen* in the introductory sentence: "Ich lief heute durch das Gebirge" (I walked through the mountains today) (*SW*, 4:141; *SS*, 30). The scenery is as "wet" and "gray" as Büchner's Alsace, but Walser's narrator couldn't care less: he even takes off his coat and—with a nod to the medieval iconographic tradition of expressing an inner state of mind through the depiction of drapery—neatly folds it together. There is nothing compulsive about him. Somebody is at peace with himself and the world here, and that peace is nourished by his wanderlust.

Walser parodies Lenz's mood swings, as rendered by Büchner, not by mocking them but by taking them seriously and retuning them against the backdrop of a scenery that facilitates rather than obstructs encounters among humans. He thus translates the etiology of Lenz's disease into an ambulatory prose that eschews the pitfalls of self-absorption and engages with the narrator's surroundings. The most powerful part of Walser's parody is his conversion of Lenz's symptoms into a rhythm of joy that reinforces itself: "Das Laufen auf der wundervollen Straße bereitete mir mehr und immer mehr Vergnügen, bald ging es *aufwärts* und bald stürzte es wieder *nieder*. Die Berge waren groß, sie schienen sich zu *drehen*" (The walk on the wonderful road gave me more and ever more pleasure; first it *went up* and then *descended* again. The mountains were huge, they seemed to *go around*) (*SW*, 4:141; *SS*, 30; emphasis added). Lenz's discontent with not being able to walk on his head is translated into the trope of mountains going around (as Tom Whalen's translation suggests) or, more accurately, revolving like a theater scenery; and indeed that is the impression corroborated in the following sentence: "Die ganze Gebirgswelt erschien mir wie ein gewaltiges Theater" (The whole mountainous world appeared to me like a huge spectacle) (ibid.; translation modified). In conversation with Lenz's narrated monologue in Büchner, Walser here takes issue with the narcissistic projection of individual desires onto nature and landscapes. As Hermann Kinder points out, the spectacle trope in Walser is an implied critique of the "eternal poetic youth" as a cultural icon in classical German-language culture. After all, "A Little Ramble" is a poetic antidote to what, according to Hermann Kinder, Walser regarded as dangerous literary predecessors: Lenz, Kleist, and Büchner "have paid with their lives for their refusal to grow up, for their desire to turn everything upside down. For Walser, they are fascinating colleagues but no role models."[2] The theater trope is clearly more than a clever *mise en abyme*.

Walking or rambling about as an antidote to the temptation of projecting oneself into landscape is a consistent topic throughout Walser's work. The literary rendition and recomposition of a landscape is also an—albeit refracted—encounter with a given natural environment and social milieu, even if the failure of this encounter is foregrounded. Thus the spinning mountains in "A Little Ramble," for example, certainly do mock the use of the Alpine scenery as spectacle; at the same time, however, the narrator emphasizes that the mountains only "seemed" to revolve. This sensory insecurity can be read as a parody of Kant's notion of the sublime and its privileging of the human faculty of conceptual thinking. Walser's carefree wanderer is blissfully unaware of the fact that he is surrounded by a scenery predestined, according to Kant, to instill a sense of superiority of the mind over the terrifying or awe-inspiring aspects of nature in him.[3] This (second) parodistic subtext is underscored in the final sentence: "Man braucht nicht viel Besonderes zu sehen. Man sieht so schon viel" (We don't need to see anything out of the ordinary. We already see so much) (*SW*, 4:142; *SS*, 31).

The visual sense, and sensory impressions in general, in Walser are about reconnecting with concrete experience rather than establishing abstract mental concepts. The last third of "A Little Ramble" deals with the narrator's joyful encounter with a young traveling apprentice who asks him about the whereabouts of two others, who "pass by with music" a little later—a convivial encounter reminiscent of Eichendorff's wanderers. Unlike Büchner's Lenz, the narrator does not seek to escape society in nature, and unlike Kleist in Walser's "Kleist in Thun," which will be discussed in the following section, he resists the temptation to use landscape as a mere projection screen for unquenchable desires. In this communicative openness, "A Little Ramble" dramatizes a close relation between the *Stimmung* of the perceiving subject (in English, "attunement," in the sense of *mood*) and the *Stimmung* of the perceived landscape (in English, "attunement," in the sense of *atmosphere*) and thus offers a playful exposition of the role of *Stimmung* in Walser's work on landscape. Otto Friedrich Bollnow introduces the term "being-attuned" (*Durchstimmtsein*) to capture the connection between the two concepts: "It is common to speak as often of the mood of the human mind as of the atmosphere of a landscape or a closed interior room—and both are, strictly speaking, only two aspects of one single homogeneous being-attuned."[4] Moments of being-attuned perforate Walser's work as moments in which experience and creativity mutually reinforce each other. In these moments, landscape emerges as both a *representational* medium and a *non-representational* set of cultural pratices that resist the total submersion into representation by participating, instead, in place-making: "Ein Dorf war besonders schön mit niedrigen Häusern dicht unter den weißen Felswänden" (A village was especially beautiful with humble dwellings set thickly under the white cliffs) (*SW*, 4:142; *SS*, 30).

This essay aims to show that scenery does not only serve as a "catalyst" of Walser's sauntering prose, as Avery remarks,[5] but also dramatizes the spatial ambiguity of the walk between scenery as "landscape" and scenery as "theater stage." This homonymy captures the deliberate dissolution of a clear boundary between a staged inner realm and a perceived outer realm. In many of Walser's texts, this ambiguity also affects the histrionics of the narrator. His poetic language traces in the physical and cultural contours of specific environs how the creative act is embedded in a dynamic between the loss and retrieval of the self. In narrating this dynamic between loss and retrieval, Walser turns *space as such* into a specific experiential *place*.

In two close readings, I will show that Walser's poetic self-reflection is not, as often suggested, simply a regurgitation of the turn-of-the-century lament about a crisis of language, but rather a decisive move beyond it.[6] "Kleist in Thun" uses the amalgamated literary figures of Lenz and Kleist to refer to a poetic self-understanding that, by insisting on the representability of concepts, harbors a potentially pathological narcissism. The narrator of this story struggles to free himself from the figure of Kleist and his legacy of compulsive identification with visual sceneries and their inherent atmospheres. This narrative struggle blurs the boundary between landscape and stage scenery, making possible alternative, nonvisual modes of relating to environs and landscape. In spite of these emancipatory efforts, however, the narrator keeps on resorting to stereotypical images of tourism brochures and the tragic trajectory of the historical Kleist. Scenery is dramatized as an ambiguous medium, vacillating between subjective affect and objective backdrop: it is both an entity one *experiences* and a composition one *creates*. "Der Spaziergang" ("The Walk") continues this discussion and offers a fully fledged narrative counter-concept to that dramaturgy of scenery. Here, Walser focuses on the tension between petrified images of scenery, or "the scenic," and the emergence of a sense of space defined by the movements that traverse it. This tension in "The Walk" is most visible in specific gestures that break open the architecture of the prose on two levels. One, the narrative is interrupted by a polysemous nonverbal expressivity that does not adhere to the conventional symbolic order of language. Two, that very expressivity is, at the same time, deprived of its potential dramatic agency, becoming instead a synesthetic enactment of physicality. Walser's walk is not only an extended metaphor for writing and poetic self-reflection; it is also—in anthropological terms—a phenomenological meditation on "the unfettered language of elementary being no longer restrained," as Max Kommerell remarks with reference to Kleist.[7]

Nonscenic Sceneries: "Kleist in Thun"

Walser's early story "Kleist in Thun" (1907) is an attempt to come to grips with a literary and psychological legacy related to the Storm and Stress movement and a romanticized ideal of poetic youth. It also manifests a profound crisis borne of equating landscape and freedom mythopoetically—be it in a political (Friedrich Schiller), social (Albrecht von Haller, Salomon Gessner), or pedagogical (Jean-Jacques Rousseau) sense. Walser engages with this distinctly modern discourse, yet pays particular attention to literary reflections that shed a precarious light on this equation, such as in Jean Paul, Georg Büchner, and Wilhelm Müller (famously set to music by Franz Schubert).[8] By hearkening back to early Enlightenment landscape escapism and its inflection throughout the nineteenth century, Walser also casts an ironic light on the habituated bourgeois forms of landscape appreciation during his lifetime. Examples include spa culture, mountain and seaside tourism, and—with a different sociopolitical index—the *Wandervogel* movement. The Alpine idyll had by this time already become a marketable asset. Its mass reproduction had changed how landscape was perceived, as Walser dramatizes in "Gebirgshallen" ("Mountain Halls"), along with how the Helvetian "ideology of integration" was visually expressed.[9] This section of the essay, accordingly, reads "Kleist in Thun" as an extended reflection on the complex relations between human imagination (and its emotional self-affection), on the one hand, and how it is embedded in cultural landscapes (and their representations), on the other. This reading provides an analysis of Walser's nonmimetic writing technique and his critique of visual representation through gestures. Gesture, as Giorgio Agamben remarks with reference to Kommerell, also does not function here as "an absolutely nonlinguistic element but, rather, something closely tied to language. It is first of all a forceful presence in language itself, one that is older and more originary than conceptual expression."[10] It is through Walser's narrative focus on the relation between the human body and that kind of linguistic gesture, or *Sprachgebärde*, that he deals with the complexities of connecting experience to creativity, and vice versa.

Walser's story is based on an episode in the life of Heinrich von Kleist.[11] In 1802, the troubled and promising dramatist, then twenty-four years old, moved to the small idyllic island Delosea in the effluent of Lake Thun into the Aare River. He lived there for several months, trying to get away from the cities of Berlin and Paris and to recalibrate his life by becoming an Alpine farmer. For the historical details, the dramatization of Kleist's language crisis and writer's block, as well as for a certain anecdotal flavor, Walser relied on the writer's letters to his sister Ulrike and others. With a mixture of empathy and distance, Walser's narrator leads the reader through the extreme amplitudes of Kleist's inner life during his spring and summer near Thun. The structure of the piece is defined by the expansions and contractions of Kleist's mind. Images of lushness and growth alternate with images of dearth and paralysis. The narrator is not immune to these mood swings, which leave their traces in the rhythm of the prose and the narrative perspective. The first paragraph is marked by a flippant lightness of tone that suggests the narrator is taking certain poetic licenses. He conjectures, for example, using a leisurely modal form of the future tense: "Darauf wird jemand die Treppen des Hauses herunterzueidechseln gekommen sein, um zu sehn, wer da sei" (Then somebody, say, came to lizard down the stairs inside, to see who was there) (*SW*, 2:70; *SS*, 17).[12] Increasingly, however, the narrator yields diegetic sovereignty to the narratee's mind, limiting his perspective to Kleist: "Es ist zum Verrücktwerden warm an der Sonne" (In the heat of the sun you could go mad) (ibid.), he remarks, and moves on by comparing the mountain scenery to a theater scenery. Kleist's agitation triggered by images of his mother and home spills over into the rhythmic flow of the narrator's prose, culminating in a snippet of stream of consciousness: "Man möchte Klötze nehmen und damit um sich heraumhauen. Weg da, weg" (One would like to seize a sledgehammer and beat a way out of it all. Get away there, get away!) (*SW*, 2:73; *SS*, 20). In the course of the final third of "Kleist in Thun" the narrator regains some of his original distance, yet refrains from marking it with the modes of narrative conjecture or playful empathy he used previously. He begins to accept that

Kleist's mental amplitudes are the symptoms of a disease rather than the side effects of poetic maturity.

The narrator's realization that Kleist wants "Unfaßliches, Unbegreifliches" (the intangible, the incomprehensible) is the turning point of the piece: Kleist is unable to grasp what is within reach because it is always already affected by his narcissistic imagination. A profound yearning for death is a direct corollary of this inability: "Er möchte in das Bild hineinsterben" (He wants to perish into the image) (*SW*, 2:77; *SS*, 22). Accordingly, as Jens Tismar emphasizes, "the attempt to render and mold an original impression of nature" is unmasked, in hindsight, as "a collective method of transfiguration."[13] In the end, the narrator reaffirms his position as an observer, commenting on the fact that Kleist's soul has been eaten away, while, at the same time, celebrating an Alpine idyll that is marked by bourgeois industriousness (*SW*, 2:81; *SS*, 25). As early as in the 1770s Jean-Jacques Rousseau had aptly described this idyll as a curious and unique "mixture of wild nature and human industry": "The whole of Switzerland is, as it were, but one big city, whose wide long streets [. . .] are planted with forests and cut across by mountains, and whose scattered and isolated houses are only connected with one another by English landscape gardens."[14]

In psychological terms, Walser's Kleist bears at least as much resemblance to Büchner's Lenz as to the historical Kleist.[15] Walser emphasizes the regressive tendencies in Kleist's personality along with the implosion of the utopian or idyllic landscape evoked by Alpine kitsch at a time of rapid urbanization. "Kleist in Thun" frustrates and deconstructs the tradition of the idyllic, utopian, and melancholic escape into the countryside but, in doing so, "defends ex negativo the experience of landscape as a compensatory form of occasional self-regulation."[16] In other words, Walser seeks to rescue landscape from the excessive visualization that comes with its touristic use and nationalistic propagation.[17]

It is true that "Kleist in Thun" was first published in the theater magazine *Schaubühne* and that it describes the Bernese mountains as an inaccessible gate to paradise, resembling the artifice of a painted scene or the sketch of a dilettante (*SW*, 2:71–72; *SS*, 18). Yet Walser erodes the calcified images of the Swiss mountains not only in order to critique the way in which they are instrumentalized; he also erodes them in order to reenvisage a lacuna underneath the visually arrested landscape clichés, a lacuna that with creative effort still makes possible authentic experience. Laying bare representational fallacies in conventional idylls becomes for Walser a form of wresting the things of nature and the experience of landscape from the limitations of visual perception. As Peter Utz observes, in Walser the "relation between subject and landscape is marked by mutual agency rather than petrifying anthropomorphism."[18]

One of the most striking aspects of Kleist's trajectory in Walser's story is the gradual loss of bodily orientation: "Er wünscht sich eine Stimme herbei, was für eine? Eine Hand, nun, und? Einen Körper, aber wozu?" (He wishes there was a voice beside him; what sort of voice? A hand; well, and? A body? But what for?) (*SW*, 2:71; *SS*, 18). A dual loss is rendered here: Kleist's loss of his lived body (which is why Kommerell aptly defines Kleist's heroes as "sentenced to be themselves")[19] and the related loss of a spatial orientation that would allow him to transform a sense of space into a sense of place. Kleist thus does not only represent an epistemological crisis (the historical Kleist's Kant crisis) and a language crisis (the writer's block of Walser's Kleist), but also a crisis of what Edward Casey terms the "panrepresentationalism" of the modern Western worldview. The "most immediate effect" of this panrepresentationalism is

> the subsumption of every sensible appearance (indeed, all appearances, including those belonging to states of mind) under a representation whose status is unremittingly mental. For any appearance whatsoever to be apprehended it must assume the format of a representation ("idea," "apperception," *Vorstellung*, etc.), and the sum total of representations is considered to make up Mind itself.[20]

Walser's Kleist text translates this panrepresentationalism into the concrete symptoms of narcissism. Kleist's compulsion to convert all appearances into predominantly visual representations, as rendered by Walser's unique narrative perspective, is one of these symptoms; his concurrently lost sense of bodily existence, another. Casey draws on Edmund Husserl's phenomenology as one of the most important critical responses to this aspect of modernity and its perpetual crisis. According to Husserl, thinking about place always implies thinking about the human body. As Casey explains:

> Although in one respect this body is merely one more physical thing (*Körper*), in another respect (as a *Leib*, a lived body), it is something extraordinary: "the bearer of the I" and the locus of sensations felt by this I. It is also extraordinary insofar as it is always experienced as "here" wherever and whenever I move.[21]

Walser's Kleist has lost vital elements of this basic experience of place. His physical body, or *Körper*, is dissociated from his lived body, or *Leib*; he experiences himself "there" rather than "here." Bereft of this basic orientation through one's body, movement, and lifeworld, Kleist is suspended between *space* and *representation* and unable to establish a sense of *place*.

This suspension between unstructured space and a compulsion to conceptualize one's being in space accounts for the jolting nature of movement in "Kleist in Thun." Walser's Kleist is trapped in sceneries without being able either to move through them or to structure them into an enriched experience:

> An Regentagen ist es entsetzlich kalt und leer. Die Gegend fröstelt ihn an. Die grünen Sträucher winseln und wimmern und regentröpfeln nach Sonnenschein. Schmutzige, ungeheuerliche Wolken gleiten den Köpfen der Berge wie große, freche, tötende Hände um die Stirnen. Das Land scheint sich vor dem Wetter verkriechen zu wollen, es will zusammenschrumpfen. (*SW*, 2:73)

> On rainy days it is terribly cold and void. The place shivers at him. The green shrubs whine and whimper and shed rain tears for some sun. Over the heads of the mountains drift monstrous dirty clouds like great impudent murderous hands over foreheads. The country-side seems to want to creep away and hide from this evil weather, to shrivel up. (*SS*, 19)

By contrast, during his sunnier moods (*SW*, 2:76–78; *SS*, 22–23), Kleist is lost in a purely panoramic perception of space and thus also dramatizes the crisis of this visual domination of space and landscape in a way that has often been associated with the late eighteenth century. In Western modernity, both paradigms—the equation of freedom and mobility, on the one hand, and the panrepresentationalism of the surveyed landscape, on the other—are inextricably intertwined. Landscape turns into a central manifestation of the internal contradictions of modernity. Walser's Kleist epitomizes some of the potential conflicts arising from this paradigmatic transformation. Rather than navigating a lived space in which experience and creativity could reinforce each other, he finds himself defenselessly exposed to the spectacle of sceneries—a spectacle he fuels by his own imagination, yet cannot turn into an inhabitable place. His sceneries are defined by rapid mood swings rather than by *Stimmung* in Bollnow's sense of "being-attuned," as dramatized in "A Little Ramble."

Walser's landscapes break with the mimetic paradigm on several levels. He turns his sceneries into scenes of sensory and bodily reflection in three distinct ways: (1) his landscapes often offer phenomenological explorations of place-making, its difficulties, and its failures; (2) in toying with and mocking the limitations of the visual rendition of *landscape*—a term that originally derives from painting—Walser draws attention to its spatial and multisensorial dimensions; and (3) underneath Walser's visual rendition of landscape there always lurks its ready-made, instrumentalized, or commodified picture postcard that jeopardizes any emphatic notion of individual experience. Even Walser's most elaborate reflections on space and place are prone to collapsing into a flat postcard reproduction at any moment. Although his landscapes may always turn out to be theater scenes and props, the play he enacts, more often than not, seeks to explore our embeddedness in space and our reliance on place.

Nondramatic Gestures: "The Walk"

One cannot talk about Walser's sceneries without talking about Walser's histrionics of walking. As Casey reminds us, "In walking, [. . .] we encounter places as much as we enliven them. The result is a place-world that is the correlate of the ambulatory body—a world constituted by the very same body that depends on it for its own ongoing localization."[22] "The Walk" (1917) is the affirmation of a poetics beyond the one Walser associates with the self-affection of the eternally young poets. It dramatizes Walser's counterpoetics: a poetics that relates bodily movement to poetic rhythm and vice versa; a poetics that enacts the conversion and translation of space into place; and a poetics that is inextricably intertwined with a kind of movement whose very momentum is its aimlessness. This section continues the phenomenological inquiry into Walser's art of perception by analyzing the relation between walking and writing within the broader context of his aesthetics of space and place. It then elaborates on the choreography of the body through the walking-writing interface and explores the role of gestures in "The Walk" as a form of breaking open dramatic narrative structures and their conditioning forces. I argue that through these aesthetic moves Walser reclaims scenery as a medium of reflection on human creatureliness and as a medium of a spatial reorientation beyond the visual landscape paradigm.

Landscape here is not a predesigned backdrop in front of which the walker promenades, but rather a space that first emerges with the rambling movement of the narrator. Walser's dramaturgy and style draw attention to the fact that (1) the experience of oneself and fellow humans cannot be separated from the experience of place; and that (2) place is neither simply given nor stable, but needs to be uncovered again and again. "Kleist in Thun" dramatizes the dislocation of humans between space and its scenic representation; "The Walk," by contrast, focuses on the coemergence of place and scenery in the related acts of writing and walking.

Accordingly, the connection between walking and writing is underscored throughout "The Walk":

> Spazieren [. . .] muß ich unbedingt, um mich zu beleben und um die Verbindung mit der lebendigen Welt aufrechtzuerhalten, ohne deren Empfinden ich keinen halben Buchstaben mehr schreiben und nicht das leiseste Gedicht in Vers oder Prosa mehr hervorbringen könnte. (*SW*, 5:50)

> Walk [. . .] I definitely must, to invigorate myself and to maintain contact with the living world, without perceiving which I could not write the half of one more single word, or produce the tiniest poem in verse or prose. (*SS*, 85)[23]

In the ensuing sequence, the narrator carefully disentangles the boundary between perceiving subject and perceived object, creation and createdness, the structure of things (noemata) and acts of recognition (noema). In his phenomenology of the human body, Maurice Merleau-Ponty locates the creation of meaning in the bodily attunement to the world. Walser, it seems to me, is concerned with a similar notion of sensual perception and cognition when his narrator dramatizes the emergence of correspondences between "lebendigen Gedichten" (living poems) and "Naturschönheiten" (natural beauties) through walking (ibid.). Mapping natural histories onto cultural histories ("Naturkunde und Landeskunde") (*SW*, 5:51),[24] the narrator stresses the methodical nature of his inquiry and the importance of close attention for an aesthetics of walking-writing:

> Ohne Spazieren und damit verbundene Naturanschauung, ohne diese ebenso liebliche wie ermahnungsreiche Erkundigung fühle ich mich wie verloren und bin es auch. Höchst liebevoll und aufmerksam muß der, der spaziert, jedes kleinste lebendige Ding, sei es ein Kind, ein Hund, eine Mücke, ein Schmetterling, ein Spatz, ein Wurm, eine Blume, ein Mann, ein Haus, ein Baum, eine Hecke, eine Schnecke, eine Maus, eine Wolke, ein Berg, ein Blatt oder auch nur ein armes weggeworfenes Fetzchen Schreibpapier, auf das vielleicht ein liebes gutes Schulkind seine ersten ungefügen Buchstaben geschrieben hat, studieren und betrachten. (*SW*, 5:51)

> Without walking and the contemplation of nature which is connected with it, without this equally delicious and admonishing search, I deem myself lost, and I am lost. With the utmost love and attention the man who walks must study and observe every smallest living thing, be it a child, a dog, a fly, a butterfly, a sparrow, a worm, a flower, a man, a house, a tree, a hedge, a snail, a mouse, a cloud, a hill, a leaf, or no more than a poor discarded scrap of paper on which, perhaps, a dear good child at school has written his first clumsy letters. (*SS*, 86)

Referring to early Enlightenment aesthetics, Walser here dramatizes the walk as an exercise in paying attention to things, in learning to see and to write like a "child at school" again. This invites a wide range of possible readings and I would like to single one of them out by returning to Merleau-Ponty. In his late work *The Visible and the Invisible*, Merleau-Ponty is concerned with a dual reversibility in human life, a reversibility which is characteristically obscured by the obsession with visual control in modernity. He reminds us that, while humans see themselves in a privileged perspective as observers, they are, in fact, constantly being seen and observed by other creatures. Furthermore, he draws attention to the reversibility between touching and being touched—the correspondence between the touching body part and the tangible organism or matter—and he stresses that one's "own movements" inadvertently "incorporate themselves into the universe they interrogate."[25] Consequently, the perceived world cannot be taken at face value, since it is hybridized with idealizations and abstractions. The awareness of the reversibility of touching and being touched is also a way of "retriev[ing] indirectly and in a negative way the perceived world that anterior idealizations had made us forget."[26] Walser is invested in this pursuit: his ambulatory prose seeks to retrieve a preconscious synaesthetic relatedness to the world, and it does so by methodically eroding the "idealizations" of compartmentalized sensual perception and conceptual abstraction. He contemplates the impulse of life in even the "smallest living thing" by reconnecting with the sensory intuitions of childhood in what Eckhard Lobsien has called the "phänomenologische Entselbstverständlichung" (phenomenonological making-non-self-evident) of landscape.[27] As Jörg Kreienbrock emphasizes, "The landscape in which [Walser's] walker moves as well as the associations connected with it are brought to him; they move—like children—towards him and carry him away. It is a mode of coming and going, in which noticing [*Aufhorchen*] and obeying [*Gehorchen*] are inextricably intertwined."[28]

In the light of these reflections, I would like to argue that "The Walk" modifies conventional perceptions of inside vs. outside on three levels: (1) it seeks to facilitate a synaesthetic, multisensory literary rendition of reality that precedes the adult division of labor among the senses and the subsequent privileging of the visual sense; (2) it defines the transformation of space into place by our ability to reverse perspectives (for which Merleau-Ponty uses the term "chiasm"), which makes possible a conceptualization of space that is also influenced by how we are seen and touched by agents in our environment; and (3) it demonstrates that this chiasm, or reversibility, does not—as Merleau-Ponty stresses—lead to a convergence or merging of inner and outer spheres, but constitutes a kind of "gap" or "wound" (*écart*), and that to acknowledge our embeddedness in relationships of mutual dependence also implies acknowledging systemic difference and differentiation as intrinsic to our embodied situation.[29]

"The Walk" opens up the world in unexpected ways, dramatizing these three aspects (synaesthesia, reversibility, nonidentity) in subtle shifts of agency and perspective in the choreography of walking. As in "A Little Ramble," the moment of interaction or exchange—the "fraternization" with things and "appearances"—takes center stage. The walker "heißt [. . .] alle sonderbaren, eigentümlichen Erscheinungen willkommen, befreundet und verbrüdert sich mit ihnen, weil sie ihn entzücken, macht sie zu gestaltenhaften, wesenreichen Körpern, gibt ihnen Seele, wie sie ihrerseits auch ihn beseelen und bilden" (welcomes all curious and peculiar phenomena, becomes their friend and brother, because they delight him; he makes them into formed and substantial bodies, gives them structure and soul just as they for their part instruct and inspire him) (*SW*, 5:54; *SS*, 88). The context of this sequence is humorous: in a conversation with a tax officer, the narrator displays all the poetic registers at his disposal in order to substantiate his claim that he qualifies for the lowest tax bracket. This does not, however, invert or subvert the poetic manifesto character of the plea. Rather, Walser's technique of ironically decomposing the sedimented imagery of cultural discourses "unleashes" the aesthetic potential of their components.[30] Even though the rhetoric serves a specific pragmatic purpose, this passage exemplifies the reversibility of perspectives that, according to Merleau-Ponty forms an important aspect of place-making. In Walser, however, this place-making is never exclusively affirmative and is always grounded in irony.

Braced by this reflection on reversibility, the narrator is now able to cross the railroad tracks, the threshold that he describes as the peak of the entire walk and story. The ensuing cascades of ready-made tropes and evocative kitsch can be read as narrative self-irony analogous to the panoramic register in "Kleist in Thun"; equally, however, they can be read as a gesture of self-emptying that ushers in a childlike opening and attention. Acoustic and visual impressions are interconnected in mock extended metaphors (later extended by haptic sensory impressions such as kissing and comforting), thus evoking a synaesthetic experience: "Wie ein bezauberndes, Tränen heraufbeschwörendes Abschiedslied lag das zarte Land mit seinen lieben, bescheidenen Wiesen, Gärten und Häusern da" (Like a song at departure that brings tears to your eyes, the gentle countryside lay there with its dear humble fields, gardens, and houses) (*SW*, 5:55; *SS*, 89). The standardized overcharged epithets both celebrate a synaesthetic relation to the world and ironize it as always already potentially sentimental: "Alles Gegenständliche schien sich in eine Seele und in eine Zärtlichkeit verwandelt zu haben" (All that was solid seemed to be transfigured into soul and into gentleness) (*SW*, 5:56; *SS*, 89). While these images and tropes engage the register of excessive kitsch, they also seem to deliberately undercut the literary attempt to harness emotions and the modernist disregard for the sentimental. Thus, extreme kitsch is juxtaposed with the sober and exuberant manifestation of the narrator's sense of fulfillment in the moment—an experience of mystical *nunc stans*: "Ich glühte und blühte selber im glühenden, blühenden Augenblick" (I glowed and flowered myself in the glowing, flowering present) (*SW*, 5:56; *SS*, 90). Both kitsch and mystical union are modes of breaking down the subject/object divide, yet the reversibility of perspectives between human and nonhuman agents in the design of environs and sceneries, as Merleau-Ponty reminds us, is always marked by a gap or wound: the acknowledgement that reversibility is not tantamount to identity. Even though "good" and "great" things emerge from the narrator's environment, the horizons do not merge: "Ich phantasierte mitten in der schönen Gegend von nichts anderem als nur eben von ihr" (In the midst of this beautiful place I dreamed of nothing but this place itself) (ibid.).

Despite his linguistic playfulness, Walser's language moves beyond the dramatic and manifests itself in poetic self-referentiality and, most importantly, gestures. Not only does Walser play with the ambiguity of scene and scenery, he also offers a narrative metacommentary on dramatic art. One of the implications of his shift from drama to scene, from narrative to situation, from fable to tableau involves a significant change in the role of the human body. This change draws particular attention to the ambiguity of human bodily existence as suspended between "the body I am" (*Leib*) and "the body I have" (*Körper*), as adumbrated above. The human body develops a story, parallel to the diegesis, about the agony of the *Leib-Körper*. It thus resists the total absorption of its manifestations into the logic of a predesigned script, plot, or drama. Accordingly, scenic actions—in particular walking—do not realize a dramatic script; they point toward a physical potentiality that resists subjection to meaning and thus take on the beauty of a purposeless gesture. In other words, while the "body I *have*" (*Körper*) is being used for representational purposes and narrative focus (agon), it is also granted resilience as the "body I *am*" (*Leib*), which strays from the agon and, instead, either suffers agony or revels in joy. It is this kind of resilience that, in many scenes in "The Walk," manifests itself in the form of polyvalent gestures.

An illustrative example can be found during the early part of the walk, where the narrator takes the reader by the hand:

> Indem du dir, lieber, gewogener Leser, die Mühe nimmst, sorgfältig mit dem Schreiber und Erfinder dieser Zeilen vorwärts in die helle, freundliche Morgenwelt hinauszumarschieren, nicht eilig, sondern vielmehr ganz behaglich, sachlich, glatt, bedächtig und ruhig, gelangen wir beide vor die bereits vorgemerkte Bäckerei mit Goldinschrift, wo wir uns bewogen fühlen, entsetzt stehenzubleiben, um auf betrübliche Weise über gröbliche Protzerei und über damit aufs engste verbundene traurige Verunstaltung des lieblichen Ländlichkeitsbildes zu staunen. (*SW*, 5:15–16)

> Since, dear kind reader, you give yourself the trouble to march attentively along with the writer and inventor of these lines, out forthwith into the bright and friendly morning world, not hurrying, but rather quite at ease, with level head, smoothly, discreetly, and calmly, now we both arrive in front of the above-mentioned bakery with the golden inscription, where we feel inclined to stop, horrified, to stand mournfully aghast at the gross ostentation and at the sad disfigurement of sweet rusticity which is intimately connected with it. (*SS*, 60)

I would like to draw attention to the two oxymoronic gestures in this passage. By combining the verb *hinausmarschieren* (to march out into) with five adverbs that do not match its semantic agency the narrator molds external ("morning world") and internal (the goal orientation of marching) agencies into one gestalt.[31] Equivocating the adverbial and adjectival attributions of perceived objects, which often adopt qualities of the subject's perception, is a common technique in Walser that can be observed as early as in the poem "Ein Landschäftchen" ("A Little Landscape").[32] The ensuing gesture of "to stop, horrified" (*entsetzt*), indicating a sudden reaction to an unexpected incident, is prepared for by "feel inclined to" (*bewogen*)—a somewhat ornate rhetorical way of suggesting a high degree of deliberation. Matching an *entsetzt*—literally, deranged or ecstatic—form of suddenness with ponderous deliberation in the same movement makes this a pure gesture that achieves two things at the same time: (1) it underscores that the implied critique of the total commodification of landscape is both a bodily *and* an intellectual reaction; and more importantly, in our context, (2) it does not exhaust itself as gesture, but rather retains a degree of unexplorable self-containment and expressive resilience.[33] The gesture of the unspeakable thus both continues (in the sense of an agon) and disrupts (in the sense of agony) the narrative. It seems to support the content while, in fact, putting its narrative coherence to the test.

The way Walser strips his text of narrative dramaturgy and reduces it to a repetitive minimum of narrative coherence foregrounds gesture as a meditation on the human body (*Leib*) and as a principal medium of spatial experience (rather than as a tool used by the mind, i.e., *Körper*). Vagrancy and sauntering are forms of relating to this dimension of the human body. Walser's gestures draw attention to the fact that landscape is "not a totality" one "can look *at*, it is rather the world *in* which we stand in taking up a point of view on our surroundings."[34] In his dramatization of sceneries, Walser thus breaks with the two most prominent and influential conceptualizations of space in modernity. He undermines the traditional position of the distant beholder dominating a panoramic view, which emerges in the eighteenth century, as well as the notion of an objectively measurable geometrical space. Both modes of relating to space suggest a position outside space and define landscape as a composition imposed onto space itself.

In this regard, Walser's "The Walk" shares an affinity with Georg Simmel's contemporaneous "Philosophy of Landscape" from 1913. The ability to attune and relate to the *Stimmung* of a particular landscape, Simmel argues, is "the intertwining of something given with our creative capacities." It is a moment when we as beholders are exposed to the fact that we are subject to our surroundings and, at the same time, experience ourselves as creators or shapers of the land—both by composing it into a land and by understanding that we are still part of the cultural praxes that shaped the land. As Simmel writes: "Thus, both the unifying move which brings landscape as such into being, and the mood that a landscape projects at us and through which we comprehend it, are merely the result of a subsequent dismantling of one and the same psychic act."[35] The perception of environments as landscape, according to Simmel, can neither be separated from one's reflection on belonging to a specific environment nor from how that belonging forms a gestalt with the beholder. What is more, Walser shows that the experience of landscape is increasingly precarious and rare under the conditions of modernity. The equally fragile and resilient gestures of "The Walk" show a lived and inhabited space that corresponds with the sensual and bodily interactions of its inhabitants.

This space is defined by the body's ability to navigate and orient itself through sensual engagement, *Stimmung*, and interaction among the inhabitants. Accordingly, cultural landscape can be conceptualized as the realm in which these dimensions overlap and interact. If they do not, there is always the danger that scenery may tilt into a theater scene. The gestalt psychologist Kurt Lewin has termed this realm of overlapping dimensions "hodological space." Gestalt psychology is interested in the totality of perception humans experience in a given moment, before this perception is compartmentalized into separate units. Lewin emphasizes the fact that this totality is defined by functional relations rather than essences. Accordingly, space interests him primarily as a fulcrum of experiencing both a total perception and the constitution of that perception through functional relations. Space thus is always already lived space, and landscape for him only exists as a dynamic field, never a static composition. Lewin's concept of hodological space designates this dynamic field; it is a space defined not as a container but as a field that emerges through its activations by the movement of traversing it.[36] Walser's sceneries dramatize a quintessentially modern conflict between landscape as hodological space and landscape as purely aesthetic experience. For landscape, as Merleau-Ponty reminds us forcefully, is not the object, but rather part of the "human world" and thus "the homeland of our thoughts."[37]

Much ink has been spilled on "The Walk" as a poetic reflection or even manifesto, in which the actual walk is ancillary to its function as a metaphor for writing; in which movement in landscape is only of interest as a reflection of the movement of a quill across a white sheet of paper; and in which the inextricable duality of scenery as both landscape and theater backdrop is inadvertently read as poetic and semiotic self-referentiality. While this notion of walking as writing certainly constitutes an important dimension, one should be cautious in reducing Walser to a constructivist exercise—one of the pitfalls of the resurgent interest in Walser throughout the 1990s and beyond. Alternatively, a phenomenological reading of Walser unearths a poetic resistance to the panrepresentationalism that undergirds the excursions of his narrators and protagonists. In Walser, our being lost in representations can be rendered manifest in literature and—in the act of writing—be temporarily overcome.

The Automobile Landscape

The fiercest enemy of Walser's walking and writing *Leib-Körper* is the automobile. Looking at playing children, the narrator of "The Walk" muses:

> Wehe dahersausenden Automobilen, die kalt und bös in das Kinderspiel, in den kindlichen Himmel hineinfahren, daß kleine unschuldige menschliche Wesen in Gefahr kommen, zermalmt zu werden. [. . .] Ich schaue da stets finster auf die Räder, aufs Ganze und nie auf die Insassen, welche ich verachte und zwar keineswegs persönlich, sondern rein grundsätzlich; denn ich begreife nicht und werde niemals begreifen, daß es ein Vergnügen sein kann, so an allen Gebilden, Gegenständen, die unsere schöne Erde aufweist, vorüberzurasen, als wenn man toll geworden sei und rennen müsse, um nicht elend zu verzweifeln. (*SW*, 5:20)

> Woe to the automobiles blustering by, as they ride coldly and maliciously into the children's games, into the child's heaven, so that small innocent human beings are in danger of being crushed to a pulp. [. . .] I always then look darkly at the wheels, at the car as a whole, but never at its occupants, whom I despise, and this in no way personally, but purely on principle; for I do not understand, and I never shall understand, how it can be a pleasure to hurtle past all the images and objects which our beautiful earth displays, as if one had gone mad and had to accelerate for fear of misery and despair. (*SS*, 63–64)

Walser's cars are not only monsters whose kinetic energy threatens to kill small children; they also jeopardize the fine kinesthetic balance of the text. The car, for Walser, is not just the epitome of urbanization, industrialization, and acceleration in modernity; it is most viscerally and immediately the destroyer of self-generating human movement (*Eigenbewegung*), that is, of a spatial experience of creativity tied to the body as both *Leib* and *Körper*. Walser's mode of writing, with its emphasis on the physical, bodily, and creaturely dimension of language and the multisensory dimension of both walking and writing, can thus be seen as ardently advocating a lived space, one created through movement rather than visual composition. At the same time, however, Walser equally ardently critiques the slavery to mobility and to the traces it leaves on and in the cultural landscape. It seems as if Walser wanted to write against Marinetti's praise, in the 1909 Futurist Manifesto, of the beauty of speed and cars, thereby anticipating recent accounts of the dissociation between body and space. What is more, the automobile in "The Walk" engages with what Peter Sloterdijk has described as a paramount feature of modernity, namely its "kinetic expressionism," the (now globalized) aestheticism of mobility in our fossil-fueled age that is, in complex ways, tied up with the genealogy of Western concepts of freedom.[38] The modern project of building an infinite civilization on a finite base has entangled itself in logical contradictions that are analogous to the epistemic contradictions of the modern gaze into landscape. Walser's walking-writing is an exemplary mode of confronting dominant features of and reactions to modernity—the

Ent-setzen (ec-stasy, dis-placement) of accelerated mobility and reification (*SW*, 5:64; *SS*, 70) in "The Walk" and the narcissistic desire to "perish into the image" (*SW*, 2:77; *SS*, 22) in "Kleist in Thun"—by engaging, in walking and writing, a radically different aesthetics of the beginner's mind, mindful of the fact that the gesture implied in walking and writing is "always the gesture of being at loss in language."[39]

Notes

1. Georg Büchner, *Lenz: Bilingual Edition*, trans. Richard Sieburth (New York: Archipelago, 2005), 2–3.

2. Hermann Kinder, "Flucht in die Landschaft: Zu Robert Walsers 'Kleist in Thun,'" in *Text und Kritik: Robert Walser*, vol. 12/12a, ed. Heinz Ludwig Arnold (Munich: Edition Text + Kritik, 2004), 100–101. Peter Huber reaches a different conclusion, asserting that Walser affirmatively identifies with Kleist; see "'Dem Dichterunstern gänzlich verfallen': Robert Walsers Kleist," in *Robert Walser und die modern Poetik*, ed. Dieter Borchmeyer (Frankfurt am Main: Suhrkamp, 1999), 140–66. For the relation between Walser and Büchner see also Regina Nörtemann, "Robert Walser und Georg Büchner: Ein Beitrag zur Rezeption und Transformation von literarischen Vorbildern," *Jahrbuch der Deutschen Schillergesellschaft* 52 (2008): 438–58. Unless otherwise noted, all translations are mine.

3. See *Critique of Judgment*, §§25–29.

4. Otto Friedrich Bollnow, *Mensch und Raum* (Stuttgart: Kohlhammer, 1963), 231.

5. George C. Avery, *Inquiry and Testament: A Study of the Novels and Short Prose of Robert Walser* (Philadelphia: University of Pennsylvania Press, 1968), 190.

6. See, for example, Claudia Albes, *Der Spaziergang als Erzählmodell: Studien zu Jean-Jacques Rousseau, Adalbert Stifter, Robert Walser und Thomas Bernhard* (Tübingen: Francke, 1999), 258–70; Elisabett Niccolini, *Der Spaziergang des Schriftstellers* (Stuttgart: Metzler, 2000), 14–15; Karl Pestalozzi, "Spazieren und Schreiben: Franz Kafka 'Der plötzliche Spaziergang' und Robert Walser 'Der Spaziergang,'" in *Franz Kafka und Robert Walser im Dialog*, ed. Vesna Kondrič Horvat (Berlin: Weidler, 2010), 31; Dierk Rodewald, *Robert Walsers Prosa: Versuch einer Strukturanalyse* (Bad Homburg: Gehlen, 1970), 187–90.

7. Max Kommerell, "Die Sprache und das Unaussprechliche: Eine Betrachtung über Heinrich von Kleist," *Das Innere Reich* 4, no. 1 (1937): 671.

8. See Kinder, "Flucht in die Landschaft," 96.

9. Peter Utz, *Tanz auf den Rändern: Robert Walsers "Jetztzeitstil"* (Frankfurt am Main: Suhrkamp, 1998), 91.

10. Giorgio Agamben, *Potentialities: Collected Essays in Philosophy* (Stanford, Calif.: Stanford University Press, 1999), 77.

11. Other literary engagements with Kleist by Walser include, for example, "Porträtskizze" (*SW*, 3:47–49), "Was braucht es zu einem Kleist-Darsteller?" (*SW*, 15:23–26), and "Kleist-Essay" (*SW*, 19:255–57).

12. Translation mine; Middleton misjudges the conjectural register.

13. Jens Tismar, *Gestörte Idyllen: Eine Studie zur Problematik der idyllischen Wunschvorstellungen am Beispiel von Jean Paul, Adalbert Stifter, Robert Walser und Thomas Bernhard* (Munich: Hanser, 1986), 88.

14. Jean-Jacques Rousseau, *Reveries of the Solitary Walker*, trans. Russell Gouldbourne (Oxford: Oxford University Press, 2011), 80–81.

15. Tismar shows how Walser manipulates quotations from Kleist's letters on a semantic, syntactic, and prosodic level, in order to create the impression that Kleist "spoke like Walser" (Tismar, *Gestörte Idyllen*, 84).

16. Kinder, "Flucht in die Landschaft," 97.

17. Utz, *Tanz auf den Rändern*, 93–102. See also Barbara Thums, "Robert Walsers 'Kleist in Thun': Zur Archäologie des touristischen Blicks auf die Schweiz als Idylle," *Literatur für Leser* 36, no. 4 (2014): 169–80.

18. Ibid., 121.

19. Kommerell, "Die Sprache und das Unaussprechliche," 663.

20. Edward S. Casey, *The Fate of Place: A Philosophical History* (Berkeley: University of California Press, 1997), 203.

21. Ibid., 217.

22. Casey, *The Fate of Place*, 228.

23. Since this reading is concerned with the first edition of "The Walk" from 1917, reference is made to Middleton's translation. Susan Bernofsky brilliantly reenvisages Walser's rewriting of the piece for the collection *Seeland* (1920) in English: *The Walk* (New York: New Directions, 2012).

24. Middleton's translation "The lore of nature and the lore of the country" (*SS*, 85) is rather misleading.

25. Maurice Merleau-Ponty, *The Visible and the Invisible*, trans. Alphonso Lingis (Evanston, Ill.: Northwestern University Press, 1968), 133.

26. Ibid., 100.

27. Eckhard Lobsien, *Landschaft in Texten: Zur Geschichte und Phänomenologie der literarischen Beschreibung* (Stuttgart: Metzler, 1981), 1.

28. Jörg Kreienbrock, *Kleiner. Feiner. Leichter: Nunancierungen zum Werk Robert Walsers* (Zurich: Diaphanes, 2010), 10. On Walser's poetics of a "childlike not yet" (ibid., 54, with reference to Davide Giuriato) and its relation to an ethics of the beginner's mind, see ibid., 53–61. In Walser, Kreienbrock asserts, walking is a form of perpetually learning to walk—an act in which beginning and exhaustion coalesce (ibid., 59).

29. Merleau-Ponty, *The Visible and the Invisible*, 123.

30. Utz, *Tanz auf den Rändern*, 82.

31. On references to World War I and the subtle subversion of military registers see Peter Utz, "Helvetische Heroik im Huber-Verlag: Robert Faesi, Paul Ilg, Robert Walser," in *Der Held im Schützengraben: Führer, Massen und Medientechnik im ersten Weltkrieg*, ed. Karl Wagner, Stephan Baumgartner, and Michael Gamper (Zurich: Chronos, 2014), 81–97.

32. *SW*, 13:20. Robert Walser, *Oppressive Light: Selected Poems*, trans. Daniele Pantano (New York: Black Lawrence, 2012), 29.

33. See Kommerell, "Die Sprache und das Unaussprechliche," for an affinity to Kleist's characters.

34. Tim Ingold, "The Temporality of the Landscape," *World Archaelogy* 25, no. 2 (1993): 171.

35. Georg Simmel, "The Philosophy of Landscape," trans. Josef Bleicher, *Theory, Culture, Society* 24, nos. 7–8 (2007): 28.
36. Kurt Lewin, "Field Theory and Experiment in Social Psychology," *American Journal of Sociology* 44 (1939): 868–97.
37. Maurice Merleau-Ponty, *Phenomenology of Perception*, trans. Colin Smith (London: Routledge, 2002), 28.
38. Peter Sloterdijk, "Wie groß ist 'groß'?," in *Das Raumschiff Erde hat keinen Notausgang: Energie und Politik im Anthropozän* (Frankfurt am Main: Suhrkamp, 2011), 97.
39. Agamben, *Potentialities*, 78.

Immersion, Interpolation, Philology

Losing Oneself in Robert Walser

Jörg Kreienbrock

> For the function of great criticism is not [. . .] to instruct by means of historical descriptions or to educate through comparisons, but to cognize by immersing itself in the object.
>
> —Walter Benjamin

I. Musil Reading Walser

In his early short essay "Novellas" (1911) Robert Musil develops a brief theory of literary genres. His schema of prose writing is organized according to a model of spheres:

> Right on the surface are characters, temperaments. A little deeper, honest people have specks of rascality, rascals specks of honesty, the great have moments of stupidity, etc. This is the sphere of the great epics, and of the depiction of great people in the drama. Here the masters are Tols[toy], Dost[oevsky], Haupt[mann], Thackeray. A little deeper still, and people dissolve in futility. It is the sphere in which one breaks off in the midst of a passionate outburst. One has the feeling that here nothing is left of oneself; there are only ideas, general relations that do not have the inclination or the capacity to form an individual. This is the sphere in which these novellas take place.[1]

On the surface of Musil's model there exist characters, well-defined figures. The deeper one moves underneath this surface and immerses oneself in the realm of the novella, the more one can observe what Gert Mattenklott calls the "fading of characters."[2] In the sphere of the novella all essences and identities are dissolved into a web of relations. In this network nothing has the tendency nor the ability to form an individual. It is a realm of "nullities." The radical relationality of the novella never crystallizes into fully developed figures, forms, or events. Characters are nothing more than insubstantial placeholders in a web of correlations, causing other critics, according to Musil, to accuse (for example) Robert Walser that his stories are "lacking character" and "ethical depth."[3] Hence, Musil calls for a mode of reading that makes it possible to perceive the pure relationality of the novella. This method would focus on the lower strata of literary production, populated by figures like Walser's Jakob von Gunten, trying to become nothing. It requires an ability to immerse oneself in the deep layers of literature as well as to read in and through relations without hastily arresting them into stable identities. Musil's observation that in the sphere of the novella "nothing is left of oneself" should be read in all of its ambiguity. Not only is the notion of identity suspended but also that of a unitary reader. In reading novellas the reader as a character becomes questionable; he or she cannot be the agent who, through an act of interpretation, establishes meaning. The reader who immerses herself in the text of the novella fades and ceases to be an individual. The stories of Walser contain "nothing [. . .] of oneself." Therefore the reader cannot project herself into the story, identifying with the characters. In this sense, Walser's novellas constitute a sharp reproach to the contemporary aesthetics of empathy. Fathoming the lower strata of literature—that is, immersing oneself in the realm of literary "nullities"—does not equal an act of identification or empathy.

In the following I will attempt to delineate both a poetics and a hermeneutics of immersion in Walser's prose writing in the light of his celebration of the minute, the surface, and the *nothing*. This notion of immersion must be understood in this context in a broad sense as referring to a process of absorption that questions the traditional concept of interpretation, according to which the "truth" of a text can be discovered beneath its surface. Walser scrambles the distinction between depth and surface, inventing a paradoxical mode of reading/writing that immerses itself *on*—not beneath—the surface.

The dissolution and abandonment that threatens the immersive reader of Walser can also be found, according to Musil, in the process of writing novellas. In this sense the phenomenon of immersion being discussed in this essay can be applied to acts of writing and reading, to an aesthetics of production and an aesthetics of reception. In both cases the writer "will remain an alien and an outcast; perhaps he will not even be a human being but a something within many."[4] The existence of the immersive writer refuses integration into human society; he remains on the periphery, an outsider, a *Sonderling*. While this definition of Walser, as someone who cannot be integrated into traditional notions of literary modernity or the community of an artistic movement, is by now a standard of Walser scholarship,[5] I would like to underscore Musil's second half-sentence: "Perhaps he will not even be a human being but a something within many." Here Musil radically questions the possibility of giving the writer a human form. Perhaps the human is too narrow of a definition for a writer who experiences the tension between self-abandonment and empathy. Perhaps this tension stresses and finally tears apart the human being. For Musil, that which remains alien in the writer, that which makes him an outcast, transcends the clear distinction between the one and the many. The writer becomes "a something within many." His essence is one of indistinction, a neutral something, an anything. This "something" lacks any definition; it has no gender, no form, no unity. It never appears as such; it has no permanent core, but instead manifests itself in the many. Therefore the writer will remain an alien to society and to himself. Writing introduces an element of self-alienation and abandonment, splitting the subject—through the act of writing—into many.

According to Musil, Walser's "extraordinary verbal command" is a nonmastery, easing "our most steadfast convictions [. . .] into a pleasant indifference."[6] It is not produced by a skill, a technique, or method over which the writer sovereignly rules, but is rooted in passivity. Walser himself expresses this ambiguity between active mastery over words and passive indifference in a short reflection titled "Über den Charakter des Künstlers" ("On the Character of the Artist"): "Daß er nie zur Sicherung oder Versicherung seiner selbst gelangt, scheint sein Los. Es ist dies weder ein sehr trübes noch ein sehr leichtes Los" (It seems to be the artist's fate that he never reaches a state of security and assurance. It is neither a very sad nor a very easy fate) (*SW*, 15:63). Lacking security and assurance, it is the artist's fate never to be completely in control of himself. There is no security, no method, no procedure that would guarantee success or even identity. The writer remains an unstable, undistinguished figure who—as an outcast—can never be sure about his status within society. He can never know whether he can actually write. The act of writing refuses to be arrested into a repeatable method.

This powerlessness, which is not necessarily the opposite of power, is the source of a writing that cannot be categorized in terms of enthusiasm or melancholy, success or failure, activity or passivity, because, as Walser continues, "weder der Erfolg noch auch der hartnäckigste Mißerfolg macht den Künstler" (neither success nor the most persistent failure makes the artist) (*SW*, 15:63). The status of the writer cannot be determined by the success of his literary production. The writing of novellas cannot be brought about intentionally; it takes place suddenly, overwhelming the writer. It is beyond the writer's intentions; it is, according to Musil, "something that befalls the writer, a tremor, not something into which one is born, but a stroke of fate [*Fügung*]."[7] The meaning of the German *Fügung* oscillates undecidedly between fate and coincidence. *Grimm's Dictionary* defines it as "the result of an action beyond all human calculation."[8] All one can say about Walser's fate as a writer, according to Musil, is that it is *beyond all human calculation.* It remains unclear whether his ability to write, his *Geschick*,[9] is preordained or a mere stroke of luck. It is this *coincidental fate* that Walter Benjamin calls Walser's "wholly exceptional fate /skill [*Geschick*]"[10] and that stigmatizes him as an outcast. The novella of a writer with an extraordinary fate and skill expresses a tremor, a rupture that renders the writer powerless. His character fades, lacking distinctive features; his fate remains one of continuous indifference, unable ever to reach a state of distinction. But how exactly does one immerse oneself in such "nullities"? How, in other words, does one read Walser?

II. Unfolding "The Walk"

In the story "Der Spaziergang" ("The Walk"), published for the first time in 1917, Walser introduces immersion as an aesthetic practice necessary for the writing of literature. The protagonist is a writer taking a walk. Suddenly his progress is interrupted and he is awoken from being immersed in his imagination. He muses:

> Zwar sehr grob ist das, wie man mich hier hindert, die feinsten Studien zu machen und mich in die vornehmsten Vertiefungen zu versenken. [. . .] Süß ist der Gedanke an das vorübergegangene Schöne und Holde [. . .] aber der Mitwelt und den Mitmenschen hat man keinen Grund deswegen den Rücken zu kehren, und man darf nicht glauben, daß man berechtigt sei, Leuten und Einrichtungen zu grollen, weil sie die Stimmung nicht berücksichtigen, die derjenige hat, der sich an Geschichtliches und Gedankliches verliert. (*SW*, 5:64–65)

> It really is most vulgar the way people impede me here from making my elegant studies and from plunging into the most superb profundities. [. . .] One has not therefore the right to turn one's back, and one may not think that one is entitled to resent people and their contrivances because they disregard the state of mind of him who is absorbed in the realms of history and thought. (*SS*, 95)

The narrator not only observes nature but also observes himself observing nature. For him the process of walking names the condition of the possibility of writing, which merges observation and second-order observation. In this sense the narrator performs what Theodor W. Adorno calls the "ability to see works of art from the inside, in their logic as artifacts."[11] Characteristic for this procedure is the fathoming of "most superb profundities," which is achieved by losing oneself. The walker's "elegant studies" are a result of immersing himself in "the realms of history and thought." In both instances the subject is absorbed, willing to give up distance to the phenomena he encounters. The method through which history and thought can be studied is identical to that which makes the observation of the natural possible: immersion.

Walser's immersed poet oscillates between poetic enthusiasm and prosaic reality. His wish to lose himself cannot be realized completely. The walking writer's merging with nature is unsustainable and continues to be interrupted. The "most superb profundities" lack permanence; they disintegrate in the moment of their emergence. It is therefore no coincidence that it is a moment of the interference of immersion that prompts the walking poet to reflect on his very immersion. The prosaic reality of modern Switzerland aggressively interrupts the *vita contemplativa* of the walker. The dreams and imaginations of the narrator are confronted by the sober realities of traffic:

> Aber es war nicht Mitternacht und weit und breit weder ein ritterliches Mittelalter, noch irgendein Jahr Fünfzehn- oder Siebzehnhundert, sondern heller Tag und dabei Werktag und ein Trupp Leute nebst einem der unhöflichsten, unritterlichsten, barschesten, impertinentesten Automobile, die mir je begegneten, störten mich an der Fülle meiner gelehrten Betrachtungen sehr und warfen mich im Handumdrehen aus aller Schloßpoesie und Vergangenheitsträumerei heraus. (*SW*, 5:64)

> But it was not midnight and far and wide neither a courtly Middle Ages nor a year 1500 or 1700, but broad daylight and a working day and a troupe of people, together with a most uncourtly and unknightly, most crude and most impertinent automobile, which came my way, rudely disturbed me at my wealth of learned and romantic observations, and threw me in a trice out of the domain of castle poetry and reverie of things past. (*SS*, 95)

The impertinence of reality persists and the narrator never completely loses himself. Hence, the immersion in the world as text, as the condition of the possibility of writing, must not be understood as a complete abandonment of subjectivity, a harmonious dissolution of the self, a merging of the subject with its surroundings. Furthermore, the process of immersion itself does not reveal essences by penetrating the interior of perceived phenomena. The way the writer immersed in the phenomena of his walk advances lacks the linearity of method or the violence of penetration. Instead, it remains superficial, resembling a fall along the surface of things: “An der Oberfläche herab stürzte ich in die fabelhafte Tiefe” (I fell along the surface, down into the fabulous depths) (*SW*, 5:57; *SS*, 90).[12] This fall of the writer does not immediately result in an immersion. He remains on the surface. Tumbling down, he does not fathom the depths of meaning. The fall, indicating an element of passivity and powerlessness, brings the writer in contact with the objects around him, but he does not breach their surface, neither merging with them nor bringing out their essences.

In an often-quoted passage from his essay on Walser, Walter Benjamin points out the superficiality of all of Walser’s characters: “These are figures who [. . .] remain so laceratingly, inhumanly, and unfailingly superficial.”[13] The superficiality of Walser’s figures is, following Benjamin, wholly inhuman. The fall along the surface of things threatens to disintegrate the human form.

Only a writer who is immersed in the fall along the surface can write the most elegant studies; but this fall also tends to disintegrate the human form. As *Sonderlinge* and "eccentrics," Walser's figures are not only outcasts of society but, in a more radical sense, outcasts of humanity. They are characterized by an uncanny superficiality that threatens to tear them apart, rendering them inhuman. In his essay on the tenth anniversary of Kafka's death, Benjamin develops a similar argument about Kafka's "Inhumans." Not surprisingly, Benjamin also mentions Walser in this context, discussing "mist-bound creatures, beings in an unfinished state."[14] Kafka's universe, like Walser's, is populated by figures in the "twilight."[15] They are formless, unfinished, held up in the process of becoming human.

The inhumanity of Walser's figures—that is, the "fading" (Mattenklott) of their character, the disintegration of their form—is a product of their *unfailing* abandonment to their fall along the phenomena of the world. The more the walker/writer gets lost in his movement, the less of a unitary, sovereign subject remains. In one of the "Short Commentaries on Proust," Adorno identifies in Proust's *Remembrance of Things Past* a "passive capacity to lose oneself in details without restraint or reservation."[16] This faculty is, according to Adorno, also characteristic for Paul Valéry, equaling a "surrendering to the object without reservations."[17] Abandoning oneself to the object and all its details is the product of a "passive capacity," not the complete abdication of agency. This surrender without reserve is seemingly reckless, but one can read this carelessness as the condition of the possibility for a different form of care. Only by showing no regard can the writer regard nature. Only by being reckless can she show care, can she be attentive to all appearances. It is a procedure that radically excludes all forms of discrimination, calling for the writer to be open and receptive to all phenomena regardless of their significance. Despite its apparent thoughtlessness and recklessness, this disposition, unrestrained and potentially boundless, resembles a form of care. It does not reduce words or things to mere carriers of meaning, but pays careful attention to the way they appear as material objects.

Although Adorno stresses the moments of a boundless and eventually groundless passivity, he nevertheless insists on calling this procedure a "capacity." Proust, according to Adorno, still maintains "the productive force that aims at unity."[18] In "The Walk" Walser writes about the walker/writer in a similar fashion: "Mühsam versucht der Erschütterte seine gesunde Besinnung aufrechtzuerhalten; es gelingt ihm, und er spaziert vertrauensvoll weiter" (Convulsed, he laboriously tries to retain his normal state of mind; he succeeds, and he walks on, full of confidence) (*SW*, 5:53; *SS*, 87). The walking writer is able to keep his consciousness; he refuses to be completely overwhelmed by the shocks of reality. He maintains a disposition that records them; that is, he lets himself be affected by the tremors of the real without being completely powerless, retaining a minimal "capacity." The peculiar faculty of the poet, his passive agency, according to Adorno and Walser, consists in the oscillation between a total abandonment of the self in nature and the exercise of control and reflection.

In another passage of "The Walk" Walser characterizes this oscillation as a reciprocity between poetic enthusiasm and prosaic reality. Again he uses the metaphors of height and depth, respectively: "Er [der Dichter] muß jederzeit des Mitleides, Mitempfindens und der Begeisterung fähig sein, und hoffentlich ist er es. Er muß in den hohen Enthusiasmus hinaufzudringen und sich in die tiefste und kleinste Alltäglichkeit herunterzusenken und zu neigen vermögen, und er kann es vermutlich" (He [the writer] must at all times be capable of compassion, of sympathy, and of enthusiasm, and it is hoped that he is. He must be able to bow down and sink into the deepest and smallest everyday thing, and it is probable that he can) (*SW*, 5:52; *SS*, 86). At first glance this model seems to follow the classical, Platonic model of artistic inspiration, which is based on an enthusiastic elevation of the genius artist above the mundane world. Walser does not follow this hierarchy, however; rather, he insists on the necessity of developing a faculty that can simultaneously elevate enthusiastically and lower prosaically. He calls for a method that combines immersion with reflection:

> Treues, hingebungsvolles Aufgehen und Sichverlieren in die Gegenstände und eifrige Liebe zu allen Erscheinungen und Dingen machen ihn aber dafür glücklich, wie jede Pflichterfüllung den Pflichtbewußten glücklich und reich im Innersten macht. Geist, Hingabe und Treue beseligen ihn und heben ihn hoch über seine eigene unscheinbare Spaziergängerperson hinaus, die nur zu oft im Geruch und schlechten Rufe des Vagabundierens und unnützen Herumstreichens steht. (*SW*, 5:52)

> Faithful, devoted self-effacement and self-surrender among objects, and zealous love for all phenomena and things make him happy in this however, just as every performance of duty make that man happy and rich in his inmost being who is aware of his duty. Spirit, devotion, and faithfulness bless him and raise him high up above his own inconspicuous walking self which has only too often a name and evil reputation for vagabondage and vagrancy. (*SS*, 86–87)

The poet ascends by losing himself. This dissolution of the self in the act of immersion Walser compares to the emotion of love. It is loyal, devoted, and diligent. Being in love, being attentive to all phenomena, elevates the writer above his empirical self as a human being. His perceptivity is heightened, including all appearances; it is boundless in its intensity as well as its extension. There is nothing the writer does not love.

In his recent reflections on philology, Werner Hamacher emphasizes a notion of *philia* that is connected to a heightened form of attentiveness.

He insists that philology should focus on details, nuances, and intervals. If philology can be understood as a technique of immersion, it becomes clear that its success in pursuing language is based on an attentiveness to gaps in the text, which become abysses of profundity for the philologist. Reading multiplies and intensifies intervals. The closer the reader looks, the more fragmented, perforated the text appears. Hamacher writes: "Philology would then be attention to that which interpunctuates, brings to a hold, creates caesuras."[19] The narrator of a posthumously published untitled Walser fragment from 1914 identifies himself with a similar form of attentiveness: "Ich bin ein achtsamer Mensch. Ich bestehe fast ganz nur aus Aufmerksamkeit. Ich muß notgedrungenermaßen auf alles acht geben, es zwingt mich, es reißt mich hin, ich kann gar nicht anders. Ich kann nicht hinwegsehen, ich kann nichts überspringen" (I am an attentive person. I am almost completely composed solely of attention. I must pay attention to everything, it forces me, it pulls me. I cannot help myself. I cannot look away. I cannot skip anything) (*SW*, 16:409). Attentiveness is not a faculty. The subject of Walser's piece is overwhelmed and subjugated. In this ravished state he consists of almost nothing but attentiveness. The phrase "fast ganz nur" (almost completely . . . solely) captures Walser's theory of attentive reading. It is neither the complete abandonment of the self in nature or of the reader in the text, nor is it a faculty of the sovereign subject, who would be in complete control of his procedure. There is a minimal element of the individual left, refusing to dissolve totally into attentiveness. The observer remains "almost completely and solely" a human being, but his existence resembles that of an eccentric, who cannot distinguish between what is important and negligible, significant and insignificant, big and small. Everything is worth paying attention to. There is no detail of a text the philologist must not investigate closely. Even a comma, as Hamacher shows for Hölderlin's remark "Look, my dear sir, a comma!," can become the subject of a "philographic"[20] attentiveness, indicating that which "is not asserted but is called and invited to *come*."[21] The attentive reader cannot jump or gloss over any detail of the text. While reading she is immersed in the text, bringing out not only those elements guaranteeing consistency and coherence, but also those—commas, lacunae, gaps—that interrupt and undermine the idea of a well-defined and ordered text. The reader is attentive to that which the text says and to that which the text does not say.

This double attentiveness requires a particular form of immersive reading, negotiating the dialectics between the superficial and the profound, the part and the whole. The surface of a text is the space of its truth. Its folds transform the text from a two-dimensional, flat surface to a three-dimensional relief. Reading traces its creases, moving along its folds. The writer as a walker flows, sinking and climbing, along this three-dimensional, folded surface of the text. Walser describes this movement in the story "Reisebericht" ("Travel Report"): "Ich hatte es mit fortwährendem Herabsinken und Hinaufsteigen, wüstem, wildem, haltlosem Hinunterfallen und-stürzen und wieder Hochemporstreben, mit Klimmen, Klettern, mich an Ästen Festhalten, Rutschen über Geröll herab [. . .] zu tun" (I had to deal with a continuous sinking and climbing, a frantic, wild falling and tumbling without footing and again an aspiration to climb and scramble, holding on to branches, sliding down rubble) (*SW*, 7:33). The movement of the walker/writer is a continuous up and down, sinking and climbing, descent and ascent. One can translate this oscillation between elevation and immersion into the distinction between the enthusiastically inspired flight of the artist and the sober, prosaic attitude of the philological reader. It is the condition of the possibility of writing "mannigfaltige Studien" (manifold studies) (*SW*, 5:52; *SS*, 87). The term "study" here refers both to the act of studying and observing and to a written text. For Walser this indistinction between process and product opens up the possibility of writing. Not only must the attentive writer be aware of the multidimensional quality of textual surfaces; his writing must also reflect the intensely folded character of the observed phenomena. This can only be achieved by an intensification of attention resulting in an increase of differentiation. The writer perceives the many, the folds in seemingly flat and unitary surfaces. These studies are not the product of an enthusiastic dissolution of the self in nature, nor a mere impressionism, but rather a process of unfolding what Michel Foucault in a reflection on the act of interpretation calls the "absolutely superficial secret"[22] of the text.

In "Naturstudie" ("Nature Study") Walser insists on the significance of exact description, correct reasoning, and firm thought:

> Wie ich nämlich annehmen zu dürfen glaube, bin ich allen diesen Dingen gegenüber weit weniger von Begeisterung und Schwärmerei, als vielmehr nur von überaus starker Aufmerksamkeit ergriffen gewesen, die mir ein Zustand zu sein scheint, wovon ich denke, daß er höher zu schätzen sei als irgendwelche Benommenheit, die über jedes exakte Beschreiben, richtige Besinnen, Einprägen und feste Denken gern hinwegschwimmt. (*SW*, 7:62)
>
> As I believe to be allowed to assume, I was much less moved by enthusiasm and rapturousness than by an exceedingly intense attentiveness, which seems to me to be a condition that I think should be valued higher than any stupor, which likes to glide over any exact description, correct reflection, inculcation, and solid thought.

The narrator, who delineates his method of observation, refrains from enthusiasm, which, according to him, glosses over the details and nuances of the observed phenomena instead developing a disposition of heightened attention. In this state he is able to see clearly and distinctly. His "Nature Study" relies on an exact and precise observation. For this reason it is not surprising that in "The Walk" Walser notes that the method of the walking writer touches an "exakte Wissenschaft, die dem scheinbar leichtfertigen Bummler niemand zutraut" (the fringes of exact science, a thing of which nobody would think the apparently frivolous wanderer capable) (*SW*, 5:52; *SS*, 87). This intense attentiveness in close proximity to the hard sciences moves from word to word, phenomenon to phenomenon, event to event, without ever relying on a given method. The writer/walker not only resembles a "leichtfertigen Bummler" (frivolous wanderer) but also a "bessere[n] Strolch, feinere[n] Vagabund, Tagedieb, Zeitverschwender oder Landstreicher" (better sort of tramp, a vagabond and pickpocket, or idler and vagrant) (*SW*, 5:27; *SS*, 69). Frivolous wandering, although it produces exact descriptions, is incalculable. The eccentric path of the rambler cannot be integrated into the straightforward progress of a scientific method. Instead it displays a precarious association with precision and levity, exactness and rambling, activity and idling.

The characterization of the rambler's "Nature Study" as bordering on science is exemplified in a passage from "The Walk" where the narrator does not aim to describe the objects of study directly. Rather, his walk moves

> neben [. . .] behaglichen Gärten vorbei, neben Obstbäumen [. . .] vorbei, neben hochaufragendem, reizendem Getreide [. . .] vorbei, neben einem Holzplatz [. . .] vorbei, neben saftigem Gras [. . .] vorbei, neben allerhand Leuten [. . .] vorbei, neben [. . .] andern gutmütigen, nützlichen Dingen vorbei, neben [. . .] an weiß Gott was sonst noch allem möglichen vorbei. (*SW*, 5:27–28)

> past all sorts of gardens, [. . .] past fruit trees, [. . .] past towering crops, [. . .] past a wood-yard, [. . .] past all sorts of people, [. . .] past many other good-hearted and useful things, [. . .] past God knows what else in the way of feasible things. (*SS*, 69)

The narrator's progress is seemingly casual: without goal, direction, or interest. He does not linger or dwell on the things he encounters but airily and carelessly moves along. There is no attempt to discover essential qualities or a deep underlying meaning. Hence, his writing becomes paraphrastic in the literal sense. It focuses on the *para*, namely that which is located next to words and things; it moves "neben" and "vorbei" and is thereby attentive to peripheral phenomena.[23] This seemingly free-floating attention, moving slightly past things, perceives what is and what might be possible. It perceives objects like gardens, trees, and crops as well as "God knows what else in the way of feasible things." What it paraphrases is not essential but accidental, circumstantial, marginal. Gilles Deleuze identifies in Lewis Carroll's *Alice in Wonderland* a similar paraphrastic writing, one that attempts "to slide the whole length in such a way that the old depth no longer exists at all, having been reduced to the opposite side of the surface."[24] According to Deleuze, this art of the surface "appears as a dismissal of depth, a display of events at the surface, and a deployment of language along this limit."[25] Depth in its literal but also its figurative meaning must not be understood as merely the opposite of superficiality; instead it appears on the surface. Profundity is a paraphrastic phenomenon, situated not under or behind the text but "neben" and "vorbei" in its margins, gaps, and folds.

In the piece "Cézannegedanken" ("Thoughts on Cézanne") Walser unfolds Cézanne's method of painting in a similar fashion. One central characteristic is what Walser calls the "Gebirgigmachung" (making mountainous) in the process of framing:

> Er [Cézanne] erhielt mit der Zeit lauernde Augen vom vielen exakten Herumschweifen rund um Umrisse, die für ihn zu Grenzen von etwas Mysteriösem wurden. Sein ganzes stilles Leben lang kämpfte er den lautlosen und, wie man versucht sein könnte zu sagen, sehr vornehmen Kampf um die Gebirgigmachung, so dürfte vielleicht der umschreibende Ausdruck lauten, des Rahmens. Der Sinn ist der, daß z.B. ein Gebiet durch Berge größer, reicher wird. (*SW*, 18, 254)

> As time went by, a secret watchfulness settled in his eyes from such precise circling of contours that became for him edges of a mystery. An entire quiet lifetime he spent fighting inaudibly and, one might be tempted to say, with nobility, to make mountainous—if such a paraphrase might suffice—the frame of things. My gist is that a region, for instance, becomes bigger and richer in a surround of mountains. (*SS*, 188)

By framing an object, that is, by "making mountainous" the frame, the painter increases the painting's complexity. Focusing on frames and contours, those elements which delimit an object, in fact makes that object appear greater and richer. Peter Utz calls this a "dialectics of amplification through limitation":

> Like the Alps in Walser's texts, the "mountainous" frame seems to open a third dimension for the two-dimensional painting that follows a dialectics of amplification through limitation. The phrase of "making the frame mountainous" is in itself a circumlocutory expression, performing that of which it speaks and thereby seemingly enlarging and enriching the area within the frame.[26]

The surface of the text transforms into a relief, a folded, alpine landscape. Walser's method of the paraphrase, which circumvents all words and things, resembles this framing. It is an act of differentiation, simultaneously folding and unfolding. Immersion and distancing thereby enrich and enlarge the observation in the paradoxical process of a "precise circling." The reader of a text as a relief not only proceeds on the flat surface of the text but traces the multiple, enfolded inscriptions of it as a mountainous space. Like the walker in an alpine landscape, the reader produces "elegant studies" by immersing herself into the "vornehmste Vertiefungen" (most superb profundities/depths) of the three-dimensional surface of the text. It is an act of deciphering the various "Aufträge aus dem Bleistiftgebiet" (instructions/layers of the pencil area),[27] to quote Elke Siegel, of exploring the "sculptural depth"[28] of writing as paraphrase and palimpsest.

In *Berlin Chronicle* Walter Benjamin compares remembering to an act of unfolding. In discussing Proust, Benjamin uses the metaphor of a fan:

> He who has once begun to open the fan of memory never comes to the end of its segments. No image satisfies him, for he has seen that it can be unfolded, and only in the folds does the truth reside—that image, that taste, that touch for whose sake all this has been unfurled and dissected; and now remembrance progresses from small to smallest details, from the smallest to the infinitesimal, while that which it encounters in these microcosms grows even mightier.[29]

By unfolding a fan and thereby revealing concealed images, the human being discovers a hidden microcosm. But no image can finally terminate the process of unfolding and thereby capture the past in a definite image. Each prospect opens to a new frame, a more minute image. In this sense, remembering is an act of indefinite intensification. Like the process of "making mountainous," the attention to the detail and the frame produces amplification. The most minute becomes "immer gewaltiger" (ever mightier/more violent). What appears to be small and negligible is characterized not only by its secret magnitude, but also by its force, even violence. The subject is drawn into to the folds of memory, losing herself in this process, which is inexorable. The more one immerses oneself in the folds of the past, the more one is drawn in. The intensification of memory, that is, the magnification of details, coincides with the minimization of the subject. The intensified (*gewaltige*) process of memory threatens to ruin the form of the human being, as Benjamin indicates in playing on the proximity of the German verbs *walten* and *falten*. One cannot sovereignly exercise (*walten*) the process of unfolding (*entfalten*). In the piece "Butterfly Hunt," Benjamin remembers how, while chasing butterflies (*Falter*), the child Walter himself metamorphosed into a butterfly. Walter resembles a *Falter*: "The more I strove to conform, in all the fibers of my being, to the animal—the more butterfly-like I became in my heart and soul."[30] This peculiar form of mimicry scrambles the distinction between what is human and what is animal. Walter, whose name alludes to the act of folding, a butterfly, and to violence, as the *Entfalter* of *Gewalt*, becomes "butterfly-like in my heart and soul." The *Falter* is characterized by an infinite number of folds, frames, limits. There is no image that could not be unfolded further, differentiated into ever more minute texture.

In the vignette "Fan" from *One-Way Street* Benjamin connects the idea of unfolding to that of the mathematical and philological method of interpolation: "The faculty of imagination is the gift of interpolating into the infinitely small, of inventing, for every intensity, and extensiveness to contain its new, compressed fullness, in short, of receiving each image as if it were that of a folded fan, which only in spreading draws breath and flourishes."[31] Imagination, according to Benjamin, is the ability to interpolate within the infinitely small. Interpolation both in philology and mathematics is a process of producing coherence and continuity by either emending the text or discovering a function whose graph would cover the gap between two known values.[32] Benjamin's enigmatic use of interpolation as a mode of reading conceives of every text as a fan that needs to be unfolded. It is through the process of interpolation that the compact, intensive fullness of the text unfolds, opening a different dimension. Unfolding as intensification is a procedure of insertion but also of separation, transforming "Auslegung" (interpretation) into an "Auseinanderlegung" in the literal sense of the German word: the reader unfolds, separates, lays bare and apart. While interpolation in mathematics and philology attempts to close gaps and produce continuity, Benjamin's interpolating method exposes discontinuities. Thomas Schestag observes, "The gesture of interpolation oscillates between the closing and tearing of gaps: the insertion of a detail, which fills a gap, tears (at least) two new gaps. Benjamin emphasizes this peculiar intermingling, which blasts open the illusion of the text as a pre-given unit in which form and content correspond."[33] To the same degree with which interpolation produces coherence, it also disrupts it. Instead of reconstructing a coherent, authentic original text, it introduces new folds, gaps, and lacunae. The more the reader becomes immersed in the text, the more creases and cracks appear on its surface. Interpolation as a form of *intensive immersion*, oscillating between the tearing and filling of gaps, produces and discovers the infinitesimally minute. Through this procedure of fathoming the "most superb profundities," the text becomes the site for a potentially infinite differentiation. Walser's fascination with the small focuses not so much on small things as such, but on minimal transitions, spaces between and within words. It is here where the profundity of literature emerges as a microcosm. It is the task of literary studies, according to Benjamin, to be concerned with the form of literary works, laying bare in their interior a microcosm: "For with this the work is transformed into a microcosm."[34]

III. A Philology of/in Ashes

One example of Walser's immersive "poetics of the minute"[35] can be found in the short piece "Asche, Nadel, Bleistift und Zündhölzchen" ("Ash, Needle, Pencil, and Little Matchstick") from 1915:

> Ich schrieb einmal eine Abhandlung über Asche, die mir nicht geringen Beifall eintrug und in welcher ich allerlei Kurioses zutage förderte, unter anderem die Beobachtung, daß Asche keinerlei nennenswerte Widerstandskraft besitzt. In der Tat läßt sich über diesen scheinbar so uninteressanten Gegenstand bei nur einigermaßen tieferem Eindringen manches sagen, was durchaus nicht uninteressant ist. (*SW*, 16:328)
>
> I once wrote an essay on ash that brought me no modicum of praise, and in which I revealed all sorts of utterly strange things, among others the observation that ash possesses no resistance at all worth naming. In fact, only by rather intensely setting upon this seemingly so uninteresting object can one say something that isn't completely uninteresting.[36]

That which appears at first glance to be irrelevant reveals, if "mit einiger Innigkeit und Sorgfalt betrachtet" (observ[ed] with some intimacy and care) (*SW*, 16:329),[37] interesting and valuable details. Using a method of deep immersion into the surface of things, the treatise about ash unearths "all sorts of utterly strange things," aspects of the phenomenon that escape our prevalent and familiar perception. In this way, the narrator—whose method resembles that of the narrator in "The Walk"—is able to perceive interesting details in seemingly uninteresting topics by looking "neben" and "vorbei." One of these details is the fact that ash does not pose any resistance. It is nothing more than a useless remainder without form and character. Walser identifies the lack of resistance characteristic of ash, its fleeting lack of substance, as inconsequential and worthless. He asks, "Kann man haltloser, schwächer und armseliger sein als Asche? [. . .] Gibt es ein Ding, das nachgiebiger und duldsamer sein könnte?" (Can one be more feeble, weak, or miserable than ash? [. . .] Is there anything that could be more yielding and tolerant?) (*SW*, 16:328).[38] How does one write about something insignificant and so small that it lacks character and essence? Ash, if touched, as Walser points out, tends "augenblicklich auseinanderzufliegen" (to instantly [. . .] go flying in every direction) (ibid.). It lacks profundity and the stability of form. It does not have the characteristics of a solid object with a distinct separation between surface and depth; therefore it cannot be penetrated. The moment an observer tries to arrest and give shape to ash it immediately disperses, falls apart, comes undone. According to his essay there are phenomena that, due to their fleeting and superficial characterlessness, do not offer themselves as objects of immersion, because immersion requires a minimal amount of substantial resistance. "Wo Asche ist," Walser writes, "ist eigentlich überhaupt nichts. Setze deinen Fuß auf Asche, und du wirst kaum spüren, daß du auf irgend etwas getreten bist" (Where ash is there is actually nothing at all. Set your foot on ash and you will hardly notice that you've stepped on anything at all) (ibid.). Ash is not just nothing, but is "actually" nothing "at all"—it is actually and essentially nothing. Walser's curious phrase expresses a double intensification of ash's nothingness and insignificance. Ash is not some thing, but nothing. It is *actually* nothing; there is no method or treatment that would turn it into something. Is there a method, a path on which the subject can walk and experience the actual nothing of ash? Is there a way to trace ash? The only element which Walser detects in the nothingness of ashes is the consciousness of its insignificance: "Asche ist die Demut, die Belanglosigkeit und die Wertlosigkeit selber, und was das Schönste ist: sie ist selbst durchdrungen von dem Glauben, daß sie zu nichts taugt" (Ash is itself humility, triviality and worthlessness, and what is most beautiful, it is totally convinced by its own belief that it is good for nothing) (ibid.). The beauty of ash—perhaps this is its minimal significance—lies in its self-reflexivity, its awareness of its own irrelevance. If one follows Walser's argument, immersion has to bring out this self-reflexive element, this knowledge of nothingness located within the phenomenon itself. Ash knows of its own uselessness and worthlessness, and it is the task of the observer to perceive this character. It is "only by rather intensely setting upon" a phenomenon that has "no resistance at all worth naming" that one brings out in it what is interesting and remarkable. Immersive observation is able to detect and excavate in a fleeting and formless form, in a characterless character, traces of resistance, ephemeral moments of reflection, figures on the edge of disfiguration.

In these moments oscillating between figuration and disfiguration, where traces present and simultaneously erase themselves, literary scholarship, according to Peter Szondi, can discover a model for its method. Through immersion into the "logic of their existence as the results of a productive process"—in other words, the inner manifold character of the work of art—understanding is possible:

> Literary study or "science" (*Literaturwissenschaft*) must not forget that it is a study, or "science," of art, which should elaborate its methodology on the basis of an analysis of the poetic process. It can hope to arrive at genuine understanding only if it immerses itself in the works themselves, in the "logic of their existence as the results of a productive process" (*die Logik ihres Produziertseins*).[39]

Szondi attempts to discover the poetic sphere through a method of immersion resembling the sphere of the novella that Musil analyzes in his review of Walser. For Musil, novellas contain "only thoughts, general relations that do not have the inclination or the capacity to form an individual."[40] But while there are no individuals, it is in this sphere where the "logic of their existence as the results of a productive process" becomes visible. Adorno, whom Szondi quotes in this passage, writes: "The ability to see works of art from the inside, in their logic as artifacts, things that have been produced—a union of action and reflection that neither hides behind naiveté nor hastily dissolves its concrete characteristics in a general concept—is probably the only form in which aesthetics is still possible."[41] Immersion here stands for the ability to see artworks from within. Only the critic who is able to enter the artwork, who is able to see the unity of "action and reflection," of folding and unfolding, has an adequate experience of art. Immersion for Adorno, far from being a purely passive merging of the recipient with the artwork, calls for the perception of the unity of theory and practice, performance and reflection. This method is neither a naive unconscious indulgence nor an abstract, generalizing approach. It focuses on the concrete determinations of the artwork. Reading as a mode of immersion, as explicated by Benjamin, Adorno, and Szondi, calls for the detection of the internal, self-reflexive structures of artworks, that is, the "logic of their existence as the results of a productive process" as a "micropoetics."[42] This logic can only be detected, as Benjamin asserts in the *Origin of the German Mourning Play*, "through immersion in the most minute details."[43] It is not an essential element of the text, but instead only appears as an unsubstantial surplus, in folds and creases, revealing the "minute precision of the work."[44]

Adorno reminds the reader in his lectures on *Philosophical Terminology* that depth and profundity must not be misunderstood as modes of vacuous self-absorption or speculation. He claims, instead, "that one can find profundity neither in the empty speculation on an absolute nor in the equally empty immersion into one's own self. It rather devolved into the force of resistance, into the force of resistance against that which is bad."[45] In modernity, old notions of profundity and immersion have been transformed into forces of resistance. Immersion, despite being without reserve (that is, a complete immersion into the phenomena without remainder), is characterized by a force. It is not mere passivity or a complete abandonment of the self. Adorno discovers profundity in acts of resistance, relinquishing aspirations to attain a transcendent realm of the absolute. These acts do not elevate the depths of profundity into something metaphysical that would assign meaning to the contingency and incommensurability of reality. Even in the complete immersion and merging without recourse and security there is a minimal element of resistance, the barely recognizable, minimal resistance of the trace. The only approach that can adequately detect minute instances of resistance in that which has "no resistance at all worth naming" is an immersive reading that would give up the scientific ideal of an objective distance and turn every text into a gray, ash-like surface. It is an immersion, which does not penetrate the text and does not search for a meaning behind or under the words, but rambles like a walker in the sphere of ashes. As such, it would approximate Benjamin's ideal of a method ("totally and unhurriedly concentrated even on the very minutest object without the slightest inhibition")[46] or Walser's "essay on ash," both of which produce an "ever more intense reappraisal of phenomena"[47] that preserves their individuality. Like the word "cinders," ashes function, to quote Jacques Derrida, as "the better paradigm for [. . .] the trace—something that erases itself totally, radically, while presenting itself."[48] For the philologist of ashes there is nothing but ashes. No ground—nothing that would arrest the trace, give it shape or a distinct outline. This fleeting groundlessness and shapelessness affects any act of writing and reading. Nothing is left of Walser's steps but traces on a ground of ashes—like a walker in the snow—always threatened to be extinguished and erased but nevertheless remaining stubbornly visible, calling for inclined readers.

Notes

The epigraph is from Walter Benjamin, "Announcement of the Journal *Angelus Novus*," in *Selected Writings*, vol. 1, ed. Marcus Paul Bullock, Howard Eiland, and Michael Jennings (Cambridge, Mass.: Harvard University Press, 2005), 293.

1. Robert Musil, "Novellas," in *Precision and Soul: Essays and Addresses*, trans. and ed. David S. Luft and Burton Pike (Chicago: University of Chicago Press, 1995), 9.
2. Gert Mattenklott, *Blindgänger: Physiognomische Essays* (Frankfurt am Main: Suhrkamp, 1986), 7.
3. Robert Musil, "The *Stories* of Robert Walser," trans. Mark Harman, in *Robert Walser Rediscovered: Stories, Fairy-Tale Plays, and Critical Responses*, ed. Mark Harman (Hanover, N.H.: University Press of New England, 1985), 141.
4. Robert Musil, "Literarische Chronik," in *Gesammelte Werke*, vol. 9, ed. Adolf Frisé (Reinbek: Rowohlt, 1978), 1466 (my translation).
5. Cf. Eva Geulen, "Autorität und Kontingenz der Tradition bei Robert Walser," in *Autorität der/in Sprache, Literatur, Neuen Medien*, ed. Jürgen Fohrmann, Ingrid Karsten, and Eva Neuland (Bielefeld: Aisthesis, 1997), 805–13; *Historismus und Literarische Moderne*, ed. Moritz Baßler et al. (Tübingen: Niemeyer, 1996), 130–34.
6. Musil, "The *Stories* of Robert Walser," 142.
7. Musil, "Literarische Chronik," 1467.
8. *Deutsches Wörterbuch*, ed. Jacob Grimm and Wilhelm Grimm, vol. 4 (Leipzig: Hirzel, 1863–78), 404: "ein aus dem in seinen verbindungen außer aller menschlichen berechnung stehenden walten hervorgehendes oder hervorgegangenes ergebnis."
9. The word *Geschick* denotes "fate" as well as "skill."
10. Walter Benjamin, "Robert Walser," in *Gesammelte Schriften*, vol. 2, ed. Rolf Tiedemann and Hermann Schweppenhäuser (Frankfurt am Main: Suhrkamp, 1977), 327 (my translation).
11. Theodor W. Adorno, "Valéry's Deviations," in *Notes to Literature*, vol. 1, trans. Shierry Weber Nicholson (New York: Columbia University Press, 1991), 138.
12. Translation modified.
13. Walter Benjamin, "Robert Walser," trans. Mark Harman, in *Robert Walser Rediscovered: Stories, Fairy-Tale Plays, and Critical Responses*, ed. Mark Harman (Hanover, N.H.: University Press of New England, 1985), 146.

14. Walter Benjamin, "Franz Kafka: On the Tenth Anniversary of His Death," in *Selected Writings*, vol. 2, ed. Michael W. Jennings, Howard Eiland, and Gary Smith (Cambridge, Mass.: Harvard University Press, 2005), 798.

15. Benjamin, "Franz Kafka," 116.

16. Theodor W. Adorno, "Short Commentaries on Proust," in *Notes to Literature*, 1:184.

17. Adorno, "Valéry's Deviations," 138.

18. Adorno, "Short Commentaries on Proust," 1:174.

19. Werner Hamacher, *Minima Philologica*, trans. Catherine Diehl and Jason Groves (New York: Fordham University Press, 2015), 28.

20. Ibid.

21. Ibid.

22. Michel Foucault, "Nietzsche, Freud, Marx," in *Aesthetics, Method, and Epistemology*, trans. Robert Hurley (New York: New Press, 1998), 273.

23. Cf. Samuel Frederick, *Narratives Unsettled: Digression in Robert Walser, Thomas Bernhard, and Adalbert Stifter* (Evanston, Ill.: Northwestern University Press, 2012), 49–50; Annette Fuchs, *Dramaturgie des Narrentums: Das Komische in der Prosa Robert Walsers* (Munich: Fink, 1993), 49–51.

24. Gilles Deleuze, *The Logic of Sense*, trans. Mark Lester (New York: Columbia University Press, 1990), 9.

25. Ibid.

26. Peter Utz, *Tanz auf den Rändern: Robert Walsers "Jetztzeitstil"* (Frankfurt am Main: Suhrkamp, 1998), 126–27.

27. Elke Siegel, *Aufträge aus dem Bleistiftgebiet: Zur Dichtung Robert Walsers* (Würzburg: Königshausen & Neumann, 2001).

28. Walter Benjamin, "Review of the Mendelssohn's *Der Mensch in der Handschrift*," in *Selected Writings*, 2:134.

29. Walter Benjamin, "Berlin Chronicle," in *Selected Writings*, 2:597.

30. Walter Benjamin, *Berlin Childhood around 1900*, trans. Howard Eiland (Cambridge, Mass.: Harvard University Press, 2006), 51.

31. Walter Benjamin, "One-Way Street," in *Selected Writings*, 1:466.

32. Peter Fenves stresses the significance of Benjamin's interest in the notion of interpolation in the context of his reading of Goethe's novella "The New Melusine" from *Wilhelm Meister's Journeyman Years*. Fenves characterizes Benjamin's philology of interpolation/interpretation as follows: "Philology seeks neither to complete a text not make its rough patches smooth; rather, 'philological interpretation,' as Benjamin emphasizes, consists in recognizing interpolation after interpolation and thus reducing the text to a point where, like Melusine in the absence of a rejuvenating 'knight,' it begins to vanish." Peter Fenves, *The Messianic Reduction: Walter Benjamin and the Shape of Time* (Stanford, Calif.: Stanford University Press, 2011), 237.

33. Thomas Schestag, "Interpolationen: Benjamins Philologie," *Philo:Xenia* 1 (2009): 50.

34. Walter Benjamin, "Literary History and the Study of Literature," in *Selected Writings*, 2:464.

35. Marianne Schuller, "Robert Walsers Poetik des Winzigen: Ein Versuch," in *Robert Walsers "Ferne Nähe": Neue Beiträge zur Forschung*, ed. Wolfram Groddeck et al. (Munich: Fink, 2007), 75–81.

36. Robert Walser, "Ash, Needle, Pencil, and Little Matchstick," trans. Samuel Frederick, in Frederick, *Narratives Unsettled*, 177.

37. Ibid., 178. On this passage Frederick writes: "The narrator [. . .] distances the ordinary act of perception in order to reawaken its significance as something that goes beyond mere passive visual apprehension. For not only is a certain kind of careful and attentive viewing required to reveal the value of the everyday things that surround us; the very value of these things lies, reciprocally, in their existence *as* objects for us to observe with intimacy and care." Ibid., 91.

38. Ibid., 177. All the following quotations of this text are from this same page.

39. Peter Szondi, *On Textual Understanding and Other Essays* (Manchester: Manchester University Press, 1986), 22.

40. Musil, "Novellas," 9.

41. Adorno, "Valérys Deviations," 138.

42. Kerstin Scheffler, *Mikropoetik: Robert Walsers Bieler Prosa* (Bielefeld: Transcript, 2010).

43. Walter Benjamin, *The Origin of German Tragic Drama*, trans. John Osborne (London: Verso, 2003), 29.

44. Ibid. A discussion of the status of the notion of *Versenkung* in Benjamin and its relation to melancholy and allegory would go beyond the scope of this essay. See Bettine Menke, *Das Trauerspiel-Buch* (Bielefeld: Transcript, 2010).

45. Theodor W. Adorno, *Philosophische Terminologie*, vol. 1 (Frankfurt am Main: Suhrkamp, 1973), 200–201. See Burkhard Meyer-Sickendieck, *Tiefe: Über die Faszination des Grübelns* (Munich: Fink, 2010).

46. Benjamin, *The Origin of German Tragic Drama*, 44–45.

47. Ibid., 45.

48. Jacques Derrida, "On Reading Heidegger: An Outline of Remarks to the Essex Colloquium," *Research in Phenomonology* 17, no. 1 (1987): 177. See Martin Roussel, *Matrikel: Zur Haltung des Schreibens in Robert Walsers Mikrographie* (Frankfurt am Main/Basel: Stroemfeld, 2011).

Parodies of Power

Robert Walser's Dramatic Scenes

Valerie Heffernan

Although Robert Walser's place on the literary scene has now, over sixty years after his death, finally been established, he is still primarily known as a writer of novels and short prose; Walser's dramatic work, by contrast, has garnered comparatively little attention from academic criticism.[1] The limited consideration devoted to the writer's dramatic work belies the fact that throughout his career, Walser wrote many short plays, dramatic scenes, and comical dramas. Indeed, one might even argue that Walser's first love was the theater. In 1895, at the age of seventeen, the young Walser attempted to make a career for himself as an actor by auditioning in front of the celebrated actor Josef Kainz.[2] By all accounts, he suffered a humiliating rejection at Kainz's hand and subsequently decided to forgo all further plans for a career on the stage.[3] Shortly after this first and last flirtation with acting, Walser wrote to his sister Lisa, "Mit dem Schauspielerberuf ist es nichts. Doch, so Gott will, werde ich ein grosser Dichter werden" (There isn't going to be any acting career, but if God so wills it, I am going to become a great poet).[4]

Even as a writer, Walser never really shook off his love of the theater and performance, and many critics have pointed to the centrality of drama and theater to his prose work. For example, Martina Schaak highlights the numerous references to the theater in Walser's prose of the Berlin period (1905–13), where the stage both plays out the tensions of modern city life and offers an idealistic reprieve from its pressures.[5] Lothar Kurzawa links the playful narrators of Walser's prose texts to the writer's interest in the dramatic form; Kurzawa speculates "that writing is a form of performance art for [Walser], that as a writer he can finally take on the countless roles (linguistic disguises) that both conceal and proliferate his identity."[6] Marion Gees takes this argument a step further and emphasizes the importance of theatricality, gesture, and masquerade for both the content and the form of Walser's writing; she relates the pose of the writing subject, who continually calls attention to his own role as producer of the written text, to a type of performance of authorship that is enacted every time Walser picks up his pen.[7] Even as a writer of prose, it seems, Walser's penchant for drama suffuses his texts.

It is noteworthy that Walser began experimenting with the dramatic form at a very early stage in his literary career. Indeed, his earliest published work includes four short dramolettes, which were published in the Munich-based literary monthly *Die Insel* between 1900 and 1902. *Die Insel* was arguably the ideal venue for the publication of what Walser would later call his "theatralisch phantasiehafte Spiele" (theatrically fantastical games).[8] Founded by Otto Julius Bierbaum, Alfred Walter Heymel, and Rudolf Alexander Schröder, the monthly magazine was, as Peter Utz observes, "one of the central literary laboratories of the avant-garde."[9] In his publications in *Die Insel*, Walser had the opportunity to test his own limits in the knowledge that his literary experiments would be read and enjoyed by a captive audience. Indeed, Heymel and Schröder seem to have been particularly fascinated by the apparent primitiveness of Walser's writing; in a letter to Bierbaum, Schröder compared Walser's raw naïveté to that of Dante or Shakespeare.[10] Moreover, Walser's involvement with *Die Insel* brought with it a certain prestige, as his work appeared alongside that of literary titans such as Hugo von Hofmannsthal, Frank Wedekind, and Rainer Maria Rilke.

Of the four plays Walser published in *Die Insel*, his dramolette *Schneewittchen* (*Snow White*), which appeared in September 1901, has received far more critical attention than the other three.[11] As early as 1929, the piece was singled out for special mention by Walter Benjamin, who highlighted it as "one of the most profound compositions in recent literature."[12] A second fairy-tale dramolette that appeared in *Die Insel*, *Aschenbrödel* (*Cinderella*), published in July 1901, was marginalized by the critics for a long time, but it too has merited some consideration in recent criticism.[13] The other two dramas, *Dichter* (*Poets*), which appeared in June 1900, and *Die Knaben* (*The Boys*), published in June 1902, have received comparatively little attention in the critical literature to date. Though these two dramas differ formally and stylistically from the two fairy-tale dramolettes, they deal with many of the same ideas as the other two, themes that would continue to preoccupy Walser throughout his career: the artist's marginal position on the threshold of life; the artificiality of romantic love; the inherent theatricality of human interaction; and the inappropriateness of socially prescribed gender roles.

The success of these first theatrical pieces does not seem to have inspired Walser to continue to engage with the dramatic form. During his years in Berlin and the early years in Biel (1913–19), Walser focused his efforts on writing novels and short prose for publication in newspapers and literary journals, and there is no evidence that he produced new dramas during this time.[14] Nevertheless, his enduring confidence in the literary quality of his early dramas—and by extension in his own abilities as a dramatist—does not seem to have waned, as is evidenced by the fact that he repeatedly approached various publishers in the 1900s and 1910s and tried to interest them in the idea of a book publication of the four early dramolettes,[15] which he presented as "kühne, freie jugendliche tänzerische Prosa- und Versspiele, Bühnenvorgänge" (bold, free, youthful dancing prose and verse plays, stage scenes).[16]

Walser's efforts were finally successful, when the volume *Komödie* (*Comedy*) was published by Bruno Cassirer in 1919.[17] The recognition afforded by the fulfillment of this literary goal seems also to have inspired Walser to return to the dramatic form again, and in the course of the 1920s he succeeded in publishing quite a few short theatrical scenes in newspapers and literary reviews. The drafts of many more dramatic scenes were discovered amongst the 526 pages of microscript texts, indicating that the dramatic form continued to fascinate Walser even in the final years of his writing career.

One concern for the critics has often been the question of how Walser's sketches and dramolettes should be understood and categorized.[18] Many seem too short or lacking in action to merit a stage performance, and others, particularly those contained in the microscripts, include stylistic quirks and far-fetched action that would seem difficult, if not altogether impossible, to depict on stage. Indeed, Walser's own explanation of how he understands his fairy-tale plays seems relevant for all of his dramatic oeuvre. In a letter to a publisher in 1912, he writes:

> Sie sind ganz Poesie, und durchaus nur für künstlerisch genießende Erwachsene. [. . .] Sie sind auf den Stil und auf die Schönheit angelegt, und der Genuß des *Buches* ist daran die Hauptsache. Ob sie je aufgeführt werden könnten, etwa mit Musik, ist ganz und gar fraglich und erscheint vorläufig völlig nebensächlich. Sie sind auf Rede und Sprache gestimmt, auf Takt und rhythmischen Genuß.[19]

> They are entirely poetry and really only for adults who appreciate artistic things. [. . .] They are constructed on style and beauty, and the enjoyment of the *book* is the main thing. Whether they could ever be put on with, for instance, music is totally questionable and seems for the present utterly beside the point. They are tempered for speech and language, to a beat and a rhythmic enjoyment.[20]

Evidently then, Walser is not concerned whether or in what form his dramas might be performed on stage; rather, he intends them to be read and enjoyed primarily as literary texts and as poetic works of art.

Dieter Borchmeyer argues that one of the main reasons Walser's enigmatic dramatic sketches are so unsuitable for the stage is that they continually reflect on their own theatricality:

> Theater's play with itself is one of its oldest motifs and one of the most effective on stage. Walser's dramas intensify the potency of this play to such an extent that it can hardly be conveyed scenically. They are a meta-theater that does not hark back to theater but rather transcends the real stage. Walser was doubtless well aware of this.[21]

Borchmeyer's contention that Walser's dramatic scenes constitute a type of metatheater will prove central to this essay. I wish to take Borchmeyer's argument a step further by relating it to Walser's mimicry of cultural norms in his work. In doing so, I argue that the self-referentiality and self-mockery of Walser's theater pieces are not merely for their own sake but can be read as a radical gesture that challenges the power structures that the writer perceives in his cultural environment.

This essay will delve deeper into the metatheatricality of Walser's drama to examine how its subversive potential enacts—in the most literal sense—a subtle subversion not just of the formal conventions of theater but also of the relationship between original and copy; the norms of human interaction; and—bearing in mind Walser's insistence that his dramas should be understood primarily as *written* texts—the conventions of the reading and writing process. It will focus on two of his lesser-known dramas from the later period of his productivity, namely the fairy-tale-like dramolette *Das Christkind* (*The Christ Child*, 1920), which is a dramatization of the nativity scene; and the microscript draft *Angela Borgia / Julio / Der Kardinal / Der Herzog / Lukrezia / Der Autor dieser Szene* (*Angela Borgia / Giulio / The Cardinal / The Duke / Lucrezia / The Author of This Scene*, 1925), a short dramatic scene based on a historical episode. Through exploring how content and form are collapsed in Walser's dramas with the reader's expectations of the dramatic form, this essay will investigate how his writing produces a space for the destabilization and subversion of power relations.[22]

Divine Intervention: *The Christ Child* (1920)

Walser's dramatic scenes of the early 1920s do not display any evidence of the fact that he had not published any new dramas in almost twenty years; in fact, in some cases, it almost seems as though the writer picked up where he left off. Some of the dramas of this period play with the same models, motifs, and forms that preoccupied the writer in his early dramolettes. A particularly pertinent example of this is a third fairy-tale dramolette, namely *Dornröschen* (*Sleeping Beauty*), which appeared in the Swiss journal *Pro Helvetia* in December 1920. Like Walser's much earlier dramatic renditions of the Grimm tales, his interpretation of the Sleeping Beauty story exploits the reader's familiarity with the Grimm pre-texts to question the rigidity of the genre. Interestingly, however, Walser published another drama in the very same month—significantly in *Die neue Rundschau*, which was one of Germany's most important literary magazines of this era. When one compares the two dramas, it is evident that the two pieces have much in common. *The Christ Child* is not, strictly speaking, a fairy tale; unlike *Snow White*, *Cinderella*, and *Sleeping Beauty*, it is not based on one of the famous fairy stories compiled by the Brothers Grimm. However, the manner in which Walser makes use of the reader's familiarity with the story on which it is based to subvert his/her expectations is very similar to the way he plays on the formalities and structures of the fairy tale to undermine its power. Daniele Pantano and James Reidel's decision to include *The Christ Child* as a fourth fairy-tale dramolette in their recent volume of translations, *Fairy Tales*, reinforces its formal, stylistic and thematic affinity to the three Grimm dramas.[23] In a translator's note included in the volume, Pantano and Reidel comment explicitly on their motivation for this decision: "The inclusion here of *The Christ Child* is our inescapable assertion that Walser intended it as a fairy tale, too, given all the devotion to the original text as the other three."[24]

Walser's short drama represents a scene that is known to most readers all over the Christian world, namely the nativity of Jesus Christ. It is significant to note that the readers' familiarity with the motifs and plot of the biblical tale is not only based on the accounts included in the Gospels of Luke and Matthew but also on numerous performances and reenactments staged at Christmastime. Indeed, the complete absence of any description of the scenery indicates that the writer fully expects that none is necessary, since the reader will already be well acquainted with the background and setting. Walser uses the reader's familiarity with the story and expectations of how it *should* go to subvert the power of the holy pre-text and offer a failed copy of its reenactment. As the following analysis will show, the metatheater inherent to the drama serves the purpose of calling into question the sanctity of the age-old tale and poking fun at its authority.

The dramatis personae of Walser's nativity scene includes the usual suspects—the simple carpenter Joseph and his virtuous wife Mary; the three wise magi who have followed a star to this humble stable; and a few shepherds and simple folk who have been guided to this holy place by a heavenly host of angels. However, all of the characters in this drama repeatedly draw attention to the theatrical elements of the scene in a manner that reminds the reader at all turns that this is yet another dramatic reenactment of a well-established story. The kings, for example, are immediately recognizable to the reader as such due to their ornate costumes; even Joseph, who initially seems quite flummoxed by the arrival of the majestic visitors, notes that their dress and regalia mean they must be men of high rank and culture. Joseph and Mary, initially rather bemused by the attitude of their visitors, comment on their appearance and demeanor, as if assessing the quality of their role-playing; they wonder if the kings are being just a little too polite and they question their words. Indeed, it is the utter conviction of their guests and the persuasiveness of their *performance* that ultimately convinces the holy couple that their visitors must be right in believing that their son is the Messiah.

Alongside the stock characters one would expect in a nativity play, Walser also includes a few additional figures whose function can only be to call attention to the theatrical quality of the scene. Three characters in particular seem a little out of place: a soldier, a vagabond, and a jester. The soldier seems to have made an appearance a little too early in this particular story; we would normally expect him to accompany Jesus to his death rather than to assist at his birth. His presence in the nativity drama reminds us that the end of this particular story is already written. The soldier reinforces the link a between birth and death that is played out elsewhere in this scene, for example when the First King accidently gives away the ending of the story to Mary by revealing that her son will suffer before his death, or when the Shepherd tells Joseph that he was drawn to the stable by angels singing "Christ ist / erstanden" (Christ is risen) (*SW*, 14:181; *FT*, 101).[25] Thus the inclusion of the soldier can be read as both reproducing the conventional story of Jesus and producing a subtle slippage designed to point to its artificiality.

The jester and vagabond, on the other hand, have no part to play in the Christmas story; they are clearly only added in for their entertainment value. The jester in particular accentuates the playacting and posturing associated with comic theater. He has little to say, but he joins in the action with gusto; he, like the other visitors, professes his zeal to see the newborn Messiah. When Joseph addresses him directly to ask him if he too is in awe of the baby, he answers "Ungemein sogar!" (Incredibly so!) (*SW*, 14:179; *FT*, 99). As is evident in this extravagant pronouncement, his performance in the scene is just a little too exaggerated and thus comes across as a pretense. The vagabond is also an interloper who has wandered into this scene from other Walser texts. As a nomad, an outsider who lives on the margins, he is always a little distant from the action; and here too, we sense an ironic detachment. His proclamation, "Ich möchte dieses Wunderkind / auch gerne sehn" (I too would very much like to see / this miracle child) (*SW*, 14:179; *FT*, 99), comes across as somewhat ambiguous, in particular because the German word "Wunderkind"—as indeed its usage in English indicates—is often used to mean a child prodigy or genius. Through his choice of wording, the vagabond thus casts doubt upon the divine status of the infant Jesus and indicates an ironic stance toward the entire scene.

The metatheatrical gesture moves beyond the self-reflexivity of theater to subvert the relationship between the story we see enacted in this scene and its relationship to its venerated pre-text. The particular ways in which Walser weaves the expectations of the reader into the fabric of his version of the scene are clearly designed to question the authority of the biblical story. Where the biblical Joseph and the Virgin Mary are from the outset aware of their roles as earthly father and mother of the Messiah and accept this responsibility without wavering, Walser's Joseph and Mary have no clue that their newborn son is special and thus are rather perplexed as to why so many visitors have arrived to welcome him into the world. Joseph seems quite astonished, but is nonetheless persuaded by the strangers' apparent conviction that his child is "der längst Ersehnte" (the Long-Awaited One) (*SW*, 14:177; *FT*, 97), so he invites them in to meet his wife so she can size them up. Mary, who seems a little more sensible than her hapless husband, tut-tuts at Joseph's gullibility:

MARIA: Bist du nicht alleweil
ein Kind, trotz deiner Jahr' und vielen
Erfahrungen; willst du, daß dich
dein Bart auslacht und deine Stirn-
runzeln sich deiner schämen? Red' nicht
so unvorsichtig. (*SW*, 14:181)

MARY: Aren't you always a child,
this despite your years and many
lessons learned? Do you want your beard
laughing at you and your brow's wrinkles
to be ashamed of you? Don't talk
so carelessly. (*FT*, 101)

Mary questions the visitors' motives: "Sind sie nicht von Betrug erfaßt?" (Have they been taken in by fraud?) (*SW*, 14:180; *FT*, 100); she is far more inclined to dismiss the suggestion that her son was born to bring happiness to all mankind as either childish fantasy or complete madness.

In Walser's other fairy-tale dramas, the characters appear all too aware of the power of the Grimm pre-text over their behavior and their fate; as the Prince insists to Cinderella, "Das Märchen will's. Das Märchen ist's / gerad', das uns verlobt will sehn" (The fairy tale wants it. It's clear, / the fairy tale will see us wed) (*SW*, 14:71; *FT*, 94).[26] In a similar vein, the various visitors who descend on Joseph and Mary are utterly convinced of their version of events, simply because that's how the story goes. There is then a peculiar split here between the "original" biblical story of the birth of Christ and its dramatic reenactment; Joseph and Mary appear to be figures in a story that the visitors have all heard before and are now coming to see acted out for them. When Joseph probes them further, the strangers cannot say who told them that the Messiah would be born here tonight, but they seem bolstered in their faith by the fact that the others have heard the same story. The characters' apparent adherence to the story line serves thus both to sustain the authority of the biblical scene and to emphasize its hollowness. In Walser's version of events, it is not entirely clear whether there is any real pre-text or whether story becomes real through the enactment of the scene on the stage. To use Borchmeyer's term, the overlapping of various theatrical layers can be understood as a kind of self-conscious metatheater, but one that destabilizes the apparently secure relationship between original and reproduction and therefore presents the Bible story as too rigid and lacking in meaning.

A remark by the First King can be read as an indirect reference to the incongruity of the many versions of this story, in which the magi are often called by different names; he comments, "die einen titulieren uns Weise, / andern erscheinen wir als Kön'ge" (Some give us the title of wise men. / To others we appears as kings) (*SW*, 14:178; *FT*, 98). This self-conscious remark draws attention to the many tellings and retellings of the story, in which the magi sometimes appear as "three kings" and at other times as "three wise men." Walser's kings point to inconsistencies in the way they have been represented in narrative, as if to undermine their own credibility. His dramatization of the nativity scene thus encourages us to question the legitimacy of the revered pre-text on which the scene is based. The story has gained power, it seems, through being retold and reenacted over and over again; but when we look for evidence of its authority, all we are left with is a bewildered couple who have little to do with the crowd of strangers who have arrived at their door to worship their newborn child.

However, the fact that the event that Walser represents here is one of the central scenes of Christian teaching adds a further dimension to his sly subversion of authority, and it is evident that there is a critique of religious faith and of organized religion at the heart of Walser's distinctive performance of the nativity scene. The repeated references to the theatrical quality of the scene as well as the fact that it is based on a story that has been passed from one generation to the next accentuate the artificiality of the stage action. Mary's remark to Joseph, "Sie sind wohl all' entweder / nicht recht gescheit oder dann selig, / vielleicht spricht Gott aus ihrem Munde?" (Likely they are all either / very mad or simply too overjoyed. / Could it be that God speaks from their mouths?) (*SW*, 14:183; *FT*, 103), suggests that she is coming around to the strangers' version of events. At the same time, no reader familiar with Walser's playful wit could overlook the tongue-in-cheek undertone of Mary's comment, which can also be read as a cunning challenge to the power of the biblical story. While her words uphold the sanctity of the religious tale and assert it to be the word of God, they also link such blind faith to madness. Even the visitors destabilize the reliability of their own story by the addition of subclauses in which they question what they see and feel and think. The Young Girl and the Old Man, transfixed at the sight of the newborn Jesus, are carried away with emotion:

> DAS MÄDCHEN: Was ist's für ein entzückend' Licht,
> Das ihm um das Gesichte leuchtet?
> Woher rührt dieser holde Strahl?
> Oder trügen mich meine Augen?
> DER ALTE: Nein, nein, auch ich seh' jetzt den Schein,
> Die ganze Stub' ist hell davon,
> Wenn nicht ein arger Wahn mich blendet. (*SW*, 14:181–82)

> YOUNG GIRL: Why is such an enchanted glow
> Shining around the face of him?
> From where beats this lovely shaft of light?
> Or do my eyes play tricks on me?
> OLD MAN: No, no, I see the glow now too.

If the whole room's not bright with it,
I'm blinded by an evil mirage. (*FT*, 101–2)

Walser is playing here on established motifs and features of the nativity scene in order to underpin the idea expressed throughout this drama that the progression of the action is always already established by the preexisting text. The image of the nativity is frequently represented in Christian art, and in many paintings, the child Jesus is depicted either bathed in light from above or with light emanating from him.[27] The image of Jesus that the characters claim to see is a clichéd copy of an image; what they see is dictated by what they have already seen. At the same time, the characters' words cast an element of doubt on the authority of the story: it is equally possible that the Young Girl's eyes are playing tricks on her or that the Old Man is blinded by an evil mirage.

In *The Christ Child*, Walser takes on one of the most authoritative and influential texts of Western culture. His reenactment of the nativity scene pays homage to its extraordinary power and vision and seems in many instances to bolster the strength of the Christmas story. However, his mimicry is always just a little too practiced, his performance a little too contrived. Though the drama features many of the characters, gestures, and props normally required to satisfy the needs of the nativity scene, the repeated emphasis on their value as elements of a staged scene severs the dramatic enactments from any apparent deeper significance. Walser's subtle and in some cases not-so-subtle parody of the story and its power to inspire and reinforce the faith of millions of followers leaves us in no doubt as to his skepticism vis-à-vis organized religion in general and Christianity specifically.

Dramatizing the Writing: *Angela Borgia / Giulio / The Cardinal / The Duke / Lucrezia / The Author of This Scene* (1925)

Walser's renewed interest in dramatic form after the publication of *Comedy* in 1919 continued for several years. In the course of the 1920s, he wrote a significant number of short plays and dramatic scenes, many of which he succeeded in publishing in prominent newspapers such as the *Prager Presse* and the *Neue Zürcher Zeitung* as well as some of the leading literary journals, including the *Neue Rundschau* and *Individualität*. His final book publication, *Die Rose* (*The Rose*, 1925) also included a number of short dialogues. The transcription of the microscripts in more recent years has also revealed that Walser drafted many more such texts that, for one reason or another, he did not submit for publication. The published volumes of the microscripts include thirty-five unpublished dramatic scenes, which, when taken together with the published texts of the Bern period and the twenty-four *Felix* scenes transcribed and published by Jochen Greven, bring Walser's dramatic output of this period to almost a hundred short dramas, sketches, and scenes.

The dramatic texts that exist only in microscript form are for the most part much shorter than Walser's published pieces, often consisting of only one scene; furthermore, the subject matter—or, in many cases, the apparent lack thereof—provides some hints as to why they were not selected for publication. The scenes are often meandering dialogues or monologues that do not appear to have a clear direction or aim. Rather, they are highly self-reflexive, playful texts that constitute a challenge to the reader; they seem to bring to the fore questions such as the connections between power and language, between tradition and revolution, or between appearance and reality. Some of the scenes are based on stories or situations from history, mythology, or literature that the reader would likely be familiar with; others are based on hierarchical constellations that the reader might have encountered in everyday life—for example, a negotiation between a landlord and a tenant.[28] Most of these scenes play with the reader's expectations of how the story usually goes or how the hierarchy normally plays out; it seems as though Walser is using the freedom afforded him by his "Bleistiftgebiet," his domain of the pencil, to try out alternative outcomes to these familiar scenes.[29] The metatheatrical gesture, which according to Borchmeyer "transcends the real stage," reaches beyond the text to expose the assumptions governing power relationships and thus to rob them of their authority.[30] As the following analysis will show, Walser's microscript dramas often go beyond the thematic and formal destabilization of the relationship between original and copy, text and pre-text that we know from his published dramas to present a more radical challenge to conventional notions of authorship and to disrupt the relationship between writer and text.

In 1925 Walser drafted a dramatic scene that draws inspiration from a renowned historical, political, and romantic conflict from sixteenth-century Rome, namely the contest between Cardinal Ippolito d'Este and his illegitimate brother Don Giulio d'Este for the affections of the beautiful Angela Borgia (*AdB*, 2:447–50). Lady-in-waiting to and close confidante of her ill-reputed cousin, Lucrezia Borgia, the Duchess of Ferrara, Angela was as renowned for her beauty as she was for her virtue, and her portrait was painted by Leonardo da Vinci in 1507. The infamous exploits of the Borgia family have of course inspired numerous literary renditions: Cesare Borgia featured as the villainous hero of Machiavelli's politico-philosophical treatise *The Prince* (1532); his sister, Lucrezia Borgia, was the subject of a drama by Victor Hugo (*Lucrezia Borgia*, 1833), which in turn was rendered in operatic form by Gaetano Donizetti (*Lucrezia Borgia*, 1833); and Alexandre Dumas devoted a volume of his *Celebrated Crimes* to the transgressions of this notorious family (*The Borgias*, 1840). Angela Borgia's story has also been portrayed in literature, notably by the Swiss poet and historical novelist Conrad Ferdinand Meyer in his final novella, "Angela Borgia" (1891).

Once again then, Walser's dramatic scene hinges on the reader's familiarity with a historical and literary pre-text—and one that provides rich material for the writer to offer his own particular perspective on the scene. The story goes that Cardinal Ippolito and his playboy brother Don Giulio were both in love with Angela, but she declared to the Cardinal that she preferred Giulio because of his striking dark eyes. Consumed by jealousy and determined to destroy his brother, the Cardinal ordered his footmen to kill Giulio and gouge out his eyes. Though the Cardinal's servants beat Giulio badly and caused him to lose the sight in one eye, he lived to tell the tale. Given the action-packed pre-text, it might be considered surprising that Walser's dramatic scene contains little action. Instead, it explores how the attraction of this particular story lies in the characterization of the figures, on the one hand, and the motifs associated with it, on the other.

Like his nativity play, Walser's Angela Borgia sketch includes the same cast as the historical plot, so that it appears to pay homage to the story's power even as it seeks to interrogate that power. The five main characters in Walser's drama bear a remarkable resemblance to their historical counterparts: the beautiful and virtuous Angela; the lecherous womanizer Giulio; the dastardly, vengeful Cardinal; the beautiful but crafty Lucrezia; and her smitten husband, the Duke. However, the blatantly theatrical quality of the scene is palpable from the beginning. The characters are presented throughout as caricatures identifiable only through these traits; indeed, the dialogue in the scene consists largely of comments in which they describe how the other characters' appearances and utterances reinforce the roles they play within the drama. The characters themselves thus seem overtly aware of their own one-dimensionality and of the way their traits have been exaggerated in the retellings of their story. Moreover, their repeated references to these characteristics suggest that the entire story, their very existence, is dependent on them. Referring to Walser's fairy-tale dramolettes, Reto Sorg argues, "When the characters speak of their existence, they stand as if beside themselves. Everything has already happened; time has stopped; life becomes reflectively stretched apart."[31] Sorg's words are even more relevant for the characters in Walser's Angela Borgia scene, who recognize themselves as players in a historical drama that has become rigid and inflexible through its numerous retellings.

The scene apparently takes place after Angela has declared her love for Giulio, but before the Cardinal has had the opportunity to exact his revenge on his half-brother. However, the characters seem already to be aware of the inevitable outcome of their interaction; because they are who they are, the story must go as it must. Thus, when Angela speaks to Giulio, her words reiterate the immorality and lasciviousness that have come to be associated with him: she pronounces,

> Die Geschichte nennt dich einen Ruchlosen, und ich gehöre zu denen, die das in Abrede stellen möchten. [. . .] Daß du mitansiehst, wie ich um dich zittere, empört mich. Sie nennen dich laut einen Verworfenen, du zuckst darüber nicht mit der Wimper. (*AdB*, 2:447)

> History calls you a reprobate and I belong to those would like to call that into question. [. . .] It appalls me that you watch as I tremble for you. They all call you depraved and you don't even bat an eyelid.

Angela's words remind Giulio of the characteristics with which he is associated; but more than this, they suggest that his character is defined by how he *has been* and *will be* defined by history. The self-reflexivity integral to Walser's metatheater is thus mobilized to perform a radical subversion of the notion of linear time. Past, present, and future seem to have blended together, so that it is not entirely clear whether the "Unglück" (misfortune) (*AdB*, 2:447) that awaits Giulio is a consequence of his actions or if his actions now are dictated by the historical events that will follow.

The Cardinal makes a barbed comment about Giulio to the Duke that expresses very well the complexity of the temporal and causal association between Giulio's character and his fate: "[Julio] lechzt nach dem Ruhm, mißhandelt worden zu sein" (Giulio lusts after the reputation of having been abused) (*AdB*, 2:449). Here, the Cardinal's words play on Giulio's reputation for being an immoral philanderer who will get his just deserts, thereby absolving him, the Cardinal, of responsibility for his violent attack on Giulio. At the same time, his words conjure up an action that *will have happened* as a result of his own reaction to Giulio's appearance and character and that will moreover dictate how he *will have been viewed* by history. The complex interweaving of past and present, imagined action and past action, and appearance and reality disrupts the concept of linear, historical time, and underlines the idea that the characters in the drama have no autonomy; they are like pawns in a game that has already been decided. The authoritative pre-text dictates their actions, their behavior, and their fate.

At the same time, there is the inevitable moment of slippage that we always find in Walser's subversion of prescribed forms: there are moments where the characters seem to go "off script" and imagine alternative endings to their collective story, and these alternative plots undermine the power of the rigid story lines within which they are compelled to function. Walser's Giulio seems particularly prone to flights of fancy; he deviates from the story line of the historical drama to tell Angela about a recent failed attempt to go to the theater—yet another overt reminder to the reader of the medium—and encourages her to look at their situation a little differently from how history dictates:

> JULIO: Der Kardinal leidet unter dem Bedürfnis, der Klügste zu sein, aber die Lebenslust ist klüger als er. Wenn etwas in mir lacht, bin ich an Weisheit nicht zu übertreffen. Er nennt mich absurd, weil er mir nicht die Hand zu geben wagt, aus Furcht, es könnte ihn kränken. Angela, tu' mir den Gefallen und liebe den Kardinal.
>
> ANGELA (*gedankenvoll*): Entweder plapperst du in's Blaue oder sprichst etwas sehr Sinnreiches aus. (*AdB*, 2:449)

GIULIO: The Cardinal suffers from a need to be the cleverest, but the lust for life is cleverer than he is. When something in me laughs, I can't be beaten in wisdom. He calls me absurd because he doesn't dare to shake my hand for fear it could offend him. Angela, do me a favor and love the Cardinal.

ANGELA (*pensively*): Either you're babbling about things you know nothing about or what you're saying is very reasonable.

Giulio's words indicate the extent to which the Cardinal is stuck in the role he is forced by the historical story into playing; his need to outperform Giulio in vying for Angela's affection is causing him suffering. By contrast, Giulio wishes to liberate himself from the constraints of the story and live and laugh, which he evidently considers a far more alluring approach to their situation. In suggesting that the Cardinal is afraid to back down, shake his hand, and bring an end to the rivalry between them, he also hints that this is something the Cardinal desires, too. His appeal to Angela to do him a favor and choose the Cardinal is thus a plea for her to enable all three of them to break through the bounds of their roles and conjure up a different ending to their story.

Walser's dramatic scenes continuously reflect on their own theatricality and drama. In the case of this pencil sketch, the characters themselves highlight the rigidity of the historical plot by repeatedly emphasizing the ways in which their own characteristics have been exaggerated through the numerous retellings and representations of their story. Moreover, they rebel against the limitations of that rigid structure by imagining an alternative ending to their shared fate, thereby belying the power of the historical pre-text. What separates this microscript drama from the published dramas of the same period however is that Walser's text also enacts a similar rebellion on a formal level, where the characters in the drama remind us of the materiality of the text *as written text*, and where, moreover, the relationship between author and the product of his authorship is destabilized.

The writing process is accentuated through the involvement of a sixth character in this particular drama, one whose presence is only announced in the stage directions at the end of the text, but whose power can be felt throughout. In many of the dramas of the Bern period, the stage directions do not conform to the norms of the genre: they contain neither instructions regarding the characters' movements or expressions nor details of the setting, lighting, or sound effects. As Marion Gees argues, they represent "subtexts" that seem to distract from rather than add to the dialogue: "The 'subtext' does not serve its supposed purpose of specifying that which is presented, but rather it often underlines the arbitrariness and insignificance of what is said, or follows it with new observations that are completely independent of the 'main text.'"[32] In some cases, these subtexts comment on the action, usually from an ironic distance; in others, they question the characters' actions or even make fun of their interaction. These self-referential subtexts remind us at all stages of the presence of an author who is writing this drama as it is being performed; they highlight the material circumstances of the textual production.

The "subtext" with which this particular drama closes can be understood as an ironic comment about the drama that has resulted from the writing; it puts the author center-stage as he looks back over the text he has produced and critically assesses what he has done:

> *Der Autor dieser Szene* (scheint sich an Conrad Ferdinand Meyer zart angeschmiegt zu haben. Wie es scheint, experimentiert er. Zum Mindesten beweist er einige Bildung und scheut vor einer gewissen Anlehnung nicht zurück. Er hält sich nichtsdestoweniger für originell, fast für zu sehr. Bekam er das häufig genug zu hören?) (*AdB*, 2:449–50)

> *The Author of this Scene* (seems to have gently nestled up to Conrad Ferdinand Meyer. It seems as though he's experimenting. At least he's demonstrating some education and he doesn't shy away from a little imitation. He nevertheless thinks he's original, maybe a little too much so. Was he told that often enough?)

The closing subtext of this scene confirms the "Author's" awareness that he is paying tribute to a literary pre-text, specifically C. F. Meyer's version of the Angela Borgia story. The self-mockery evident in his remarks that he has "gently nestled up to" Meyer in writing this scene is indicative of the exaggerated—and thus ironic—homage he pays to his literary predecessor. At the same time, the subsequent lines imply a sense of satisfaction that he has done something different with the story. The additional comment that he has been "maybe a little too" original in his approach to the story—specifically by imagining an entirely different ending for the characters—may be read as depicting the author who wonders about the marketability of a text that strays so far from the reader's expectations of literary as well historical convention. No doubt Walser's originality was praised many times in the course of his literary career; but there is a fine line between originality and peculiarity, and many of Walser's texts stray a little too far into the territory of the peculiar to be considered suitable for common consumption.

Walser's pencil draft of a drama emphasizes the revolutionary potential of the space that is opened up through his dramatic writing. His self-conscious imitation of theatrical forms reveals its slippage at every turn; the characters themselves comment on their characterization and assess each other's capacity to stay on character and fulfill the roles laid out for them. His rendering of the Angela Borgia story—or to be more accurate, his imitation of C. F. Meyer's rendering of the Angela Borgia story—nods to the historical and literary pre-texts and yet rejects the one-dimensionality of their characters and the limitations of the story line.

It is in writing himself into the drama though, in giving himself the part of "Author" of his own text, that Walser enacts his most radical mimicry, in that he self-consciously disrupts his own authority as author. His dramatization of the writing process and of his own role within it points to the power structures that permeate the literary text, even at the point of its production: the text is always already potentially publishable, and the author must always cast a cool editorial eye over what he has just produced to assess its quality. At the same time, his inclusion of himself as a player in his little drama lays bare his own paradoxical role as its producer and director; yet he calls attention to his authority only to undermine it. Walser's dramatic performance of the process of writing his draft ultimately reveals the material circumstances of the production of his text and destabilizes his own power as author.

Conclusion

Walser's affection for the theater is evident in the playful eccentricity of his dramatic scenes, which endures from his very first attempts at drama to the pencil drafts of scenes that he writes in diminutive microscript form. His insistence that his dramas are intended to be read rather than performed is evident in the way in which the scenes repeatedly draw attention to their own theatricality, a characteristic that Borchmeyer has captured in his identification of the metatheatrical quality of Walser's dramas. Beyond this self-conscious takeoff of the dramatic form, the texts also incorporate other mimetic elements. As shown in this essay, Walser parodies the power structures and hierarchies that pervade social and cultural norms. The dramas discussed here use the space offered by the inevitable slippage between faithful imitation and parodic simulation to subvert conventional notions of power and authority. In Walser's mimicry of literary forms, his innovative retellings undermine their authoritative pre-texts even as they seem to replicate their conventions. Indeed, one might argue that the tension between freedom and discipline, conformism and rebellion that pervades all of Walser's oeuvre finds its most intense expression in his dramatic scenes. The dramas also allow the writer space to explore his own agency as writer and producer of the dramatic text and to chip away at the power associated with authorship: to perform a subtle deconstruction of that power and a subversive play with authority.

Notes

1. Walser's poetry has also tended to be neglected by academic criticism, as Samuel Frederick argues in his essay in this volume.

2. Jochen Greven casts doubt on the probability that Walser actually auditioned for Kainz, since there is no record of him having performed in Stuttgart. Greven

suggests that it is more likely that Walser auditioned for Eleonore Benzinger-Wahlmann: Greven, " 'Er fährt nach dem Schwabenland': Robert Walsers Jahr in Stuttgart," presentation at the annual meeting of the Robert Walser Society, June 23, 2007. Available at http://www.robertWalser.ch/fileadmin/redaktion/dokumente/jahrestagungen/vortraege/Greven-2007.pdf (accessed July 6, 2016).

3. Walser writes this scene into several of his literary texts—for example, "Die Talentprobe" ("The Audition") (*SW*, 2:67–69) and "Wenzel" (*SW*, 2:81–91), as well as the early dramatic scene "Die Knaben" ("The Boys") (*SW*, 14:7–17).

4. Cited in Robert Mächler, *Das Leben Robert Walsers: Eine dokumentarische Biographie* (Frankfurt am Main: Suhrkamp, 2003), 41.

5. Martina Schaak, *"Das Theater ein Traum": Robert Walsers Welt als gestaltete Bühne* (Berlin: Wissenschaftlicher Verlag Berlin, 1999). Bernhard Böschenstein estimates that around fifty of Walser's prose pieces published between 1902 and 1912 deal directly or indirectly with the theater: Böschenstein, "Theatralische Miniaturen: Zur frühen Prosa Robert Walsers," in *Probleme der Moderne: Studien zur deutschen Literatur von Nietzsche bis Brecht*, ed. Benjamin Bennett, Anton Kaes, and William J. Lillyman (Tübingen: Niemeyer, 1983), 67.

6. Lothar Kurzawa, "'Ich ging eine Weile als alte Frau': Subjektivität und Maskerade bei Robert Walser," in *Robert Walser*, ed. Klaus-Michael Hinz and Thomas Horst (Frankfurt am Main: Suhrkamp, 1991), 168.

7. Marion Gees, *Schauspiel auf Papier: Gebärde und Maskierung in der Prosa Robert Walsers* (Berlin: Erich Schmidt, 2001).

8. Letter to the Rascher Verlag, April 14, 1918 (*Briefe*, 132).

9. Peter Utz, *Tanz auf den Rändern. Robert Walsers "Jetztzeitstil"* (Frankfurt am Main: Suhrkamp, 1998), 39.

10. Schröder quoted in Kurt Ifkovits, "Der Kreis um *Die Insel*," in *Robert Walser-Handbuch: Leben-Werk-Wirkung*, ed. Lucas Marco Gisi (Stuttgart: Metzler, 2015), 22.

11. Mark Harman's introduction to the English translation of the fairy-tale plays offers a useful starting point for the English-speaking reader: Harman, "Introduction: A Reluctant Modern," in *Robert Walser Rediscovered: Stories, Fairy-Tale Plays, and Critical Responses*, ed. Mark Harman (Hanover, N.H.: University Press of New England, 1985), 1–14. Jan Plug also includes a chapter on Walser's *Snow White* in his book *They Have All Been Healed: Reading Robert Walser* (Evanston, Ill.: Northwestern University Press, 2016).

12. Walter Benjamin, "Robert Walser," trans. Mark Harman, in *Robert Walser Rediscovered*, 146.

13. See in particular Andrea Hübner, *Ei', welcher Sinn liegt im Unsinn? Robert Walsers Umgang mit Märchen und Trivialliteratur* (Tübingen: Stauffenberg, 1995); Utz, *Tanz auf den Rändern*, 23–52.

14. Cf. Tobias Lambrecht, "Theater," in Gisi, *Robert Walser-Handbuch*, 383.

15. Jens Hobus mentions no less than six separate occasions when Walser offered his book of dramas to various publishers. Jens Hobus, "*Komödie* (1919)," in Gisi, *Robert Walser-Handbuch*, 83.

16. *Briefe*, 132.

17. This publication should not be confused with volume 14 of the Suhrkamp edition of Walser's work. That volume, which is also entitled *Komödie*, contains the four dramas published in 1919, along with the unpublished drama *Der Teich*

(*The Pond*, ca. 1900/1902, written in Bernese dialect), a number of other dramatic scenes that Walser published in the early 1920s, including *The Christ Child*, and the *Felix* scenes from the microscripts.

18. Susanne Andres compares the scenes to the open drama of the modernist period, due to the alienating effect of their lack of clear purpose and content. Susanne Andres, *Robert Walsers arabeskes Schreiben* (Göttingen: Cuvillier, 1997), 87. Ulf Bleckmann suggests that Walser's attentiveness to language in his dramas—at the expense of setting and action—prefigures Samuel Beckett's privileging of language in his absurdist plays such as *Waiting for Godot*. Bleckmann, *". . . ein Meinungslabyrinth, in welchem alle, alle herumirren . . .": Intertextualität und Metasprache als Robert Walsers Beitrag zur Moderne* (Frankfurt am Main: Peter Lang, 1994), 191.

19. Letter from Robert Walser to the E. Rowohlt / K. Wolff Verlag dated December 12, 1912 (*Briefe*, 59; emphasis in original).

20. This translation is taken in part from Reto Sorg, foreword to *Fairy Tales: Dramolettes* (New York: New Directions, 2015), vii, and is in part my own.

21. Dieter Borchmeyer, "Robert Walsers Metatheater: Über die Dramolette und szenischen Prosastücke," in *"Immer dicht vor dem Sturze . . .": Zum Werk Robert Walsers*, ed. Paolo Chiarini and Hans Dieter Zimmermann (Frankfurt am Main: athanäum, 1987), 135.

22. Walser's ambivalence toward and disruption of authority in his work is explored further in Valerie Heffernan, *Provocation from the Periphery: Robert Walser Re-examined* (Würzburg: Königshausen & Neumann, 2007).

23. *FT*, 97–108.

24. Sorg, foreword, xi. Sorg also argues that *The Christ Child* too can be read as a fairy tale. Ibid., viii.

25. Jochen Greven attributes this line to a prophetic slip of the tongue and suggests that the line should read "Christ ist geboren" (Christ is born). *SW*, 14:256. While this might seem more appropriate for the nativity scene, I would argue that the confusion of various elements of the Christ story is deliberate.

26. For a discussion of Walser's play with the Grimm pre-texts in his works based on fairy tales, see Heffernan, *Provocation from the Periphery*, 30–43.

27. This can be seen in well-known paintings such as Rubens's *Adoration of the Magi* (1609), Rembrandt's *Adoration of the Shepherds* (1646), as well as in many nineteenth-century Bible illustrations.

28. For a detailed an analysis of just such a scene, see the discussion of Walser's "Grieder/Grunder" dialogue in Heffernan, *Provocation from the Periphery*, 70–76.

29. For further information on Walser's "domain of the pencil," see Kai Evers's essay in this volume.

30. Borchmeyer, "Robert Walsers Metatheater," 135.

31. Sorg, foreword, ix.

32. Gees, *Schauspiel auf Papier*, 64.

Robert Walser and Violence

Strange Excursions into the Microscripts

Kai Evers

A man and a woman quarrel. Outraged by his impertinence, the woman decides to cut off the very thing from where "seine Lebenslust, sein beleidigendes Prangen und Lachen herrührte" (arose his lust for life, his offensive boastfulness and laughter).[1] While he sleeps, she gets a sharp instrument and "entfernte [. . .] von seinem Wesen, was ihrer Meinung nach keinesfalls dazu paßte" (removed from his being what in her opinion did not belong there). Sliced off, the man's manhood resembles "mehr einem Würstchen als dem Lauf einer Kanone" (rather a small sausage than the barrel of a cannon). The woman takes it to the kitchen, drops it in a pan, and fries it like a bratwurst. "Glaubt ihr, daß es ihr schmeckte, als sie's aß? Muß das eine Lust gewesen sein hineinzubeißen. Sie aß es vor seinen Augen glatt auf" (Do you believe she savored it when she ate it? What a pleasure it must have been to take a bite. She finished it right before his eyes). The man just sits there, watching her enjoying the cannibalistic meal.

One might expect such a bizarre sequence of events in the notoriously cruel and grotesque novellas of Hanns Heinz Ewers (1871–1943), but not in stories of his contemporary Robert Walser. When Thomas Mann read Walser's *Die Rose* (*The Rose*, 1925) shortly after its publication, he sent Walser a now-lost letter. Still incensed, Walser summarized this letter by "Herr Dr. Thomas Mann" to Frieda Mermet: "Ich sei in dem Buch 'Die Rose' klug wie ein sehr, sehr feines, vornehmenes, artiges und unartiges Kind, vielleicht demnach also gescheit und dumm" (that in the book "The Rose," I was clever like a very, very delicate, refined, well-behaved and mischievous child, therefore perhaps both smart and dumb) (*Briefe*, 226). Thomas Mann's characterization of him as not yet mature, mischievous but innocent, playful, light, and charming, angered Walser but continues to describe accurately the prevalent perception of his work.

The phallophagic scene from "Vor Wut über ihre Wut war sie grün" ("With Anger about Her Anger She Was Green," 1928) does not fit Walser's popular image. Nor does the cannibalistic story suit readings that note the darker regions below the surface of Walser's charming prose. Martin Walser read Robert Walser's writings as a paradigm for a literature of self-denial, echoing Walter Benjamin's observation that each of Walser's sentences is written to make the previous one be forgotten.[2] Had Benjamin seen Walser's posthumous papers, he would have learned how aware the Swiss author had been of his tendency for self-erasure; as one of his poetic alter egos comments, "Von Prosastück zu Prosastück ich husche / womit ich, was ich einmal war, vertusche, / wenn unerwünschte Sentiments mir nah'n" (From prose piece to prose piece I race / to erase what I once have been / when undesired sentiments approach) (*AdB*, 6:425). Most readers of Walser arrive at the same conclusion regarding the specific nature of these unpleasant sentiments that drive Walser's narrative voices to cancel out what they have just said. Benjamin and W. G. Sebald detected anxiety and despair lurking below the distractingly beautiful surfaces of Walser's sentences. Elias Canetti called Walser "the most concealed of all writers," whose works exemplify "an incessant attempt to keep silent about fear."[3]

The anxiety hidden below Walser's chatty prose has been analyzed in the context of Walser's stance toward power and authority. Despite an agreement on the sentiment propelling Walser's creativity, critics and fellow writers could not be more incompatible in their consideration of how such anxiety relates to Walser's representation of power and authority. Those tempted to interpret Walser's prose, often written in the first person, as deeply intertwined with its author's life and opinions, find in his writings predominantly an escape from power and authority into self-denial and silence. As Canetti argued, Franz Kafka took his most important lesson about power from Walser's example: the scheme of becoming smaller and smaller. Even the elegant and spacious calligraphy of Walser's early manuscripts shrinks to a minuscule and barely decipherable script in his later writings. It is as if Walser followed the dream of Jakob von Gunten, the eponymous hero of his third novel, to become nothing but a zero (*SW*, 11:8; *JvG*, 5). Walser's withdrawal from the public, his initially voluntary institutionalization, his decision to stop writing altogether—a literary silence lasting for more than twenty years—transformed him into one of European modernism's sacrosanct figures of innocence. Left alone and forgotten, Walser hid away from a world that would soon erupt into mass violence and destruction. Kafka and Walser are, as Canetti writes, "the better ones," experts in power who never succumbed to its temptations: "[Walser] is everything I am not: helpless, innocent and in an enchantingly trivial way truthful."[4] Without intending to, Canetti suggests, Walser resisted power by moving and being moved to the margin of society. First silenced by neglect and then silent by choice, he became one of the enduring writers of the twentieth century. By never seeming to come to the point in his narratives, with sentences that delay, defer, and renounce, Walser created one of literature's rare authentic oeuvres. As Canetti wrote, "He is truthful without making steps towards the truth; he becomes the truth by circling around it."[5]

Analyzing Walser's representation of power and authority, J. M. Coetzee offered a more sinister interpretation for Walser's figures of powerlessness and self-denial. Differentiating more insistently than Canetti between author and literary creation, Coetzee completes the characterization of Jakob von Gunten with aspects and features Canetti never commented on: he lauds

> Jakob's cynicism about civilization and about values in general, his contempt for the life of the mind, his simplistic beliefs about how the world really works (it is run by big business to exploit the little man), his elevation of obedience to the highest of virtues, his readiness to bide his time, awaiting the call of destiny, his claim to be descended from noble, warlike ancestors [. . .], as well as his pleasure in the all-male ambience of the boarding school and his delight in malicious pranks.[6]

Rather than avoiding or resisting power, Walser's protagonist turns himself into a submissive servant to authority, ready to follow commands, dreaming of the moment when he will be told to lash out against others. *Jakob von Gunten*, Coetzee suggests, points "prophetically toward the petit-bourgeois type that, in times of greater social confusion, would find Hitler's Brownshirts so attractive."[7]

Though diametrically opposed in their readings of Walser's representations of power and authority, ample evidence supports both Canetti's and Coetzee's theses. As much as their conclusions differ, however, they do not present the entire spectrum of Walser's writings on power, violence, and the self. Alongside strategies of deferral and avoidance, of submission and longing for suppression, one encounters again and again moments when Walser's stories dispel the spectral beauty of their meandering sentences with accounts of unremitting cruelty, mutilation, and sadistic pleasure. How do we reconcile these moments when Walser's first-person narrator relishes cruel and brutal acts of violence against others? Recently, scholars have suggested that they occur primarily in Walser's micrographic writings. Safely hidden under the veil of undecipherability, these stories break taboos and transgress all boundaries of propriety because no one but Walser was ever supposed to read them.[8] Should these moments of cruelty and detailed destruction be treated as curiosities in Walser's writings, or might they open up a path toward a more comprehensive understanding of the role of violence and power in Walser's work? These widely differing moments of withdrawal from authority, of submissive longing for the power of absolute destruction, and of pleasure drawn from cruelty against others fit together if one understands Walser's concept of the self not primarily as one of self-denial but as one of high placidity and malleability. The main focus of this investigation are texts drawn from Walser's microscripts, which are chosen because of their explicit focus on violence and cruelty and which, I argue, lead to a fuller understanding of Walser's concept of the self. These texts are not representative of all of Walser's microscripts, nor are they marginal exceptions. They not only illuminate peculiar aspects of his works, but also clarify why Walser holds a unique position in German modernism.

What Are Walser's Microscripts?

To answer this question, one has to distinguish between microscripts as material objects and microscripting as a method of writing. It remains uncertain how many microscripts once existed and when Walser started producing them. Jochen Greven estimates that at least two-thirds of Walser's entire work originated as microscripts.[9] Susan Bernofsky observes that Walser experimented as early as 1902 with tiny but still legible handwriting in his correspondence and might refer to the method of microscripting already in a passage from *Geschwister Tanner* (*The Tanners*, 1907), his first novel.[10] Walser's own account of the beginning of his microscripting is both imprecise and riddled with contradiction. In a letter to Max Rychner, he offered in June 1927 his most detailed account of the reasons for his new writing method:

> Sie sollen erfahren, mein Herr, dass ich vor ungefähr zehn Jahren anfing, alles, was ich produziere, zuerst scheu und andächtig mit Bleistift hinzuskizzieren, wodurch der Prozeß der Schriftstellerei naturgemäß eine beinahe in's Kolossale gehende, schleppende Langsamkeit erfuhr. [. . .] Für mich [. . .] hat die Bleistifterei eine Bedeutung. Für den Schreiber dieser Zeilen gab es nämlich einen Zeitpunkt, wo er die Feder schrecklich, fürchterlich haßte, wo er ihrer müde war, wie ich es Ihnen kaum zu schildern imstand bin, wo er ganz dumm wurde, so wie er sich ihrer nur ein bißchen zu bedienen begann, und um sich von diesem Schreibfederüberdruß zu befreien, fing er an zu bleistifteln, zu zeichnelen, zu gfätterlen. Für mich ließ es sich mit Hülfe des Bleistiftes wieder besser spielen, dichten; es schien mir, die Schriftstellerlust lebe dadurch von neuem auf. Ich darf Sie versichern, dass ich (es begann dies schon in Berlin) mit der Feder einen wahren Zusammenbruch meiner Hand erlebte, eine Art Krampf, aus dessen Klammern ich mich auf dem Bleistiftweg mühsam, langsam befreite. (*Briefe*, 300–301)

> You should know, sir, that approximately ten years ago I began to first shyly and reverentially sketch out in pencil everything I produced, which naturally imparted a sluggishness and slowness to the writing process that assumed practically colossal proportions. [. . .] The pencil method has great meaning for me. The writer of these lines experienced a time when he hideously, frightfully hated his pen, I can't begin to tell you how sick of it he was; he became an outright idiot the moment he made the least use of it; and to free himself from this pen malaise he began to pencil-sketch, to scribble, fiddle about. With the aid of my pencil I was better able to play, to write; it seemed this revived my writerly enthusiasm. I can assure you (this all began in Berlin) I suffered a real breakdown in my hand on account of the

> pen, a sort of cramp from whose clutches I slowly, laboriously freed myself by means of the pencil.[11]

Facing a creative crisis Walser adapted his way of writing to the new situation. His creative self proved flexible enough to fully regain his literary productivity. What Walser probably got wrong, as Bernofsky notes, is the when or where of the initial crisis.[12] Walser moved to Berlin in 1905 and returned to Switzerland in 1913. If the writer's block occurred in Berlin, then he overcame it with his pencil method not ten years earlier, in 1917, but maybe fourteen or even twenty years earlier. More importantly, and rather typical for Walser, he never mentioned the strangest aspect of his pencil method. To write first drafts in pencil is hardly unusual. But by writing in pencil Walser reduced the scale of his script so drastically that his scribbling and fiddling not only slowed him down, but made the micrographic drafts illegible to anyone except him. Of the surviving microscripts, Walser transcribed about one-third into normal script in preparation for publication.[13] Knowing the difficulty of deciphering what he wrote in pencil, Walser must have anticipated that any draft he did not transcribe would be lost to posterity.

Walser exposed all of his microscripts to the risk of likely destruction, and an unknown number have been lost. Of those written between 1924 and 1933, the only period from which microscripts survive, up to 40 percent might have been destroyed, according to Bernhard Echte, one of the editors and decipherers of these texts.[14] The surviving ones comprise a total of 526 leaves of paper. Of them, 117 are larger (13 × 21.5 cm) and on higher-quality material, paper generally meant for art prints. Another 158 leaves come from a daily calendar of 1926: Walser cut its pages in half and used them as writing material. Other paper sources are even more accidental and ephemeral, including envelopes, letters of rejection from publishers, and torn-off scraps of paper. Until 1933, the year of the last surviving microscript, Walser drafted on these papers a novel, love stories, literary portraits, essayistic stories, fictional letters, poems, and dramatic scenes as well as stories based on daily life events or responding to his readings of trivial literature.[15]

During his last two decades Walser undertook little to secure or publish these texts. In 1929, when he admitted himself into a sanatorium, he left some of the microscripts in his sister's house, not telling her what they were or what to do with them. Walser remained secretive about those he kept and added to them until 1933. After Lisa Walser's death in 1944, Carl Seelig became his second legal guardian. Starting in 1936, Seelig visited Walser in the sanatorium at Herisau. During their walks, he talked with him about literature, Walser's life, and current events. According to Seelig's account of these conversations, neither of them ever alluded to the existence of the microscripts.[16] When Walser died in 1956, by then long forgotten by the public, sanatorium officials discovered a shoebox filled with papers of varying sizes and quality, many of them yellowed and browned by age, most of them densely covered with scribblings too small to be legible. Left without instructions, they did not discard the box, as they easily could have done; instead, eight months later they sent everything to Seelig.

While Walser left the survival of the microscripts to chance, Seelig wrote instructions for their destruction. During the last decades of Walser's life, he was his literary executor, republishing new editions of Walser's works. Seelig showed little interest, however, in the contents of the shoebox he received in 1957. In October 1957 he compiled for the Swiss cultural magazine *Du* a beautifully illustrated portfolio in memory of his deceased friend and ward. Along with photographs of Walser and previously unpublished texts, it included the reproduction of a microscript in its original size. Next to it, Seelig placed a magnified excerpt to demonstrate its illegibility. He published these images not to distribute a work of literature, but as evidence of Walser's mental illness. The black-and-white reproductions were accompanied by his short, erroneous, and almost dismissive commentary.

> The self-invented indecipherable secret code that the poet used during the 1920s and later, at the onset of his mental illness, should be interpreted as the shy escape from the public's eye and as a calligraphically enchanting means of camouflage to hide his thoughts from it. In later years this secret code was abandoned once more in favor of normal script, but it could not be said that Robert Walser produced anything creatively new in it.[17]

This single reproduction in the journal *Du* could have very well become the sole surviving trace of Walser's microscripts. After examining the journal's facsimile, Jochen Greven, at the time a graduate student living in Cologne, wrote to Seelig. He included in his letter a transcription of the microscript, suggesting that Seelig might possess a treasure trove of unknown works by Walser. Rather than pursuing the lead, Seelig set up his last will, forbidding his heirs to publish any of Walser's manuscripts. All microscripts and all unpublished manuscripts should be burned upon his death. Evidently, Seelig believed Walser's creative powers had withered long ago and assumed that the microscripts, even if they could be deciphered, contained nothing worth preserving. Seelig died in 1962, and his lawyer ignored these instructions. Greven eventually became the editor of Walser's collected works, publishing thirteen volumes between 1966 and 1975, including, in 1972, two extensive transcriptions from Walser's microscripts: the novel *The Robber* and the *Felix* scenes. To get an idea of the sheer volume of texts hidden in Walser's minute handwriting, it is important to note that the novel and the *Felix* scenes together filled fewer than thirty-five pages of the entire packet of microscripts.

More than a decade after Greven's editorial work, Bernhard Echte and Werner Morlang made the best possible case for the preservation Walser's microscripts. They examined all 526 leaves once more and published, over fifteen years, six volumes under the title *Aus dem Bleistiftgebiet* (*From the Pencilscape*). One volume contained revised versions of *The Robber* and the *Felix* scenes, the other five volumes presented a plethora of previously unknown texts. But Echte and Morlang decided not to publish everything they could decipher. They did not, for instance, publish drafts of texts Walser had transcribed and revised himself. In 2008 the publishers Stroemfeld and Schwabe started a critical edition of Walser's complete works. Fourteen volumes are planned for the microscripts alone, including every text found on these 526 leaves of paper, regardless of whether the microscript had previously been published or prepared for publication by Walser. With this new edition of Walser's works another development in the reception of the microscripts will come to a conclusion.

What Walser kept in a shoebox and Seelig intended to destroy have since become objects of veneration. These papers of often poor quality, covered with a script illegible to the untrained eye, are considered today as much works of art as works of literature. With the reproduction of a microscript in the journal *Du*, Seelig started this trend rather unintentionally. The six volumes of the Echte and Morlang edition contain similar black-and-white facsimiles on high-quality paper intended to document the original size of the microscripts. But in furthermore using them for the design of the covers and bindings of the hardback edition, the microscripts were already treated as aesthetic objects in their own right. While the Echte and Morlang edition concentrated first and foremost on the content of Walser's writings, more recent editions of small selections from the microscripts in Germany and the United States emphasize much more prominently their visual quality. Each transcription or translation is accompanied by a facsimile of the microscript in color. The German edition (and sometimes also the English translation) provides an image of the reverse side of the microscript as well, even when the reverse has been left empty.[18] The new edition announced by Schwabe and Stroemfeld will contain high-quality facsimiles in color and transcriptions of every microscript page. All contents will be available electronically, allowing readers to magnify the microscripts as much as they like.[19] Without plan or intention, Walser's oeuvre has kept growing for more than eighty years after he (apparently) stopped writing in 1933. This new edition means that his literary universe will expand for at least another two decades.

The Microscripts and the Grace and Disgrace of Walser's Literary Immortality

Being treated with neglect and contempt by one's contemporaries improves a writer's chance for literary immortality. In his essay "Etwas von der Schande" ("Something about Disgrace"), a text placed right at the porous border between Walser's published works and his microscripts, Walser offers his contribution to the theory of literary canonization (*SW*, 18:192–94). At the time of writing, he was wrong to apply it to himself. Today it speaks with strange precision to the premature end of his literary career, his death, and especially the posthumous fate of his microscripts. As boastful and inaccurate as Walser was when writing the essay, the passing of time has turned it into an accurate prediction of his literary afterlife. In support of his theory, Walser points to the cases of Gottfried Keller and Oscar Wilde. Keller, he notes, suffered the reading public's indifference as well as the indignities of involuntary bachelorhood. Put on trial for his sexuality, Wilde was publicly shamed and sentenced to prison. After their deaths, however, such disgraced writers were capable of metamorphosing into objects of public veneration:

> Mit der Zeit verwandelt sich so eine Schmach und Schande in etwas Rührendes, ja beinahe Schönes und Gutes. [. . .] Als [Wilde] aber von dannen gefahren war, schmückte man ihn, ich möchte sagen, mit einem Heiligenschein, den er sicher in jeder Beziehung, d. h. auf das redlichste verdiente. Das Schicksalhafte ist es, das einen Dichter in die Unvergeßlichkeit hebt, ihn zu einer immer jungen, grünenden Erscheinung macht. (*SW*, 18:193–94)

> Over time such disgrace and shame transforms into something touching, almost beautiful and good. [. . .] When [Wilde] passed away, he was adorned, I am tempted to say, with a gloriole, one he certainly and in every respect deserved most righteously. Such fatefulness lifts the poet into immortality, makes him a forever young, ever greening appearance.

Walser never questions the quality of Keller's and Wilde's writings. They deserve literary immortality. But they assured their position in the literary canon with their biographies, their suffering of either the public's indifference or contempt. Without such suffering writers of no less literary quality find themselves in the dustbin of literary history, or, more accurately, rarely touched on a university library bookshelf. With his last sentence, Walser reveals the personal interest in his theory of literary canonization: "Wie man sieht, bin ich hier in einer illustren Gesellschaft" (As one can see, here I am in illustrious company).

Walser wrote the essay on disgrace in 1926. At that time he did not belong by any means in the company of neglected or disgraced authors. He might have been a voluntary or involuntary bachelor, but as a writer he enjoyed a period of high productivity and renewed popular appeal. Three years later, Walter Benjamin noted in his essay on Walser: "We can read much by Walser, but nothing about him."[20] While Benjamin's second claim should be approached with some caution—Walser received public recognition in regular reviews of the *Neue Züricher Zeitung* (*NZZ*), Switzerland's most influential newspaper, as well as by colleagues like Robert Musil and Franz Blei—his first claim is easily confirmed. Walser does so himself in a response to a survey of the *NZZ*. The same year he wrote his essay on disgrace, the newspaper asked him and other well-known writers, Who are the "unrecognized authors among us?" In typical fashion, Walser's answer missed the point while being right on target. Instead of taking the opportunity to bring underappreciated fellow writers into the public spotlight, or to demand more attention for his own works, Walser boasts how much success he has with women and publishers:

> Was mich betrifft, so habe ich mich keineswegs über Verkanntheit zu beklagen. [. . .] Frauen von nicht zu mißverstehender gesellschaftlicher Bedeutung freuen sich, wenn ich nur in geringem Grad artig zu ihnen bin. [. . .] Meine Verleger teilen mir mit, sie seien entzückt von mir. Meine dichterischen Produkte reisen munter und zirkulieren unentwegt durch die Presse. (*SW*, 18:276–77)

> With regard to myself, I do not have to complain at all about a lack of recognition. [. . .] Women whose social standing cannot be misunderstood are overjoyed when I am just a bit polite to them. [. . .] My publishers tell me that I delight them. My poetic products travel cheerfully and circulate incessantly in the press.

One might hear a fear of rejection under the sound of Walser's loud bragging. But in 1926 his poetic productions swam indeed like a school of fish through the German print media. The *NZZ* published him four times, the *Berliner Tageblatt* twelve times, and the *Prager Presse* at least thirty-five times, as did other newspapers and journals. The previous year he had enjoyed similar success in newspapers and published *The Rose*, a collection of stories and dialogues, with the Ernst Rowohlt Verlag. Walser's publications of the mid-1920s fill several volumes. In 1925 and 1926 Walser did well enough that any struggling author might have heard a patronizing callousness when Walser concluded:

> Meiner Meinung nach werden die Dichter im großen und ganzen nur beinahe zu gern und zu rasch anerkannt. [. . .] Allgemein gesprochen halte ich nichts für so gesund, als eine kräftige Portion Verkennung, die gewiß auch Nachteile haben mag, aber aus fröhlicher Verarbeitung dessen, was nachteilig ist, wächst Vorzügliches. (Ibid.)

> In my opinion, writers are all in all almost too eagerly and quickly recognized. In general, I consider nothing healthier than a hearty portion of disregard, which certainly might have its disadvantages, but out of the joyful processing of what's detrimental grows the exceptional.

Only if one applies Walser's own theory of literary canonization to his popular success does one find cause for concern. His omnipresence in

German-language newspapers might have drastically diminished his chances of ever being recognized as an exceptional author.

Today the essay on disgrace has turned into an accurate prediction of the regretfully early end of Walser's literary career and his by now safely secured posthumous fame and worldwide recognition as one of the preeminent writers of the twentieth century. The volume *The Rose* failed to find an audience in 1925; it became the last book Walser published during his lifetime. In 1929, the year of Benjamin's essay, Walser withdrew into a sanatorium and began to experience fully the public's neglect. After 1933, he occasionally published in newspapers older texts that he transcribed from microscripts. But newspaper editors no longer showed much interest in Walser's work. After his death in 1956, about three hundred texts were found that he had prepared for publication, works that would appear only decades later.[21] Walser's essay "Something about Disgrace" is an exception to the rule of rejection. Written in 1926, Walser sold the essay ten years later to the *Prager Presse*. With an irony that must have hurt, the claim of its last sentence was now fully backed by Walser's biography. By now, Walser was indeed a neglected and disgraced author, sorting recyclables for a pittance in the Herisau sanatorium. The extent of the neglect found its clearest expression in the *NZZ*'s obituary for Walser: "We received from Carl Seelig the news of Robert Walser's death on Christmas Day. The report confused us—one had lived already with this poet's oeuvre, sensing he had departed from our globe some time ago. A man died for a second time."[22] Walser died alone during a walk on Christmas Day 1956. The police took pictures of the outstretched, frozen corpse. Ever since the press printed these photos, Walser scholars and admirers have reproduced them, turning his solitary death quite shamelessly, as J. M. Coetzee noted, into a spectacle.[23] These disgraceful publications transformed the death of a disregarded author, as Walser unknowingly predicted in 1926, into "something touching, almost something beautiful and good" for many of his posthumous admirers (*SW*, 18:229). The American paperback edition of a small selection from Walser's microscripts includes an artistic re-creation of one such photo.[24] Next to the image of Walser's corpse, one reads, "I am hoping that he is not / Dead, just enjoying a Refreshing / Lie-down in the snow. But the caption, sadly, says he is dead."[25] Like the images of his corpse, Walser's microscripts were, after decades of neglect and near destruction, objects of veneration, carefully reproduced in exquisite editions. Unlike the images of the dead body, the microscripts deserve careful study, particularly when Walser deals explicitly with the role of violence in history.

Walser, Violence, and the Malleable Self

To analyze the role of violence and power in Walser's microscripts more closely, I return to the phallophagic scene from "With Anger about Her Anger

She Was Green," the microscript quoted at this essay's opening. Unlike the stories of decadent writers like Villiers de L'Isle-Adam, Barbey d'Aurevilly, or Ewers, Walser's excursions into cruelty rarely end with a blatantly shocking revelation of murder, madness, or incest. Indeed, in this text Walser's narrator arrives at a seemingly anticlimactic conclusion. Neither the castration nor the act of cannibalism has changed the man or the woman in any noticeable way.

> Ganz derselbe war er. Solange er das Ding hatte, besaß er's, und jetzt, wo es ihm nicht mehr gehörte, war's nicht mehr sein. Sie wunderte sich sehr, wie sie sich hatte ereifern können. Er war nicht anders, auch sie nicht, indem es Dinge geben kann, denen man zu viel Wert beimißt, da es auf eine Eigentümlichkeit mehr oder weniger nicht so viel ankommt, wie die meisten Menschen meinen. (*AdB*, 5:125)

> He was just the same. As long as he had the thing, he possessed it, and now, when it no longer belonged to him, it was no longer his. She was very surprised how she could have gotten so excited. He was no different, nor was she, as there can be things to which one attributes too much importance, since contrary what most people assume, little depends on one more or one less peculiarity.

After this act of violence and humiliation, the man exhibits no signs of pain, shock, or trauma. Neither is the woman emboldened by her exercise of power. As if there were nothing inside them that could undergo permanent change, life goes on for both. The fear of castration turns out to have been baseless for Walser's subjects, and Freudian theories are not the only ones that do not apply. When the woman takes the man's genitals she believes she literally holds his strength and power, his aggressive and boastful lust for life, in her hands. Her decision to eat this part of his body recalls what ethnologists reported in Walser's lifetime about so-called primitive religions. E. S. C. Handy, for instance, described the idea of *mana* among the Marquesas in Polynesia. By eating parts of the defeated enemy's body, the warriors of the Marquesas incorporated his *mana*, his strength and power, into their bodies.[26] Even though Walser's woman enjoys her meal with an "eigenthümliche Art von Freude" (a peculiar kind of joy), as the mutilated man believes, the act does not make her more powerful or self-confident (*AdB*, 5:125). Her inner being, just like the man's, remains unchanged.

The lack of change within the characters does not mean, however, that these events have no consequence. A comparison with Musil's and Freud's lessons regarding the relation between violence and the self allows for a better understanding of the woman's and the man's nonchalant responses to her act of castration and cannibalism as well as Walser's peculiar concept of the self. In *Timely Observations on War and Death* (1915), Freud expresses his initial shock and disbelief at the brutality Europeans exhibited during the

First World War. His contemporaries exposed themselves as cultural "hypocrites."[27] They had clearly failed to internalize the norms of civilized behavior, preferring instead to live out their unconscious wishes of being "like primeval man, a gang of murderers."[28] While Freud argues for the continued presence of a primitive self within the modern subject, Musil dealt a decade earlier with an even stranger relation between the self and the experience of violence. In *The Confusions of Young Törless* (1906), Musil's first novel, the character Basini is caught stealing by his fellow students Beineberg, Reiting, and Törless. Threatening to report him to the authorities, the friends use their power over Basini for a series of violent experiments. Törless, especially, wants to learn whether extreme experiences like rape and torture shatter one's sense of self: "What is happening inside you? Does something explode in you? Tell me! Suddenly, like a piece of glass that suddenly explodes into a thousand splinters before it's shown so much as a crack? The image you've made of yourself, isn't it extinguished by a breath?"[29] As painful as Basini's suffering is, he never experiences such an explosion of the self. Törless is terrified by the possibility of a self that does not shatter under such violent and shameful circumstances. He believes in a clear sense of character and righteousness. Basini's example suggests the self might not be anything like a precisely definable single core (or a coherent narrative) that cracks (or unravels) under extreme pressure. Instead of being something firm, enduring, predictable, but also breakable, the self might be malleable. It might be capable of adapting to any situation without losing its sense of continuity and normality. Törless responds to Basini's testimony—to the suggestion that one can live through devastating events without being devastated—with shock and disbelief, especially when Basini suggests that he, Törless, "would do exactly the same as I do."[30]

The relation between the experience of violence and the self in "With Anger about Her Anger She Was Green" is closer to Musil than to Freud. Walser's story suggests no return to a primitive self à la Freud's band of murderers or the *mana* of the Marquesas. There is no primitive core that survives below a brittle crust of civilized behavior. Nothing of the self has to stay in the same shape; the continuity of the self depends on no single peculiarity. But while Musil's account bears similarities to the concept of the self that emerges in Walser's story, the responses to this discovery of a malleable self are utterly different. Walser's story registers nothing like Freud's disappointment in the collective brutality of his contemporaries or Törless's shock that Basini simply lives on after the beatings and sexual abuse he suffered. Walser's story disturbs because it neglects to do what almost every other text on violence attempts to do. It offers no cause for the violence. No narrator blames the violence on a less civilized other and implies for himself (and the reader) a superior position in the civilizing process. And the text assigns no historical, cultural, or psychological significance to the suffering of violence. Walser's story continues to disturb because it ignores the reader's expectations. After noticing momentarily with surprise that nothing changed after the phallophagic scene, life goes on, seemingly undisturbed.

A last comparison further situates Walser's unique position among his contemporaries in terms of his depiction of violence and its relationship to the self. One of Kafka's most illuminating autobiographical reflections begins with the sentence "Every human is peculiar [*eigentümlich*] and because of his peculiarity [*Eigentümlichkeit*] is called upon to have an effect; but he has to acquire a taste for his peculiarity."[31] While not denying aspects of sameness and universality, Kafka stresses the nonidentical potential of each individual human being with the not-fully-translatable term *Eigentümlichkeit*, a word that shares the positive connotations of "uniqueness" with the more questionable overtones of "peculiarity." Little else is for Kafka of greater importance or exposed to a greater risk in modern society than the acknowledgment and preservation of such peculiarity.[32] Walser's text, however, refers to a situation in which no such struggle for recognition and influence of one's identity remains significant. Without even a shrug, the removal of individual peculiarity is accepted. Neither the narrator nor the woman remembers what all the fuss had been about, since "es auf eine Eigentümlichkeit mehr oder weniger nicht so viel ankommt" (little depends on one more or one less peculiarity) (*AdB*, 5:125).

Peter Utz and Reto Sorg note a related phenomenon in Walser's contribution to—or, rather, subversion of—contemporary utopian and apocalyptical discourses. When Utz reads the ending of Walser's seemingly apocalyptical story "Feuer" ("Fire"), he observes how a catastrophic event, which at one moment seems to change the whole world around it, dissipates anticlimactically "into the banality of daily life."[33] Sorg calls this tendency of Walser's writing its "dedramatization."[34] Walser's response to the malleable self repeats a similar gesture of dedramatization. Neither the threat of returning to a primitive self nor the utopian promise of a new man are enacted in Walser's texts.[35] One encounters instead a malleable self without any regret for the disappearance of human peculiarity. The renunciation of the individual's unique potential, of his or her "Eigentümlichkeit," and the desire to become nothing but a zero, runs through Walser's entire oeuvre, particularly his microscripts.

Taking Detours: Walser and the Civilizing Process

In "Grausame Bräuche, Sitten, Gewohnheiten usw." ("Cruel Rites, Customs, Habits etc."), probably written in 1926, Walser delivers an incisive critique of several certainties on which the progressive narrative of modernity relies, including the notion of the modern self as a coherent and stable entity (*AdB*, 4:178–81). The prevailing narratives of modernity have anticipated the elimination of war and violence as means of conflict resolution on every level of social life, from the interpersonal to the international. Whether one consults classics of political thought from Hobbes to Kant and Marx, or sociologists and cultural theorists like Weber, Freud, and Elias, one sees that they all adhere, despite their differences, to a similar story line regarding the relationship between violence and progress in modernity. These thinkers imagine the prehistoric origin of social organization as a response to situations of extreme violence. Whether as a state of nature where man is a wolf to man, or as the story of a band of brothers murdering their father, ghastly brutality surrounds these narratives of the inception of social and political order.[36] Each of these thinkers conceives of history as a slow march toward less and less violent interaction—with the possibility of one last cataclysmic event ahead, an event to end all wars, battles, and struggles. From the perspective of a present plagued by occasional violent conflicts, a peaceable future seems nonetheless within reach, offering the prospect of global cooperation. Actually occurring events of violence and destruction are met with disappointment, but not considered as integral elements of modernity. They are explained as unfortunate but necessary responses to attacks from a barbaric outside, or disparaged as negligible exceptions to the general trend toward peaceful interaction. Norbert Elias argues that the internal logic of war and violence guides historical development toward the eventual abolition of warfare. With hindsight, each war of the past converts into another stepping stone, slowly paving the path to a global order of nonviolent competition and collaboration. While past battles provide evidence of Western societies' supposed advancement in the civilizing process, current instances of hostility in and between modern societies are set aside as atavistic throwbacks or passing inconveniences without lasting cultural impact.[37] Steven Pinker, a recent proponent of Elias's theory of the civilizing process, sees even the destructions of the twentieth century as part of an inevitable decline in violence in human history. Starting once more with lurid tales of prehistoric violence, the death toll of two world wars, including the Holocaust, becomes little more than "an isolated peak in a declining saw tooth—the last gasp in a long slide of major war into historical obsolescence."[38] As Zygmunt Bauman notes with some sarcasm, such theories manage to view wars and acts of genocide as mere "hiccups of barbarism" in modernity's progression toward peace and prosperity.[39]

As a historical argument, Walser's "Cruel Rites, Customs, Habits etc." seems to subscribe to this narrative of a civilizing process. In just three pages the narrator moves, like Hobbes, Freud, or Pinker, from vivid accounts of past human cruelty to claims of an ever more cultured modernity. The narrator will claim that the slightest social infractions nowadays send shockwaves through the truly civilized subject of a magnitude that less civilized subjects did not and do not experience even during the most gruesome spectacles of cruelty. Walser's chatty narrator never doubts his own refinement and sophistication while he supplies his audience with a long and detailed series of grisly customs of the past. His claim that modernity is the least violent stage in human history exists side by side with the apparent enjoyment he takes in watching the supposedly less civilized suffer. While the narrator insists emphatically on the existence of a steady decline in cruelty and brutality over the course of history, Walser's story exposes the precariousness of modernity's self-image as the most civilized stage of human history.

Laying out the path of Western history, Walser's cultural historian moves from warfare between Germanic and Slavic tribes in late antiquity and the early medieval period to Inquisition, Reformation, and the Peasants' War, interspersing his chronicle with vivid images of cut-off noses, gouged-out eyes, impalements, bones broken on the wheel, and men sawn in half or burned at the stake. Once the narrator arrives at the French Revolution, he pauses for a moment to emphasize the importance of this step in the "Enwicklungsgang[] der Zivilisation" (historical development of civilization): "Die Guillotinen der großen Revolution verfuhren, früheren Strafarten gegenübergehalten, wesentlich humaner, das leuchtet augenblicklich ein" (Compared to earlier forms of punishment, it is immediately evident that the guillotines of the Great Revolution proceeded substantially more humanely) (*AdB*, 4:179). With its less painful and faster methods of execution, modern society departed once and for all from the lengthy and brutal displays of death and dying. By 1926, the time of Walser's essayistic story, the distance to the times and cultures of cruel spectacles had become so vast, the narrator claims, that past rites and customs have moved outside of the reach of contemporary imagination. Referring to the condemned man fixed to planks of wood, awaiting to be sawn in half, he comments, "Wie sich so einer in solcher Lage vorgekommen sein muß! So etwas vermögen sich Leute von heute kaum auszudenken" (How such a person must have felt in this situation! People of today are hardly capable of thinking of it) (*AdB*, 4:180). The continual reduction in public violence in Western history has rendered the modern subject incapable of fathoming such early acts of cruelty. Woodcarvings, paintings, and literary representations of these customs exist, but the suffering represented has become inaccessible to the modern subject.

Having risen to the zenith of the civilizing process, the narrator asserts the existence of an unbridgeable experiential distance from most humans—his assumed readership excepted—to all those who never rose to his level of sophistication, be they premodern Europeans or contemporary colonial subjects. Through no fault of his own, as he suggests, his superior position in the civilizing process prevents him from feeling empathy for those who have suffered in the past or are currently being mistreated in the non-European world. Instead of feeling their pain, he rather enjoys the tales of their suffering as absurd, comical, and delightful. The medieval cutting off of noses makes him laugh; the practice of widow burning in India is even more hilarious. Fully expecting his readers to share his delight, he asks of the custom of widow burning: "Sollte ich der einzige sein, dem es als etwas

Pompöskomisches vorkommt?" (Should I be the only one to whom it appears as rather pompously comical?) (*AdB*, 4:178). To legitimize his enjoyment, Walser's narrator questions whether past human beings truly experienced pain: "Grausame Bräuche, Sitten, Gewohnheiten usw. haben ja, unsentimental betrachtet, etwas Naives, Drolliges, vielleicht beinah etwas Puppenhaftes, als wenn körperlicher Schmerz im Grund gar nicht so schlimm wäre" (If looked at without sentiment, cruel rites, customs, habits etc. have something naive, something droll about them, possibly something dollish, as if bodily pain were basically not so bad) (ibid.). Not yet fully human and a bit like puppets, his European ancestors and Asian or African contemporaries require only a tiny measure of empathy and might as well serve as a source for amusement.

The narrator is well aware how he should respond to past and current acts of violence and humiliation: "Die Geschichte der bei den verschiedenen Völkerschaften oder Nationen und zu verschiedenen Zeiten vorgekommenen Grausamkeiten ist natürlich vorwiegend ernsthafter Art" (The history of cruelties occurring at different times and among different ethnic groups and nations is of course first and foremost of a serious nature) (*AdB*, 4:179). But he pays no more than lip service to a code of conduct he falsely believes to have internalized. The pretense drops when he imagines the details of acts of cruelty. In the case of widow burning, his pleasure stems not from the pomp and circumstance of funeral rites, but from his rich imaginings of the suffering: "Wie doch solche Fraueli, die zuweilen jung und hübsch waren, eine Möglichkeit, an der man nicht zu zweifeln Anlaß hat, gewinselt haben müssen, als wenn's arme Hundchen oder Käuzchen oder Täubchen oder Spätzchen gewesen wären" (How such women—young and pretty ones from time to time, no reason to doubt such a possibility—must have whimpered as if they were poor little puppies or owlets or doves or sparrows) (*AdB*, 4:178). He thoroughly enjoys what he claimed never quite existed, namely the excruciating pain of the supposedly less civilized. The narrator imagines their agony with all his senses. He hears the women's screams and whimpers, smells the stink of their roasted flesh, its "nasenflügelbeklemmende Geruch" (nostril-constricting scent), and scrutinizes the faces of those fried and boiled to death: "Die Gesichter, die sie in ihren Pfannen oder erhitzten Kübeln geschnitten haben mögen! Gott bewahre mich davor, daß ich je[ne] Grimasse schneiden müßte" (The faces they might have made in their pans or heated-up pots! God save me from ever having to make such a face) (*AdB*, 4:179).

Walser's narrator demonstrates great plasticity and versatility in imagining acts of physical destruction. He moves back and forth between the position of an observer who inspects closely the distorted faces of the dying and that of the perpetrator who tortures and kills with relish. He is with the slave trader who goes below deck and shoots "ohne daß er dabei zu zielen brauchte" (without needing to take aim) into a crowd of slaves where "ein

Murren der Unzufriedenheit enstanden sein konnte" (a grumble of dissatisfaction might have come about) (*AdB*, 4:181). And he sides with the slave owner who whipped African slaves to death "mit der größten vernichtenden Gemütlichkeit" (with the greatest obliterating congeniality) (*AdB*, 4:180). In other accounts whose memory he cherishes, slaves have their ribs broken and are tied to the ground. Together with their owner our narrator stays and waits until they will be eaten alive by hyenas: "Im Zustand ihrer Zerbrochenheit wurde es ihnen erlaubt, liegen zu bleiben, bis sie von Hyänen sauber aufgegessen worden waren, jede Űberbleibsel durchweg verschwindend machend" (In the state of their brokenness they were allowed to stay on the ground until they had been cleanly eaten up by hyenas, making every leftover disappear without exception) (ibid.). Unspectacular deaths offer too little to his voracious imagination. When he mentions drowning as a particularly popular method of execution, he writes with some regret that "jeder Einsichtsvolle zugeben muß, daß solche Tötungsart gelinde genannt zu werden verdient" (every judicious person has to admit that such killing method deserves to be called a gentle one) (*AdB*, 4:179), and he quickly moves on to the next cruelty.

While Walser's narrator transports himself with ease into the position of any past perpetrator of cruelty, he returns just as quickly to the position of the civilized modern subject, sitting in judgment over those who ordered and arranged these bygone spectacles of punishment. Once again the reader encounters Walser's move of letting his narrator insist emphatically on one hard truth while the story exposes the reader to the brittle foundation of the narrator's argument. Fully subscribing to the state's capacity to weed out violence and achieve global peace and cooperation, the narrator has to explain the fact that cruel rites of the past were often orchestrated by state officials. He finds an answer by declaring the past spectacles as the pathological acts of misguided individuals. By identifying a nonsystemic cause for these cruel customs, he shifts the blame from the state and its institutions to the aberrant behavior of its inadequate representatives. This interpretative task is imbued with such urgency and necessity that Walser's narrator appears not to notice the destabilizing circularity of his argument:

> Viele solcher Richtenden, Urteilenden mögen entweder bereits seit "längerer Zeit" krank gewesen sein oder sind es dann im Verlauf ihres ziemlich sicher sehr anstrengenden Lebens und während ihrer doch wohl ziemlich peinlichen Berufsausübung geworden, so daß sie nicht umhin konnten, sich für krank zu halten. (*AdB*, 4:179)
>
> Many of those who judge and sentence might have been ill already for a "longer time" or became ill in the course of their quite certainly very strenuous life and during the quite painful exercise of their profession so that they could not avoid considering themselves to be ill.

To preside over such cruel rites makes one ill, and this illness led judges and state officials to arrange cruel executions. By regarding these rites and customs as symptoms of an illness, Walser's narrator holds a small group of individuals and not the institution of the state responsible for the spectacles. At the same time he releases these state officials from much of their responsibility, since they must have been ill at the time. The utter confusion of his argument is apparent in the narrator's added afterthought. Despite their pathologies, the judges of the past must have already known what the present narrator holds to be true: "They could not avoid considering themselves to be ill."

At the end of the essayistic story, Walser's narrator offers one final proof for the existence of a successful civilizing process, claiming once more for himself and his readers the position of the fully civilized modern subject. While the past was defined by cruelties and pathologies, the modern subject suffers due to his high sensitivity to violence. Living at the height of the civilizing process means being in agony over the smallest infraction of social convention. Leopold von Sacher-Masoch's works and their reception serve Walser's cultural historian as evidence so conclusive that he ends his deliberations here, certain of having made his case to the reader:

> Auf was ich hier hindeuten will, ist, daß sich die Grausamkeiten Gott Lob und Dank überaus verfeinert haben. Beim bekannten Grausamkeitsautor Sacher-Masoch finden sich bloß noch von Schloßfrauen ihren sie anhimmelnden Kammerzofen zuteil werden lassende sanfte, zarte, intelligente Ohrfeigen. Mit diesem Hinblick auf den Beweis, daß sich unsere Anschauungen und unsere Handlungsweisen von Jahr zu Jahr oder vielleicht sogar von Stunde zu Stunde ausglätten und -gleichen, ziehe ich mich aus dem Gemach der Aufführungen, womit ich mich Ihnen hier präsentiert habe, achtungsvoll zurück. (*AdB*, 4:181)
>
> As I would like to point out here, thanks and praise be to the Lord, cruelties have become exceedingly refined. In the works of the well-known cruelty author Sacher-Masoch one encounters just gentle, tender, intelligent slaps in the face that chatelaines deliver their adoring chambermaids. In view of the proof that from year to year, if not from hour to hour, our opinions and our conduct is flattening and smoothing out, I respectfully take leave of the chamber of my explanations, in which I presented myself to you.

Living at the pinnacle of the civilizing process, minimal transgressions have become as shocking to Walser's contemporaries as past spectacles of cruelty might have been to their bystanders. The audience of the early twentieth century is no longer shocked by its own actions and observations, but only by mediated literary and artistic representations. Rather than seeing, hearing, and smelling the cutting, breaking, and burning of human bodies, the civilized modern reader is deeply appalled by visualizing Sacher-Masoch's account of a gentle slap in the chambermaid's face. For members of a fully civilized society, populated by Walser's narrator and his assumed audience, social interaction has flattened out so smoothly that not only the slightest transgression, but even the slightest *imagined* transgression, sends shock waves through its citizenry. With this observation as final proof for the success of the civilizing process, Walser's narrator takes his bow, closes the curtain, and concludes his argument.

Yet throughout the entire story he never gave a hint that such a slap would shock him, or even hold his interest for more than a moment. Tracing a historical development from an initial situation of extreme violence to the staging of public cruelties as spectacles and deterrents, to today's shock at a mere slap in the face, Walser's narrator might have offered a stronger case for a triumphant civilizing process if he had refrained from taking such pleasure in past cruelties. As an exemplary modern subject who never harms anyone personally and always keeps a reading distance from acts of violence, Walser's narrator appropriates and transforms all of human history into a ready spectacle of cruelty and misery, always at hand for his enjoyment, mockery, and fake outrage, always at hand to confirm his own ethical and cultural superiority. The more this narrator insists on his superior position in the civilizing process, the clearer his inner contradictions become to Walser's readers. Instead of confirming the existence of a united and coherent self, Walser's protagonists tend to alternate like Jakob von Gunten between dreams and fantasies of becoming a zero and of being part of absolute power over life and death.[40]

In Walser's microscripts, however, one comes across not only figures who cannot live up to the ideal of their self-image, whether that means becoming a zero or claiming to be part of the most civilized generation in human history. Most prominently, one encounters in the final words of the *Felix* scenes an awareness and acceptance of the malleability of the self, an affirmation of constant change and lasting uncertainty: "Keiner von uns kann wissen, ob er nicht Schlimmeres ist" (None of us can know whether he is not something worse) (*AdB*, 3:190).

Even though Walser discloses inherent instabilities of any assurances of a steady and successful civilizing process, he never simply moves in an opposite direction, succumbing to apocalyptical narratives or stories of a necessary decline of modern civilization. Instead, Walser acknowledges an equally modest and radical understanding of the self and the varied directions human history has taken already and in the future might take. Rather than expounding certainties about the course of history, Walser formulates in one of his earliest surviving microscripts little more than a personal preference for less warfare: "Was Kriege betrifft, so wünschte ich, sie würden vermieden werden können, aber an ihr Aufhören glaube ich nicht. [. . .] Ich glaube an die Grausamkeit und an die Schönheit und an die sehr angenehme Notwendigkeit, aufzupassen, achtzugeben" (With regard to wars I wish they could be avoided but I do not believe in their disappearance. [. . .] I believe in cruelty and beauty and the delightful necessity to take care and to pay attention) (*AdB*, 1:261–62). Walser does not subscribe to a grand vision of a civilizing process guiding human history step by step toward global cooperation and ever more peaceful conflict resolution. War is neither an unavoidable necessity in history nor a barbaric anomaly that will eventually disappear from international relations. War and violence should be avoided, but their disappearance from history cannot be expected or predicted. Just as the individual self remains malleable and always exposed to changing circumstances, the future course of history stays open and remains uncertain. The only necessity Walser acknowledges is the delightful one of staying alert, of paying enough attention so that the next occasion for war and violence might be avoided. One has to remember, however, that most of Walser's fictional characters are easily distracted and fail to stay focused. While Walser acknowledges in his microscripts the possibility of reducing the future occurrence of war and violence, such a prospect remains a fragile one in his universe. It remains nothing more but also nothing less than a personal preference others are invited to share.

Notes

1. All quotations on this page are from *AdB*, 5:125.

2. Walter Benjamin, "Robert Walser," in *Selected Writings*, vol. 2, ed. Michael W. Jennings, Howard Eiland, and Gary Smith (Cambridge, Mass.: Harvard University Press, 1999), 258.

3. Elias Canetti, *Die Provinz des Menschen* (Munich: Hanser, 1973), 289.

4. Elias Canetti, *Das Geheimherz der Uhr* (Munich: Hanser, 1987), 38.

5. Ibid.

6. J. M. Coetzee, *Inner Workings: Literary Essays 2000–2005* (New York: Viking, 2007), 19–20.

7. Ibid., 20.

8. Lucas Marco Gisi, Reto Sorg, and Peter Stocker, "Nachwort," in Robert Walser, *Mikrogramme* (Berlin: Suhrkamp, 2011), 209.

9. Jochen Greven, "Schatzkammer und Papierkorb: Die Bleistiftentwürfe sind die Grundlage von Walsers vielseitigem Werk," *Du: Die Zeitschrift der Kultur* 62, no. 730 (2002–3): 64.

10. Susan Bernofsky, "Secrets, Not Code: On Robert Walser's Microscripts," in Robert Walser, *Microscripts* (New York: New Directions / Christine Burgin, 2012), 17.

11. The translation of this passage is Susan Bernofsky's and quoted ibid., 11–12.

12. Ibid., 16–17.

13. Bernhard Echte, "Editorischer Bericht," in *AdB*, 2:575.

14. Ibid., 574–76.

15. Werner Morlang, "Nachwort," in *AdB*, 2:517–21.

16. Carl Seelig, *Wanderungen mit Robert Walser* (Frankfurt am Main: Suhrkamp, 1977).

17. Carl Seelig, "Die Handschrift des Dichters," *Du: die Zeitschrift der Kultur* 17, no. 10 (1957): 46, http://www.e-periodica.ch/digbib/view?pid=dkm-001:1957:17#775.

18. Walser, *Mikrogramme*; Walser, *Microscripts*.

19. Barbara von Reibnitz and Wolfram Groddeck, "Editorisches Nachwort," in *Kritische Ausgabe sämtlicher Drucke und Manuskripte. Band I2: Geschwister Tanner (Erstdruck)*, by Robert Walser (Basel: Stroemfeld, 2008), 309–32.

20. Benjamin, "Robert Walser," 257.

21. Greven, "Schatzkammer und Papierkorb," 64.

22. Robert Walser, *Jakob von Gunten*, ed. Wolfram Groddeck and Barbara von Reibnitz (Basel: Stroemfeld, 2013), 483.

23. Coetzee, *Inner Workings*, 15.

24. Walser, *Microscripts*, 148.

25. Ibid., 149.

26. E. S. C. Handy, *Polynesian Religion* (Honolulu: The Museum, 1927), 31.

27. Sigmund Freud, "Thoughts for the Times on War and Death," in *The Standard Edition of the Complete Psychological Works of Sigmund Freud*, 24 vols., trans. and ed. James Strachey (London: Hogarth, 1957), 14:278.

28. Ibid., 297.

29. Robert Musil, *The Confusions of Young Törless*, trans. Shaun Whiteside (New York: Penguin, 2001), 117.

30. Ibid., 118. For an extensive reading of Törless's panicked response to Basini's experience of violence, see Kai Evers, *Violent Modernists: The Aesthetics of Destruction in Twentieth-Century German Literature* (Evanston, Ill.: Northwestern University Press, 2013), 65–68.

31. Franz Kafka, *Nachgelassene Schriften und Fragmente II*, ed. Jost Schillemeit (Frankfurt am Main: Fischer, 1992), 7.

32. Gerhard Neumann, *Kafka-Lektüren* (Berlin: De Gruyter, 2013), 55–75.

33. Peter Utz, *Tanz auf den Rändern: Robert Walsers "Jetztzeitstil"* (Frankfurt am Main: Suhrkamp, 1998), 142.

34. Reto Sorg, "Abschied von Europa? 'Kulturentrückung' bei Robert Walser," in *Utopie und Apokalypse in der Moderne*, ed. Reto Sorg and Stefan Bodo Würffel (Munich: Wilhelm Fink, 2010), 171.

35. Ibid., 165–66.

36. Heinrich Popitz, *Phänomene der Macht* (Tübingen: Mohr Siebeck, 1992), 62.

37. Norbert Elias, *The Civilizing Process: Sociogenetic and Psychogenetic Investigations*, ed. Eric Dunning, Johan Goudsblom, and Stephen Mennell, trans. Edmund Jephcott (Oxford: Blackwell, 2000), 445–46.

38. Steven Pinker, *The Better Angels of Our Nature: Why Violence Has Declined* (New York: Viking, 2011), 192.

39. Zygmunt Bauman, *Modernity and the Holocaust* (Ithaca, N.Y.: Cornell University Press, 2001), 13.

40. *SW*, 11:108–10, 137–38; *JvG*, 115–17, 146–47. On the zero, see Peter Utz's essay in this volume.

Robert Walser's *The Robber*

An Exercise in Camp

Anne Fuchs

I

Robert Walser wrote his last novel in 1925, one year after Thomas Mann's *The Magic Mountain* appeared, three years after the publication of James Joyce's *Ulysses*, and one year before Robert Musil announced his monumental *Man without Qualities*. Kafka's *The Trial* and *The Castle* were posthumously published in 1926, and the last part of Proust's *In Search of Lost Time—Time Regained*—appeared in 1927. Sandwiched between these epochal figures of high modernism, Walser looks like an oddity. While Mann, Proust, Musil, and Joyce experimented with extreme modes of epic narration, Walser's domain was the miniature prose piece whose status was ephemeral and, in Walser's own view, without lasting value.[1] For example, in "Meine Bemühungen" ("My Endeavors"), a piece from Walser's Bern phase, the narrating self mentions his dubious reputation as a "Kurzgeschichtenschreiber" (a stenographer of short stories) before qualifying his modest self-appraisal: after conceding that in all likelihood the short story only induces short-term admiration, he then explains that he only became an author because his beautiful handwriting had been applauded by his schoolteachers (*SW*, 20:427, 428). According to Walser's alter ego, then, it was not his creative imagination but merely the craft of handwriting—in the age of mechanical reproduction an increasingly obsolete skill—that stimulated his writerly production. After this typically Walserian deflation of the very notion of creative authorship, the piece tracks Walser's pathway from his early novels *Geschwister Tanner* (*The Tanners*, 1907), *Der Gehülfe* (*The Assistant*, 1908), and *Jakob von Gunten* (1909) to the production of prose pieces for daily consumption and finally to the "Bleistiftgebiet" (domain of the pencil) of the microscripts. Retrospectively, Walser chronicles here a poetics of reduction that began with the disavowal of epic coherence and ended with an extreme notion of smallness that became a graphic feature of his textual production. From 1924 to 1933 Walser produced more than five hundred so-called microscripts, drafts of prose texts in pencil in a tiny hand of approximately two millimeters in height. Smallness does not, however, relate only to his tiny handwriting, but also to his choice of writing material: he used a pencil on scraps of paper, invoices, receipts, envelopes, and calendar pages.[2] Walser's microscripts mark his withdrawal from the competitive world of the literary market into a space of private resistance where, without self-censorship, he could explore his insecure position in the literary market and in society at large.

The Robber (*"Räuber"-Roman*)—the German title was assigned to the manuscript by the pioneering Walser editor Jochen Greven—stands at the beginning of Walser's retreat into the domain of the pencil. Greven and Martin Jürgens painstakingly deciphered this microscript and published a first version in 1972 that was then superseded by Bernhard Echte and Werner Morlang's new transcription in 1986.[3] A third edition will appear as part of the new critical edition of Walser's entire oeuvre (*Kritische Robert Walser-Ausgabe*). While the belatedness of the publication and reception of *The Robber* may, to a degree, explain why it has not yet been fêted as a masterpiece of twentieth-century literature, its marginal place in the international canon of modernism surely also comes from its decentered and, as I argue below, "camp" mode of narration. The narrative enacts precisely the deterritorialization of literature that, according to Gilles Deleuze and Félix Guattari, is the defining feature of "minor literature."[4] Writing within the context of a major literature, the writer of minor literature rejects the transcendental signification of major literature through a marginal or eccentric idiom that subverts conventional notions of coherence, power, and of the sovereign subject. In line with this paradigm of subversion, Walser's *The Robber* consists of thirty-five discontinuous and apparently rambling paragraphs that explode all conventional notions of a stable subject and of storytelling.[5] Martin Jürgens describes the novel as "a piece of literary recklessness" because it confronts the reader with a disorienting perception and experience of reality.[6] Samuel Frederick calls it a work of "nearly unrelenting asides, a novel that sacrifices story in its onslaught of hesitations, prolepses, deliberations, non sequiturs, meta-commentary, retractions, contradictions, exhausting inattentiveness, apologies and a seemingly limitless supply of other dilatory tactics."[7] Peter Utz notes that the text entangles both the first-person narrator and the reader in a labyrinthine structure that circumvents all conventional notions of a sensible narrative world.[8] Commenting on the relationship between the first-person narrator and his elusive protagonist, Christoph Bungartz remarks that both figures are lacking in precise contours.[9]

The ensuing essay analyzes the narrator's and Robber's joint quest for enhanced financial capital and social standing through the coauthorship of a love story, the conventions of which they simultaneously evoke and thwart. By employing the commonplace narrative format of the romance, the narrator signals his willingness to fulfill the reader's basic expectations. However, it soon becomes apparent that this promise is a mere ploy: while both the narrator and his protagonist seemingly conform to their prescribed literary and social roles, in reality they mobilize and exploit the reader's desire for narrative and erotic suspense to very different effect. The verbosely digressive narrative mode not only negates linear, plot-based storytelling but also, in so doing, displaces narrative and erotic desire and the very notion of textual and sexual consummation. His exuberant loquaciousness and armory of rhetorical devices fuel narrative deferral, thereby forestalling the finality of signification. Walser's narrator could thus be seen as a precursor or older relative of Beckett's Winnie in *Happy Days* (1960): in both cases the protagonists' palaver asserts their presence against the threat of silence. While such plotless chattering is in both texts a matter of life and death, in Walser's *The Robber* the frivolous and exuberant style is deliberately camp: it overturns the heteronormative expectations that conventionally underpin romance. "Camp," writes Susan Sontag, "is a vision of the world in terms of style—but a particular kind of style. It is the love of the exaggerated, the 'off,' of things-being-what-they-are-not." Further, "camp is the consistently aesthetic experience of the world. It incarnates a victory of 'style' over 'content,' 'aesthetics' over 'morality,' of irony over tragedy."[10] In what follows I suggest that Walser's camp mode of writing replaces heteronormative desire with the playful performance of a mode of eroticism that pulverizes oedipal conflict. We shall also see that the camp style is heightened by narrative *mise en abyme* that constantly collapses only to reerect the difference between the narrator and his Robber.[11]

II

From the first paragraph on, Walser's deviant strategy plays with narrative mode, characterization, and emplotment.

> Edith liebte ihn. Hiervon nachher mehr. Vielleicht hätte sie nie zu diesem Nichtsnutz, der kein Geld besitzt, Beziehungen anbahnen sollen. Es scheint, daß sie Abgeordnetinnen, wie sollen wir sagen, Kommissärinnen nach ihm aussendet. Er hat überall so seine Freundinnen, aber es ist nichts mit ihnen, und vor allen Dingen ist wieder nichts mit diesen sozusagen berühmten hundert Franken. Einst ließ er aus nichts als Nachgiebigkeit, aus Menschenfreundlichkeit hunderttausend Mark in den Händen anderer liegen. Wenn man ihn auslacht, so lacht er mit. Schon das allein könnte an ihm bedenklich erscheinen. Nicht einmal einen Freund hat er. Während "all dieser Zeit," die er hier unter uns zubringt, ist es ihm zu seinem Vergnügen, nicht gelungen, sich unter der Herrenwelt Wertschätzungen zu erwerben. Ist das nicht eine der gröbsten Talentlosigkeiten, die man sich denken kann. (*AdB*, 3:11)

> Edith loves him. More on this later. Perhaps she never should have initiated relations with this good-for-nothing who has no money. It appears she's been sending him emissaries or—how shall we put

> it—ambassadresses. He has ladyfriends everywhere, but nothing ever comes of them, and what nothing has come of this famous, as it were, hundred francs! Once out of sheer affability, benevolence, he left one hundred thousand marks in the hands of others. Laugh at him, and he'll laugh as well. This alone might make a dubious impression. And not one friend to show for himself. In "all this time" he's spent here among us, he's failed—which delights him—to gain the esteem of gentlemen. (*TR*, 1)[12]

While the opening sentence appears to set in train the romantic plotline, the narrator's ensuing interjections suspend established genre conventions in favor of a running metacommentary that interweaves his own evaluations of his protagonist with society's overwhelmingly negative judgments. A string of negations dislodges the reader's basic expectation of characterization: rather than a descriptive introduction to his main protagonist, the narrator piles on the abuse. The Robber is denounced as a good-for-nothing, because he has no money, has no best male buddy, and is bereft of all esteem in the world of gentlemen. To make things worse, he deviates from the norms of masculine virility because, as the narrator already hints, his relationships with women are entirely nonsexual.

Criminological theories of deviance often approach the concept from the perspective of a normative society that aims to limit behavior through control mechanisms, ranging from silent or explicit disapproval to official punishment. Deviance is thus a stigmatized form of difference that, in the modern age, mobilizes a slick Foucauldian machinery of surveillance, prosecution, and punishment backed up over time by ever more refined diagnostic tools and sanctions. The modern state deindividualized the deviant other through a basic distinction between two types of deviance: the criminal and the pathological.[13] Revolutionary theory, by contrast, may legitimize deviance, but only if the deviant social actor is seen to serve an emancipatory political cause.[14] In revolutionary discourse, deviance from the political mainstream is seen as a form of political resistance in the service of the common good. In Walser's novel, however, the Robber challenges this taxonomy of deviance because he neither engages in overtly criminal activity nor embodies revolutionary practice. While he does indeed offend the code of acceptable conduct by, for example, shouting "Hoch der Kommunismus" (Long live Communism!) (*AdB*, 3:16; *TR*, 6) in the midst of the good burghers of Bern, or by throwing a cigarette butt into the gaping mouth of a man who is yawning in public (*AdB*, 3:52; *TR*, 43), in reality he is persecuted because his deviance fails to conform to established definitions of a proper offense.[15] Furthermore, it quickly becomes apparent that, despite the Robber's seemingly amorous pursuits, he is emasculated as he fails to convert erotic playfulness into heterosexual conquest. The public is therefore deeply upset by the Robber's refusal to adopt a fixed and recognizable identity. He is scolded not only for failing to conform to the bourgeois lifestyle but also for spectacularly frustrating the expectations aroused by the supposedly reckless but manly "Abenteurernatur" (adventurer type) (*AdB*, 3:81).[16] Halfway through the novel, a woman exclaims: "Ihrer Gestalt fehlt eine Etikette, Ihrem Lebenswandel eine Abstempelung" (Your person lacks a label, your way of living shows no particular stamp) (*AdB*, 3:81; *TR* 72). The evident mismatch between the romantic ideal of the heroic outlaw and the Robber's deviance is compounded by the following register of sins: the Robber loves eating semolina pudding (*AdB*, 3:17; *TR*, 7); he engages in acts of "Löffeliliebkosung" (teaspoon fondling) (*AdB*, 3:22),[17] a point to which I return later; he stuffs himself with the "Brotbröckeli" (scraps of bread) (*AdB*, 3:34; *TR*, 24) that his landlady left scattered on the dinner table and gobbles up her half-eaten apples (*AdB*, 3:34; *TR*, 24); he darns his own trousers, a habit that is deemed a "niewiedergutzumachender Verstoß" (an irreparable offense) (*AdB*, 3:50; *TR*, 41); he blows his nose with his bare fingers rather than with a handkerchief (*AdB*, 3:44; *TR*, 34); he reads newspaper advertisements with indecent eagerness (*AdB*, 3:45; *TR*, 35), and—above all—his marriage proposals are lacking in seriousness (*AdB*, 3:44; *TR*, 34).

At first it seems that the first-person narrator speaks for society in calling the Robber names[18] and demonstrates his narrative authority by regularly dressing him down: "Wir aber schnauzen ihn für Verfehlungen stetsfort kalt an. Er befindet sich bei uns sozusagen in festen Händen, denn uns scheint, er habe es nötig" (We, however, shall go on coldly castigating him for his lapses. With us he is situated, so to speak, in firm hands, which he appears to require) (*AdB*, 3:28; *TR*, 18). In the attempt to distinguish himself from his inadequate protagonist he makes a point of introducing himself to the reader as a "vornehme[r] Autor" (a refined sort of author) (*AdB*, 3:12; *TR*, 2), who will disclose nothing unseemly—a servile act of self-ingratiation that is, however, immediately undermined by the ensuing concession that his narrative is likely to contain numerous "Unvornehmheiten" (crude episodes) (*AdB*, 3:12).[19] Evidently the narrator is unreliable: the incessant interruptions, exclamations, and asides about the Robber's multiple failings produce a theatrical rant quite out of keeping with the narrator's supposed social conformity. In reality the Robber is the narrator's accomplice who carefully collects his fellow citizens' remarks (*AdB*, 3:13; *TR*, 3), reports everything that passes between him and Edith, and even helps with the composition of the book until he is "ganz bleich vor lauter Dichten" (ghostly pale from all his writing) (*AdB*, 3:133; *TR*, 125). As Malcolm Pender has remarked, the split between narrator and his Robber is a device that "permits the narrator to examine the interaction with society of some of his own attitudes, while he himself ostensibly retains views more in keeping with a writer who is conforming to his social role by writing a book."[20] Proclamations about a fundamental antithesis between the narrator and his protagonist are scattered throughout the text: the narrator reveals that he has to be careful not to confuse himself with the Robber: "Ich will doch keine Gemeinschaft mit einem Räuber haben" (After all, I wouldn't want to make common cause with a robber) (*AdB*, 3:71; *TR*, 62); "Er und ich sind jedenfalls zweierlei. Wir halten ihn für einen Löl, weil es ihm an Geld gebricht" (In any case, he and I are completely different. We think him a loser because of his lack of cash) (*AdB*, 3:148–49);[21] and "Ich bin ich, und er ist er. Ich habe Geld und er hat keins" (I am I, and he is he. I have money, and he has none) (*AdB*, 3:149; *TR*, 141).[22] This split creates a Brechtian distancing effect that projects the writer's social alienation onto the Robber; it also enables Walser to employ *mise en abyme* by mirroring the two figures. And so it is that both narrator and his Robber are under huge social and financial pressure to produce books of epic length for a demanding literary public. At the beginning of the novel the narrator had emphasized the Robber's financial independence: an inheritance from an uncle in Batavia, we are informed at the start, allows the Robber to lead an independent life:

> Und auf Grund dieser unalltäglichen und doch wieder alltäglichen Existenz baue ich hier ein besonnenes Buch auf, aus dem absolut nichts gelernt werden kann. Es gibt nämlich Leute, die aus Büchern Anhaltspunkte fürs Leben herausheben wollen. Für diese Sorte schreibe ich demnach zu meinem riesiggroßen Bedauern nicht. (*AdB*, 3:14–15)

> And on the basis of this extraordinary and yet also quite ordinary existence, I am constructing here a judicious book from which nothing at all can be learned. There are, to be sure, people, who wish to extract from books pointers for their lives. For this type I am therefore not writing to my gigantic regret.[23]

The narrator's emphatic assertion that his book will not furnish the reader with lessons for life implicitly rejects the ancient notion that literature should provide profitable pleasure (Horace famously advised poets "either to benefit or to amuse, or to utter words at once both pleasing and helpful for life").[24] On the one hand, the narrator's dismissal of the very idea of poetic profitability, in Horace's sense, aligns his writing with pure pleasure; on the other hand, he keeps returning to the burning issue of his diminishing material, social, and cultural capital.[25] Neither the Robber nor the narrator is financially independent: we already know that the Robber is a good-for-nothing without money, and the narrator too confesses that he needs money and connections (*AdB*, 3:15; *TR*, 5). This explains why the narrative is littered with references to money: the recurring motif of the hundred francs which is already introduced in the fifth sentence is therefore far more than one of the countless dead ends created by the narrator's digressive strategy.[26] As a persistent leitmotif, it reveals that the need to attain capital—monetary, social, and cultural—fuels the engine driving the narrator's and Robber's joint efforts. Halfway through the story the narrator concedes that he needs to produce a book of some length to repair his damaged reputation:

> Diese Umschweife, die ich da mache, haben den Zweck Zeit auszufüllen, denn ich muss zu einem Buch von einigem Umfang kommen, da ich sonst noch tiefer verachtet werde, als ich bereits bin. Es kann unmöglich so weitergehen. Hiesige Lebeherren nennen mich einen Torebuben, weil mir keine Romane aus den Taschen herausfallen. (*AdB*, 3:84)

> These detours I am making serve the end of filling time, for I really must pull off a book of considerable length, otherwise I'll be even more deeply despised than I am now. Things can't possibly go on like this. Local men of the world call me a simpleton because novels don't tumble out of my pocket. (*TR*, 75)

Rather than providing profitless pleasure, then, the narrator's digressions are prompted by the social and financial pressure to produce a book of some length, that is, a material object that can be exchanged for enhanced social and cultural capital. In sharp contrast to the earlier passage where he scoffed at the very notion of profitable literature, the production of a novel is rendered here as an act of economic and social productivity through which he hopes to overcome his deep sense of anguish and hurt about his own social degradation. But the Robber, too, needs to acquire monetary and social capital through writing: we learn that, on more than one occasion, members of the public have written to him, urging him not to stop performing the duties "seines so nützlichen Standes: 'Wo sind Ihre einst so gesucht und so glänzend honoriert gewordenen Räubereien?' hieß es" (of his so useful vocation: "Whatever has become of your once so sought-after and splendidly remunerated robberies?" they asked) (*AdB*, 3:30; *TR*, 20). What is at stake, then, is precisely the exchange of one form of capital for another through which, according to Pierre Bourdieu, social actors enhance their social status: literary works are a cultural currency that can be converted into monetary reward.

And so it is that the narrator and Robber team up to coauthor a love story that draws on popular literary models. In addition to exploiting the conventions of romance as embodied in the penny dreadful, the narrative also draws on the figure of the lovable bandit as represented by Rinaldo Rinaldini:

> Welch ein Unterschied besteht zwischen unserem Bürschchen und einem Rinaldini, der ja wohl seinerzeit Hunderten von guten Staatsbürgern den Kopf gespaltet hat, der Reichen den Reichtum abzapfte und solchen der Armut zugut kommen ließ. Muss das ein Idealist gewesen sein. (*AdB*, 3:20)

> What a difference there is between this lad of ours and a Rinaldini, who, of course, in his day, no doubt split open the heads of hundreds of good citizens, sapped the wealth from the wealthy and caused it to benefit the poor. What an idealist he must have been. (*TR*, 10)

Paradoxically, the narrator's very denial that his Robber is a modern version of Rinaldo Rinaldini, the noble-minded protagonist of Christian August Vulpius's eponymous 1799 novel, places his protagonist squarely in a popular literary tradition.

Schiller's tragedy *The Robbers* is another parodic intertext that recurs in Walser's oeuvre. For example, in the early sketch "Berühmter Auftritt" ("Famous Stage Appearance"), Franz Moor is no longer driven by sibling hatred, as in Schiller's text, but instead is bogged down by ennui and the awareness that the plot of Schiller's play is rather clunky and forced. Walser's preoccupation with Schiller as a literary model, prompting parodic repetition, continued well into his Bern years: "Die Tragödie" ("Tragedy"), a quirky summary of Schiller's *The Robbers*, replaces the psychological depth of Schiller's characters with a comically allegorical rendition of their dominant character traits.[27] Walser often generates parody by deflating the pathos of Schiller's tragedies in this way.[28] In line with this parodic tendency Walser's Robber explains that writing consists of firing shots "auf unsere hochgeschätzten Modelle" (at our highly esteemed models) (*AdB*, 3:134; *TR*, 125). Although Walser's late novel contains no direct allusion to Schiller, this narrative too accentuates the Robber's parasitic literariness. We are told that he walks about in a robber's fancy-dress costume, wearing wide and pale blue trousers with a dagger in his belt, a sash wrapped around his hips, and a threadbare, fur-edged coat. While his hat and hair embody "das Prinzip der Unerschrockenheit" (the principle of intrepidity) (*AdB*, 3:20; *TR*, 10), the pistol in his hand appears decorative: "Er glich dem Produkt eines Aquarellisten" (He resembled the product of a watercolor painter) (*AdB*, 3:20; *TR*, 10). This description is based on a watercolor by Walser's brother Karl, the famous stage designer who worked with Max Reinhardt at the Theater am Schifferbaudamm in Berlin. Titled "Nach der Natur" ("After Nature"), it showed the fifteen-year-old Robert dressed up as a robber.[29] Such intermedial allusions make writing a form of theft that abandons authenticity in favor of a parasitic notion of originality. Accordingly, the Robber's only theft consists in the story lines that he snatches from trivial literature.[30]

III

The novel exploits the genre conventions of a love story by ostensibly recounting the Robber's emotional conflict between love for a waitress named Edith and love for the teenager Wanda, whose name alludes to the heroine of Sacher-Masoch's *Venus in Furs* (1870).[31] In addition to this love triangle, the narrator peoples his story with a whole gallery of other female characters who—with the exception of the "Abgetane," a female outcast and the Robber's occasional companion—invariably represent the heteronormative social order. For example, early on the so-called Henri-Rousseaufrau berates the Robber for his antisocial behavior, as evident in his self-sufficient ability to remain happy in spite of severe social censure. Toward the end of her rant, the Henri-Rousseaufrau implores the Robber "im Namen der Zivilisation" (in the name of civilization) to believe that he was made for her: "Ich sehe dir an, daß du Ehemannstugenden hast" (I can see that you have husbandly virtues) (*AdB*, 3:18; *TR*, 9). Social conformity through matchmaking is a narrative thread that runs through the text as a whole: when he takes up lodgings with a landlady called Stalder, she too attempts to coax him into marrying one or—as the narrator sarcastically comments—both of her daughters on the spot (*AdB*, 3:56; *TR*, 47). The Robber escapes entrapment in a false Swiss idyll by coauthoring a romance that sidesteps the social enforcement of heterosexuality through marriage. With a sleight-of-hand the narrator and Robber filter such prevailing social expectations though the hackneyed literary format of the romantic penny dreadful, in order then to defer and ultimately circumvent sexual consummation by way of a disruptive stream of digressions.

The staged rivalry between Wanda and Edith, who seemingly compete for the Robber, is a narrative ploy that enables the team of coauthors simultaneously to mobilize and defer the reader's expectation of some sort of narrative climax. Time and again, *mise en abyme* saves the Robber from sexual surrender. The Robber's professed adoration of the schoolgirl Wanda evokes pedophilic eroticism. We are told that before she reached the age for long skirts he was "mit Haut und Knochen, mit Leib und Seele 'unter' Wanda" (skin and bone, body and soul "under" Wanda) (*AdB*, 3:53; *TR*, 44). However, this overtone gains a burlesque dimension when, with characteristic hyperbole, the Robber is prepared to throw himself into the Tower of Hunger from Dante's *Inferno* because Wanda is "der lieblichste Kitsch auf der Erde" (the sweetest bit of kitsch on the planet) (*AdB*, 3:53; *TR*, 44). This comical chain of association accentuates the Robber's camp role-play: by exposing Wanda as a piece of literary kitsch, the Robber gives eroticism a camp edge. As a pastiche of various clichés that range from the innocent schoolgirl or the unreachable Empress of Russia, to the titillating dominatrix, the figure of Wanda allows the Robber to perform romance as role-play without heterosexual desire. In Walser's *The Robber*, however, *mise en abyme* works both ways: it not only exposes Wanda's status as a literary figure but also allows for Wanda's transformation back into a plump character with far-too-chubby lips (*AdB*, 3:55; *TR*, 45).

After abandoning Wanda, the Robber moves on to Edith, who will also be caught up in such narrative loops. Toward the end of the novel, the Robber informs Edith's protector, an unnamed figure who is described as a mediocre but otherwise perfectly solid individual, that Edith is the main character in a smallish but meaning-packed novel he is writing (*AdB*, 3:134; *TR*, 125). Originally he had planned to compose this novel under the eyes of his beloved in the public house where Edith worked as a waitress, but his romantic resolve came to nothing (*AdB*, 3:39; *TR*, 30). His failure to produce a romance in Edith's presence thus brings to the fore the logic of erotic deferral, which feeds on fantasy and distance. And so it is that the Robber considers it indispensable "so um seine Edith herum, an die er nicht herankam oder vielleicht aus sich heraus gar nicht herankommen wollte, Schwärmereien zu haben, gleichsam Nebenschönheiten" (to entertain besides Edith, to whom he could not get close or perhaps never really wanted to get close, infatuations, secondary queens, as it were) (*AdB*, 3:69).[32] Such calculated displacement of desire allows the Robber both to perform publicly the role of romantic lover and to fuel the engine of the literary romance with erotic deferral.

It comes as no surprise, then, that toward the end, the Robber confesses publicly that he has already received an honorarium for all the stories about Edith that he has made up (*AdB*, 3:143; *TR*, 134). Edith's earlier misgivings that the Robber is colluding with a known author in the writing of a love story about her are thus entirely justified:

> Und nun ist er zu einem anerkannten Autor gegangen, hat diesem alles berichtet, und jetzt dichten und schreiben sie mit vereinten Anstrengungen über mich, und ich kann mich nicht wehren, und niemand setzt sich für mich ein. Ich muß mir die Dichtereien dieses Bettlers gefallen lassen, der nicht einmal hundert Franken aus dem Portemonnaie hat fallen und hinausgleiten lassen. (*AdB*, 3:134–35)

> And now he's gone to a respected author and told him everything, and now the two of them are composing and writing about me with combined efforts and I am powerless to defend myself and there's no one to stand up for me. I have to put up with the scribblings of this beggar who wouldn't even let a hundred francs come tumbling and sliding out of his wallet. (*TR*, 126)

The female protagonist emerges as the real victim of the Robber and narrator's joint plot to exploit Edith's erotic appeal. By coauthoring a love story about her, they conspire to convert pleasure into material and social capital. As a writer the Robber is a thieving rascal in more than one sense: he not only steals his story lines from the trivial literature that he regularly consumes, but also leaves Edith empty-handed by converting her promised payment into a fictional currency. The narrator declares rather triumphantly that the hundred francs were purely literary in nature: "Er erzählte nämlich einmal in einem Manuskript er habe einer Saaltochter hundert Franken ins Händchen gedrückt, und nun warteten alle Saaltöchter dieser Stadt auf Aushändigung dieses poetischen Geldes" (For he once, in manuscript, described having placed one hundred franks in the little hands of a waitress, and now every barmaid in the city was awaiting delivery of this poetic sum) (*AdB*, 3:65; *TR*, 55). Evidently, Walser's play with *mise en abyme* not only swallows up Edith's payment but also the prospect of the Robber's and narrator's financial profit. Because both the Robber and the narrator are entangled in the same *mise en abyme* structure as Edith, their investment in the narrative too produces a poetic currency without a material value outside the text.

The comical performance of such hackneyed romances allows the team of narrator and Robber to coproduce precisely a book of "some length" with which, against all odds, they want to regain lost social and financial ground. But the narrative also features instances of the Robber's genuine erotic pleasure. Of central importance in this regard is the episode in which the Robber licks his landlady's used teaspoon:

> Neben dem Schüttstein ruhte und träumte in seiner Tasse das Löffeli, das die Witwe zum Kaffeetrinken benutzt hatte. "Das Löffeli ist von ihr zum Mund hineingesteckt worden. Ihr Mund ist bildhübsch. Das übrige an ihr ist hundertmal weniger hübsch als gerade ihr Mund, und ich sollte zaudern können, dieses Hübsche, das sie an sich hat, dadurch hochzuschätzen, daß ich jetzt dieses Löffeli gleichsam küsse?" Solchergestalt lauteten seine literarischen Ausführungen. Er sprach da gleichsam einen geistvollen Essay und hatte natürlich seine Freude daran. [. . .] Einen Freudensprung mindestens wird er wohl ausgeführt haben nach seiner Löffeliliebkosung. (*AdB*, 3:22)

> Beside the sink and dreaming in its cup reposed the spoon which the widow had used when she drank her coffee. "This little spoon has been placed by her in her mouth. Her mouth is as pretty as a picture. Everything else about her is a hundred times less lovely than her mouth, so how could I possibly hesitate to pay homage to this prettiness by kissing, as it were, this little spoon?" Such were his literary observations. He was giving voice, so to speak, to an insightful essay, which, of course, gave him delight. [. . .] We can assume he executed at least one leap of joy following his teaspoon fondle.[33]

At first sight the episode appears as a classic case of a fetishistic performance through which the Robber would enact the disavowal of his castration anxiety. The narrator himself calls the Robber's licking of the teaspoon "a stattliche Leistung auf erotischem Gebiet" (an impressive feat in the field of eroticism) (*AdB*, 3:22; *TR*, 12), thus outing his protagonist as a kinky fetishist who depends on substitutes for his sexual kicks. For Freud, the male child's shocking discovery that women don't have a penis leads to castration anxiety, which then unleashes a conflict between this troubling discovery and its disavowal. By substituting the lacking organ, the fetish offers a compromise: it erects a permanent memorial to this traumatic discovery, simultaneously providing protection against the threat of castration while giving expression to the triumph over it.[34] Fetishism is thus characterized by the irresolvable ambivalence between the acceptance that castration has taken place and its disavowal. According to Freud, stockings, shoes, underwear, and bits of fur are often the preferred objects of the fetishist's desire. But is the "teaspoon fondle" really an example of fetishism in Freudian terms? And is the "Löffeli" (spoon) a suitable fetish?

The point of the above episode is not the Freudian enactment of Oedipal castration anxiety so much as the disavowal of the phallus as prime signifier of the symbolic order. Rather than substituting the phallus, his landlady's used teaspoon evokes the oral pleasure of feeding that precedes any Oedipal desire. At the heart of the episode is thus a polymorphous eroticism that psychoanalysis would designate regressive. As a performance at the kitchen sink, that is, the location where wives and mothers tend to clean up, the "teaspoon fondle" upstages Freud's script which, in misogynistic fashion, revolves around the dramatic discovery of a lack in women. In contrast to the Freudian fetishist, who is driven by castration anxiety, the Robber also indulges in gender-jumping and camp cross-dressing: whenever he wears an apron, he is thrilled by his transformation into a maid and his effeminate looks (*AdB*, 3:108; *TR*, 99–100). Evidently the Robber inhabits a pre-Oedipal sphere of pleasure that is untouched by the economy of heterosexual love.

The Robber's lack of heterosexual response is also conveyed through the leitmotif of a pre-Oedipal childlike quality which, as the narrator speculates, might be another reason for his persecution (*AdB*, 3:51; *TR*, 41). In Walser's oeuvre, the motif of "Kindlichkeit" (childlikeness) designates an energetic spontaneity and unruly buoyancy that are unharnessed by the rules of the symbolic order. It stands for the exhilarating creativity and élan that Walser associates with a new language of love that has the potential to disrupt the phallic economy of human sexuality. However, when an Englishman claims that lack of sex can cause long-term problems, above all "eine Art von Vertrottelung" (a sort of mental degeneration) (*AdB*, 3:66),[35] the Robber and his narrator do get worried. Eventually the narrator dispatches the Robber to consult a doctor, to whom he confesses that he has never felt any sexual aggression or lust. He explains that a sort of child resides in him and that he often feels like a girl who loves her household duties, declaring that this has never troubled him or made him unhappy. Even though he has never felt the urge to spend a night with a woman (*AdB*, 3:112–13; *TR*, 103–5), the Robber's "Fond an Liebeskraft" (reservoir of love) (*AdB*, 3:114)[36] is immense. He further reveals that he can engage in romance only by making up stories in which he plays the part of the "unterliegende, gehorchende, opfernde, bewachte, bevormundete Teil" (the subordinate, obedient, sacrificing, scrutinized, and chaperoned party) (*AdB*, 3:115; *TR*, 106).

At first sight this therapeutic confession appears to corroborate the Freudian notion of masochism, according to which it is the male child's pathological response to the Oedipal threat by the father. For Freud, Oedipal castration anxiety turns into masochistic perversion if this fear translates into a passive sexual role.[37] In a later essay Freud linked feminine masochism in men explicitly to infantilism: sexual infantilism and femininity are deemed to be pathological and perverse precisely because they are characterized by passivity.[38] Although Freud mentions in passing the idea of a playful performance of feminine masochism,[39] for him this phenomenon is determined by the presence of sadistic impulses in the masochist. By contrast, Gilles Deleuze returns to the literary sources of sadomasochism, the works of Marquis de Sade and Sacher-Masoch, to explore masochism's dramaturgical and staged dimension. While Freud merely acknowledges playful masochism in passing, for Deleuze such playfulness is a quintessential dimension that imposes a formal structure onto the masochistic scenario.[40] As Thamen and Wallenberg argue, "Masochism's formality is inscribed explicitly in the contract governing masochist relations between two partners. This contract invests masochism with strict rules, roles and directions. The contract is a narrative in itself already replete with a scenario, a story and dramatis personae."[41] In line with the scripted dimension of masochism, the Robber's metaconsciousness calls attention to the theatrical performance of playful masochism. He knows all too well that his erotic thrills derive from dramatic suspense rather than from real humiliation. At the end of the consultation with the doctor, the latter therefore gives him the following advice in defiance of psychoanalytic orthodoxy: "Lassen Sie sich so, wie Sie sind, leben Sie so weiter, wie Sie bisher gelebt haben. Sie kennen sich ja anscheinend ausgezeichnet, finden sich ausgezeichnet mit sich ab" (Remain as you are, go on living the way you live. You seem to know yourself, and to have come to terms with yourself exceedingly well) (*AdB*, 3:115; *TR*, 106). With his final assessment the doctor thus endorses the Robber's performance of playful female masochism and his lack of heterosexual desire.

Rather than a clinical symptom, then, the "teaspoon fondle" is a central episode that liberates pleasure from sexual consummation. While for Freud fetishism merely serves to underline the status of the phallus in the symbolic order, here we are dealing with a pre-Oedipal form of eroticism and a camp transmutation of the Robber's oral pleasure at the kitchen sink into the reader's aural delight. With its alliterations and Swiss diminutive, the prime signifier of the "Löffeliliebkosung"—the English translation "teaspoon fondle" does not manage to communicate this—is therefore not the phallus but the idea of a language of poetry that generates pleasure. The conversion of the Robber's pre-Oedipal eroticism into literary pleasure is already alluded to in the scene quoted above: his erotically charged thoughts about his landlady's used teaspoon are, after all, "literarische Ausführungen" (literary observations), framed by "ein beständiges Poesiezwielicht" (enduring poetic twilight) (*AdB*, 3:22; *TR*, 22).[42] And when, later on, the Robber confesses his transgression to his landlady, his disclosure is motivated neither by a sense of guilt nor by his exhibitionistic tendencies but rather by a discussion about Joan of Arc, the "Jungfrau von Orleans"—another literary figure associated with Schiller. Accordingly, the real purpose of the confession is the enactment of literary roles. It thus comes as no surprise that, in the eyes of the Robber, the landlady leaves the stage like a queen: "Man kann sagen, daß sie wie ein Bild ausgesehen habe. Sie hatte da so etwas Kupferstichhaftes, wie sie so den Korridor entlang ging, indigniert und sicher nicht ganz ungeschmeichelt" (One might say she looked exactly like a picture. There was something about her reminiscent of an etching, the way she retreated down the corridor, offended, yet also, surely, just a little bit pleased) (*AdB*, 3:35; *TR*, 25).

IV

We have seen that throughout the narrative, the coauthoring team of narrator and Robber employ extremely hackneyed notions of social and literary popularity—the romantic lover and the heroic robber who fights on behalf of the poor—to boost their own reputation.[43] But their plan to exploit such genre conventions for financial and social capital collapses because of Walser's employment of a range of metanarratological devices that disrupt the plot structure of the conventional romance. *Mise en abyme*, narrative deferral, and intertexuality bring into play a camp style that liberates pleasure from the normative idea of a narrative and sexual climax. That the digressive style of this narrative does indeed offer an escape route from the prison house of genre conventions that are steeped in heterosexual norms can be gleaned from the narrator's observation toward the end: "Das ganze kommt mir übrigens vor wie eine große, große Glosse, lächerlich und abgründig" (The whole thing seems to me, by the way, like a big prose sketch, ridiculous and unfathomable) (*AdB*, 3:148).[44] With this final transmutation of the epic form of the novel into a mere "Glosse," marginal note or pithy commentary, the narrator calls attention to his decentered, camp mode of writing, one that formally replicates the Robber's mode of social deviance.

The narrator's apparent downgrading of his novel is much more than a throwaway remark. Its poetological significance finds full articulation in "Die Glosse" ("Marginal Note"), in which Walser foregrounds and stages with typical hyperbolic humor the diminution and marginalization of his writing in a harsh literary market. At the beginning of this text the author is depicted as a mere "Glossenschmied," a toiling blacksmith of marginal notes, whose exhausted "Skizzenhervorbringerseele" (sketch-producing soul) has to contend with a contemptuous literary public. While the grand form of the novel aims to achieve a totality of historical representation, the transient form of the "marginal note" is deemed a "Verkommenheit" (depravity) that bogs him down in the quagmire of literary deviance. However, the narrating self then overturns this negative judgment though an increasingly burlesque metaconsciousness that stages marginality as a creative vantage point: placing his finger on his "geistvolle Nase" (thoughtful nose), he realizes that it is not so much epic form and polished style that matter, but the intention of "irgend etwas Lesenswertes, Aufheiterndes segelschiffwimpelnd ins liebe Publikumsmeer hinauszusenden" (floating something that is well worth reading and entertaining like the bunting of a boat sailing out into the sea of the lovely public) (*SW*, 19:287). Surrounded by the "Engel der Prosapoesie" (angels of poetry in prose), the self then recognizes that his small texts have the power to resonate with the public precisely because of his ability to explode literary conventions (*SW*, 19:288).

The Robber concludes with the narrator recommending the Robber to a discerning minority: "Und so unlogisch das auch scheint, bin ich des Glaubens und erkläre mich mit all denjenigen einverstanden, die meinen, es sei schicklich, daß man den Räuber angenehm finde und daß man ihn von nun an kenne und grüße" (And, illogical, as it may seem, I hold the belief and concur with all those who maintain that it is only proper that the Robber be found agreeable and that from now on he be recognized and greeted) (*AdB*, 3:150;*TR*, 141). However, the convoluted mannerism of this final gesture makes the envisaged mutual assent an extremely fragile construct. To be sure, by inviting the public to greet his protagonist, the narrator seeks to procure the Robber's social rehabilitation. On the other hand, the mannerist sentence structure pushes the realization of the desired approval from the social sphere into the realm of the literary work. In the final analysis, Walser envisages rehabilitation as a form of literary partisanship that can be enacted only through the reader's pleasure in a camp mode of narration. Rather than a mere strategy to produce a lengthy novel, the narrator's digressions and loquaciousness enact an infectious playfulness that relishes precisely the "theatricalization of experience" that for Sontag marks camp style.[45] In so doing the text envisages a community between narrator, protagonist, and reader that dethrones heteronormative designations, roles, and expectations. As Sontag notes, "Camp is a solvent of morality. It neutralizes moral indignation, sponsors playfulness."[46] With his final deliberation, the narrator envisages the reader as a recipient who is open to such camp sensibility. However, it cannot be overlooked that, by contrast to his earlier writings, during his Bern years Walser could enact such dialogic gestures only within the confines of his "Bleistiftgebiet," that is, the private domain of his pencil. For the Walser of the Bern years, the communicative function of his camp style was in jeopardy.

Notes

1. On Walser's poetics of smallness see Anne Fuchs, "Why Smallness Matters: The Problem of Attention in Franz Kafka's and Robert Walser's Short Prose," in *Kafka und die kleine Prosa der Moderne / Franz Kafka and Short Modernist*

Prose, ed. Ritchie Robertson and Manfred Engel (Würzburg: Königshausen & Neumann, 2011), 167–81. On the small form in German literature see Günter Oesterle, "'Unter dem Strich': Skizze einer Kulturpoetik des Feuilletons," in *Das schwierige neunzehnte Jahrhundert: Germanistische Tagung zum 65. Geburtstag von Eda Sagarra im August 1998*, ed. Jürgen Barkhoff, Gilbert Carr, and Roger Paulin (Tübingen: Niemeyer, 2000), 230–50; Andreas Huyssen, "Modernist Miniatures: Literary Snapshots of Urban Spaces," *PMLA* 122, no. 1 (2007): 27–42; Dirk Göttsche, *Kleine Prosa in Moderne und Gegenwart* (Münster: Aschendorff, 2006); Dirk Göttsche, "Epistemology, Poetics and Time in Modernist Short Prose around 1900," in *Time in German Literature and Culture, 1900–2015: Between Acceleration and Slowness*, ed. Anne Fuchs and J. J. Long (Basingstoke, U.K.: Palgrave Macmillan, 2016), 71–92.

2. On these manuscripts see Bernhard Echte and Werner Morlang, "Editorischer Bericht," in *AdB*, 6:701–11. Also see their "Nachwort" in the same volume, 568–84, as well as Kai Evers's essay in this volume.

3. Werner Morlang and Bernhard Echte, "Editorische Vorbemerkung," in *AdB*, 3:5–8.

4. Gilles Deleuze and Félix Guattari, *Kafka: Toward a Minor Literature*, trans. Dana Polan (Minneapolis: University of Minnesota Press, 1986).

5. Michael Böhler, "Dichten aus der Peripherie des Schreibens: Überlegungen zu Robert Walsers kulturpolitischem Ort im deutschsprachigen Raum," in *"Wärmende Fremde": Robert Walser und seine Übersetzer*, ed. Walter Lenschen and Peter Utz (Bern: Peter Lang, 1994), 31–44.

6. Martin Jürgens, *Seine Kunst zu zögern: Elf Versuche zu Robert Walser* (Münster: Oktober, 2006), 79, 80.

7. Samuel Frederick, "Stealing the Story: Robert Walser's *Robber*-Novel," in *Digressions in European Literature: From Cervantes to Sebald*, ed. Alexis Grohmann and Caragh Wells (Basingstoke, U.K.: Palgrave Macmillan, 2010), 131.

8. Peter Utz, *Tanz auf den Rändern: Robert Walsers "Jetztzeitstil"* (Frankfurt am Main: Suhrkamp, 1999), 408–23.

9. Christoph Bungartz, *Zurückweichend vorwärtsschreiten: Die Ironie in Robert Walsers Berner Prosa* (Frankfurt am Main: Peter Lang, 1988), 55. See also Thomas Bürgi-Michaud, *Robert Walsers mühseligkeitsüberschüttetes Kunststück* (Frankfurt am Main: Peter Lang, 1996), 139, 168.

10. Susan Sontag, "Notes on 'Camp,'" in *Against Interpretation and Other Essays* (New York: Delta, 1966), 279, 287.

11. *Mise en abyme* refers to various narrative mirroring devices, including inset narratives, ekphrasis, remediations of nonverbal media, etc., that create narrative self-reflexivity and undermine the mimetic effect of the fictional world. See Lucien Dällenbach, *The Mirror in the Text*, trans. Jeremy Whitely with Emma Hughes (Cambridge: Polity, 1989); Linda Hutcheon, *Narcissistic Narrative: The Metafictional Paradox* (Waterloo, Ont.: Wilfried Laurier University Press, 1980); Brian McHale, "En Abyme: Internal Models and Cognitive Mapping," in *A Sense of the World: Essays in Fiction, Narrative and Knowledge*, ed. John Gibson, Wolfgang Huemer, and Luca Pocci (New York: Routledge, 2007), 189–206.

12. Bernofsky's translation used throughout. Occasionally I provide my own translations where I deem a more literal translation necessary. In these cases the corresponding passages in Bernofsky's translation are provided in the endnotes.

13. Michel Foucault, *Discipline and Punish: The Birth of the Prison* (New York: Random House, 1984).

14. See Davie Downes and Paul Rock, *Understanding Deviance*, 6th ed. (Oxford: Oxford University Press, 2011).

15. The Robber commits one of his greatest offenses after the murder of Walther Rathenau: "Und was tat da der wundervolle, seltsame Fötzel, er klatschte in die Hände, anstatt daß er vor Schreck und Trauer umgesunken wäre bei solch niederschmetternden Benachrichtigung" (And what did this marvellous, weird scoundrel do now? He clapped his hands, when he ought to have sunk to the ground in horror and grief at this shattering announcement) (*AdB*, 3:21; *TR*, 11). Here the expected display of public piety is overturned in favor of a carnivalesque celebration of death as a leveler of social differences. Later the Robber exclaims: "Herrlich dieser Abschluß einer Karriere!" (Wonderful, this ending of a great career!) (*AdB*, 3:23; my translation, cf. *TR*, 12). On Walser's preoccupation with Rathenau see also the prose piece "Zwei Männer" ("Two Men"), in *SW*, 16:194–204. See also Daniel Medin's essay in this volume.

16. My translation. Cf. *TR*, 72.

17. My translation. Cf. ibid., 12.

18. These include "Peruaner" (Peruvian), "Schafskopf" (simpleton), "Löl" (loser, moron), "Lümmel" (scoundrel), "Abgetaner" (down-and-out), "Trappi" (twit), and "Fötzel" (crook).

19. My translation. Cf. *TR*, 2.

20. Malcolm Pender, "A Writer's Relationship to Society: Robert Walser's *Räuber*-Roman," *Modern Language Review* 78 (1983): 104.

21. My translation. Cf. *TR*, 140.

22. On the split between narrator and robber see Jürgens, *Seine Kunst zu zögern*, 81–86.

23. My translation. Cf. *TR*, 4–5.

24. Cited in Robert Matz, *Defending Literature in Early Modern England: Renaissance Literary Theory in Social Context* (Cambridge: Cambridge University Press, 2000), 2.

25. On pleasure in Walser see Lucia Ruprecht, "Pleasure and Affinity in W. G. Sebald and Robert Walser," *German Life and Letters* 62, no. 3 (2009): 311–26.

26. Frederick, "Stealing the Story," 136.

27. In other prose pieces Walser interweaves laconic plot summaries of various plays with the narrator's running commentary about the theatrical costume and behavior of Schiller's characters: see "Schiller I" (*SW*, 20:328).

28. Besides Schiller's *Die Räuber*, Walser also made Wilhelm Tell the subject of parodic prose pieces that subvert the Swiss national myth. See Valerie Heffernan, *Provocation from the Periphery: Robert Walser Re-examined* (Würzburg: Königshausen & Neumann, 2007), 43–51; Monika Lemmel, "Angelesen?—Robert Walsers Schiller-Texte," in *Bildersprache—Klangfiguren: Spielformen der Intermedialität bei Robert Walser*, ed. Anna Fattori and Margit Gigerl (Munich: Fink, 2008), 193–200.

29. A reproduction can be found in *Die Brüder Karl und Robert Walser: Maler und Dichter*, ed. Bernhard Echte and Andreas Maier (Stäfa: Rothenhäusler Verlag 1990), 44.

30. On Walser's play with trivial literature see Annette Fuchs, *Dramaturgie des Narrentums: Das Komische in der Prosa Robert Walsers* (Munich: Wilhelm Fink, 1993), 103–32; Andrea Hübner, "'Das Märchen ja sagt . . .'—Märchen und Trivialliteratur im Werk von Robert Walser," in *Robert Walser und die moderne Poetik*, ed. Dieter Borchmeyer (Frankfurt am Main: Suhrkamp, 1999), 167–86.

31. According to Gilles Deleuze, Sacher-Masoch was the first novelist to make suspense an essential ingredient of romantic fiction precisely because masochism requires the postponement of pleasure. See Gilles Deleuze, *Masochism: Coldness and Cruelty*, trans. Jean McNeil (New York: Zone Books, 1991), 33–35.

32. My translation. Cf. *TR*, 60.

33. My translation. Cf. ibid., 12.

34. Sigmund Freud, "Fetishism," in *The Standard Edition of the Complete Psychological Works of Sigmund Freud*, 24 vols., ed. and trans. James Strachey (London: Hogarth, 1953–74), 21:154.

35. My translation. Cf. *TR*, 56.

36. My translation. Cf. ibid., 105.

37. Sigmund Freud, "A Child Is Being Beaten," in *The Standard Edition*, 17:189–91.

38. Sigmund Freud, "The Economic Problem of Masochism," in *The Standard Edition*, 19:159–70.

39. Ibid., 375.

40. Deleuze, *Masochism*, 69–89.

41. Torkild Thamen and Louise Wallenberg, "Buggering Freud and Deleuze: Toward a Queer Theory of Masochism," *Journal of Aesthetics and Culture* 2 (2010), http://www.tandfonline.com/doi/full/10.3402/jac.v2i0.4642.

42. Translations: "literary observations" (Bernofksy); "enduring poetic twilight" (mine).

43. Much debate in Walser criticism therefore concerns the perceived conflict between the subject's autonomy and subjugation in Walser's late novel. For Ernst Osterkamp the delivery of the novel enacts a social custodianship that controls and ultimately stifles the Robber's rebellious subjectivity. See Ernst Osterkamp, "Commis, Poet, Räuber: Eigengesetzlichkeit und Selbstaufgabe bei Robert Walser," in *Robert Walser*, ed. Klaus-Michael Hinz and Thomas Horst (Frankfurt am Main: Suhrkamp, 1991), 235. By contrast, Peter Utz argues that the labyrinthine structure of this narrative defies such a simple surrender to the formal intention of writing a novel. Utz, *Tanz auf den Rändern,* 419.

44. My translation. Cf. *TR*, 139.

45. Sontag, "Notes on 'Camp,'" 286.

46. Ibid., 290.

WORKS CITED

Works by Robert Walser

The following editions are cited using the indicated abbreviations, followed by a volume number where applicable:

AdB *Aus dem Bleistiftgebiet*. Edited by Bernhard Echte and Werner Morlang. 6 vols. Frankfurt am Main: Suhrkamp, 1985–2000.

Briefe *Briefe*. Edited by Jörg Schäfer with Robert Mächler. Frankfurt am Main: Suhrkamp, 1979.

SW *Sämtliche Werke in Einzelausgaben*. Edited by Jochen Greven. 20 vols. Frankfurt am Main: Suhrkamp, 1985–86.

ASD *A Schoolboy's Diary and Other Stories*. Translated by Damion Searls. New York: New York Review Books, 2013.

FT *Fairy Tales: Dramolettes*. Translated by Daniele Pantano and James Reidel. New York: New Directions, 2015.

JvG *Jakob von Gunten*. Translated by Christopher Middleton. New York: New York Review Books, 1999.

SS *Selected Stories*. Translated by Christopher Middleton and others. New York: Farrar, Straus and Giroux, 2012. (Note: The New York Review Books reprint of *Selected Stories* has a slightly different pagination.)

TA *The Assistant*. Translated by Susan Bernofsky. New York: New Directions, 2007.

TR *The Robber*. Translated by Susan Bernofsky. Lincoln: University of Nebraska Press, 2000.

TT *The Tanners*. Translated by Susan Bernofsky. New York: New Directions, 2009.

Other editions of, texts by, and translations of Walser:

Fragments of Imaginary Landscapes: Joan Nelson and Robert Walser. Swiss Institute of New York, 1994. Exhibition catalogue.

Pencil Sketches: Dickinson/Walser. New York: The Drawing Center, 2014. Exhibition catalogue.

Schütte, Thomas. *Watercolors for Robert Walser and Donald Young*. With poems by Walser, translated by Damion Searls. Paris: Editions Cahiers d'art, 2014.

Walser, Robert. "Ash, Needle, Pencil, and Little Matchstick." Translated by Samuel Frederick. In *Narratives Unsettled: Digression in Robert Walser, Thomas Bernhard, and Adalbert Stifter*, by Samuel Frederick, 177–78. Evanston, Ill.: Northwestern University Press, 2012.

———. *The Assistant*. Translated by Michael Bullock. London: Calder and Boyars, 1969.

———. *Berlin Stories*. Translated by Susan Bernofsky. New York: New York Review Books, 2012.

———. *Girlfriends, Ghosts, and Other Stories*. Translated by Tom Whalen with Nicole Köngeter and Annette Wiesner. New York: New York Review Books, 2016.

———. *Jakob von Gunten*. Edited by Wolfram Groddeck and Barbara von Reibnitz. Basel: Stroemfeld, 2013.

———. *A Little Ramble: In the Spirit of Robert Walser*. New York: New Directions / Christine Burgin, 2013.

———. *Looking at Pictures*. Translated by Susan Bernofsky, with additional translations by Lydia Davis and Christopher Middleton. New Directions / Christine Burgin, 2016.

———. *Masquerade and Other Stories*. Translated by Susan Bernofsky. Baltimore: Johns Hopkins University Press, 1990.

———. *Microscripts*. Translated by Susan Bernofsky. New York: New Directions / Christine Burgin, 2012.

———. *Oppressive Light: Selected Poems by Robert Walser*. Translated by Daniele Pantano. Pittsburgh: Black Lawrence, 2012.

———. *Der Schnee fällt nicht hinauf: Dreiunddreißig Gedichte ausgewählt und kommentiert von Urs Allemann*. Frankfurt am Main: Insel, 2009.

———. *Speaking to the Rose: Writings 1912–1932*. Translated by Christopher Middleton. Lincoln: University of Nebraska Press, 2005.

———. *Thirty Poems*. Translated by Christopher Middleton. New York: New Directions, 2012.

———. *Vor Bildern: Geschichten und Gedichte*. Edited by Bernhard Echte. Frankfurt am Main: Suhrkamp, 2006.

———. *The Walk*. Translated by Christopher Middleton with Susan Bernofsky. New York: New Directions, 2012.

———. *The Walk and Other Stories*. Translated by Christopher Middleton. London: Calder and Boyars, 1957.

Secondary Literature

Adorno, Theodor W. *Notes to Literature*. 2 vols. Translated by Shierry Weber Nicholson. New York: Columbia University Press, 1991.

———. *Philosophische Terminologie*. Vol. 1. Frankfurt am Main: Suhrkamp, 1973.

Aebli, Adriano. "'Diese Art von belächelnswerten Sächelchen': Ein Vorschlag zur Lektüretechnik des Bleistiftgebiets." In Arnold, *Text und Kritik*, 181–91.

Agamben, Giorgio. *The End of the Poem: Studies in Poetics*. Translated by Daniel Heller-Roazen. Stanford, Calif.: Stanford University Press, 1999.

———. *Potentialities: Collected Essays in Philosophy*. Stanford, Calif.: Stanford University Press, 1999.

Albes, Claudia. *Der Spaziergang als Erzählmodell: Studien zu Jean-Jacques Rousseau, Adalbert Stifter, Robert Walser und Thomas Bernhard*. Tübingen: Francke, 1999.

Amann, Jürg. "Liebe Frau Mermet: Eine Art Liebesbrief nach Briefen von Robert Walser." In Jürg Amann, *Pornographische Novelle*, 67–98. Cologne: Tisch 7, 2005.

———. *Robert Walser*. Zurich: Arche, 1995.

Andres, Susanne. *Robert Walsers arabeskes Schreiben*. Göttingen: Cuvillier, 1997.

Arnold, Heinz Ludwig, ed. *Text und Kritik: Robert Walser*. 4th ed. Vol. 12/12a. Munich: Edition Text + Kritik, 2004.

Audiberti, Marie-Louise. *Le vagabond immobile: Robert Walser*. Paris: Gallimard, 1996.

Avery, George C. "Focus on Reality in the Novels of Robert Walser." Ph.D. diss., University of Pennsylvania, 1959.

———. *Inquiry and Testament: A Study of the Novels and Short Prose of Robert Walser*. Philadelphia: University of Pennsylvania Press, 1968.

Bachmann, Ingeborg. *"Todesarten"-Projekt*. Edited by Robert Pickl. Vol. 1 of *Kritische Ausgabe*, edited by Monika Albrecht and Dirk Göttsche. Munich and Zurich: Piper, 1995.

Barthes, Roland. *A Lover's Discourse: Fragments*. Translated by Richard Howard. New York: Hill and Wang, 1978.

———. *Writing Degree Zero*. Translated by Annette Lavers and Colin Smith. New York: Hill and Wang, 1998.

Baßler, Moritz, Christoph Brecht, Dirk Niefanger, and Gotthart Wunberg, eds. *Historismus und literarische Moderne*. Tübingen: Niemeyer, 1996.

Bauman, Zygmunt. *Modernity and the Holocaust*. Ithaca, N.Y.: Cornell University Press, 2001.

Benjamin, Walter. *Berlin Childhood around 1900*. Translated by Howard Eiland. Cambridge, Mass.: Harvard University Press, 2006.

———. *The Origin of German Tragic Drama*. Translated by John Osborne. London: Verso, 2003.

———. "Robert Walser." Translated by Mark Harman. In *Robert Walser Rediscovered*, edited by Mark Harman, 144–47.

———. "Robert Walser." In *Gesammelte Schriften*, vol. 2, edited by Rolf Tiedemann and Hermann Schweppenhäuser, 324–28. Frankfurt am Main: Suhrkamp, 1977.

———. *Selected Writings*. Vol. 1. Edited by Marcus Paul Bullock, Howard Eiland, and Michael Jennings. Cambridge, Mass.: Harvard University Press, 1996.

———. *Selected Writings*. Vol. 2. Edited by Michael W. Jennings, Howard Eiland, and Gary Smith. Cambridge, Mass.: Harvard University Press, 1999.

Bernofsky, Susan. *Robert Walser: Clairvoyant of the Small*. New Haven, Conn.: Yale University Press, forthcoming.

———. "Secrets, Not Code: On Robert Walser's Microscripts." In *Microscripts*, by Robert Walser, 9–20. New York: New Directions / Christine Burgin, 2012.

Bernofsky, Susan, and Lucas Marco Gisi. "USA, England." In Gisi, *Robert Walser-Handbuch*, 396–400.

Bernofsky, Susan, and Tom Whalen, eds. "Robert Walser." Special issue, *Review of Contemporary Fiction* 12, no. 1 (spring 1992).

———. "Introduction." *Review of Contemporary Fiction* 12, no. 1 (1992): 7–15.

Binder, Thomas. *Zu Robert Walsers frühen Gedichten: Eine Konstellation von Einzelanalysen*. Bonn: Bouvier Verlag Herbert Grundmann, 1976.

Bleckmann, Ulf. "*. . . ein Meinungslabyrinth, in welchem alle, alle herumirren . . .": Intertextualität und Metasprache als Robert Walsers Beitrag zur Moderne*. Frankfurt am Main: Peter Lang, 1994.

Blei, Franz. "Robert Walser." *Prager Presse*, April 21, 1935.

Bloemen, Henri. "Durch die 'inneren Gemächer' geführt: Zur Lektüre von Robert Walsers *Jakob von Gunten*." In *Bild-Sprache. Texte zwischen Dichten und Denken*, edited by Luc Lambrechts and Johan Nové, 51–66. Leuven: Universitaire Pers Leuven, 1990.

Böhler, Michael. "Dichten aus der Peripherie des Schreibens: Überlegungen zu Robert Walsers kulturpolitischem Ort im deutschsprachigen Raum." In *"Wärmende Fremde": Robert Walser und seine Übersetzer*, edited by Walter Lenschen and Peter Utz, 31–44. Bern: Peter Lang, 1994.

Bollnow, Otto Friedrich. *Mensch und Raum*. Stuttgart: Kohlhammer, 1963.

Borchmeyer, Dieter. *Dienst und Herrschaft: Ein Versuch über Robert Walser*. Tübingen: de Gruyter, 1980.

———. "Robert Walsers Metatheater: Über die Dramolette und szenischen Prosastücke." In Chiarini and Zimmermann, *"Immer dicht vor dem Sturze . . . ,"* 129–43.

Böschenstein, Bernhard. "Sprechen als Wandern: Robert Walsers *Aus dem Bleistiftgebiet*." In Chiarini and Zimmermann, *"Immer dicht vor dem Sturze . . . ,"* 19–23.

———. "Theatralische Miniaturen: Zur frühen Prosa Robert Walsers." In *Probleme der Moderne: Studien zur deutschen Literatur von Nietzsche bis Brecht*, edited by Benjamin Bennett, Anton Kaes, and William J. Lillyman, 67–81. Tübingen: Niemeyer, 1983.

Bottigheimer, Ruth B. "Review of *Robert Walser Rediscovered*." *German Quarterly* 60, no. 2 (1987): 306.

Brod, Max. *Über Franz Kafka*. Frankfurt am Main: Fischer, 1974.

Brotbeck, Roman. "Musik." In Gisi, *Robert Walser-Handbuch*, 391–94.

Buchan, Suzanne. *The Quay Brothers: Into a Metaphysical Playroom*. Minneapolis: University of Minnesota Press, 2011.

———. "The Quay Brothers: Choreographed Chiaroscuro, Enigmatic and Sublime." *Film Quarterly* 51, no. 3 (1998): 2–15.

Bucheli, Roman. "Deutschsprachige Literatur." In Gisi, *Robert Walser-Handbuch*, 371–80.

Buchholz, Paul. "Monologue Overgrown: Revising the World with Speech in Franz Kafka, Robert Walser, and Thomas Bernhard." Ph.D. diss., Cornell University, 2010.

———. *Private Anarchy: Impossible Community and the Outsider's Monologue in German Experimental Fiction*. Evanston, Ill.: Northwestern University Press, 2018.

Büchner, Georg. *Lenz*. Bilingual ed. Translated by Richard Sieburth. New York: Archipelago, 2005.

Bungartz, Christoph. *Zurückweichend vorwärtsschreiten: Die Ironie in Robert Walsers Berner Prosa*. Frankfurt am Main: Peter Lang, 1988.

Bürgi-Michaud, Thomas. *Robert Walsers mühseligkeitsüberschüttetes Kunststück*. Frankfurt am Main: Peter Lang, 1996.
Canetti, Elias. *Das Geheimherz der Uhr*. Munich: Hanser, 1987.
———. *Die Provinz des Menschen*. Munich: Hanser, 1973.
Casey, Edward S. *The Fate of Place: A Philosophical History*. Berkeley: University of California Press, 1997.
Chiarini, Paolo, and Hans Dieter Zimmermann, eds. *"Immer dicht vor dem Sturze . . .": Zum Werk Robert Walsers*. Frankfurt am Main: Athanäum, 1987.
Coetzee, J. M. *Inner Workings: Literary Essays, 2000–2005*. New York: Penguin, 2007.
Colwell, Constance. "Robert Walser, *Der Räuber*: A Study of the Narrative Structure." Ph.D. diss., Cornell University, 1977.
Dällenbach, Lucien. *The Mirror in the Text*. Translated by Jeremy Whitely with Emma Hughes. Cambridge: Polity, 1989.
Deleuze, Gilles. *The Logic of Sense*. Translated by Mark Lester. New York: Columbia University Press, 1990.
———. *Masochism: Coldness and Cruelty*. Translated by Jean McNeil. New York: Zone Books, 1991.
Deleuze, Gilles, and Félix Guattari. *Kafka: Toward a Minor Literature*. Translated by Dana Polan. Minneapolis: University of Minnesota Press, 1986.
Denneler, Iris. "'Erzähle ich eine Geschichte, so denke ich ans Essen': Zur kulinarischen Poetologie Robert Walsers." *Wirkendes Wort* 49 (1999): 167–295.
Derrida, Jacques. "On Reading Heidegger: An Outline of Remarks to the Essex Colloquium." *Research in Phenomonology* 17, no. 1 (1987): 171–85.
Deutsches Wörterbuch. Edited by Jacob Grimm and Wilhelm Grimm. Leipzig: Hirzel, 1863–78.
Downes, Davie, and Paul Rock. *Understanding Deviance*. 6th ed. Oxford: Oxford University Press, 2011.
Echte, Bernhard. *Robert Walser: Sein Leben in Bildern und Texten*. Frankfurt am Main: Suhrkamp, 2008.
Echte, Bernhard, and Andreas Meier, eds. *Die Brüder Karl und Robert Walser: Maler und Dichter*. Stäfa: Rothenhäusler Verlag, 1990.
Echte, Bernhard, and Werner Morlang. "Editorischer Bericht." In Robert Walser, *Aus dem Bleistiftgebiet*, edited by Echte and Morlang, 6:701–11. Frankfurt am Main: Suhrkamp, 2000.
———. "Editorische Vorbemerkung." In Robert Walser, *Aus dem Bleistiftgebiet*, edited by Echte and Morlang, 3:5–8. Frankfurt am Main: Suhrkamp, 1992.
———. Nachwort (Afterword) to Robert Walser, *Aus dem Bleistiftgebiet*, edited by Echte and Morlang, 6:568–84. Frankfurt am Main: Suhrkamp, 2000.
Eiden-Offe, Patrick. "Männlichkeitsvertreter: Figurationen von Männlichkeit in der späten Prosa Robert Walsers. Eine exemplarische Lektüre des Prosastücks 'Es war einmal.'" Paper presented at the "2. Tagung AIM Gender" (November 7–9, 2002). https://www.fk12.tu-dortmund.de/cms/ISO/de/arbeitsbereiche/soziologie_der_geschlechterverhaeltnisse/Medienpool/AIM-Beitraege_zweite_Tagung/eiden.pdf. Accessed October 1, 2015.
Elias, Norbert. *The Civilizing Process: Sociogenetic and Psychogenetic Investigations*. Edited by Eric Dunning, Johan Goudsblom, and Stephen Mennell. Translated by Edmund Jephcott. Oxford: Blackwell, 2000.

Elon, Amos. *The Pity of It All: A Portrait of the Jewish-German Epoch, 1743–1933*. New York: Picador, 2002.

Engel, Manfred. "Außenwelt und Innenwelt: Subjektivitätsentwurf und moderne Romanpoetik in Robert Walsers *Jakob von Gunten* und Franz Kafkas *Der Verschollene*." *Jahrbuch der deutschen Schillergesellschaft* 30 (1986): 533–70.

Evans, Tamara. "'Ein Künstler ist hier gezwungen aufzuhorchen': Zu Robert Walsers Kunstrezeption in der Berliner Zeit." In *Bildersprache, Klangfiguren: Spielformen der Intermedialität bei Robert Walser*, 107–16. Munich: Wilhelm Fink, 2008.

———, ed. *Robert Walser and the Visual Arts*. New York: CUNY Press, 1996.

———. *Robert Walsers Moderne*. Bern: Francke, 1989.

———. "'A Paul Klee in Prose': Design, Space, and Time in the Work of Robert Walser." *German Quarterly* 75, no. 1 (1984): 27–41.

Evers, Kai. *Violent Modernists: The Aesthetics of Destruction in Twentieth-Century German Literature*. Evanston, Ill.: Northwestern University Press, 2013.

Fattori, Anna. "Forschungsgeschichte." In Gisi, *Robert Walser-Handbuch*, 417–30.

Fenves, Peter. *The Messianic Reduction: Walter Benjamin and the Shape of Time*. Stanford, Calif.: Stanford University Press, 2011.

Fischer, Uve. "Armut und Schnee in den frühen Gedichten Robert Walsers." In Chiarini and Zimmermann, *"Immer dicht vor dem Sturze . . . ,"* 68–79.

Foucault, Michel. *Discipline and Punish: The Birth of the Prison*. New York: Random House, 1984.

———. "Nietzsche, Freud, Marx." In *Aesthetics, Method, and Epistemology*, translated by Robert Hurley, 269–78. New York: New Press, 1998.

Frederick, Samuel. "An Antlered Adaptation: Stag Iconography and Animal-Human Hybridity in the Quay Brothers' *Institute Benjamenta*." *Literature/Film Quarterly* 43, no. 3 (2015): 202–16.

———. "A Bursting Zero of Unknowing: Overcoming the Paradox of Infinite Knowledge in Heinrich von Kleist's 'Über das Marionettentheater' and Robert Walser's *Jakob von Gunten*." *Germanic Review* 88, no. 4 (2013): 375–90.

———. *Narratives Unsettled: Digression in Robert Walser, Thomas Bernhard, and Adalbert Stifter*. Evanston, Ill.: Northwestern University Press, 2012.

———. "Redemption of the Miniature: The Quay Brothers and Robert Walser." In *Institute Benjamenta, or This Dream People Call Human Life*, directed by the Quay Brothers, 1–6 (booklet). DVD/Blu-ray, British Film Institute, 2010.

———. "Stealing the Story: Robert Walser's *Robber*-Novel." In *Digressions in European Literature: From Cervantes to Sebald*, edited by Alexis Grohmann and Caragh Wells, 130–42. Basingstoke, U.K.: Palgrave Macmillan, 2010.

Freud, Sigmund. "A Child Is Being Beaten." In *The Standard Edition of the Complete Psychological Works of Sigmund Freud*, 24 vols., edited and translated by James Strachey, 17:175–204. London: Hogarth, 1953–74.

———. "The Economic Problem of Masochism." In *The Standard Edition*, 19:159–70. London: Hogarth, 1953–74.

———. "Fetishism." In *The Standard Edition*, 21:147–57. London: Hogarth, 1953–74.

———. "A Note upon the 'Mystic Writing-Pad.'" In *The Standard Edition*, 19:225–32. London: Hogarth, 1953–74.

———. "Thoughts for the Times on War and Death." In *The Standard Edition*, 14:274–300. London: Hogarth, 1953–74.

Frey, Hans-Jost. *Lesen und Schreiben*. Basel: Urs Engeler, 1998.

Frisch, Efraim. "Ein Jüngling: Jakob von Gunten." In Kerr, *Über Robert Walser*, 1:71.

Fröhlich, Elio, and Robert Mächler, eds. *Robert Walser zum Gedenken*. Frankfurt am Main: Suhrkamp, 1976.

Fuchs, Anne. *Dramaturgie des Narrentums: Das Komische in der Prosa Robert Walsers*. Published under the name Annette Fuchs. Munich: Wilhelm Fink, 1993.

———. "Why Smallness Matters: The Problem of Attention in Franz Kafka's and Robert Walser's Short Prose." In *Kafka und die kleine Prosa der Moderne / Franz Kafka and Short Modernist Prose*, edited by Ritchie Robertson and Manfred Engel, 167–81. Würzburg: Königshausen & Neumann, 2011.

Gabrisch, Anne. "Robert Walser in Berlin." In Hinz and Horst, *Robert Walser*, 30–55.

———. "Robert Walser und Franz Blei—Oder: vom Elend des literarischen Betriebs." Presentation at the annual gathering of the Robert Walser-Gesellschaft, Berlin, October 22–24, 1999, http://www.robertWalser.ch/fileadmin/redaktion/dokumente/jahrestagungen/vortraege/gabrisch99.pdf.

Gass, William H. Introduction to Robert Walser, *Masquerade and Other Stories*, ix–xix. Baltimore: Johns Hopkins University Press, 1990.

Gass, William H., and Jürg Laederach. *Über Robert Walser: Zwei Essays*. Salzburg: Residenz, 1997.

Gees, Marion. "Robert Walsers galante Damen: Fragmente einer Sprache der höfischen Geste." In Arnold, *Text und Kritik*, 142–54.

———. *Schauspiel auf Papier: Gebärde und Maskierung in der Prosa Robert Walsers*. Berlin: Erich Schmidt, 2001.

Geulen, Eva. "Autorität und Kontingenz der Tradition bei Robert Walser." In *Autorität der/in Sprache, Literatur, Neuen Medien*, edited by Jürgen Fohrmann, Ingrid Karsten, and Eva Neuland, 805–13. Bielefeld: Aisthesis, 1997.

Gilman, Sander L. *Jewish Self-Hatred: Anti-Semitism and the Hidden Language of the Jews*. Baltimore: Johns Hopkins University Press, 1986.

Gisi, Lucas Marco, ed. *Robert Walser-Handbuch: Leben—Werk—Wirkung*. Stuttgart: Metzler, 2015.

Gisi, Lucas Marco, Reto Sorg, and Peter Stocker. Nachwort (Afterword) to Robert Walser, *Mikrogramme*, 203–13. Berlin: Suhrkamp, 2011.

Giuriato, Davide. "Kindheit, Naivität, Dilettantismus." In Gisi, *Robert Walser-Handbuch*, 337–40.

———. "Robert Walsers Kinder." In Groddeck et al., *Robert Walsers "Ferne Nähe,"* 125–32.

Glauser, Friedrich. *Gourrama: Ein Roman aus der Fremdenlegion*. Edited by Bernhard Echte. Zurich: Limmat, 1997.

Gößling, Andreas. *Abendstern und Zauberstab: Studien und Interpretationen zu Robert Walsers "Der Gehülfe" und "Jakob von Gunten."* Würzburg: Königshausen & Neumann, 1992.

———. *Ein lächelndes Spiel: Kommentar zu Robert Walsers "Geschwister Tanner."* Würzburg: Königshausen & Neumann, 1991.

Göttsche, Dirk. "Epistemology, Poetics and Time in Modernist Short Prose around 1900." In *Time in German Literature and Culture, 1900–2015: Between Acceleration and Slowness*, edited by Anne Fuchs and J. J. Long, 71–92. Basingstoke, U.K.: Palgrave Macmillan, 2016.

———. *Kleine Prosa in Moderne und Gegenwart*. Münster: Aschendorff, 2006.

Grenz, Dagmar. *Die Romane Robert Walsers: Weltbezug und Wirklichkeitsdarstellung*. Munich: Wilhelm Fink, 1974.

Greven, Jochen. "Die beklatschte Tragödie: Robert Walser und Walther Rathenau—Versuche einer Rekonstruktion." *Allemande* 16, nos. 50/51 (1996): 11–30.

———. "'Er fährt nach dem Schwabenland': Robert Walsers Jahr in Stuttgart." Presentation at the annual meeting of the Robert Walser Society, June 23, 2007, http://www.robertWalser.ch/fileadmin/redaktion/dokumente/jahrestagungen/vortraege/Greven-2007.pdf. Accessed July 6, 2016.

———. *Existenz, Welt und reines Sein im Werk Robert Walsers*. Munich: Wilhelm Fink, 2009.

———. "Schatzkammer und Papierkorb: Die Bleistiftentwürfe sind die Grundlage von Walsers vielseitigem Werk." *Du: Die Zeitschrift der Kultur* 62, no. 730 (2002–3): 64–67.

Groddeck, Wolfram. "Masochismus." In Gisi, *Robert Walser-Handbuch*, 332–36.

———. "Weiss das Blatt, wie schön es ist? Prosastück, Schriftbild und Poesie bei Robert Walser." *Text: Kritische Beiträge* 3 (1997): 23–41.

Groddeck, Wolfram, Reto Sorg, Peter Utz, and Karl Wagner, eds. *Robert Walsers "Ferne Nähe": Neue Beiträge zur Forschung*. Munich: Fink, 2007.

Gronau, Peter. *"Ich schreibe hier dekorativ": Essays zu Robert Walser*. Würzburg: Königshausen & Neumann, 2006.

Hamacher, Werner. *Minima Philologica*. Translated by Catherine Diehl and Jason Groves. New York: Fordham University Press, 2015.

Hammer, Gerd. *Momente des Kindlichen im Werk Robert Walsers*. Frankfurt am Main: Griedel, 1989.

Handy, E. S. C. *Polynesian Religion*. Honolulu: The Museum, 1927.

Harman, Mark. "Introduction: A Reluctant Modern." In *Robert Walser Rediscovered*, edited by Mark Harman, 1–14.

———, ed. *Robert Walser Rediscovered: Stories, Fairy-Tale Plays, and Critical Responses*. Hanover, N.H.: University Press of New England, 1985.

Hauschner, Auguste. "Gebrüder Tanner." *Die Zukunft* 59 (1907): 99–101.

Heffernan, Valerie. *Provocation from the Periphery: Robert Walser Re-examined*. Würzburg: Königshausen & Neumann, 2007.

Heiniger, Urs. "Ich entwickle mich nicht: Das ist ja nun so eine Behauptung. Zur Tagebuchstruktur von 'Jakob von Gunten.'" Ph.D. diss., University of Bern, 1996.

Henke, Silvia. "Eigensinnige Briefe: Zwischen Literatur- und Medienwissenschaft." In *Weiterlesen: Literatur und Wissen*, edited by Ulrike Bergermann and Elisabeth Strowick, 174–98. Bielefeld: Transcript, 2007.

Henking, Irene Weber. "Überblick." In Gisi, *Robert Walser-Handbuch*, 394–95.

Hiebel, Hans H. "Robert Walsers *Jakob von Gunten*: Die Zerstörung der Signifikanz im modernen Roman." In Hinz and Horst, *Robert Walser*, 240–75.

Hildesheimer, Wolfgang. *Masante*. Vol. 2 of *Gesammelte Werke*, edited by Christiaan L. Hart Nibbrig and Volker Jehle. Frankfurt am Main: Suhrkamp, 1991.

Hinz, Klaus-Michael. "Robert Walsers Souveränität." In Chiarini and Zimmermann, "*Immer dicht vor dem Sturze . . .*," 153–71.

———. "Wo die bösen Kinder wohnen: Robert Walsers Melancholie. Mit einer Fussnote zu Franz Kafkas Spielsachen." In Hinz and Horst, *Robert Walser*, 310–22.

Hinz, Klaus-Michael, and Thomas Horst, eds. *Robert Walser*. Frankfurt am Main: Suhrkamp, 1991.

Hobus, Jens. "*Komödie* (1919)." In Gisi, *Robert Walser-Handbuch*, 82–90.

———. *Poetik der Umschreibung: Figurationen der Liebe im Werk Robert Walsers*. Würzburg: Königshausen & Neumann, 2011.

Hofmiller, Josef. "Jakob von Gunten: Gedichte." In Kerr, *Über Robert Walser*, 1:51.

Horst, Thomas. "Robert Walser, ein Forschungsbericht." In Hinz and Horst, *Robert Walser*, 376–452.

Huber, Peter. "'Dem Dichterunstern gänzlich verfallen': Robert Walsers Kleist." In *Robert Walser und die modern Poetik*, edited by Dieter Borchmeyer, 140–66. Frankfurt am Main: Suhrkamp, 1999.

Hübner, Andrea. "'Das Märchen ja sagt . . .'—Märchen und Trivialliteratur im Werk von Robert Walser." In *Robert Walser und die moderne Poetik*, edited by Dieter Borchmeyer, 167–86. Frankfurt am Main: Suhrkamp, 1999.

———. *Ei', welcher Sinn liegt im Unsinn? Robert Walsers Umgang mit Märchen und Trivialliteratur*. Tübingen: Stauffenberg, 1995.

Huster, Alexandra. "Going One's Own Way: The Literary Construction of the Oddball in German Literature (Jean Paul, Franz Grillparzer, Robert Walser)." Ph.D. diss., New York University, 2007.

Hutcheon, Linda. *Narcissistic Narrative: The Metafictional Paradox*. Waterloo, Ont.: Wilfried Laurier University Press, 1980.

Huyssen, Andreas. "Modernist Miniatures: Literary Snapshots of Urban Spaces." *PMLA* 122, no. 1 (2007): 27–42.

Ifkovits, Kurt. "Der Kreis um *Die Insel*." In Gisi, *Robert Walser-Handbuch*, 21–24.

Ifrah, Georges. *Histoire universelle des chiffres*. Paris: Robert Laffont, 1981.

Ingold, Tim. "The Temporality of the Landscape." *World Archaeology* 25, no. 2 (1993): 152–74.

Jürgens, Martin. *Robert Walser: Die Krise der Darstellbarkeit*. 2nd ed. Kronberg: Scriptor Verlag, 1973.

———. *Seine Kunst zu zögern: Elf Versuche zu Robert Walser*. Münster: Oktober, 2006.

Kafka, Franz. *Gesammelte Werke*. 12 vols. Edited by Hans-Gerd Koch. Frankfurt am Main: Fischer, 1994.

———. *Nachgelassene Schriften und Fragmente II*. Edited by Jost Schillemeit. Frankfurt am Main: Fischer, 1992.

Kammer, Stephan. *Figurationen und Gesten des Schreibens: Zur Ästhetik der Produktion in Robert Walsers Prosa der Berner Zeit*. Tübingen: Max Niemeyer, 2003.

———. "Gestörte Kommunikation: Robert Walsers Briefschreibspiele." In "*Ich an Dich": Edition, Konzeption und Kommentierung von Briefen*, edited by

Werner M. Bauer and Wolfgang Wiesmüller, 229–45. Innsbruck: Universität Innsbruck, 2001.

———. "'Lib/e/ri': Walsers poetologisch souveräne Kinder." In Groddeck et al., *Robert Walsers "Ferne Nähe,"* 133–40.

———. "'Sorgsam übersetzt?': Robert Walser als 'Verdeutscher von Verlaine.'" In *Edition und Übersetzung: Zur wissenschaftlichen Dokumentation des interkulturellen Texttransfers*, edited by Bodo Plachta and Winfried Woesler, 149–64. Tübingen: Max Niemeyer, 2002.

Kandinsky, Wassily. *On the Spiritual in Art.* Translated by Hilla Rebay. New York: Solomon R. Guggenheim Foundation, 1946.

———. *Über das Geistige in der Kunst.* 8th ed. Bern: Benteli Verlag, 1965.

Kaufmann, Herbert L. "The Narrative Structure in Robert Walser's *Geschwister Tanner, Der Gehülfe, Jakob von Gunten.*" Ph.D. diss., New York University, 1969.

Kaufmann, Vincent. *Post Scripts: The Writer's Workshop.* Translated by Deborah Treisman. Cambridge, Mass.: Harvard University Press, 1994.

Keckeis, Paul. "Fritz Kocher's Aufsätze (1904)." In Gisi, *Robert Walser-Handbuch*, 90–94.

Kerr, Katharina, ed. *Über Robert Walser.* 3 vols. Frankfurt am Main: Suhrkamp, 1978–79.

Kinder, Hermann. "Flucht in die Landschaft: Zu Robert Walsers 'Kleist in Thun.'" In Arnold, *Text und Kritik*, 95–105.

Kleist, Heinrich von. *Sämtliche Werke und Briefe.* 9th ed. Edited by Helmut Sembdner. Munich: Carl Hanser, 1993.

Kommerell, Max. "Die Sprache und das Unaussprechliche: Eine Betrachtung über Heinrich von Kleist." *Das Innere Reich* 4, no. 1 (1937): 654–97.

Kreienbrock, Jörg. *Kleiner. Feiner. Leichter: Nunancierungen zum Werk Robert Walsers.* Zurich: Diaphanes, 2010.

Kurzawa, Lothar. "'Ich ging eine Weile als alte Frau': Subjektivität und Maskerade bei Robert Walser." In Hinz and Horst, *Robert Walser*, 167–79.

Lambrecht, Tobias. "Theater." In Gisi, *Robert Walser-Handbuch*, 381–84.

Lemmel, Monika. "Angelesen?—Robert Walsers Schiller-Texte." In *Bildersprache—Klangfiguren: Spielformen der Intermedialität bei Robert Walser*, edited by Anna Fattori and Margit Gigerl, 193–200. Munich: Fink, 2008.

———. "Robert Walsers Poetik der Intertextualität." In *Robert Walser und die modern Poetik*, edited by Dieter Borchmeyer, 83–101. Frankfurt am Main: Suhrkamp, 1999.

Lewin, Kurt. "Field Theory and Experiment in Social Psychology." *American Journal of Sociology* 44 (1939): 868–97.

Lobsien, Eckhard. *Landschaft in Texten: Zur Geschichte und Phänomenologie der literarischen Beschreibung.* Stuttgart: Metzler, 1981.

Mächler, Robert. *Das Leben Robert Walsers: Eine dokumentarische Biographie.* 2nd ed. Frankfurt am Main: Suhrkamp, 2003.

Malkmus, Bernhard F. *The German Picaro and Modernity: Between Underdog and Shape-Shifter.* New York: Continuum, 2011.

Marks, Laura. "The Quays' *Institute Benjamenta*: An Olfactory View." *Afterimage* 25, no. 2 (September/October 1997): 11–13.

Marx, Karl. "Wage Labor and Capital." In *The Marx-Engels Reader*, edited by Robert Tucker, 203–17. New York: W. W. Norton, 1978.

Mattenklott, Gert. *Blindgänger: Physiognomische Essays*. Frankfurt am Main: Suhrkamp, 1986.

Matz, Robert. *Defending Literature in Early Modern England: Renaissance Literary Theory in Social Context*. Cambridge: Cambridge University Press, 2000.

McHale, Brian. "En abyme: Internal Models and Cognitive Mapping." In *A Sense of the World: Essays in Fiction, Narrative and Knowledge*, edited by John Gibson, Wolfgang Huemer, and Luca Pocci, 189–206. New York: Routledge, 2007.

Menke, Bettine. *Das Trauerspiel-Buch*. Bielefeld: Transcript, 2010.

Merleau-Ponty, Maurice. *Phenomeology of Perception*. Translated by Colin Smith. London: Routledge, 1962.

———. *The Visible and the Invisible*. Translated by Alphonso Lingis. Evanston, Ill.: Northwestern University Press, 1968.

Mermet, Frieda. "Frau Frieda Mermet erzählt." *Neutralität* 5, no. 3 (1967): 15–19.

Meyer-Sickendieck, Burkhard. *Tiefe: Über die Faszination des Grübelns*. Munich: Fink, 2010.

Meyers großes Konversations-Lexikon. 6th ed. Leipzig: Bibliographisches Institut, 1906.

Middleton, Christopher. "The Picture of Nobody: Some Remarks on Robert Walser with a Note on Walser and Kafka." *Revue des langues vivantes* 24 (1958): 404–28.

Morlang, Werner. Afterword (Nachwort) to Robert Walser, *Aus dem Bleistiftgebiet*, edited by Bernhard Echte and Werner Morlang, 2:517–21. Frankfurt am Main: Suhrkamp, 1990.

———. "Gelegenheits- oder Verlegenheitslyrik? Anmerkungen zu den späten Gedichten Robert Walsers." In Hinz and Horst, *Robert Walser*, 115–33.

———. *Robert Walser in Bern: Auf den Spuren eines Stadtnomaden*. Oberhofen: Zytglogge, 2009.

Morse, J. Mitchell. "Fiction Chronicle." *Hudson Review* 23, no. 2 (1970): 331.

Müller, Dominik. "Text und Bild." In Gisi, *Robert Walser-Handbuch*, 283–89.

Musil, Robert. *The Confusions of Young Törless*. Translated by Shaun Whiteside. New York: Penguin, 2001.

———. *Gesammelte Werke*. 9 vols. Edited by Adolf Frisé. Reinbek: Rowohlt, 1978.

———. *The Man without Qualities*. Vol. 1. Translated by Sophie Wilkins. New York: Knopf, 1996.

———. "The Mathematical Man." In *Precision and Soul: Essays and Addresses*, by Robert Musil, edited and translated by Burton Pike and David S. Luft, 39–42. Chicago: University of Chicago Press, 1990.

———. "Novellas." In Robert Musil, *Precision and Soul: Essays and Addresses*, edited and translated by Burton Pike and David S. Luft, 9–10. Chicago: University of Chicago Press, 1990.

———. "Sketch of What the Writer Knows." In *Precision and Soul: Essays and Addresses*, by Robert Musil, edited and translated by Burton Pike and David S. Luft, 61–65. Chicago: University of Chicago Press, 1990.

———. "The *Stories* of Robert Walser." Translated by Mark Harman. In Harman, *Robert Walser Rediscovered*, 141–43.

Naguib, Nagi. *Robert Walser: Entwurf einer Bewußtseinsstruktur*. Munich: W. Fink, 1970.

Neumann, Gerhard. *Kafka-Lektüren*. Berlin: De Gruyter, 2013.

Niccolini, Elisabett. *Der Spaziergang des Schriftstellers*. Stuttgart: Metzler, 2000.

Nietzsche, Friedrich. *Dithyrambs of Dionysus*. Translated by R. J. Hollingdale. London: Anvil Press Poetry, 1984.

———. *The Gay Science: With a Prelude in German Rhymes and an Appendix of Songs*. Edited by Bernard Williams; translated by Josefine Nauckhoff. Cambridge: Cambridge University Press, 2001.

———. *Thus Spake Zarathustra: A Book for Everybody and Nobody*. Translated by Graham Parkes. Oxford: Oxford University Press, 2005.

Nörtemann, Regina. "Robert Walser und Georg Büchner: Ein Beitrag zur Rezeption und Transformation von literarischen Vorbildern." *Jahrbuch der Deutschen Schillergesellschaft* 52 (2008): 438–58.

Nußbaum, Fritz. "Professor Hermann Walser." *Geographische Zeitschrift* 26, no. 3 (1920): 65–67.

Oesterle, Günter. "Commis, Poet, Räuber: Eigengesetzlichkeit und Selbstaufgabe bei Robert Walser." In Hinz and Horst, *Robert Walser*, 217–39.

———. "'Unter dem Strich': Skizze einer Kulturpoetik des Feuilletons." In *Das schwierige neunzehnte Jahrhundert: Germanistische Tagung zum 65. Geburtstag von Eda Sagarra im August 1998*, edited by Jürgen Barkhoff, Gilbert Carr, and Roger Paulin, 230–50. Tübingen: Niemeyer, 2000.

Pelletier, Nicole. *Franz Kafka et Robert Walser: Étude d'une relation littéraire*. Stuttgart: Heinz, 1985.

Pender, Malcolm. "A Writer's Relationship to Society: Robert Walser's *Räuber-Roman*." *Modern Language Review* 78 (1983): 103–12.

Pestalozzi, Karl. "Spazieren und Schreiben: Franz Kafka 'Der plötzliche Spaziergang' und Robert Walser *Der Spaziergang*." In *Franz Kafka und Robert Walser im Dialog*, edited by Vesna Kondrič Horvat, 23–39. Berlin: Weidler, 2010.

Philippi, Klaus-Peter. "Robert Walsers 'Jakob von Gunten.'" In *Provokation und Idylle: Über Robert Walser*, edited by Jochen Greven, 51–70. Stuttgart: Klett, 1971.

Piniel, Gerhard. *Robert Walsers "Geschwister Tanner."* Zurich: Juris, 1968.

Pinker, Steven. *The Better Angels of Our Nature: Why Violence Has Declined*. New York: Viking, 2011.

Plug, Jan. *They Have All Been Healed: Reading Robert Walser*. Evanston, Ill.: Northwestern University Press, 2016.

Popitz, Heinrich. *Phänomene der Macht*. Tübingen: Mohr Siebeck, 1992.

Puig, Teresa Vinardell. "'In unaufrichtigster, dafür aber schimmerndster Hochachtung': Überlegungen zu Robert Walsers Briefen an Verleger und Redakteure." In *WortKulturen TonWelten: Festschrift für Alfonsina Janés zum 70. Geburtstag*, edited by Marisa Siguan, M. Loreto Vilar, and Rosa Pérez Zancas, 101–14. Marburg: Tectum, 2014.

Reibnitz, Barbara von, and Wolfram Groddeck. "Editorisches Nachwort." In *Kritische Ausgabe sämtlicher Drucke und Manuskripte. Band I.2: Geschwister Tanner (Erstdruck)*, by Robert Walser, 309–32. Basel: Stroemfeld, 2008.

Reinacher, Pia. *Die Sprache der Kleider im literarischen Text: Untersuchungen zu Gottfried Keller und Robert Walser*. Frankfurt am Main: Peter Lang, 1988.

Rimbaud, Arthur. *A Season in Hell and The Drunken Boat*. Translated by Louise Varèse. New York: New Directions, 1961.

Rodewald, Dierk. *Robert Walsers Prosa: Versuch einer Strukturanalyse*. Bad Homburg: Gehlen, 1970.

Roser, Dieter. *Fingierte Mündlichkeit und reine Schrift: Zur Sprachproblematik in Robert Walsers späten Texten*. Würzburg: Königshausen & Neumann, 1994.

Rossbacher, Karlheinz. "Mathematik und Gefühl: Zu Robert Musils 'Die Verwirrungen des Zöglings Törless.'" In *Österreichische Literatur des 20. Jahrhunderts: Französische und österreichische Beiträge*, edited by Sigurd Paul Scheichel and Gerald Stieg, 127–39. Innsbruck: Institut für Germanistik der Universität Innsbruck, 1986.

Rotman, Brian. *Signifying Nothing: The Semiotics of Zero*. Basingstoke, U.K.: Palgrave Macmillan, 1987.

Roulet, Daniel de. "Wandern, Schreiben, Lieben." Translated by Marion Gees. In Arnold, *Text und Kritik*, 44–51.

Rousseau, Jean-Jacques. *Reveries of the Solitary Walker*. Translated by Russell Gouldbourne. Oxford: Oxford University Press, 2011.

Roussel, Martin. *Matrikel: Zur Haltung des Schreibens in Robert Walsers Mikrographie*. Frankfurt am Main and Basel: Stroemfeld, 2011.

———. "Schreibszenen (Schreiben, Materialität, Schriftbild)." In Gisi, *Robert Walser-Handbuch*, 261–68.

Ruprecht, Lucia. "Film." In Gisi, *Robert Walser-Handbuch*, 385–87.

———. "Pleasure and Affinity in W. G. Sebald and Robert Walser." *German Life and Letters* 62, no. 3 (2009): 311–26.

Rüsch, Lukas. *Ironie und Herrschaft: Untersuchungen zum Verhältnis von Herr und Knecht in Robert Walsers Roman "Der Gehülfe."* Königstein: Forum Academicum, 1983.

Sauvat, Catherine. *Vergessene Weiten: Eine Robert Walser-Biographie*. Frankfurt am Main: Suhrkamp, 1995.

Schaak, Martina. *"Das Theater ein Traum": Robert Walsers Welt als gestaltete Bühne*. Berlin: Wissenschaftlicher Verlag Berlin, 1999.

Schaffner, Jakob. *Hans Himmelhoch*. Berlin: Fischer, 1909.

Scheffler, Kerstin. *Mikropoetik: Robert Walsers Bieler Prosa*. Bielefeld: Transcript, 2010.

Schestag, Thomas. "Interpolationen: Benjamins Philologie." *Philo:Xenia* 1 (2009): 33–99.

Schiller, Friedrich. *On the Aesthetic Education of Man in a Series of Letters*. Translated by Elizabeth M. Wilkinson and L. A. Willoughby. Oxford: Clarendon, 1982.

Schuller, Marianne. "Briefe an Frieda Mermet." In Gisi, *Robert Walser-Handbuch*, 224–30.

———. "Robert Walsers Poetik des Winzigen: Ein Versuch." In Groddeck et al., *Robert Walsers "Ferne Nähe,"* 75–81.

Schwahl, Markus. *Die Wirklichkeit und ihre Schwestern: Epistemologische Ideologiekritik und ihre ethischen Implikationen im Werk Robert Walsers*. Frankfurt am Main: Peter Lang, 2001.

Schwarz, Anette. *Melancholie: Figuren und Orte einer Stimmung*. Vienna: Passagen Verlag, 1996.

Schwerin, Kerstin Gräfin von. "'Kolossal zierliche Zusammengeschrobenheiten von durchweg abenteuerlichem Charakter': In den Regionen des Bleistiftgebiets." In Arnold, *Text und Kritik*, 161–80.

Searls, Damion. "That Old Goat! Robert Walser's Scrupulous Art of Translation." *Paris Review* blog, September 30, 2015, https://www.theparisreview.org/blog/2015/09/30/that-old-goat/. Accessed August 8, 2017.

Sebald, W. G. *Logis in einem Landhaus: Über Gottfried Keller, Johann Peter Hebel, Robert Walser und andere*. Munich: Hanser, 1998.

———. *A Place in the Country*. Translated by Jo Catling. New York: Random House, 2014.

Seelig, Carl. "Die Handschrift des Dichters." *Du: Die Zeitschrift der Kultur* 17, no. 10 (1957): 45–46, http://www.e-periodica.ch/digbib/view?pid=dkm-001:1957:17#775. Accessed May 2017.

———. *Wanderungen mit Robert Walser*. Frankfurt am Main: Suhrkamp, 1981.

Seidel, Robert. *Aus Kampfgewühl und Einsamkeit: Gedichte*. Stuttgart: J. H. W. Dietz, 1895.

Siegel, Elke. *Aufträge aus dem Bleistiftgebiet: Zur Dichtung Robert Walsers*. Würzburg: Königshausen & Neumann, 2001.

Siegert, Bernhard. *Relays: Literature as an Epoch of the Postal System*. Translated by Kevin Repp. Stanford, Calif.: Stanford University Press, 1999.

Simmel, Georg. "The Philosophy of Landscape." Translated by Josef Bleicher. *Theory, Culture, Society* 24, nos. 7–8 (2007): 20–29.

Sloterdijk, Peter. *Das Raumschiff Erde hat keinen Notausgang: Energie und Politik im Anthropozän*. Frankfurt am Main: Suhrkamp, 2011.

Sontag, Susan. "Notes on 'Camp.'" In *Against Interpretation and Other Essays*, 275–92. New York: Delta, 1966.

———. "Walser's Voice." In *Selected Stories*, by Robert Walser, translated by Christopher Middleton and others, vii–ix. New York: Farrar, Straus and Giroux, 2012.

Sorfa, David. "The Illusory Architext of the *Institute Benjamenta*." *Adaptation* 5, no. 1 (2011): 88–101.

Sorg, Reto. "Abschied von Europa? 'Kulturentrückung' bei Robert Walser." In *Utopie und Apokalypse in der Moderne*, edited by Reto Sorg and Stefan Bodo Würffel, 161–78. Munich: Wilhelm Fink, 2010.

———. Foreword to *Fairy Tales: Dramolettes*, by Robert Walser, vii–x. New York: New Directions, 2015.

Sorg, Reto, and Lucas Marco Gisi. "'Er gehorcht gern und widersetzt sich leicht': Zur Figur des Angestellten bei Robert Walser." In *Im Bureau: Aus dem Leben der Angestellten*, by Robert Walser, 129–42. Berlin: Insel, 2011.

Spengler, Oswald. *The Decline of the West*. Translated by Charles Francis Atkinson. New York: Knopf, 1927.

———. *Der Untergang des Abendlandes*. Munich: Beck, 1922.

Spitteler, Carl. *Imago*. Edited by Werner Stauffacher. Frankfurt am Main: Suhrkamp, 1990.

Sprengel, Peter. *Geschichte der deutschsprachigen Literatur, 1900–1918: Von der Jahrhundertwende bis zum Ende des Ersten Weltkriegs*. Munich: C. H. Beck, 2004.

Stapleton, Amy. "Review of *Robert Walser Rediscovered*." *South Atlantic Review* 53, no. 4 (1998): 161.

Steffen, Albert. "Robert Walser: Große kleine Welt." In Kerr, *Über Robert Walser*, 1:146–47.

Stiemer, Hendrik. *Über scheinbar naïve und dilettantische Dichtung: Text- und Kontextstudien zu Robert Walser*. Würzburg: Königshausen & Neumann, 2013.

Stocker, Peter. "Adressaten und Adressierungen in Robert Walsers Briefen und ihre editorische Behandlung in der Kommentierten Berner Ausgabe (KBA)." *Germanistik in der Schweiz* 9 (2012): 57–78.

———. "Korpus, Brieftypen, Deutungsaspekte." In Gisi, *Robert Walser-Handbuch*, 217–24.

Szondi, Peter. *On Textual Understanding and Other Essays*. Manchester: Manchester University Press, 1986.

Thamen, Torkild, and Louise Wallenberg. "Buggering Freud and Deleuze: Toward a Queer Theory of Masochism." *Journal of Aesthetics and Culture* 2 (2010), http://www.tandfonline.com/doi/full/10.3402/jac.v2i0.4642. Accessed May 2017.

Thums, Barbara. "Robert Walsers 'Kleist in Thun': Zur Archäologie des touristischen Blicks auf die Schweiz als Idylle." *Literatur für Leser* 36, no. 4 (2014): 169–80.

Tismar, Jens. *Gestörte Idyllen: Eine Studie zur Problematik der idyllischen Wunschvorstellungen am Beispiel von Jean Paul, Adalbert Stifter, Robert Walser und Thomas Bernhard*. Munich: Hanser, 1986.

Tobler, Konrad. "Gegenwartskunst." In Gisi, *Robert Walser-Handbuch*, 387–90.

Treichel, Hans-Ulrich. "Über die Schrift hinaus: Franz Kafka, Robert Walser und die Grenzen der Literatur." In Hinz and Horst, *Robert Walser*, 292–309.

Unglaub, Erich. "Flora Ackeret und Robert Walser: Poetisierung oder Poetologisierung einer Beziehung?" In Chiarini and Zimmermann, "*Immer dicht vor dem Sturze . . .* ," 106–12.

Utz, Peter. "Ausgeplauderte Geheimnisse: Die Verwandtschaft von Brief und Feuilleton am Beispiel Robert Walsers." In *Briefkultur: Transformationen epistolaren Schreibens in der deutschen Literatur*, edited by Isolde Schiffermüller and Chiara Conterno, 181–99. Würzburg: Königshausen & Neumann, 2015.

———. "Die Kalligrafie des 'Idioten.' " In Arnold, *Text und Kritik*, 106–18.

———. "Helvetische Heroik im Huber-Verlag: Robert Faesi, Paul Ilg, Robert Walser." In *Der Held im Schützengraben: Führer, Massen und Medientechnik im ersten Weltkrieg*, edited by Karl Wagner, Stephan Baumgartner and Michael Gamper, 81–97. Zurich: Chronos, 2014.

———. "La fringale épistolaire de Robert Walser." In Robert Walser, *Lettres de 1897 à 1949*, translated by Marion Graf, 5–18. Geneva: Éditions Zoé, 2012.

———. "Robert Walser: Stück ohne Titel." In Groddeck et al., *Robert Walsers "Ferne Nähe,"* 49–60.

———. "Robert Walsers *Jakob von Gunten*: Eine 'Null'-Stelle der deutschen Literatur." *Deutsche Vierteljahrsschrift für Literaturwissenschaft und Geistesgeschichte* 74, no. 3 (2000): 488–512.

———. *Tanz auf den Rändern: Robert Walsers "Jetztzeitstil."* Frankfurt am Main: Suhrkamp, 1998.

Vannette, Charles M. "'Wir pröbeln und schneidern mit Dingen, die in der Brust anderer Menschen gesund und geheimnisvoll und unangetastet ruhen . . .': Narrative Observation and Hyperreflexivity in the Works of Robert Walser." Ph.D. diss., Ohio State University, 2011.

Vila-Matas, Enrique. *Bartleby & Co.* Translated by Jonathan Dunne. New York: New Directions, 2004.

Vollmer, Hartmut. "Die erschriebene Kindheit: Erzähllust, Sprachzauber und Rollenspiel im Werk Robert Walsers." *Euphorion: Zeitschrift für Literaturgeschichte* 93, no. 1 (1999): 75–98.

von Matt, Peter. "Die Schwäche des Vaters und das Vergnügen des Sohnes: Voraussetzungen der Fröhlichkeit bei Robert Walser." In Hinz and Horst, *Robert Walser*, 182–98.

———. "Wer hat Robert Walsers Briefe geschrieben?" In Chiarini and Zimmermann, *"Immer dicht vor dem Sturze . . . ,"* 98–105.

———. "Wie weise ist Walsers Weisheit?" In Groddeck et al., *Robert Walsers "Ferne Nähe,"* 35–47.

Wagner, Karl. *Herr und Knecht: Robert Walsers Roman "Der Gehülfe."* Vienna: Braumüller, 1980.

Walser, Martin. *Selbstbewußtsein und Ironie: Frankfurter Vorlesungen.* Frankfurt am Main: Suhrkamp, 1981.

Walt, Christian. "'Den Lyrikern empfehl' ich dringend, / sich dem Zwang des Reims zu unterziehen . . .': Zur Übererfüllung von Gattungsnormen in Robert Walsers späten Gedichten." In *"Ich beendige dieses Gedicht lieber in Prosa": Robert Walser als Grenzgänger der Gattungen*, edited by Anna Fattori and Kerstin Gräfin von Schwerin, 157–72. Heidelberg: Universitätsverlag Winter, 2011.

———. "Schreibprozesse: Abschreiben, Überarbeiten." In Gisi, *Robert Walser-Handbuch*, 268–73.

Weitzmann, Erica. *Irony's Antics: Walser, Kafka, Roth, and the German Comic Tradition.* Evanston, Ill.: Northwestern University Press, 2014.

Widmann, Joseph Viktor. "Gebrüder Walser." In Kerr, *Über Robert Walser*, 1:13–16.

———. "Geschwister Tanner: Roman von Robert Walser." In Kerr, *Über Robert Walser*, 1:17–23.

———. "Robert Walsers Schweizerroman Der Gehülfe." In Kerr, *Über Robert Walser*, 1:25–29.

Zellweger, Katja. "Familie Walser." In Gisi, *Robert Walser-Handbuch*, 16–18.

Zmegac, Victor. "Robert Walsers Poetik in der literarischen Konstellation der Jahrhundertwende." In *Robert Walser und die moderne Poetik*, edited by Dieter Borchmeyer, 21–36. Frankfurt am Main: Suhrkamp, 1999.

Zollinger, Albin. "Robert Walsers Roman *Der Gehülfe*." In Kerr, *Über Robert Walser*, 1:132–38.

"Zur Geschichte der Null." *Schweizerisches Familien-Wochenblatt* 45 (February 6, 1926).

CONTRIBUTORS

Susan Bernofsky directs the program in literary translation at Columbia University's School of the Arts. Her translations include eight books by Robert Walser, as well as works by Yoko Tawada, Jenny Erpenbeck, Franz Kafka, Hermann Hesse, and others. The recipient of numerous awards (most recently the Independent Foreign Fiction Prize, the Oxford-Weidenfeld Translation Prize, and the Schlegel-Tieck Prize for her translation of Erpenbeck's *The End of Days*), she blogs about translation at www.translationista.com. Her biography-in-progress of Robert Walser is forthcoming from Yale University Press.

Paul Buchholz is an assistant professor of German Studies at Emory University. He is the author of *Private Anarchy: Impossible Community and the Outsider's Monologue in German Experimental Fiction* (Northwestern, 2018). After receiving his Ph.D. in German Studies from Cornell University in 2010, he held a postdoctoral position at New York University and worked as an assistant professor in the German Departments at Scripps College and the University of California, Berkeley. Buchholz's research focuses on German-language prose of the twentieth and twenty-first centuries, with an emphasis on how the experiments with narrative form complicate commonplace ideas of human community.

Kai Evers is an associate professor of German at the University of California, Irvine. He is the author of *Violent Modernists: The Aesthetics of Destruction in Twentieth-Century German Literature* (Northwestern, 2013) and has published on Robert Musil, Franz Kafka, Elias Canetti, Hannah Arendt, Peter Weiss, and Gert Neumann, among others. His current research analyzes attempts to anticipate new forms of warfare in literary and nonliterary discourses of interwar Europe.

Samuel Frederick is an associate professor of German at the Pennsylvania State University. He is the author of *Narratives Unsettled: Digression in Robert Walser, Thomas Bernhard, and Adalbert Stifter* (Northwestern, 2012), as well as articles on Friedrich von Blanckenburg, Oswald Egger, Oskar Fischinger, Theodor Fontane, Jeremias Gotthelf, Heinrich von Kleist (in relation to Walser), Gerhard Meier, and the Quay Brothers, among others. With Graham Foust he has translated three volumes of Ernst Meister's late poetry.

Anne Fuchs (FBA, MRIA) is a professor of German and director of the Humanities Institute at University College Dublin. She has published widely on cultural memory, modernist and contemporary literature, and the modern experience of time. Her monographs include *After the Dresden Bombing: Pathways of*

Memory, 1945 to the Present (2012), *Phantoms of War in Contemporary German Literature, Films and Discourse* (2008, 2010), and *Die Schmerzensspuren der Geschichte: Zur Poetik der Erinnerung in W. G. Sebalds Prosa* (2004). Recent coedited volumes include (with J. J. Long) *Time in German Literature and Culture, 1900–2015* (2016) and (with Ines Detmers) a special issue titled "Ästhetische Eigenzeit in Contemporary Literature and Culture," *Oxford German Studies* 46, nos. 3–4 (2017).

Valerie Heffernan is a senior lecturer in German Studies at the National University of Ireland Maynooth. She is the author of *Provocation from the Periphery: Robert Walser Re-examined* (2007). She has also published widely on contemporary German-language literature, with a particular focus on German-speaking Swiss writers and women writers. Heffernan is coeditor of *Schweiz schreiben: Zu Konstruktion und Dekonstruktion des Mythos Schweiz in der Gegenwartsliteratur* (2010) and coeditor of *Transitions. Emerging Women Writers in German-language Literature* (2013).

Jörg Kreienbrock is an associate professor of German and comparative literature at Northwestern University. His research focuses on German literature from the eighteenth to the twenty-first centuries, with an emphasis on literary theory, contemporary literature, the history of science, and popular culture. Professor Kreienbrock is the author of *Kleiner. Feiner. Leichter: Nuancierungen zum Werk Robert Walsers* (2010) and *Malicious Objects, Anger Management, and the Question of Modern Literature* (2012) and coeditor of *Die Amerikanischen Götter: Transatlantische Prozesse in der Deutschsprachigen Popkultur seit 1945* (2015).

Bernhard F. Malkmus is a professor of German at the University of Newcastle. His research focuses on narratives of modernity, aesthetic theories of text-image relations, and the environmental humanities. He is the author of *The German Picaro and Modernity: Between Underdog and Shape-shifter* (2011). Currently he is working on a book entitled *The Twilight of Man: On Living in an Anthropomorphic World*. His favorite pastime is walking.

Daniel Medin is an associate professor of comparative literature and English at the American University of Paris. His research is principally concerned with modern fiction from Germany, Austria, and Switzerland, with an emphasis on the work and global reception of Franz Kafka. He is associate director of AUP's Center for Writers and Translators and one of the editors of its *Cahiers Series* (published jointly with Sylph Editions in London).

Anette Schwarz is an associate professor of German Studies at Cornell University. She is the author of the monograph *Melancholie: Figuren und Orte einer Stimmung* (1997). She has published articles on Rainer Maria Rilke, Sigmund Freud, Martin Heidegger, Theodor Storm, Theodor Fontane, Albert Vigoleis Thelen, Walter Benjamin, and Peter Szondi. She is currently working on a book about notions of sociality and kinship in twentieth-century philosophy and psychoanalysis (especially Heidegger, Freud, and Benjamin).

Elke Siegel is an associate professor in the Department of German Studies at Cornell University. She is the author of *Aufträge aus dem Bleistiftgebiet: Zur Dichtung Robert Walsers* (2001) and *Entfernte Freunde: Nietzsche, Freud, Kafka und die Freundschaft der Moderne* (2009). Further publications include articles on twentieth-century and contemporary German-language literature; literature and film; writing and the Internet; the diaristic as interface between life and writing, subject and world, self and history, fiction and nonfiction.

Peter Utz is a professor of German at the University of Lausanne. His research interests include modern German literature from the eighteenth century, Swiss German literature, and literary translation. He is the author of *Tanz auf den Rändern: Robert Walsers "Jetztzeitstil"* (1998) and the editor of several French translations of Walser's work. Utz is also editor of *Wärmende Fremde: Robert Walser und seine Übersetzer im Gespräch* (1994) and coeditor (with Wolfram Groddeck, Reto Sorg, and Karl Wagner) of *Robert Walsers "Ferne Nähe": Neue Beiträge zur Forschung* (2008). Other monographs include *Anders gesagt—autrement dit—in other words: Übersetzt gelesen; Hoffmann, Fontane, Kafka, Musil* (2007), *Kultivierung der Katastrophe: Untergangsszenarien in den Literaturen der Schweiz* (2013) and *"Nachreife des fremden Wortes": Hölderlins "Hälfte des Lebens" und die Poetik des Übersetzens* (2017).

INDEX

Entries in **boldface** refer to extended discussions of individual works.

Works by Robert Walser (English titles)

"Adage," 43
"Always at the Window," 37, 39–40
Angela Borgia / Giulio / The Cardinal / The Duke / Lucrezia / The Author of This Scene, 214, **219–25**
Annotated Bernese Edition, 14–15, 47, 61n2
"As Ever," **66–68**, 85n6. *See also* "No Way Out"
"Ash, Needle, Pencil, and Little Matchstick," **203–7**, 209n37
Assistant, The, 9–10, 12, 32–33, **125–31, 134–40,** 143, 251
"At the Window (I)." *See* "Always at the Window"
"Audition, The," 226n3

"Before Bedtime," 37
"Berlin and the Artist," 164–65
Berlin Stories (English collection), 10
"Berühmter Auftritt," 258
Boys, The, 212, 226n3
"Brightness," 37, 39, 43

"Casserole," 63n38
Chord and Longing, 66, 71–73
Christ Child, The, **214–19**, 227n17, 227n24
Cinderella, 212, 214, 217
Comedy, 212–13, 219, 226n15, 226–27n17
Critical Robert Walser Edition, 14, 252
"Cruel Rites, Customs, Habits etc.," **241–47**

"Doctor Franz Blei," 41–42

Fairy Tales (English collection), 10, 215
"Famous Stage Appearance," 258
Felix scenes, 219, 227n17, 234–35, 247
"Fire," 241
"Frau Bähni," 112–13
Fritz Kocher's Essays, 10, 13, **87–103,** 110, 113
From the Domain of the Pencil (collection of microscripts), 14, 119, 219, 234–35
"Future!," **26–27**, 38

"Gloomy Neighbor," 37–38
"Goodbye," 162–63

"Harden," 108
"Hot Porridge, The," 152

Jakob von Gunten, 4, 6–7, 9, 10, 12, 16n24, 62n20, 86n34, 110–11, 117, 125, **143–69**, 192, 230, 231, 247, 251
"Johanna," 22, 44n4

"Kleist in Thun," 173, **174–78**, 179, 182, 187

"Letter to Alfred Kerr," 106
"Little Berliner, The," 113
"Little Landscape, A," 37–39, 184
"Little Ramble, A," 171–73, 178, 181
"Little Turtle Thine," **78–80**
Looking at Pictures (English collection), 10
"Louise," 27–29, 31, 32, 44n4, 45n32

"Marginal Note," 264–65
Masquerade and Other Stories (English collection), 3, 10
"Meadow Green," **69–71**, 72

Microscripts (English collection), 10
"Minotaur," 152
"Mountain Halls," 110, 174
"My Endeavours," 251

"Nature Study," 199–200
"No Way Out," 37, 84n6. *See also* "As Ever"

"On the Character of the Artist," 193

"Painter's Life, A," 107
Poems (1909), 66, 84n6
"Poems (II), The," 35–36
Poets, 212
Pond, The, 226–27n17
"Portrait of a Businessman," 113–14
"Potpourri," 107

"Rathenau was in a somewhat melancholy mood," 119–20
Robber, The, 4, 10, 12, 13, 118–19, 123n29, 143, 165, 234–35, **251–68**
Rose, The, 219, 229, 237, 238

"Secretary, The," 112
Schoolboy's Diary and Other Stories, A (English collection), 10
Seeland, 17n27, 188n23
Sleeping Beauty, 214
"Snow (II)," 68–69, 72, 73
Snow White, 212, 214, 226n11
"Something about Disgrace," 235–36, 238
Speaking to the Rose (English collection), 10
"Study (I)," 163

Tanners, The, 10, 12, 33, 62n20, 107, 118, **125–31**, **134–40**, 141n28, 143, 157, 232, 251
Thirty Poems (English collection), 10
"This minister more or less probably had too meticulous an upbringing," 121
"Thoughts on Cézanne," 153, 201–2
"Time," **71–72**
"Tragedy," 258
"Travel Report," 198–99
"Two Men," 117–18, 121, 267n15

"Walk, The," 7, 9, 10, 12, 18n39, 174, **179–87**, 188n23, **194–207**
"Wenzel," 226n3
"Winter Rain," 69
"With Anger about Her Anger She Was Green," 229, 238–41

Works by Robert Walser (German titles)

"Abschied," 162–63
"Am Fenster (I)." *See* "Immer am Fenster"
"andere Junggeselle, Der," 62n28
Angela Borgia / Julio / Der Kardinal / Der Herzog / Lukrezia / Der Autor dieser Szene, 214, **219–25**
"Asche, Nadel, Bleistift und Zündhölzchen," **203–7**, 209n37
Aschenbrödel, 212, 214, 217
"Auflauf," 63n38
Aus dem Bleistiftgebiet (collection of microscripts), 14, 119, 219, 234–35

"Beiseit." *See* "Spruch"
"Berlin und der Künstler," 164–65
"Brief an Alfred Kerr," 106

"Cézannegedanken," 153, 201–2
Christkind, Das, **214–19**, 227n17, 227n24

Dichter, 212
"Dieser Minister erhielt vielleicht gleichsam eine zu sorgfältige Erziehung," 121
"Doktor Franz Blei," 41–42
Dornröschen, 214

"Etwas von der Schande," 235–36, 238

Felix-Szenen, 219, 227n17, 234–35, 247
"Festzug," 45n28
"Feuer," 241
"Frau Bähni," 112–13
Fritz Kochers Aufsätze, 10, 13, **87–103**, 110, 113
"fünfzigste Geburtstag, Der," 45n28

"Gebirgshallen," 110, 174
Gedichte (1909), 66, 84n6
"Gedichte (II), Die," 35–36
Gehülfe, Der, 9–10, 12, 32–33, **125–31**, **134–40**, 143, 251
Geschwister Tanner, 10, 12, 33, 62n20, 107, 118, **125–31**, **134–40**, 141n28, 143, 157, 232, 251
"Glosse, Die," 264–65
"Grausame Bräuche, Sitten, Gewohnheiten usw.," **241–47**
"Gute schrieb, Der," 45n28

"Harden," 108
"heiße Brei, Der," 152
"Helle," 37, 39, 43

"Ich weiß zur Stunde nicht recht," 45n32
"Immer am Fenster," 37, 39–40

Jakob von Gunten, 4, 6–7, 9, 10, 12, 16n24, 62n20, 86n34, 110–11, 117, 125, 143–69, 192, 230, 231, 247, 251
"Johanna," 22, 44n4

"Kein Ausweg," 37, 84n6. *See also* "Wie Immer"
"Kleine Wanderung," 171–73, 178, 181
"kleiner Berlinerin, Die," 113
"Kleist in Thun," 173, 174–78, 179, 182, 187
Knaben, Die, 212, 226n3
Kommentierte Berner Ausgabe, 14–15, 47, 61n2
Komödie, 212–13, 219, 226n15, 226–27n17
Kritische Robert Walser-Ausgabe, 14, 252

"Landschäftchen, Ein," 37–39, 184
"Leben eines Malers," 107
"Louise," 27–29, 31, 32, 44n4, 45n32

"Meine Bemühungen," 251
"Minotauros," 152

"Naturstudie," 199–200

"Porträt eines Kaufmannes," 113–14
"Potpourri," 107

"Rathenau war von etwas melancholischem Gemüt," 119–20
Räuber, Der, 4, 10, 12, 13, 118–19, 123n29, 143, 165, 234–35, **251–68**
"Reisebericht," 198–99
"Rosa," 45n32
Rose Die, 219, 229, 237, 238

Saite und Sehnsucht, 66, 71–73
"Schildkrötelein," **78–80**
"Schnee (II)," 68–69, 72, 73
Schneewittchen, 212, 214, 226n11
Seeland, 17n27, 188n23
"Sekretär, Der," 112
"Spaziergang, Der," 7, 9, 10, 12, 18n39, 174, **179–87**, 188n23, **194–207**
"Spruch," 43
"Studie (I)," 163

"Talentprobe, Die," 226n3
Teich, Der, 226–27n17
"Tragödie, Die," 258
"Trüber Nachbar," 37–38

"Über den Charakter des Künstlers," 193

"Vor Schlafengehen," 37
"Vor Wut über ihre Wut war sie grün," 229, 238–41

"Weihnachtsgeschichte I," 45n28, 45n32
"Wenzel," 226n3
"Wie Immer," **66–68**, 84n6. *See also* "Kein Ausweg"
"Wiesengrün," **69–71**, 72
"Winterregen," 69

"Zeit, Die," **71–72**
"Zukunft!," **26–27**, 38
"Zwei Männer," 117–18, 121, 267n15

General Index

abstraction, 67–68, 147, 158, 181
Ackeret, Flora, 34, 48–49, 52, 62n26

Ackermann, Otto, 33
adaptation (of Walser's work), 6–7
Adorno, Theodor W., 194–5, 196–7, 205–7
affect, 9, 13, 56–57, 67, 72, 90, 126–27, 130–37, 139, 174–76, 179. *See also* emotion
Africa, 163, 164, 244–45
Agamben, Giorgio, 71–72, 73, 175, 187
agency, 56, 78, 174, 176, 181, 183, 196–97, 225
aggression, 129, 133, 164, 262
Aimée, Suzanne, 113
Allemann, Urs, 85n26
Alps, 172, 174, 176, 201
Altenberg, Peter, 43–44
ambiguity, 164, 173–74, 183, 192–93, 216
ambivalence, 72, 109, 126, 136, 227n22, 262
anarchism, 45n14, 127, 139
Andres, Susanne, 227n18
Arabia, 145–46, 160, 161
Arbeiterstimme (socialist newspaper), 24–25
artificiality, 66, 74, 90, 93, 176, 212, 216
Ashbery, John, 3
Asia, 153, 163, 244
authority, 131–32, 134, 215–20, 225, 227n22, 230–31, 240, 255
authorship, 57–60, 89, 93–94, 154–55, 211, 220, 223–25, 251–52, 255–60
autobiography, 125, 140n3, 141n28, 146, 147, 155
avant-garde (historical movement), 33, 212
Avery, George C., 11, 126, 131, 173

Bachmann, Ingeborg, 164
Barbey d'Aurevilly, Jules, 239
Barthes, Roland, 140n5, 165
Baudelaire, Charles, 163
Bauer, Felice, 49, 60
Bauman, Zygmunt, 242
Beckett, Samuel, 11, 164, 227n18, 253
Benjamin, Walter, 3, 4, 14, 47, 62n19, 84–85n22, 94–95, 98, 103n12, 121, 141n12, 191, 193, 195–96, 202–3, 206, 208n32, 212, 229–30, 236, 238
Benn, Gottfried, 8
Benzinger-Wahlmann, Eleonore, 225–26n2
Berliner Tageblatt (newspaper), 237
Berlin period, 12, 14, 34–35, 65, 105–7, 125, 141, 164–65, 211–12, 232–33
Berlin Secession, 91, 106, 111–13, 118
Bernofsky, Susan, 3, 4, 8, 10–13, 17n33, 18n39, 21–46, 62n22, 135, 141n28, 188n23, 232–33
Bern period, 10, 12, 65, 125, 152, 219–20, 223, 251, 258, 265
Bible, 31, 161, 214–19, 227n27
Biel period, 10, 12, 53–54, 63n32, 65, 94, 212
Bierbaum, Otto Julius, 212
bildungsroman, 146–47. See also *Entwicklungsroman*
Binder, Thomas, 67, 84n11
Bismarck, Otto von, 115–16
Bleckmann, Ulf, 227n18
Blei, Franz, 40–43, 46n51, 121, 236
Bodmann, Emanuel von, 33
body, 13, 56, 81–82, 132, 175, 177, 179–81, 183–87
Bollnow, Otto Friedrich, 173, 178
Borchmeyer, Dieter, 167n25, 213–15, 217, 220, 225
Borgia family, 214, 219–20, 224
Börne, Ludwig, 33, 108, 115–16
Böschenstein, Bernhard, 86n33, 226n5
Bourdieu, Pierre, 257
Brahms, Johannes, 36
Brecht, Bertolt, 7–8, 91, 256
Breitbach, Therese, 48, 114–15
Brentano, Clemens, 41
Broch, Hermann, 8
Brod, Max, 83n2, 110
Buchholz, Paul, 12, 13–14, 18n52, 125–41
Büchner, Georg, 41; *Lenz* (novella), 171–74, 176
Bullock, Michael, 9
Bund, Der (newspaper), 36–37, 41, 43, 66, 88–89
Bungartz, Christoph, 252
Burgin, Christine, 5–6

Calasso, Roberto, 130
Camus, Albert, 165

Canetti, Elias, 3, 230–31
canon, literary, 7–9, 11, 15, 235–37, 252
capital, 134, 137, 252, 256–57, 260, 264
Carroll, Lewis, 200
Casey, Edward, 177, 179
Cassirer, Bruno, 106–7, 109, 110–11, 122, 125, 213
Cassirer, Paul, 106, 111–17, 118, 122n23
Catling, Jo, 4
Cézanne, Paul, 111, 153, 201–02
Childish, Billy, 5
childlikeness, 83, 87, 91, 94–95, 102n9, 262–63
Coetzee, J. M., 3, 4–5, 117, 230–31, 238
comical elements, 13, 30, 44, 181–82, 211, 243–44, 258–59, 261, 264
Corinth, Lovis, 111

Dada, 85n24
dance, 87, 102n3
Dante, 23, 212, 259
Daumier, Honoré, 115–16
Davey, Moyra, 6
Davies, Siobhan, 7
deciphering, 94, 101, 202, 233–35
deferral, 52–53, 231, 253, 260, 264
Dehmel, Richard, 33
Deleuze, Gilles, 19n65, 86n33, 200–1, 252, 263, 268n31
Derrida, Jacques, 207
desert, 143–44, 146, 152–54, 160–65. *See also* landscape
Dickinson, Emily, 6
digression, 13, 151, 252–53, 256–57, 259, 254–65
Döblin, Alfred, 8
Donizetti, Gaetano, 220
Dostoevsky, Fyodor, 4, 107, 191
dramatic scenes/dramolettes, 6, 7, 10, 12, 13, 65, **211–27**, 233
dream, 4, 6, 39–40, 92, 95, 126, 130, 143, 151–53, 157–63, 165, 182, 195, 230–31, 247, 261
Du (journal), 234, 235
Duchamp, Marcel, 62n28
Dumas, Alexandre, 220
Durieux, Tilla, 113

Echte, Bernhard, 11, 19n56, 32, 45n28, 46n54, 107, 109, 233, 234–35, 252
education, 35, 37, 59, 89, 94–95, 99–101, 120, 144–45, 148, 156–58, 167n25, 180
Eichendorff, Joseph von, 141n12, 173; *Life of a Good-for-Nothing*, 127
Eiden-Offe, Patrick, 57
Elias, Norbert, 242
emotion, 92, 122, 126, 128–30, 131–32, 135–37, 175, 182, 197, 218, 258–59. *See also* affect, empathy
empathy, 175, 192, 243–44
Entwicklungsroman, 155–56
eroticism, 13, 54, 56, 252–54, 259–64
Europe, 137, 145, 160–61, 162–65, 239–40, 243–44
Evans, Tamara S., 5, 11, 16n20, 19n53, 126
Evers, Kai, 12, 14, 227n29, 229–49
Ewers, Hanns Heinz, 229, 239

fairy tales, 7, 10, 129, 212–15, 217, 221, 226n11, 227n24, 227n26
female characters, 22, 27–29, 31, 32–33, 62n20, 128, 138–39, 259, 263
Fenves, Peter, 208n32
fetishism, 261–63
feuilleton, 36, 43, 49, 61n2, 66, 105, 107, 109, 111–12, 116, 154–55, 265–66n1
film, 6–7, 16n20, 17n26
Fischer, Samuel, 107, 111, 122
Flaubert, Gustave, 107
Foucault, Michel, 199, 254
Frederick, Samuel, 12, 13, 16n24–25, 55, 65–86, 209n37, 225n1, 252
French Revolution, 162, 243
Freud, Sigmund, 100, 239–40, 242, 261–63
Frey, Hans-Jost, 72–73, 84n22
Frisch, Efraim, 110–11, 122, 143, 150
Frisch, Fega, 111, 122
Fuchs, Anne, 12, 13, 85n32, 167n21, 251–68
Futurism, 186

Galiani, Ferdinand, 41
Gass, William H., 3–4, 5
Gees, Marion, 211, 223

gender, 40, 49, 56–58, 193, 212, 262
George, Stefan, 7
Gessner, Salomon, 174
gesture, 174–75, 179, 182–85, 187, 211, 219–20
Gilman, Claire, 6
Gilman, Sander L., 123n24
Gisi, Lucas Marco, 10–11, 17n33, 140–41n11
Giuriato, Davide, 95, 103n12
Glauser, Friedrich, 164
Goethe, Johann Wolfgang von, 49. WORKS: *Faust*, 31; *Wilhelm Meister's Apprenticeship*, 155–56; *Wilhelm Meister's Journeyman Years*, 156, 208n32
Gold, Alfred, 91
Gößling, Andreas, 155–56, 167n26
Gotthelf, Jeremias, 63n30
Graham, Rodney, 6
Greven, Jochen, 11, 14–15, 219, 225–26n2, 227n25, 232, 234, 252
Grimm, Jacob and Wilhelm, 193, 207n8, 214–15, 217, 227n26
Groddeck, Wolfram, 14
Guattari, Félix, 252

Haller, Albrecht von, 174
Hamacher, Werner, 197–98
Handy, E. S. C., 239
Harden, Maximilian, 107–9, 122
Harman, Mark, 10–11, 19n53, 226n11
Hauptmann, Gerhard, 121, 191
Heffernan, Valerie, 12, 13, 19n65, 62n18, 211–27
Hegel, G. W. F., 62n18
Heine, Heinrich, 33, 115–16
Henckell, Karl, 33
Herisau, 6, 47, 60, 62n20, 233, 238
Hesse, Hermann, 3, 8, 34, 109
heterosexuality, 254, 259, 262–64
Heym, Georg, 79–80
Heymel, Alfred Walter, 212
Hiebel, Hans H., 147, 162
hierarchy, 23, 35, 126, 136–37, 139, 197, 220, 225
Hildesheimer, Wolfgang, 164
Hilton, David, 7
Hinrichsen, Otto, 41
Hitler, Adolf, 231
Hobbes, Thomas, 242
Hobus, Jens, 226n15
Hodler, Ferdinand, 36
Hofmannsthal, Hugo von, 8, 109, 121–22, 212
Hofmiller, Josef, 143, 154
Hölderlin, Friedrich, 198
Horace, 256
Hugo, Victor, 220
humiliation, 211, 239, 244, 263
humor. *See* comical elements
hunger, 29, 48–52, 55, 60, 63n38, 116, 259
Husserl, Edmund, 177

Ibsen, Henrik, 74, 85, 122
inanity, 66, 74, 81–83, 86. *See also* unknowing
India, 160–61, 243
Individualität (journal), 219
infinity (the infinite), 149, 154, 157–60, 162, 186, 202–3
Insel, Die (journal), 212
Insel Verlag, 61n2, 88, 110
intertextuality, 9, 211, 217–19, 221, 258, 264
irony, 4, 8, 30, 40–41, 72, 74, 78, 91, 106, 109, 114–15, 136, 147, 148, 162, 174, 182, 216, 223–24, 253

Jacobsohn, Siegfried, 108–10, 114, 122
Jakobowsky, Ludwig, 33
Jean Paul, 174
Jelinek, Elfriede, 3
jester, 8, 215–16
Joyce, James, 251
Jünger, Ernst, 7
Jürgens, Martin, 252, 267n22

Kafka, Franz, 3, 7–8, 13, 14, 23, 49, 60, 62n28, 87, 110, 164, 196, 230, 241, 251, 265–66n1
Kainz, Josef, 211, 225n2
Kalckreuth, Count Leopold von, 110
Kammer, Stephan, 47
Kandinsky, Wassily, 158
Kant, Immanuel, 172, 177, 242
Kaufmann, Vincent, 48, 60
Keller, Gottfried, 36, 236
Kerr, Alfred, 81–82, 105–6, 122

Kinder, Hermann, 172
kitsch, 176, 182, 259
Klee, Paul, 5, 11, 95
Kleist, Heinrich von, 31, 172–78, 187n2, 187n11, 188n15, 188n33
Kommerell, Max, 174–75, 177
Köngeter, Nicole, 10
Kraus, Karl, 8
Kreienbrock, Jörg, 12, 13, 167n20, 181, 188n28, 191–209
Kunst und Künstler (journal), 107
Kurzawa, Lothar, 211

labyrinth, 9, 152, 163–64, 252, 268n43
Laederach, Jürg, 165
landscape, 38–40, 128–29, 164, 172–76, 177–81, 183–87, 201–2. *See also* desert
Lasker-Schüler, Else, 8
Lenz, J. M. R., 41, 171–73
Leonardo da Vinci, 220
Lerner, Ben, 5
Lesezirkel, Der (journal), 21, 44n1
Lewin, Kurt, 185
Liebermann, Max, 107, 111
Literarische Welt (journal), 115
literary market, 53, 57, 224, 252, 264
Lobsien, Eckhard, 181

Machiavelli, Niccolò, 220
Mächler, Robert, 47, 84n2, 122, 140n3
Malkmus, Bernhard, 12, 13, 171–89
Mann, Thomas, 7–8, 229, 251
marginality, 8, 11–12, 14–15, 19n65, 105, 122, 146, 151–55, 167n21, 192, 200–1, 212, 216, 230, 252, 264–65
Marinetti, Filippo Tommaso, 186
Marx, Karl, 137, 140n6, 242
masculinity, 60, 231, 254, 261–63
masks, 8, 30, 91–92, 95–96, 176, 211
masochism, 63n35, 78, 263, 268n31
mathematics, 23, 145–51, 155–59, 203
Mathews, Harry, 3
Mattenklott, Gert, 191, 196
May, Karl, 163
McElheny, Josiah, 6
meaninglessness, 145, 148, 217
Medin, Daniel, 12, 14, 105–23, 267n15
melancholy, 33, 37, 67–68, 116, 119, 121–22, 138, 164, 176, 193, 209n44
mental illness, 6, 14, 62n20, 130, 171, 175–76, 230, 233, 234, 238
Merleau-Ponty, Maurice, 180–82, 185
Mermet, Frieda, 47–49, 53–60, 63n32, 63n36, 64n54, 83n1, 229
metaphor, 78, 82, 153, 157, 159, 164, 174, 182, 185, 197, 202
metonym, 49, 56
Meyer, Conrad Ferdinand, 220, 224
microscripts, 5–6, 10, 12, 14–15, 65, 75–76, 85n24, 100–101, 103n26–27, 109–10, 114, 119, 121, 123n29, 145, 213, 214, 219–20, 223, 225, 226n17, 231–36, 238–39, 241, 247–48, 251–52. *See also* pencil method, writing process
Middleton, Christopher, 4, 8–11, 17n27, 18n39, 145, 151, 187n12, 188n23–24
mimicry, 69, 202, 214, 219, 225
minimizaton (or miniaturization), 76, 145, 202, 206, 208n32, 233, 251
mise en abyme, 172, 253, 256, 259, 261, 264, 266n11
modernism, 3, 5, 7–9, 10–11, 12, 14–15, 65, 122, 165, 182, 227n18, 230–31, 251, 252
Monet, Claude, 111
monologue, 13–14, 126, 156, 163–65, 171–72, 220
Montaigne, Michel de, 146, 155
Morgenstern, Christian, 107, 111, 163
Morlang, Werner, 11, 86, 234–35, 252, 266n2
Müller, Wilhelm, 174
Muschg, Adolf, 11
music, 5, 11, 16n20, 39, 105, 116, 173, 174, 213
Musil, Robert, 3, 8, 14, 122, 155, 157–60, 191–94, 205, 236, 239–40, 251. WORKS: *The Confusions of Young Törless*, 157–58, 240, 249n30; *The Man without Qualities*, 122, 159–60, 251

naïveté, 8, 66, 89, 91, 205–06, 212, 244
narrative technique, 3–4, 143, 174–75, 179, 230, 251–65. *See also* deferral, digression, nonlinearity, self-reflexivity
narrative voice, 9, 29, 44, 87–88, 230
National Socialism, 7–8

negation, 68–69, 125–6, 130, 146–49, 151–52, 155, 160, 164–65, 166n8, 168n49, 252, 253–54. *See also* nothing, zero
Nelson, Joan, 5
Neue Rundschau (journal), 110, 113, 143, 162, 214, 219
Neue Züricher Zeitung (NZZ), 236
newspapers, 15, 24, 36, 40, 45n14, 58, 59–60, 66, 88, 100–01, 154, 212–13, 219, 236–38
Nietzsche, Friedrich, 56, 157, 163–64
nonlinearity, 4, 195, 222, 252–3. *See also* digression
nothing (or nothingness), 68–69, 73, 76, 84n13, 137, 144–45, 148, 150, 151–52, 155, 156, 160–62, 164, 182, 191–92, 204–05, 207, 230, 241, 254, 256. *See also* negation, zero
Novalis, 41

Oppenheim, Méret, 6
Orient, 160–65
Oulipo, 86n33
outsider (or outcast), 8, 9, 13–14, 22–23, 105, 122, 131–32, 136, 145, 192–94, 196, 216, 259

Pantano, Daniele, 10, 70, 84n5, 215
parody, 15, 74, 75–76, 85n32, 106, 113, 117, 155, 172, 219, 225, 258, 267n28
passivity, 193, 195–96, 206, 209n37, 263
pedagogy. *See* education
pencil method, 4, 6, 10, 99–101, 202, 220, 225, **232–35**. *See also* microscripts, writing process
Pender, Malcolm, 255
phenomenology, 13, 174, 177–81, 185
Pick, Otto, 57, 106, 108
Pinker, Steven, 242
pleasure, 25, 30, 36, 51–52, 55, 58, 78, 80–82, 89, 100, 119, 172, 229, 231, 244, 247, 256–57, 260–65, 267n25, 268n31
poetry (or poems), 5, 6, 7, 10, 12, 19, 21–22, 25–27, 32, **35–44**, 46n54, 48, 52, 57, **65–86**, 109–10, 179, 180, 184, 211, 225n1, 233, 263, 265
Polgar, Alfred, 155
power, 13, 32, 49, 56–57, 72, 111–12, 137, 161–63, 164, 193–94, 195–96, 214–15, 217–25, 230–31, 238–40, 247, 252, 260
powerlessness, 72, 137, 193–94, 195–96, 230–31, 260
Prager Presse, 57, 83n2, 106, 108, 113, 219, 237, 238
precariousness, 21, 49, 60, 127, 136–7, 163, 243
Pro Helvetia (journal), 214
proletariat, 28, 33, 118, 127, 137–38. *See also* socialism, Workers' Movement
Proust, Marcel, 196, 202, 251

Quay Brothers, 6–7, 17n26

Rascher Verlag, 61n2
Rathenau, Walther, 117–23, 267n15
refusal, 8, 14, 80, 98, 101, 114, 125–40, 172, 192–93, 196, 198, 254
Reidel, James, 10, 215
Reinhard, Max, 105
religion, 30–31, 39, 161–62, 215–19, 227, 239
Renfer, Paul Hans, 33, 34
Renoir, Auguste, 111
repetition, 38, 44, 66–74, 80, 83, 258
rhyme, 25, 30, 38–40, 50, 66, 67, 70–72, 74–80, 83
Rilke, Rainer Maria, 7, 8, 33, 212
Rimbaud, Arthur, 163–64, 168n51
Roser, Dieter, 62n19
Rotman, Brian, 146
Rousseau, Jean-Jacques, 4, 174, 176
Roussel, Martin, 96
Rowohlt Verlag, 237
Rubens, Peter Paul, 227n27
Rychner, Max, 81, 232

Sacher-Masoch, Leopold von, 78, 246–47, 258–59, 263, 268n31; *Venus in Furs*, 78, 80, 259
Sade, Marquis de, 263
Sauvat, Catherine, 13
Schaak, Martina, 211
Schäfer, Jörg, 47
Schaffner, Jakob, 157, 159

Schätzle, Rosa, 32–34, 41
Schaubühne (journal), 108–10, 176
Schestag, Thomas, 203
Schiller, Friedrich, 174, 264, 267n27–28. WORKS: *On the Aesthetic Education of Man*, 156; *The Robbers*, 5, 23, 258, 267n28
schizophrenia, 171. *See also* mental illness
Schnitlzer, Arthur, 8
school. *See* education
Schröder, Rudolf Alexander, 212
Schubert, Franz, 174
Schuller, Marianne, 56, 62n21
Schwahl, Markus, 126
Schwarz, Anette, 12, 13, 87–103
Schweizer, Louisa, 32–33
Searls, Damion, 10, 85n31, 103n15
Sebald, W. G., 3, 4, 5, 140n3, 230
Seelig, Carl, 9, 33, 83, 83n2, 106–07, 108, 110, 111, 165, 233–35, 238; *Walks with Robert Walser*, 111
Seidel, Robert, 24–31, 33, 34, 40, 42, 44, 45n14; *Aus Kampfgewühl und Einsamkeit*, 25, 27, 45n14
self-reflexivity, 4, 9, 57, 83, 152, 205–06, 216, 220, 222, 266n11
sexuality, 119, 121, 236, 254, 259, 261–64
Shakespeare, William, 212
Siegel, Elke, 12, 13, 47–64, 202
Siegert, Bernhard, 48
silence, 6, 163, 230, 253
Simmel, Georg, 184–85
simplicity, 9, 66, 77, 89–91, 93, 231
Slavona, Maria, 33
Slevogt, Max, 110, 111
Sloterdijk, Peter, 186
smallness, 5, 6, 80, 83, 180–81, 197–98, 202–04, 230, 251–52, 264, 265–66n1
Smith, Stevie, 11
socialism, 24–28, 33, 45n14, 137–40, 141n28. *See also* proletariat, Workers' Movement
Sontag, Susan, 5, 10, 11, 253, 265
Sorg, Reto, 18n45, 46n46, 140n11, 221, 227n20, 227n24, 241
sovereignty, 57, 86n33, 134, 150, 175, 193, 196, 198, 202, 252
Spengler, Oswald, 158–59
Spitteler, Carl, 36; *Imago*, 156–57, 159
Stauffer-Bern, Karl, 34
Steffen, Albert, 156
Stendhal, 110
Stern, Maurice Reinhold von, 33, 41
Stocker, Peter, 61n2
Storm and Stress (movement), 174
subjectivity, 130–31, 146, 149–50, 155–60, 164, 195, 268n43
subjugation, 198, 268n43
subversion, 56, 62n18, 76, 86, 98, 126, 182, 188n31, 214–16, 218, 222, 225, 241, 252, 267n28
Süddeutsche Monatshefte (journal), 143
Suhrkamp Verlag, 14, 119, 226n17
Switzerland, 8, 21, 36, 40, 53, 61n2, 63n32, 105, 111, 122, 128, 130, 195, 233, 236, 267n28; as idyll, 174, 176, 259
Szondi, Peter, 205–6

Tales of Hoffmann, The (opera), 106
Thackeray, William Makepeace, 191
theater, 29, 31, 36, 105–07, 172–78, 185, 211–16, 217, 222, 225, 226n5, 258
theatricality, 33, 134, 211–13, 215–18, 220–25, 263, 265, 267n27
Tismar, Jens, 176, 188n15
Tolstoy, Leo, 191
tradition, 7, 11, 13, 65, 73, 76, 125, 127, 141n12, 146, 154, 156, 165, 171, 176, 184, 192, 220, 258
tragedy/tragic, 90, 174, 253, 258
transcription, 14, 109, 202, 219, 233–35, 238, 252
transgression, 13, 54, 77, 220, 231, 246–7, 263
translations (of Walser's work), 3, 4, 7–12, 14, 18n39, 85n31, 188n23, 215, 235, 269–70
trivial literature, 233, 258, 260, 268n30

Uhland, Ludwig, 30, 50
unknowing, 9, 13, 76, 78, 81–82. *See also* inanity
Utz, Peter, 7, 12, 19n65, 47–48, 50, 53–54, 63n32, 97–99, 101, 103n27, 143–69, 176, 188n31, 201, 212, 241, 252, 268n43

vagabond, 117–18, 125, 127, 197, 200, 215–16
Vahltreich, Julius, 45n14
Valéry, Paul, 196
Van Gogh, Vincent, 111
Velásquez, Diego, 146
Verlaine, Paul, 75, 85n31, 163
Vermeer, Johannes, 146
Vienna, 14, 43
Vila-Matas, Enrique, 125–26
Villiers de L'Isle-Adam, Auguste, 239
violence, 14, 80–81, 195, 202, 222, 229–48
von Matt, Peter, 47, 56–57, 60
Vulpius, Christian August, 258; *Rinaldo Rinaldini*, 257–58

Waldau, 62n20
walking, 3, 4, 13, 87, 102n3, 130, 171–74, 179–87, 188n28, 194–202, 206–07, 238
Wallinger, Mark, 6
Walser, Fanny, 48
Walser, Hermann, 36–37
Walser, Karl, 5, 21, 23, 31–35, 37, 40, 52, 88, 91, 105–7, 111, 116, 121, 258
Walser, Lisa, 25, 29–31, 36, 37, 44, 48, 49–52, 53–55, 62n20, 63n36, 211, 233
Walser, Martin, 3, 11, 148–49, 229–30
Walser, Robert: biography, 12, 13, 19, 21–44, 47–60, 65, 105–22, 125, 162, 232–35, 238; death, 5, 6, 14, 234, 236, 238; letters, 13, 15, 23–25, 27–31, 33–34, 36–37, **41–44**, **47–64**, 81–83, 83n1, 101, 107, 109–11, 114–16, 118, 163, 212, 213, 229, 232–34; photographs of, 5, 46n51, 234, 238; published biographies of, vii, 13, 19, 236; published works, *see separate indexes*; reception of, 3–11, 17n33, 65, 83n2, 87, 89, 110, 130, 212, 224, 235–38
Walt, Christian, 85n26, 86n33, 100
Wandervogel (movement), 174
Weber, Max, 140n11, 242
Wedekind, Frank, 8, 212
Weimar Republic, 117
Weiß, Emil Rudolf, 118
Weltbühne (journal), 109
Western culture/society, 146, 154, 158–59, 177–78, 186, 219, 242–43
Wethli, Louis, 29
Whalen, Tom, 10, 172
Widmann, Joseph Viktor, 36–37, 39, 40–41, 43, 88–94, 98, 100, 141n13
Widmann, Max, 36
Wiener Rundschau (journal), 43
Wiesner, Annette, 10
Wilde, Oscar, 236
Workers' Movement, 24–28, 33, 137–40. *See also* proletariat, socialism
World War I, 53, 108, 188n31, 239–40, 242
World War II, 23, 108, 242
writing process, 100, 223–25, 232–35. *See also* microscripts, pencil method

Young, Donald, 5–6

zero, 7, 16n25, 76, 143–65, 166n5, 166n10, 230, 241, 247. *See also* negation, nothing
Zukunft, Die (literary journal), 107–8, 123n31
Zurich period, 19, 21–24, 29–35, 40–42, 49, 129